WHAT THEY SAY ABOUT 'HODGEY'

For sixty years Alan has operated at the highest level of football. People talk of legends of sport, but often the term is used without the recipient having the credibility and stature to merit such a description. In the case of Alan Hodgkinson there is absolutely no doubt he is truly deserving of the accolade.

Craig Brown

He was not only a great goalkeeper but a county level cricketer and squash player. Alan was one of the great goalkeepers in an era of great goalkeepers. His experience and contacts in the game are second to none. The best goalkeeping coach there is.

Jim Smith

Alan was my goalkeeping coach and played a highly significant role in my career at Manchester United, coaching me and offering me the benefit of his unparalleled expertise and experience. He helped me mature and settle into a much higher grade of football than I had been used to. I shall be forever grateful to him.

Peter Schmeichel

Alan was not only my first professional goalkeeping coach, he was THE first goalkeeping coach. He was instrumental in helping me as a goalkeeper and ultimately as a goalkeeping coach. He is a very special man both on and off the field.

Eric Steele, Senior Goalkeeping Coach, Manchester United

He was more than the club's goalkeeper, he was part of the match day at Bramall Lane. He was a local lad who knew his audience. He was a remarkable player. His reflexes defied explanation and his bravery was never in question. Few players in the history of Sheffield United are remembered with as much affection as 'Hodgey'.

Sean Bean, actor

Having worked with Alan at the highest level I consider myself privileged to have witnessed his preparation, organisation and attention to detail. He has been totally dedicated to the art and science of his trade – he's a one-off.

Gordon Milne

The specialist work Alan did with the Scotland goalkeepers was outstanding. The fact he worked for the Scottish FA for 17 years is testament to his quality of coaching. He transformed top goalkeepers in Scotland. A brilliant goalkeeping coach.

Andy Roxburgh

Alan was one of my boyhood heroes. All these years on, nothing has changed in that respect. He is a modest, warm, fine man and a true Blades legend. He is always welcome at Bramall Lane – his spiritual home.

Kevin McCabe, Chairman, Sheffield United FC

Alan worked for me for several years as goalkeeping coach and was a conscientious worker. He set excellent standards for every goalkeeper he coached based on technique and hard work. His most important role was on deciding the potential of a young Danish goalkeeper. When Alan kept coming back with better and better reports I had to put the question to him, one that had always bothered me regarding Continental goalkeepers, 'Can he play in the English game?' Alan replied, 'He will be an absolute certainty at Manchester United.' That was Peter Schmeichel – enough said.

Sir Alex Ferguson

Alan was the first professional goalkeeping coach. In 1981–82 when Watford gained promotion to what was then Division One, I made one of my best ever managerial decisions. I appointed him as our goalkeeping coach. He was a top-class goalkeeper who became a top-class coach, but, just as importantly, he is a top-class man.

Graham Taylor

I can never recall Hodgey wearing gloves. Yet the ball stuck to his hands like a Teflon coating to a pan. He was a great goalkeeper in an era when England produced truly great goalkeepers.

Jimmy Greaves

When Alan played at Goodison Park he would often take a young lad from the crowd and invite the lad to 'keep goal' with him in the pre-match kick-in. I'm sure the lad never forgot the experience and Everton fans appreciated it too. You can't imagine such a thing happening these days, football is bereft of such simple, yet wonderful gestures towards ordinary fans.

Jimmy Gabriel, Everton FC

Hodgey was a truly superb goalkeeper. I was recently asked if Alan was better than the goalkeepers we now see in the Premier League. I had to be honest and say, 'Not quite ... then again, Alan has turned 76!'

Tommy Smith

Sixty years in professional football is a truly remarkable achievement. Alan Hodgkinson is unique and the longevity of his career in football may never be bettered.

Michel Platini

Hodgey is the 'daddy' of all goalkeeping coaches. He instigated and created the content for the UEFA Goalkeeping Licences. His expertise and experience are respected throughout the world.

Ian Rush

Sixty years in professional football is a phenomenal achievement. Alan has not simply 'worked with' the best, his efforts and expertise made those goalkeepers the best.

Paul Ince

It was said I developed into a 'world class' goalkeeper. If that's true, then I owe it all to Alan Hodgkinson. The best goalkeeping coach in the world.

Andy Goram

A superb goalkeeper, Hodgey was not content with that, he went on to become arguably the best goalkeeping coach there has ever been.

Gordon Banks

Between the Sticks

| THE AUTOBIOGRAPHY |

Alan Hodgkinson MBE

HarperSport
An Imprint of HarperCollins*Publishers*

www.harpercollins.co.uk

First published by HarperCollins*Publishers* 2013

1 3 5 7 9 10 8 6 4 2

A catalogue record of this book is
available from the British Library

ISBN 978-0-00-750387-2

Printed and bound in Great Britain by
Clays Ltd, St Ives plc

MIX
Paper from
responsible sources
FSC® C007454

FSC™ is a non-profit international organisation established to promote
the responsible management of the world's forests. Products carrying the
FSC label are independently certified to assure consumers that they come
from forests that are managed to meet the social, economic and
ecological needs of present and future generations,
and other controlled sources.

Find out more about HarperCollins and the environment at
www.harpercollins.co.uk/green

*This book is dedicated to Brenda, the love of my life,
and to our loving family.*

| CONTENTS |

CHAPTER ONE	1
CHAPTER TWO	35
CHAPTER THREE	63
CHAPTER FOUR	91
CHAPTER FIVE	113
CHAPTER SIX	155
CHAPTER SEVEN	179
CHAPTER EIGHT	205
CHAPTER NINE	227
CHAPTER TEN	243
CHAPTER ELEVEN	267
CHAPTER TWELVE	293
CHAPTER THIRTEEN	305
Acknowledgements	315
Index	317

'It is a wise man that knows his own child.'

The Merchant of Venice

14 October 1967: George Best at Bramall Lane

In 1967, George Best had it all. There is hardly anything that can be done with a football that Best could not do. He is part of an elite group that includes Pele, Johan Cruyff, Diego Maradona, Stanley Matthews and Lionel Messi, players who have taken their place in the pantheon of the football gods.

Genius is a word bandied around far too often in football, but for George it was wholly appropriate. And he was, of course, unbelievably handsome. Teenage girls worshipped him, and women of all ages adored him. There are some people who look effortlessly stylish and elegant no matter what they wear – dress them in an old potato sack and they'll still exude elan. George was such a person. It was this heady cocktail of football genius and dashing good looks (along with the fact that he was a really nice guy) that resulted in George being the first footballer to achieve fame outside the game. I remember, how, on a visit to France in the sixties, I saw George on the cover of *Paris Match* and thought, 'This lad has really made it.'

It is for his genius as a footballer that I like to remember George. For me, his secret weapon was his acceleration. In all my years in the sport I have never seen a footballer move as fast as Best from a standing start – not Alan Shearer, Thierry Henry, Robin Van Persie;

no one. When it comes to leaving your marker for dead, the first three yards are the most important, and the first yard is in your head. Add in the skill, agility and dexterity that throws opponents off balance and George became uncatchable.

I have never come across a player, then or since, who did it all so easily and, apparently, instinctively. George was a superb exponent of the almost lost art of dribbling. He scribbled football history with his feet and it was nothing to see him leave four, even five men standing off-balance and bemused.

Countless words have been written and spoken about George's genius as a footballer. All of them wholly deserved. One thing I have never heard mentioned, however, was how thick and effective his neck muscles were. The power he generated from the neck enabled him to head a ball as well as the most potent striker or towering centre-back, and he was strong enough to look after himself when the going got tough, as it often did for him.

What is also often overlooked about George's game is that he was a terrific defender and tackler. It was part of his job to track back and defend, and he did so to tremendous effect. But it was for his audacious attacking flair that he was best known and loved, and it was this skill that left an indelible mark on the minds of all who were lucky enough to see him play.

When George burst onto the international scene as a teenager with Northern Ireland, the former Spurs and Northern Ireland captain Danny Blanchflower was approached outside Windsor Park by *Daily Mirror* football reporter Vince Wilson and asked for his opinion of the young George Best. Most players would have replied with a list of insipid superlatives. Not the astute, aesthetic and articulate Blanchflower, the Oscar Wilde of Windsor Park.

'George makes a greater appeal to the senses than Stan Matthews or Tom Finney did,' said Danny, in characteristic fashion. 'His movements are quicker, lighter, more balletic. He offers grander surprises to the mind and eye. Though seemingly insouciant on the pitch, he has ice in his veins, warmth in his heart and hitherto unseen timing and balance in his feet.'

Vince Wilson looked up from his notebook, somewhat agitated.

'Yes, yes, yes, Danny,' said Vince, pen still poised, 'but do you rate Best as a player?'

I played against George on numerous occasions and was lucky enough to observe at first hand his development from teenager of outstanding natural talent to a true football genius. In October 1967, following a game at Stoke, I chatted to Gordon Banks about Best, because Manchester United were Sheffield United's next opponents.

'United play to his speed,' Gordon informed me. 'When we played them, Charlton and Crerand played the ball through the channels between and behind our back four for George to run on to. He times his runs to perfection, so he doesn't get offside. He's like lightning. He leaves defenders in his wake. You're left with a one-on-one with him. He'll really test you because he's ice cool, clever, unbelievably skilful and very, very quick.'

I always felt that one of the strongest aspects of my game was when faced one-on-one with an advancing forward. I had, over the years, spent countless hours on the training ground working to improve that ability. In the 1960s clubs did not have specialist goalkeeping coaches. I did the normal daily training with the rest of the first-team squad but felt I needed more. As there was no one at Sheffield United to help me in this, I did it myself, mostly in the afternoons. Keepers at other clubs were also developing their skills, making what, in essence, was a journey of self-discovery, among them Tony Waiters (Blackpool), Peter Bonetti (Chelsea), Alex Stepney (Manchester United), Jimmy Montgomery (Sunderland) and the young-bloods: Peter Shilton (Leicester City) and Pat Jennings (Tottenham Hotspur). They were all working hard to improve their game and, in so doing, the standard of goalkeeping in England.

Though working in isolation we each devised personal training schedules to improve positioning, angles, reflexes, distribution, collecting, punching, dead-ball kicks, dealing with corners and free-kicks, organising the defence and so on. At the time the greatest exponent and the man who can be credited with turning the art of goalkeeping into a science was Banks, widely accepted as the best goalkeeper there has ever been.

You will have heard the phrase, 'the goalkeepers' union'. There is, of course, no union as such; it is simply a phrase to explain the bond goalkeepers enjoy with one another. As a specialist position it demands specific skills and attributes, but it also applies pressures that no other position in the team carries. An outfield player can make mistakes and get away with them; he can make a wayward pass and teammates will, more often than not, rectify his error as play unfolds. Not so with a goalkeeper. Mistakes here invariably result in a goal for the opposition. It is the knowledge and pressure of this that invokes in goalkeepers a common bond, and even in the days before teams were requested to shake hands prior to a game, goalkeepers always shook hands when they passed one another after the ritual tossing of the coin before a match.

When the teams met for a drink after a game I always made a point of chatting to the opposing goalkeeper. Quite often he would reveal a little nugget about a player he had encountered and I would try and reciprocate, hence my chat to Banksy about George Best.

Indecision in a goalkeeper gives away more goals than any other flaw, so I always tried to let my defenders know exactly where I was and what I wanted them to do. Nowhere is indecision more catastrophic than in a one-on-one. Quite often a striker is through before the danger can be seen. Call it intuition or instinct, but a goalkeeper must see the opening before a forward and, without hesitation, sprint out to cut down the angle and force the forward wide. It is all about alertness, anticipation and the ability to read a game.

'You know, as well as I do, what to do in a one-on-one,' said Banksy, 'but Best is so quick and skilful, you need a special strategy. Anticipation is the key. You have to be out there, your position and angle spot on when he sets off, because he's so quick. He'll weigh you up in an instant, and his ability to change pace and direction is phenomenal. So get out to him as quickly as you can. Stay on your feet and make sure you force him wide to his left. He's good with both feet, but prefers his right, so get him so the ball is on his left. Jockey him. He'll twist and turn, but stay on your feet. Just keep jockeying him across to his left, boss it. Eventually he'll try and switch and give you a glimpse of the ball, and that's when you go down to collect.'

I thanked Bansky for his advice. It was more or less what I had figured, but hearing it from him made me believe my strategy would be the right one.

Just over an hour into our game against Manchester United at Bramall Lane, Pat Crerand played the defence-splitting ball Banksy had warned me about. George was on it in a flash, but I had taken to my toes a split second before.

George bore down on me. I had taken a position in the left-hand channel of my area, halfway between the penalty spot and the edge of the penalty area, a very good position. I made a half-turn to my right, inviting George across my penalty area. He immediately swerved away to his left, the way I wanted him to go. Excellent. No sooner had he done this than, in more or less the same movement he veered back to his right. I instantly re-adjusted my position. Staying on my feet, I angled my body to force George back onto his left. Got him! I had him switching the ball back onto his left foot, George nudged the ball some nine inches away from his left boot – just what I wanted him to do. I seized my opportunity, went to ground and made a lunge for the ball. I grasped fresh air. In the split second it took for me to hit the deck George switched his right leg across, dragged the ball back with the sole of his right boot, then, with the toe of the same boot, flicked the ball away to his right and my left. Anxious to regain my feet and catch him, I over-balanced and fell backwards onto my backside. Instinctively I stuck out my left arm, but George was gone. I turned in time to see him behind me, in more space than Captain Kirk ever enjoyed. I watched helplessly as he side-footed the ball into the empty net courtesy of his favoured right foot.

George raised one arm in the air and smiled benignly as he walked slowly back towards his rejoicing teammates.

'Bloody hell, George. You gave me spiral blood,' I said as he passed me.

'Ah, you had me going there, Hodgey,' he replied. A smile as wide as a slice of melon broke across his face. 'Had a bitta luck.'

Luck didn't come into it. It was brilliant play on his part. No other player had ever turned me over in a one-on-one with such consummate ease as George did that day. What's more, no player ever did again.

A couple of months later, I fell into conversation with Banksy after we had played Stoke City at Bramall Lane. During our chat I recalled my experience with George.

'Did just as you said. To the letter,' I informed Banksy. 'Forced him across goal and onto his left foot. Stayed on my feet, forced him further to his left till he gave me a glimpse of the ball. He dumped me on my arse and tapped the ball in the net. Made me look a right Charlie.'

Bansky rubbed his chin with the thumb and forefinger of his right hand.

'Yeah, thought he would,' said Banksy, emitting a sigh, 'he did exactly the same to me.'

*   *   *

George Best was a football genius and, sadly, there is no true genius without a tincture of madness. I have nothing but fond memories of George and, as I will also later recall, found him to be a very intelligent, immensely witty, amiable and caring guy who, for all his fame and exploits, was surprisingly shy.

I have now reached an age where I increasingly find myself recalling the great players, great games and even the not-so-great names and games that provided the essence to my sixty-year career in professional football. I am, if nothing else, a very lucky guy indeed. To have enjoyed – and I emphasise the word 'enjoyed' – sixty years as a player and coach in professional football, is a journey I could never, in my wildest dreams, have envisaged making when I first signed for Sheffield United back in the days when the only thing that came ready to serve were tennis balls, and it was girls that brought me out in a sweat and not tandoori chicken.

Football has been my life and it has blessed me with a treasure trove of memories. Memory tempers prosperity, mitigates adversity, controls youth and, as I am now discovering, delights one in the seasoned years. The true art of memory is the art of attention. During the course of their careers many players never take note or commit to memory the characters, games, unguarded asides, humour, friendships, golden moments and angst they experience – quintessentially what makes football so entertaining and the greatest team game on the planet. I had the presence of mind to document my career: I kept and logged every press report of every game I was ever involved in, from my salad days as a teenage amateur with Worksop Town via Sheffield United and England, to my role as a coach with myriad top clubs and both Scotland and England.

I also kept the match programmes of every game I was involved in. These and my personal collection of scrapbooks and notebooks have proved to be invaluable now that I have decided to commit my story to paper. I have never written a book before but, after sixty years of continuous employment in the game, I felt the time was right.

During the course of my career I have seen football change irrevocably, from a working man's leisure pursuit to the multi-billion-pound industry that it is today. Self-appraisal is no guarantee of merit, I know, but rather than being one of those former players who believe football past was far better than football present, I would like to believe I have not only moved with the times but, in my field of goalkeeping, have always been an innovator. In recent years the ideas I introduced to my UEFA coaching sessions attended by the likes of José Mourinho, Harry Redknapp, Rafael Benitez and Felipe Scolari have, I would like to think, in some small way enhanced their expertise as coaches in the modern game. Football past was great, but so too is football present. That I have continued to contribute in a positive way to the game I love so much is a constant source of joy to me.

Though now in my eighth decade, I do not feel old. On the contrary, the fact I have continued to work in the game has kept me young of mind and heart. A friend once said to me, 'How old would you put yourself at, if you didn't know how old you were?' It's a good question. Thanks to my long career in football I would put myself at an age far younger than my actual years. That is just one of the great gifts and benefits football has given me and one of the reasons why I am so grateful to the game that has, and always will have, a special place in the best of all possible worlds.

*   *   *

I was born on 16 August 1936. Little over two weeks later King Edward VIII abdicated, Nazi troops occupied the Rhineland and civil war broke out in Spain. An unfortunate sequence of events, but I have it on good authority that none of these was due to me having entered the world.

I was born into a hard-working and principled working-class family. My dad, Len, was a loving father, though something of a stickler for discipline. He was also an enigma in our home town of Laughton Common, which is equidistant between Sheffield and Rotherham, being as he was a miner at Dinnington Colliery and also an accomplished concert pianist.

When it comes to playing the piano some people can carry a tune but appear to stagger under the load. Not so Dad. Those strong, gnarled hands that hewed coal for eight hours on a daily basis would suddenly be transformed into deftly gliding fingers that lovingly caressed the piano keys. So popular was he as a pianist that Dad often gave recitals at civic halls and theatres throughout South Yorkshire and, in the summer, entertained holidaymakers at Butlin's holiday camps. I would listen to him play and be totally transfixed. He not only reproduced the piece perfectly but he seemed to capture its very essence and that of its composer.

Given his talent, I have often wondered whether if he had been born into a middle-class family in, say, the leafy suburbs of Betjeman's London rather than a working-class family in the South Yorkshire coalfields, his musical destiny would have been different. Dad was born at the turn of the twentieth century, when working people accepted their lot. There was little, if any, recognition of a working person's musical talent by the great and good of classical music. Dad would never have had the wherewithal nor was he offered the opportunity to develop his talent at a musical college or academy. A great pity, not least because a bill poster proclaiming, 'The Conservatoire Collier plays Chopin', would have had a wonderful alliterative ring to it.

Dad began working down the pit at the age of fourteen and continued to do so until he retired at the age of sixty-five. He hadn't missed a day's work and, what's more, in fifty-one years as a miner Dad was never once late. On his retirement, the well-meaning folk at the colliery bought him a clock.

My mum was called Ivy. She was a very loving and attentive mother who, in keeping with most mothers of that era, worked impossibly long hours cooking, washing, ironing, cleaning, mending and shopping for her family. Long before the phrase was invented, women were 'multi-taskers', quite simply because their role of looking after the home and children and everything to do with domesticity was labour intensive.

I was fortunate in having a mother and father who took an interest in me, my brothers and sister. I felt Dad knew me and what made me tick. Most of the other dads I knew were also miners but they spent little time with their kids. In the 1940s, as now, a mother knew everything about her children – the scabs, nits, bad teeth, best friends, favourite foods, constipation, shoes that didn't fit properly, romances, secret fears, hopes and dreams – but most fathers were only vaguely aware of the small people living in the house. Not so my dad.

Home was a two-up-two-down red-brick terraced house on Station Road in Laughton Common. People stayed in their jobs in those days and they stayed in their houses too. It was unheard of for couples to set up home before they were married. Once they had, the vast majority stayed put until the time came for their children to call the funeral director. There were no nursing homes, no managed flats for the elderly. A house was bought or rented and turned into a home by women like my mum. At various times it was also a nursery (though no one ever used the term 'nursery' in the 1940s), a hospital, classroom, party function room, music hall stage, a rest home and, in the vast majority of cases, in the end, a chapel of rest for those who had purchased the house in the first place.

Internally and externally, the houses took on the character of their occupants. From either end of Station Road the terraced houses all looked the same, but as a boy I soon learned the subtle individualities of each one. It was the small touches – invariably the mother's – that gave them their identity. The highly polished brass letterbox on the front door of the Coopers'; the pristine gold-leaf house number on the fanlight over the front door of the Cartwrights' (as a boy I had no idea why this number had survived intact when all the others had become mottled and flaked with age); the net curtains in the front window of the Thompsons', gathered rather than hanging straight as in every other home; the red glass vase, no more than four inches high, that balanced precariously on the narrow window ledge in the Smiths' front window.

Those surnames were all traditional, straightforward, dependable, no-nonsense names, most of which owed their origin to some trade or other. When I was a boy it was said Sheffield boasted more Smiths than anywhere else in England, until, as Dad once joked, the title was taken one weekend by a cheap hotel in Brighton.

Fresh flowers were a rarity in the houses. In the summer, Mum would occasionally give me a threepenny bit (just over 1p) and send me across to the allotments which were, in the main, rented by miners. I would ask the allotment owner, 'Have you any chrysanths you don't want?' Chrysanths – that was all the miners who ran the allotments seemed to grow in the way of flowers. With their football-like blooms (there was even a species called 'Football Mums') and tall stems, these flowers dominated the small living rooms of the houses they fleetingly graced.

Keen to make threepence and offload my surplus flowers, I would find myself skipping home with an enormous bunch of earwig-infested chrysanths. Mum would indeed marvel at them before cutting their stems and displaying them in two or often three vases around the house. I only realised their full name, chrysanthemums, when I was in my mid-teens. True, chrysanths runs off the tongue a lot easier but, looking back, there might have been another reason for the shortened name. Chrysanthemum sounds Latin, something only posh kids learned. In Sheffield and Rotherham in the forties such class distinction was as clearly drawn by the working class as it was by the middle and upper classes, and you wouldn't want to be accused of getting above your station.

Mum organised the house and family life and we functioned to a tried-and-tested routine. We had no bathroom; we washed twice daily at the kitchen sink, usually with cold water. In keeping with every family I knew, Friday night was bath night. Dad would take down the tin bath from its hook in the backyard shed. It would be placed on newspaper in front of the living-room fire and laboriously filled by Dad with kettles of hot water. First to go was Dad, then my sister, followed by my two brothers, then me. Being the fifth user of the same bath water it's a wonder I didn't get out dirtier than when I got in.

It seems unbelievable now, but Friday night was the only time in the week when I changed my underpants and vest. Again, we were not unique in this, every family I knew changed underwear weekly. There were no modern labour-saving devices such as washing machines. Mum washed our clothes every Monday, in the kitchen, with a tub and dolly, after which she would hand-rinse everything then put all the washing through a hand-operated wringer before hanging it out to dry, or, in the event of rain, on wooden clothes horses which were dotted around the living room or placed in front of the 'range' fire. Come Tuesday they were dry. On Wednesday they were ironed and then put away in wooden drawers that smelled of lavender and mothballs, ready for us to wear again on Friday after our bath, and so the cycle was repeated. Mum's life must have been as monotonous as mutton, as regular as the roll of an army drum. That my childhood was such a happy one, secure and filled with a warm heart is to her eternal credit.

Saturday was football day, but for the vast majority of Laughton Common women and, I would suggest, women everywhere, it was the day they had their hair done. It was the time of 'Twink' perms for women and an entirely different type of perm for the menfolk.

Come the weekend, the women of Laughton Common would buy a Twink perm in their quest to have glamorous hair, if only for a couple of days. I recall my mother and neighbouring women spending most of Saturday with myriad purple plastic grips in their hair which to me looked like small chicken bones. Around these purple 'bones' they wrapped strands of hair and tissue paper. I never knew the reason for the tissue paper and still don't; it was minutiae from a mysterious female world that, for all it touched mine, was to remain beyond my ken.

The permed hair would be protected from the elements and sooty Sheffield air with a headscarf. Just about every woman in Laughton Common sported a headscarf on a Saturday, though the effect alluded more to 'Old Mother Riley' than Grace Kelly in an open-top sports car.

On a Saturday it was not only the women who talked of perms but the menfolk too, though the perms the men discussed were far removed from the Twink variety. For most working men the only way to escape their frugal lifestyle and the daily grind of work at the colliery would be to win the 'Pools'. The Pools, or 'coupon' as they were also known, was the dream ticket out of a life of working drudgery.

I was three years old when war was declared, and nine when it ended. It would be an exaggeration to say the tranquillity of life was shattered; war in all its horror didn't descend on Laughton Green, but it is equally true to say that life was never the same again. There were no dog fights in blue skies strewn with the spaghetti of vapour trails. No trains departing from Station Road with carriages full of husbands and sons waving to the tear-stained faces of loved ones. No wailing air-raid sirens. No need for us to take to the Anderson shelter every night. No houses or factories ablaze.

But if our village didn't warrant the destructive attention of the Luftwaffe, Sheffield, the city built on steel manufacture, was an entirely different matter. On several occasions I can recall my family and me joining neighbours in a back garden to witness the city suffer a horrendous pounding four miles away. The sloe-coloured sky hummed to the drone of bombers from which there seemed no respite. Ack-ack guns thumped away in the dark distance. The sky flashed and flared. The sound of thunder beset Sheffield most nights. I remember one particular night when I was around seven years old, the thunderous sound was accompanied by a thin red line in the sky above Sheffield. Within half an hour it had billowed into a crimson aura that lit up the surrounding countryside for miles. Sheffield, the city where my football heroes dwelled, was ablaze. Only then did the ghostly droning sound in the darkness of the sky depart.

As a miner, Dad was considered essential to the war effort, which meant he could not be called up. The raw materials needed to help fight the war included leather. Even after the war, it remained scarce, so leather footballs were non-existent around Laughton Common. Even if the 'sell everything' shop on Station Road had stocked leather footballs, I doubt if the hard-pressed budgets of most parents could have run to buying one.

The father of one of my pals worked in the local butcher's. The bladder of a pig is not too dissimilar to the rubber bladder that was inserted inside the leather 'casey' or caseball. From as early as I can remember, until I was around ten or eleven years of age, we boys played football on the local rec with a pig's bladder.

Pigs' bladders are surprisingly durable. Given that we mostly wore hobnailed boots, those pigs' bladders came in for some hammer, but they could last a couple of games. That was some going as our football matches on the rec lasted for anything up to three hours between teams of up to fifteen players. A boy who wanted to join the game would have to wait for another boy to accompany him. The pair would then decide who was 'chalk' and who was 'cheese'. As the game continued, the pair would then present themselves before the rival captains, one of whom would choose 'chalk or cheese'. There were variations such as 'beef or pudding', 'jam or tart', all with foody connotations, like the ball we played with. I have since learned that many lads of my generation played football through the war years with a pig's bladder. If you hit the bladder really hard, sometimes it would burst on impact, hence the term, 'he really bladdered it', when a player hits a really hard shot at goal.

When the pig's bladder did eventually give up the ghost, you simply went to the local butcher's to ask for another. Someone then blew it up and tied the bladder's 'tube' into a knot, like a balloon. No one ever had any fear of catching a disease from it – we never considered such a thing possible. And, gruesome and unhygienic as it might sound to put a raw pig bladder in your mouth, I can't recall a lad ever being taken ill from having done so.

Many of the lads who played football on the local rec were older than me. As a seven-year-old it is difficult when most of the boys are three or four years older because the physical difference is so pronounced. So I could feel I was fully participating in these games, I always opted to go in goal. There was always plenty for both goalkeepers to do in kick-about matches but, as time went by, I became conscious of the fact that I really enjoyed being a goalkeeper. What's more, I began to display something of a talent for it.

I had a go at every sport at school and seemed to do okay at most. I represented my school and the district at football, cricket, badminton, basketball, table-tennis, swimming and athletics. I was, however, very keen on gymnastics and in time I became a good gymnast, good enough to represent the city and South Yorkshire. Gymnastics helped me achieve things other small lads could not, such as greater agility, flexibility, the ability to stretch, reach and dive to longer distances – all essential to good goalkeeping.

The recreation pitch we played on would not have been out of place in the foothills of the Himalayas. Any team playing up the slope was in need of Sherpas and oxygen masks to stand any chance of making progress. The pitch had been laid on what had once been a Victorian rubbish tip and, as the pounding of hobnailed boots took their toll on the topsoil, the rubbish tip beneath began to give up its treasures. Many a game was halted while one of my pals unearthed something peculiar. The most striking find was a cast-iron Victorian bicycle dug up from the sea of mud in the bottom goalmouth.

It was during the post-war years, in what has been termed 'football's golden age' when Football League attendances hit a record high, that I first began to collect items of football memorabilia. The first item I treasured was a scrapbook made from sheets of brown paper filled with newspaper photographs and cuttings of my heroes, which I diligently affixed to the pages with a glue I made from mixing flour and water.

I realise as I look at them now, that most of my childhood heroes in those scrapbooks were goalkeepers. Ted Burgin of Sheffield United was an acrobatic goalkeeper with a thick mop of black hair who had written to United for a trial when with non-League Alford Town (Lincolnshire). The amazing thing about Ted was his height; he was only 5 foot 7 inches. You simply will not see a professional goalkeeper of that height in today's game, where clubs are looking to develop goalkeepers of 6 foot 2 and more. Sam Bartram, a keeper who served Charlton Athletic for twenty-five years, was considered a giant of a man at the time at 5 foot 11. Frank Swift (Manchester City), the first goalkeeper to captain England, was a larger-than-life character and a fabulous goalkeeper. He had fingers like bananas and many a supporter of a certain age is willing to testify to having seen Frank's 'party piece': catching and holding a thunderous shot with one hand.

When I was thirteen to fourteen years of age, my book of goalkeeper heroes expanded to include Jimmy Cowan (Morton and Sunderland). Jimmy had an outstanding game against England at Wembley in 1949 when his heroics helped the Scots to a famous 3–1 victory. I listened to the match on the radio and can well remember Raymond Glendenning's rich and plummy commentary peppered with superlatives in praise of Cowan's performance.

Bert Trautmann, the former German paratrooper and POW who stayed on in England after the war to carve a great career for himself with Manchester City, was another hero of mine. As was the dependable Ronnie Simpson of Newcastle United who, much later, at the age of 39, kept goal when Celtic became the first British club to win the European Cup in 1967.

Looking back, the press cuttings I collected tell of a game that is alien to the football of today. It wasn't better or worse, just so very different. They also reveal that during the war, when football was regionalised, the game was also mighty different to that of the immediate post-war period. The Football League North Division of 1944, for example, comprised an eye-watering 54 clubs, albeit each club played only eighteen matches. Huddersfield Town were crowned champions and, as one glances down a league table that seems to go on forever, there, to the eternal delight of Liverpool fans, I am sure, is Manchester United, in the bottom half, two places behind Crewe Alexandra and Rochdale.

As a small boy I went to Laughton Council School, then to Dinnington Secondary Modern. Unbelievably now, the class I was in at Laughton Council School comprised forty-seven children, and what's more our teacher had no assistance. It's a wonder any of us learned anything at all – by the time she had taken the register it was nearly playtime! I was never an outstanding scholar, more fair to middling. At Dinnington Secondary Modern my favourite subjects were PE, of course, English (I love to read), music and history. Though something of a scamp, I was never a source of trouble at school.

I had a really happy childhood. My dad harboured the hope that I might one day become a concert pianist and paid for me to go to piano lessons. My piano teacher was a genteel old lady who did her best with me, but the lure of football was too great in the end. Although I never played truant from school, piano lessons increasingly got in the way of games of football on the rec. I would set out for my piano teacher's house with good intentions only to then bump into a few mates who would say, 'Fancy a game?' Without exception, any inclination I had to play Schubert's 'The Trout' would play second fiddle to me trying to be be Bert Trautmann.

I suppose there was more than an element of Dad wanting me to live out his dream of being a top-class concert pianist. To this day I still feel a tinge of sadness that I couldn't do that, but I hope my long career in football in some way compensated him for me not being able to be the Victor Borge of Sheffield.

When I was around thirteen the family moved some three miles to Sawnmoor Avenue in Thurcroft. It was to be a house move that would have a fantastic and life-long effect on me for, when we moved into our new house, I caught sight of a young girl who lived opposite. Even at the tender age of thirteen, I realised there and then that I had seen the girl of my dreams.

Being a gregarious lad, I made friends quickly in my new neighbourhood. I started to go about with a group of young lads and girls, and to my excitement and delight one of the young girls was my neighbour from across the road who, I quickly learned, was called Brenda. Our group, surprisingly unisex considering we were all around thirteen years of age, liked to meet up on a Saturday night and go dancing at the village welfare hall in Thurcroft. When it came to dancing I made a beeline for Brenda and couldn't believe my good fortune when it became apparent she appeared to like me as much as I liked her.

In the ensuing weeks we spent as much time as we could in one another's company. What today people may refer to as 'chemistry' was perfect between us. I had never had a girlfriend to speak of, nor had Brenda had a boyfriend of any note; we were incredibly naive but I was aware that every moment I spent in her company was magical and special for me.

In time we graduated from the dances at the local village hall and broadened our horizons by travelling the four or so miles to the local swimming baths in Rotherham where, on a Saturday night, the swimming pool was covered with boards to form a dance floor. The attraction of the dances at Rotherham Baths was the music provided by a proper dance band, The Clifton Group, as opposed to a quintet at the village hall. The Saturday dance at the swimming baths was a great attraction for the young people of Rotherham, the place was invariably packed, full of atmosphere and the optimism and anticipation that one can only find at the edge of a dance floor. The type of dancing we did was ballroom dancing, the foxtrot, dashing white sergeant and, later in the night, when things got wild, we jitterbugged. From a lad's point of view, the great advantage to ballroom dancing was it enabled you to hold the girl you were dancing with. Much modern dancing involves couples not touching at all; not so in those days. For many a lad, when a girl consented to dance and he placed his arm around her waist it was a great thrill, albeit, in many cases, this proved to be the extent of their sex life until he married her.

Brenda was widely considered to be one of the most fashionable girls who attended the dance. In the post-war years there was little to be had in the way of fashion as far as young working-class people were concerned, but when it came to clothes and her appearance, Brenda possessed the all-important attribute of imagination. I recall her once wearing a fulsome skirt in what was known as a 'tulip cut' with a netted skirt underneath. With her hair in a bubble cut courtesy of a Twink perm, I remember feeling very special with her on my arm as we walked about the dance hall and she attracted admiring looks from other lads, some even in their late teens. Like the majority of other lads, I dressed in a short-sleeved V-neck sweater of the Fair Isle variety, shirt, tie and baggy trousers purchased off the peg from the Co-op. I longed to own a suit, as did every lad, but family budgets didn't go to suits for sons. Though I felt I never dressed as stylishly as Brenda, she didn't seem to mind. She liked me for who I was, which, pardon the pun, suited me fine.

In addition to playing in goal for my school, the District team, Sheffield Boys and Hallamshire County, I also played on a Saturday afternoon for my local youth club before, at the age of fourteen, gaining my first taste of 'open-age' football when I signed for the Dinnington Colliery Welfare team.

The Colliery Welfare team played in a league consisting of other colliery welfare clubs and works teams in the South Yorkshire area. In addition to miners, the various local leagues comprised teams for steel-workers, smelters, cutlers, engineers, railway workers, tram and bus drivers, firemen, policemen, painters and decorators, even milkmen. There was, however, not one team from any of the professions. Football was considered the property of the working classes and the notion was that it should be played by them because they were the only people with the talent to play it.

I remember being very excited at the prospect of playing at enclosed grounds whose pitches boasted goals with nets and were bordered by a wooden railing, rather than on a park pitch situated among up to half-a-dozen other pitches. The colliery welfare teams contained the usual characters one will find in any football team at that level of the game. The cultured inside-forward, who wore his hair a little longer than everyone else and played with the air of a grammar school boy among elementary school pupils.

The bull-in-a-china-shop centre-forward who was expected to run through a brick shit-house and expected to be roundly abused if he shirked it. The wingers: on one wing a tall, skinny flyer who was all bone and elbow whilst, on the other flank, as if to balance things out, a small and squat winger with bandy legs who, although lacking the pace of his counterpart, was full of trickery. The full-back who never spoke, went about his business in silent efficiency and showed such a lack of emotion you were left to wonder what, if any, enjoyment he got from football at all. The hard-man wing-half, with shin-pads like castle doors who never buttoned his shirt even on the coldest of days, his chest hair protruding from his shirt like stuffing from a burst sofa. The towering centre-half with a granite chin and a forehead hammered flat through contact with a thousand muddy footballs, whose muscular legs would protrude from his cotton shorts like bags of Portland cement. The niggler wing-half who, from the kick-off kept up an incessant verbal harassment of the referee – 'Bloody hell, Ref, get a grip. Hey, Ref, hand-ball, you missed that. Ref, you're having a bad one. Hey, Ref, handball. Bloody hell, Ref, he was late. Hey, Ref, he's all over me. 'king hell, Ref, I never touched him. Hey, Ref, your linesman missed that. Come on, Ref, he's having the shirt off me back. Bloody hell, Ref, you can't give that. Hey, Ref, offside, a mile off! Thank you!'

Even at the age of fourteen I never felt overawed at the prospect of playing against men in their twenties and thirties. I think this had much to do with the fact since early childhood I had always played against boys who were older than me. I relished the challenge of pitting myself against what were very decent amateur players, some of whom enjoyed legendary status in local Sheffield football. It was a standard of football far removed from school and youth club football; it was far and away quicker, more physical, more aggressive. Players would swear loudly as they chased the ball across a Lowry landscape and, joy of joys, thumbnail reports of these matches would appear in the *Sheffield Star*. As a boy of fourteen, the first time I saw my name in print in the *Sheffield Star* I must have read the match report a hundred times, before cutting it from the sports page and carefully gluing it into a virginal exercise book, on the cover of which I had somewhat optimistically written,

'Match Reports'.

On leaving school in 1951 at the age of fifteen, I got a job in the local Co-op store as a butcher's assistant with a view to one day learning the trade. I was very half-hearted about the prospect of being a butcher, though I never dared tell Dad; I took the job because I finished work at noon on a Saturday, which meant I was then free to play football in the afternoon.

Saturday was a long day. I was up with the sparrows' fart at a quarter past four, started work at the Co-op at five, where my first job would be to defrost the freezer then arrange the various cuts of meat, sausages, pork pies and what have you on the display counters. Before the store opened the manager would come and inspect my handiwork, and would indicate that everything was in order simply by a single nod of his head. I would then do a variety of jobs around the shop and help out behind the counter until noon, when I collected my wages: the princely sum of £1. 2/6d (£1.12½p). That done, I would head for home, pay Mum my board and lodging and have a bite to eat before setting off to play football. In the evening, I would collect Brenda and we would go off dancing with our friends.

In the event my time with the Colliery Welfare team was short-lived. After twenty or so games I was approached by non-League Worksop Town and, keen to try my hand at a higher level of football, signed for a club where, unbeknown to me, serendipity would shape my future career and life.

For working-class people there was no such thing as fashion in 1952, after all, what could you possibly wear during rationing? We relied on functional clothes, mostly woollen hand-me-downs, previously worn by parents, older siblings or, in many instances, both. In the early fifties a young person's taste in fashion was dictated by what was least itchy.

If you were a lad in your mid-teens and wanted to appear grown-up and smart, the crowning ambition was to own a suit. They were worn only on special occasions: to church on Sundays, for weddings, funerals, christenings, hot dates and to celebrate a Sheffield United away win. (I'm joking about the latter, but only a little...)

Most adult men owned a suit and the vast majority had been given it by the government when they were 'demobbed' from the forces at the end of World War Two. Demob suits, as they were known, were of plain cloth in either dark blue or brown and came in only two sizes – too small or too big.

As was the case with every other lad too young to have served in the war, I didn't enjoy this dubious distinction. As a lad of sixteen, however, I longed to have a suit of my own and not simply because I wanted to appear smart. It offered real kudos in Laughton Common and the same was true of Sheffield and Rotherham. If you were young and owned a suit, other lads were in awe of you and, more importantly, you found yourself very popular with the girls.

I was still working as a butcher's assistant at the local Co-op store when I signed as an amateur for Worksop Town. Such was my desire to own a suit that I hit upon the plan to buy one by saving some money from my weekly wage, still just £1. 2/6d, from the Co-op. I reasoned that once I had paid my mum for my board, deducted necessary personal expenses such as train and bus fares to and from Worksop Town for training and matches, ceased going to the cinema once a week, stopped buying fish 'n' chips on a Friday night, went dancing every third Saturday night and continued to wear an old pair of football boots handed down to me by an uncle rather than buying a new pair, I would have saved enough to buy a suit in five years. Obviously, another way had to be found.

Sheffield FC was formed in 1857 and is the oldest football club in the world, but Worksop Town were only four years behind them. Even when I joined Worksop in 1952, the club had a long history. It was also as broke as the Ten Commandments.

Worksop Town played in the Midland League but, because they ran six teams, were always pleading poverty. The word was, Worksop had been saddled with debt for over thirty years but had somehow managed to struggle on.

In the 1907–08 season, Worksop had reached the first round proper of the FA Cup, the equivalent today of the third round of the competition. The club was drawn away to Chelsea, and though hammered 9–1, it found some consolation in a bountiful share of the revenue from a bumper attendance of 70,184 at Stamford Bridge. The money from the Chelsea game sustained Worksop for nigh on a decade until, once again, the club fell upon hard times.

During 1920 and into 1921 they enjoyed another good run in the FA Cup which resulted in a plum tie away to Tottenham Hotspur.

Worksop produced the shock of that season's competition, a doughty performance earning them a goalless draw and unprecedented head-lines in the sports pages of national newspapers. The town was suddenly galvanised. The thought of playing host to mighty Spurs before a record attendance at Central Avenue had even non-football fans excited.

The club directors, rather than keeping one eye on the future, focused exclusively on money. They made a highly controversial decision to concede home advantage and return to White Hart Lane for the replay. According to those around at the time, Worksop stood a chance of beating Spurs on a home pitch that in mid-winter resembled molasses. But there was more chance of hell freezing over than achieving another favourable result at White Hart Lane.

To a man, and woman, the town believed the club's directors had sacrificed the chance of beating Spurs, thereby earning lasting fame for the town, by opting instead to line their own pockets.

The result of the replay was as emphatic as the fall-out from the decision proved catastrophic. Worksop lost 9–0 before a White Hart Lane crowd of just 12,000 which meant the club's share of the gate revenue was far less than anticipated. Town councillors and the local press berated the directors for their decision, and the town's population exacted their revenge by boycotting subsequent matches.

Attendances for matches at Central Avenue plummeted, and once people lost the habit of going along to watch their local team, they never again returned in the numbers they had prior to the Tottenham furore. Thirty-two years on, when I joined the club, Worksop Town were still struggling to make ends meet and were burdened by debt.

The Midland League was semi-professional and its members included the reserve teams of, amongst others, Nottingham Forest, Notts County, Hull City, Rotherham United, Scunthorpe United, Bradford City and Doncaster Rovers as well as crack non-League clubs such as Peterborough United, Corby Town, Boston United, Scarborough and Grantham.

I was a month short of my sixteenth birthday when I joined Worksop in the summer of 1952. I began the 1952–53 season play-ing in goal for the club's youth and reserve teams but my perfor-mances were such that I soon made the first team. That season we finished six places above bottom club Wisbech Town but won the Sheffield Senior Cup, the club's first trophy of any significance since winning the same competition way back in 1924.

Every summit marks the brink of an abyss, and two days after the club's Sheffield Senior Cup success, the club announced an annual loss of £145. It may not appear much by today's standards, but in 1952 that sum would have covered my wages behind the butcher's counter at the Co-op for the best part of three years.

In July 1953, as part of Worksop's pre-season programme, the club organised a friendly at Central Avenue for the youth team against Sheffield United's youth side. Although I was now Worksop's recognised first-team goalkeeper, I was still not yet seventeen, so I was delighted when manager Fred Morris selected me to play in goal.

The fact it was the youth team didn't matter at all. As far as I was concerned, I was playing against Sheffield United, and all their players were heroes to me. United had won the Second Division title the previous season and were preparing for life in the First Division (Premiership equivalent), so to play in this match was a tremendous thrill.

One-way traffic had yet to be introduced to Britain's road systems, but those present at Worksop Town that night witnessed its football equivalent. I can't recall much about the game itself but for the fact I was very busy indeed. Apart from having kicked off, I don't think Worksop managed to venture into Sheffield's half of the field for the majority of the first half. But, minutes before half-time and against the run of play, we broke out of defence and scored.

The second half mirrored the first. It was like the Alamo as wave after wave of red-and-white striped shirts laid siege to my goal. I had to pull off save after save to preserve our lead. Eventually, we broke away and, to my utter joy, scored again. This served only to annoy the United players even more. Their retribution was a constant pressure on my goal. United did pull a goal back but, after a period of desperate defending, we managed to snatch a third goal a minute from time.

The dressing room after the game was joyous. The final score in no way reflected the balance of play, but that's football. I'd lost count of how many saves I'd had to make but, as far as I was concerned, that was my job, even if I wasn't being paid.

Two days later, when I reported for evening training, I was asked to call in to Fred Morris's office. 'Office' was too grand a word for the cubby-hole under the main stand where Fred conducted his business of part-time football management. Forming the underneath of the tiered floor of the grandstand, the ceiling sloped at such an acute angle that anyone coming into the room could only take two paces before having to lower their head and shoulders. Fred's response was always to nod his head in recognition of what he perceived to be deference.

I knew something was up the moment I entered Fred's snuggery and bowed my head. He was seated at his desk, flanked on either side by a crouching club director. Not one to stand on ceremony, or upright in that cubby-hole, Fred told me straight off that Sheffield United had been so impressed by my performance against them they wanted to sign me.

I was flabbergasted. I loved playing football but never, at any time, had I ever thought about trying to make a career in the professional game. I simply didn't think I was good enough.

I was told by one director that the club would be more than happy for me to stay should I want to, but subsequent phrases such as 'once-in-a-lifetime opportunity', 'a golden chance to make something of yourself' and 'you'd be a fool to turn this offer down' suggested they couldn't wait for me to put pen to paper.

With my mind still whirling, I told Fred I would go home and discuss the matter with my parents and let him know my decision.

'That's the sensible thing to do, take as much time as you want. There's no rush,' said Fred, 'I'll call round your house at six tomorrow morning.'

Neither of my parents were great followers of football. I had two brothers and a sister and none of them was into it either. Having discussed the opportunity with Mum and Dad, they both said the decision should be entirely mine, but that they would support me in whatever I decided.

I slept on it and, when I awoke the next morning, felt the same as I had the night before.

I just didn't think I had the talent to make a go of it in the professional game. I thought about going to Sheffield United to play alongside junior players who had represented the county and England at schoolboy and, in some cases, Under-18 level, and felt I would be way out of my depth.

Fred dutifully arrived at our house on his way to work. When I informed him of my decision his chin fell to his chest. Undaunted, he left saying he would give me more time to 'think it over'. When Fred had left our house, I spoke to my dad.

'The decision is entirely yours, son,' he told me, 'but I know you, and by that token I know whichever decision you come to, it will prove to be the right one.'

Later that day I bumped into a teammate and it was from my conversations with him I discovered why the club were so keen for me to go to Bramall Lane. I was an amateur player but, according to my pal, Sheffield United had offered Worksop a fee of £250 for me. That was a huge amount of money, enough to erase the recent annual loss with enough left over to put a welcome hundred quid into the club's coffers.

When I reported for evening training I was again summoned to Fred's anticlinal office, where once again I informed him and the two stooping directors that I felt I wasn't good enough for professional football at any level, let alone with a First Division club.

'They think you are,' said Fred, 'and the fact that a club the stature of Sheffield United think you are good enough, should be good enough for you.'

I hadn't thought of that. It got me thinking.

The conversation continued and I began to hover. Sensing I was having second thoughts, Fred then played his ace.

'Tell you what,' he said. 'You know that United have offered £250 for you. You're an amateur so we can't make a payment to you, but, if you sign for them, as a sort of signing-on fee from us, Worksop will buy you a brand new suit out of the fee we receive.'

'A suit?' I repeated, feeling my heart flutter and my eyes widen as I said the words.

'A brand new suit, from a proper tailor?'

'None of that demob stuff,' said Fred, 'one that'll fit you like bark on a tree.'

This time I was aware of his eyes widening.

I started to reason that if Sheffield United felt I had the kind of talent as a goalkeeper they could possibly develop, the least I could do was to respect their view and let them try. I saw for the first time this was indeed a 'once-in-a-lifetime opportunity' and, should things not work out for me, I could always get a job on a building site. Sheffield had been heavily bombed during the war and the city had implemented a massive re-building programme. Jobs in the building trade were plentiful. Should United release me, I was still young enough to learn a trade and, of course, I could always return to non-League football.

All these thoughts ran through my mind as I stooped in contemplation in Fred's office, but it was the promise of the suit that swung it.

As my hand hovered over the signing-on form, I re-affirmed with Fred that Worksop would buy me the suit I craved.

'Made to measure, from a bespoke tailor,' confirmed Fred. 'The best that money can buy, well, from round here at any rate.'

That was good enough for me. I put pen to paper and signed for Sheffield United.

Fred reached into a drawer of his desk and threw a cloth tape measure to one of the directors.

'Arms out,' said the director.

With my face beaming I thrust out both arms and the director ran the tape along one of them.

'We'll send all your measurements to the tailor. It'll be a suit fit for a king,' Fred boasted, his face now a mixture of relief and joy.

That is how my career in professional football began

Sixty years on, I'm still waiting for the suit.

*   *   *

I wasn't quite done with the butchery business, though, because I began my career at Sheffield United as an amateur. I trained at Bramall Lane twice a week, on a Tuesday and Thursday night, in the company of some fourteen other amateur players and a few semi-professionals. I had, of course, been to Bramall Lane before but only as a spectator, not only for football, but also to watch cricket, as the ground hosted both Sheffield and Yorkshire County Championship games. The first evening I turned up for training my body was wracked with a mixture of awe, excitement and nerves.

It was still the summer. In 1953 the steel and building industries and their affiliated businesses were working around the clock to rebuild not only the city but the nation, so there was as much work going on in the evening as there was during the day. As I walked from the bus station to Bramall Lane, tramcars clattered along cobbled streets and hissed like ganders as they stopped to pick up passengers. The ugly fingers of soot-blackened chimneys forever pointing at the sky belched great fugs of yellowy-brown smoke into the atmosphere. Though evening, there was the bustle of a city whose industry lived cheek by jowl with the homes of its work-force. Not far off I could hear the sound of a thousand hammers echoing in cavernous corrugated-iron-roofed factories. The fiendish chatter of electric riveters. The sudden squeal of tortured metal. Occasionally I would catch a glimpse inside a partly open door and see a shower of sparks followed by great plumes of grey smoke. In the air an acrid mix of fired coal, sulphur-tainted steam and human sweat fought for ascendency with the yeasty odour of the nearby Wards' brewery. Amidst all this stood Bramall Lane, where many of the folk who sweated for little reward would escape to on a Saturday afternoon in the hope of inhabiting, for ninety minutes at least, a better world.

Sheffield United and, yes, Sheffield Wednesday too, provided the workers of the city with conflict and art. On the terraces, the smelter or foundry man was turned into a critic. Happy in his judgement of the finer points of what Tony Waddington would later refer to as 'the working man's ballet'. Ready to analyse a defensive formation; to estimate the worth of a slide-rule cross-field pass; a mesmerising dribble down the touchline, a bullet header or a crunching tackle. I knew how these supporters felt because I was one of them. On the terraces at Bramall Lane we turned into partisans, drawing breath when a shot from the opposition whistled past our goal; elated, exultant and ecstatic when a thunderous shot from one of our forwards turned the opposition net into a gumboil. Just as with every supporter the length and breadth of the land, smiling, scowling, laughing, longing, delirious, downcast, rabid, rapturous, vitriolic and victorious by turns at the fortunes of our team, as the players and a leather ball shaped Iliads and Odysseys before our very eyes, created our memories and myths and sprinkled stardust on harsh working lives.

Reg Wright looked after the amateurs and semi-pros at Sheffield United; Reg was an old pro who had stayed on at the club upon his retirement as a player to fulfil myriad roles. Reg took the training on Tuesday and Thursday nights, and he was also in charge of the 'A' team which played on a Saturday morning. Today, an academy team can have half a dozen backroom staff and more; Reg was their manager, coach, trainer, masseur, doctor and kit-man; and, just in case anyone felt he wasn't putting in a good shift at the club, during the week he also acted as physio to the full-time pros and helped out in the training of the first team.

I warmed to Reg Wright immediately. He was a hard taskmaster, but fair. His philosophy did not embrace the molly coddling of young players; you either did what he asked of you or you were out on your ear. Through his whole narrative ran a steel cable of tenacious durability, you had to be hard because football was hard, and football was hard because life was hard. With his Brylcreemed hair parted down the centre and topped by a flat cap worn at a jaunty angle, a baggy roll-neck sports jumper that looked every inch like the one you see the garrulous trainer's second wearing in one of those Laurel and Hardy shorts when Olly has persuaded Stan to get into a boxing ring to fight a frightening hulk, there was more than a little of the anachronistic about Reg Wright, even in 1953.

Reg exemplified the notion that football is a simple game and he embraced a simplistic evaluation of young talent. According to Reg, young players came in only three categories: 'Quick burn, slow burn, never to burn'. I can only assume Reg assessed me as being worthy of the former category for, after only a handful of games in goal for the 'A' team, I graduated to the youth team and, again, after only half a dozen or so matches, found myself promoted to the reserves.

I couldn't believe how quickly my life had changed. In little over a year I had progressed from the local Colliery Welfare team via the various teams at Worksop Town to Sheffield United reserves team via their 'A' and youth teams. I wasn't going to qualify with any team for a long-service award, that much I knew.

Sheffield United reserves played in the Central League, which was a massive step up from Youth and 'A' team football as it boasted the reserve teams of Wolverhampton Wanderers, both Manchester clubs, Liverpool, Everton, Newcastle United, Bolton Wanderers, Sheffield Wednesday, Stoke City, West Bromwich Albion and Aston Villa, to name but a few.

In those days the manager picked twelve players for the first team on a Saturday, the eleven who would play plus a standby reserve – there being no substitutes, of course. The remaining first-team squad players turned out for the reserves along with any regular first-teamers playing their way back following injuries, young hope-fuls such as myself and, a category of player you just don't have nowadays, the 'loyal foot soldier' who had years of service at the club but few, if any, first-team appearances to his name.

It was not uncommon in the fifties to find these loyal foot soldiers at most clubs. One of the most notable examples was Arthur Perry, who signed for Hull City in 1947 and left the club a few months short of ten years later without ever making a first-team appear-ance. Arthur spent his entire Hull career playing for the reserves before being transferred to Bradford in 1956. It's interesting to note that, under the rules of the time, should Arthur have completed the ten years he would have qualified for a Testimonial. Poor Arthur missed out, by a matter of months, on what for him would have been a big pay-out. That said, should Arthur have qualified for a Testimonial match, the mind boggles at Hull supporters turning up to honour a player many of them had never seen play.

Playing in the Central League it was not uncommon that I found myself playing against internationals coming back from injury and players out of favour in the first team but with League appearances under their belt that stretched into three figures. My debut for United reserves took place at Goodison Park and it was something of an ignominious debut as far as I was concerned – we lost 5–2 to Everton. For all I had conceded five goals I was told, however, I had acquitted myself well and, to my delight, kept my place in the reserves the following Saturday when I felt a whole lot better about life as we beat Manchester City's second string 1–0.

For me, every reserve team match, particularly those away from home, was exciting and an adventure. I hadn't travelled out of the Sheffield area much in my life, bar the occasional holiday to Skegness. For me, journeys to the likes of Manchester United, Preston or Aston Villa filled me with awe and wonder. I had only read about these clubs and their grounds, and never visited let alone seen them in these pre-television days. On arriving at such places I would accompany reserve team stalwarts of the day such as Graham Shaw and Willie Toner for the ritual inspection of the pitch, only I would not be staring down at the grass. My eyes would pan around the ground itself, taking in the detail of grandstands and alp-like terracing. I'd find myself saying something like, 'So this is Old Trafford? Where Johnny Carey and Stan Pearson play.' It was totally magical to me. I know you may feel I am conveying a romantic and idealised view of these reserve team matches, but they were romantic and idealised to me. I was not yet seventeen years of age and I was in awe and wonder of everyone I met and everywhere I visited.

When I reached my seventeenth birthday, the United manager, Reg Freeman, called me into his office. It was the first time I had ever been in the manager's office and probably only the third time he had spoken to me directly. Reg Freeman said he had 'news' for me and his news was music to my ears. He told me that, such had been my progress, the club were going to sign me as a full-time professional. This time, I had no hesitation in accepting. When he told me, I didn't hear his follow-up words for the sound of angels singing. My immediate thought was I would have to tender my resignation from my job as a butcher's assistant at the Co-op. It never occurred to me to ask what sort of wage I would be on, but when Reg got around to talking money, my legs did a fine impersonation of a cocktail shaker held aloft by a barman who takes real pride in his work. With my jaw almost resting on my middle shirt buttons, I listened as Reg told me I was to receive a £50 signing-on fee and a weekly wage of £7 during the season and £5 in the close-season. It was more money than I had ever seen in my life. A few days later, when the secretary paid me my signing-on fee, he did so with white fivers and I dutifully took the money straight home to Mum and Dad. As I carefully laid each fiver out on the kitchen table, Mum and Dad stood staring at the money in mute silence, their faces exuding the sort of wonder Columbus must have felt on realising he hadn't sailed over the end of the Earth.

I spent 1953 and 1954 as the regular reserve team goalkeeper and got to know well the unique culture of reserve team matches. Today

Premiership teams have squads; players not in the starting eleven or on the bench watch from the stands, as if it is beneath them to be asked to play for the reserves. Not that there is such a thing as a Premiership reserve team nowadays. The very term 'reserves' is considered to have negative overtones. They call them 'Development' squads now and no doubt someone was paid handsomely for coming up with that term. In a sense, I suppose, Development squad is more apposite, seeing as their ranks are filled with players under the age of 21.

With the passing of reserve teams, a small and lesser-spotted ritual of football disappeared. In terms of support, reserve team matches were the preserve of the die-hard supporter and children. In the fifties and well into the sixties, many a child's first visit to their local football ground was to a reserve team game. Parents or older brothers would take along little Johnny to their first football match, a reserve team game, as the crowd would not be intimidating and the child was guaranteed a good, unobstructed view of proceedings. It was also a good way for a boy to get to know the local ground as, quite often, supporters could change ends at half-time or, should it be raining, forgo the terraces and take shelter in the paddock of grandstands that overlooked the flanks.

In comparison to a first-team match, a reserve team game often seemed to take place in an eerie canyon. Even if there were 2–3,000 present, which often there were in grounds such as Goodison Park and Old Trafford, or even Bramall Lane, such a number appeared lost on the cold, grey slabs of terracing. They would hang from crash barriers munching monkey nuts and howling their grievances. Some preferred to take up the normal place in the ground they would inhabit for match days, and such lone fans would lean against the barriers high up at the very back of the terracing like guillemots perched on cliff faces. Whichever ground you visited there was always a raucous knot of seasoned supporters on either side of the ground overlooking the halfway line. Whilst behind the goal, a row of boys would cling to the perimeter fencing and try to make conversation with me when play was concentrated down the other end of the field.

Though my concentration was total during games, there was the odd occasion when I would acknowledge a question from one of the boys behind my goal. I did so in the hope he would be as thrilled as I would have been as a boy, should a footballer ever have spoken to me. Amongst his collection of personal memorabilia, Gordon Banks has a photograph taken of him on the occasion of his debut for Leicester City reserves against Swansea. The black-and-white snapshot shows a young, smiling Banksy, hands on hips, standing in between his posts. The photograph was taken by a boy who simply left his place on the perimeter fence behind the goal, walked onto the pitch during the pre-match kick-in and asked Banksy to pose, which he duly did. The lad later posted a copy of the print to Banksy care of the club and it serves as a happy reminder of his very first appearance in Leicester City colours. As Banksy says, 'It would never have occurred to me to say "No", even with a minute or so to go to kick-off.' Young supporters could do that kind of thing at reserve team games then; sadly, not so nowadays.

At the end of the 1953–54 season, Sheffield United reserves finished in exactly the same position in the Central League as they had in the previous season – fourth from bottom – not that it mattered. In all competitions, however, the reserves conceded twenty-seven fewer goals. I never gave this a thought at the time, but my performances in goal in what was my first season with Sheffield United must have indicated to Reg Freeman that I was developing along pleasing lines because, during the first week of April, I received a message to report to his office for what would be the fourth occasion he had spoken to me.

When it came to being a manager, Reg Freeman was one of the old school. We players never saw him at training; that was taken by Eric Jackson aided by Reg Wright, who was fast becoming the Swiss Army knife of the club. Reg Freeman seemed to spend most of his week in his office, emerging late on Thursday afternoon or early Friday morning to pin up the various team sheets for the forthcoming matches on the Saturday.

There were five League matches of the season remaining. Sheffield United had just about consolidated in our return to the First Division and were lying fourth from bottom, a place above Sheffield Wednesday, with Middlesbrough and Liverpool looking like favourites for relegation. For all that there was a buzz around Bramall Lane for the simple reason the club was due to unveil their floodlights. Floodlights were nothing new. Many top continental grounds boasted lights, but in 1954 very few English clubs had floodlights, even Wembley and Hampden Park didn't have them, so Sheffield United was considered one of the most forward thinking and go-ahead clubs in British football, and the unveiling of their floodlights was an auspicious occasion that would afford the club national publicity. (An experimental game under lights had taken place at Bramall Lane once before, way back in 1878, with lamps erected on wooden towers powered by Siemens dynamos, but thereafter the notion of playing matches under lights had literally receded into the shadows.)

To celebrate this new addition to the pitch, the club had arranged a floodlit friendly against Clyde. Today a Premiership club would never arrange a friendly against Clyde because it would not be a money spinner and also, with all due respect, because Clyde would not be a big attraction to Premiership supporters. Clyde are, after all, a club whose record club transfer paid dates back over forty years to 1966 to the £14,000 paid to Sunderland for Harry Hood.

In 1954 it was different. Clyde was a top-four team in Scotland. They boasted current Scottish internationals and one of the most memorably named of all footballers: Harry Haddock.

In the days of fledgeling television, fans could only read about teams such as Clyde, so they held a certain mystique for English supporters. Anglo-Scottish rivalry was still intense, with both the respective Football Associations misguidedly believing British football was still the best in the world. As such, a meeting of teams from either side of the border was a very attractive fixture, one sure to draw in a good crowd, especially on a novelty occasion such as an inaugural floodlit game.

To my delight and astonishment, Reg Freeman informed me that my form had been such for the reserves he was going to give me an outing with the first team, in the game against Clyde. I was both excited and elated. Friendly it might be, but I was determined to grasp this opportunity to show everyone I was capable of playing in the first team.

When I returned home I couldn't wait to tell my parents and Brenda my good news. My dad, as I have said, was never a keen follower of football. I reckon he had only attended but two football matches in his life, but when he heard I was to play for the first team against Clyde told me he 'wouldn't miss it for the world'. What's more, until he passed away, Dad would attend just about every future game I would play for United – and England.

The date was 6 April 1954. Bramall Lane was packed to the rafters for the visit of Clyde. Half an hour before kick-off, in a ceremony performed by local dignitaries and United chairman, Blakeo Yates, the massed ranks of United supporters cooed and ah'd as if watching a grand display of fireworks as our brand new floodlights flickered into full illumination.

Even in 1954, Bramall Lane had rich history to it. In 1883 it was the venue for England's first home international match outside London (versus Scotland), albeit Sheffield United as a club was not formed until six years later. The main grandstand was the work of the renowned architect Archibald Leach, its main feature being, on the roof of the John Street stand, a mock-Tudor gable which contained the press box. Ten bombs had hit Bramall Lane during the Second World War which destroyed most of the John Street stand, the Kop, and left a forty-foot deep crater in the centre of the pitch. It was to take several years for the club to make good the damage. A new double roof had been erected over the Kop in 1948 and the inaugural floodlit game against Clyde also marked the opening of the new John Street stand with, alas, the old gable stripped down to a flat-roofed press box. Bramall Lane, however, was still a three-sided ground, with the cricket pavilion on the far side separated from the football pitch by the cricket wicket and outfield. Rather than relishing the unusual layout of their home ground, the majority of United supporters disliked the open fourth side to the ground, which I could understand: even on such an auspicious occasion with a capacity crowd present, the open far side seemed to be a drain on the fervent atmosphere.

I wasn't overawed by the crowd, in fact, I was later to realise the bigger the occasion the better I liked it. As I changed next to my teammates I was riddled with nerves but, once I crossed that white line, my concentration was total and my nervousness dissipated. For a friendly it was a keenly contested game. There was, after all, Anglo-Scottish pride at stake. The game ended 1–1 and I readily recall the Clyde goal being scored by their international winger,

Tommy Ring. Little did I know then, Tommy was to come back and haunt me, albeit for a short time, on the occasion of another auspicious debut in my football career.

I felt pleased with my performance, though I was more relieved than anything at the fact I had not made any telling errors. Reg Freeman appeared pleased too, though in keeping with the man, he didn't say as much. When I entered the home team changing room at the end of the game, he simply patted me on the back.

Sheffield United's star player was Jimmy Hagan, an immensely talented inside-forward of considerable artistry whose talent deserved far more than the meagre reward of one official cap for England. Jimmy, like so many of his generation, had had his foot-ball career sacrificed to the war. He was the inspirational leader of the team, a man who always thought deeply about the game. Knowing Reg Freeman was not one to offer praise to players, never mind lavish it, Jimmy came up to me and complimented me on my performance. Such a compliment from a player of Jimmy's stature made me feel ten feet tall.

'You did well, Alan, son,' Jimmy informed me. 'The boss thinks so too, but you'll find out what he is like. Getting words of praise out of him is like knitting with sawdust.'

In light of Jimmy's kind words I couldn't wait for the following Friday when Reg Freeman pinned up the various teams for the games on Saturday. When he did so, my heart flopped. Ted Burgin, the reg-ular first-team goalkeeper, was reinstated for the game at home to Preston North End. I was back with the reserves at Newcastle United.

I saw out the remaining five matches of the season with the reserves, but wasn't too disheartened. In my first season at Sheffield United I had established myself as the regular reserve team goal-keeper and had enjoyed a brief flirtation with the first team, albeit for a friendly.

I couldn't believe that my whole attitude to my football had changed so much and so irrevocably in a little over a year. From not thinking I was good enough to sign for Sheffield United, I now believed my development, application and attitude were such that I was good enough to claim the number one jersey. I could see light at the end of the tunnel and I knew, in my heart of hearts, that it wasn't a train coming.

| CHAPTER TWO |

'Follow your spirit, and, upon this charge, cry,
'God for Harry! England and St George.'

Henry V

To keep myself reasonably fit, I spent most of the summer of 1954 playing cricket for Thurcroft Main in the Bassetlaw League. Somewhat appropriately, given I was a goalkeeper, I kept wicket for Thurcroft, whilst my batting was good enough to see me in the higher order. When pre-season training began with Sheffield United I felt in pretty good shape, confident, should my personal game continue to improve, I would be knocking on the door for the first-team jersey.

As things turned out, 1954–55 had an inauspicious start for yours truly. On the opening day of the season I found myself keeping goal for the reserves at Newcastle United. Sheffield United fielded several youngsters in the team of which, of course, I was one. Newcastle, on the other hand, named a strong team, too strong for us. We found ourselves overrun from the word go. Try as we did, we proved incapable of mounting anything but sporadic attacks. We were totally outplayed and the Newcastle reserves ran out easy winners 4–0. For all I had conceded four goals I felt I had given a very good account of myself. In addition to executing a string of saves, I managed to save a second-half penalty from Alan Monkhouse, who had recently been signed by Newcastle from Millwall for the princely sum of £11,000.

One of the first things reserve team players do when entering the dressing room at the end of a game is to find out the result of the first-team match. We are all human. Whilst one part of a reserve team player wants to see the first team do well, as we all want to be part of a successful club, another part of him secretly hopes the first team will turn in a bad performance as that will increase his chances of a call-up. No one openly admits to this, of course, but that's how the reserve team player thinks and, I imagine, such a state of mind is true irrespective of the standard of football you play. On this particular day we learned the first team had drawn 2–2 at home to Everton, which served as no indication whatsoever as to what Reg Freeman might do in terms of the line-up for Sheffield United's following match. I felt I would have to produce not simply good, but outstanding displays for the reserves to be even considered for the first team. The way things stood I was going to have plenty of opportunity to do that.

Sure enough, I was back in action with the reserves the following Monday when we entertained our old rivals from 'up the road', Leeds United. The Leeds team included George Meek, who has the distinction of being the first ever 'loan' player, following a spell at Walsall, and a former Sheffield United favourite, Albert Nightingale. Albert wouldn't be singing that night, though, as we cruised to a 4–0 victory which, in light of our defeat at Newcastle, rather evened things up. What is more, I kept a clean sheet and turned in what I felt was another good performance.

On the Wednesday, the United first team travelled to Manchester City and found themselves on the wrong end of a 5–2 scoreline. Sheffield United had flirted with relegation the previous season; following the defeat at Maine Road, even though only two matches had been played, the press were predicting United were in for 'another long, hard season'. I imagined what Reg Freeman's face would be like when he read that – like Louis Armstrong sucking on a lemon whilst a steamroller ran over his foot.

Sheffield United's next game was at Newcastle United, a trip which would necessitate an overnight stay. When United were due to stay over, the team sheets were pinned up on a Thursday afternoon to allow players time to pack a bag for the journey the following day. The reserves were scheduled to play at home to West Bromwich Albion. When I sauntered along to the notice board to read the team sheet, for a moment I thought I had looked at the wrong one. There, at the head of the team to play West Brom with the number one next to it, was the name 'Burgin'. My eyes immediately darted to the adjacent team sheet. Written in blue biro was the name 'Hodgkinson' and, above it: 'First Team. Away to Newcastle United'.

I stood staring at my name in disbelief. No one had said anything to me. I had been given no indication whatsoever that I was going to make my Football League debut. It was a complete and utter surprise. I stood as spellbound as a small boy whose father is telling him a wonderful story. My forehead prickled. My hands were clammy and my mouth was so parched and dry David Lean could have shot *Lawrence of Arabia* in it. I looked at the team sheet again, then glanced across to the other team sheet. There was no mistake. I was going to make my Sheffield United debut.

I was so stupefied I didn't notice two people arrive behind me. Sensing someone's presence, I turned to see regular first teamers Jimmy Hagan and Tommy Hoyland.

'Well done, Alan, son. You deserve your chance,' said Jimmy.

'Aye, good luck. You'll be fine, have every confidence in you,' Tommy added.

I managed to thank them and said I hoped I wouldn't let anybody down.

'You won't,' said Jimmy. 'Besides, we'll look after you.'

My mind was a whirl. I told Jimmy and Tommy no one had spoken to me about this and asked what the arrangements were for reporting to the ground and travel.

'It tells you there, underneath the line-up,' said Jimmy pointing to the team sheet.

'Oh, didn't see that,' I said, feeling not a little foolish.

'Bloody hell, Alan, I hope your eyesight's a damn sight better on Saturday,' Tommy quipped.

I burst out laughing but it was more a nervous laugh than anything to do with Tommy's wit. The arrangements were simple enough. Players were to pack an overnight bag and report to Bramall Lane on Friday at 11am. We were catching the noon train to Newcastle from Sheffield Midland station. Collar and tie to be worn.

I wasted no time in getting home. When I told Mum she was so happy for me she was close to tears. When Dad came in from his shift at the pit and I told him my news, I may have been mistaken but I thought I saw his chest swell. Dad was in no doubt as to what he was going to do. He told me he would go down to Sheffield station the next day, find out the train times to and from Newcastle and buy a ticket to travel up on the Saturday. Brenda too was delighted for me and said she wanted to accompany Dad to see me play. I was thrilled to bits. I arranged to meet Dad and Brenda at the players' entrance at St James's Park so that I could give them a couple of complimentary tickets.

When I reported to Bramall Lane on the Friday morning I was met by a sports reporter from the *Sheffield Star* who asked for my reaction to my debut. I still have the cutting of that report. The headline reads, 'Thrilled To Bits' (see, I told you I was), beneath which is a photograph of a smiling yours truly in my goalkeeper's jersey. The piece quotes me as saying my selection 'came as a complete surprise', which it did. The report then goes on to say my visit to St James's Park would be my second in successive Saturdays, 'having kept goal for the club's Central League side in their 4–0 defeat last week'. Not exactly the sort of thing a debutant wishes to read, albeit I am also quoted as saying, 'I hope this trip will not have the same result.' A quote which appears to have come straight from the John Cleese 'School of the bleedin' obvious'. The report also mentions the fact I joined United 'a year ago' and, somewhat curiously, ends by mentioning my cricket exploits with Thurcroft Main.

The team kit, boots, shin-pads and everything else required for an away game – first aid box, bottles of liniment, trainers' bucket and sponge, towels, soaps and so on – was carried in a large wicker basket known as 'the skip'. The skip was about the size of a small dining-room table and of similar depth. It was lugged on and off the train by the trainer and his assistant, or by the travelling reserve player, but when the kit came back soaking wet the weight of the skip doubled so that it became a four-man job to carry it.

As our Newcastle-bound train pulled out of Sheffield station I idly watched the platform glide by with increasing speed. In those days of steam trains, even though it had not rained for some days, the platform was wet, shining Bible-black and dotted with puddles.

At daily training the first team changed in the 'home' dressing room, the reserves in the other, so I didn't know any of the first team players particularly well, certainly not well enough to engage them in conversation unless I was spoken to. About an hour had passed when our train stopped at York for a change of engine. In that hour I had hardly spoken a word to anyone. I had listened, though. The players' talk was all of football and horse racing, some of it spoken amidst a game of cards. My silence was noticed by Joe Shaw, our centre-half.

'Come on, Alan, son,' said Joe, as he sat himself down opposite me. 'You're going to make your debut, put a smile on your face. Make your dream come true.'

' I think I'm a bit anxious,' I replied, 'I don't want to let anyone down.'

'Let me tell you something, Alan, and this applies to life not just football,' said Joe, his face adopting a serious look, 'Whether you think you can, or whether you think you can't, you'll be right.'

I mulled that one over.

'I don't just think I can, I know I can.' I eventually replied.

Joe leaned in closer and slapped me once on the knee with his hand.

'Good lad!'

There are moments in everyone's life that make you set the course of who you will be. I have learned that sometimes they are small, insignificant moments you do not immediately recognise as being pivotal and transitional. Sometimes they are big moments. I knew my debut at Newcastle was a very big moment in my life. Everyone needs one day, one chance to grasp the opportunity they have longed for. As Joe Shaw told me, a day to put a smile on their face, and make the dream come true. It's funny how one day, ninety minutes even, can do so much. No one asks for their life to change, but I felt mine was about to. What's more, I knew it was what I would do afterwards that would count. That's when I would find out who and what I was. Deep down I was confident I would give a good account of myself in my League debut, but I was conscious this was just a start. I would have to continue to progress, to get better as a goalkeeper with each and every game if I was to achieve my dream of making a career in the game. I had learned a lot in my first year at Sheffield about goalkeeping and, the more I learned, the more I realised how much there was to learn. I calmed my nerves by convincing myself my debut was not an ordeal to overcome but a doorway to the future.

We stayed at the Station Hotel which, you'll not be surprised to know, is next door to the station, St James's Park being only half a mile away on the periphery of Newcastle's city centre. After an early sitting for dinner our party took off to the Empire theatre. At a time when very few people owned a television set, theatres would present a bill boasting all manner of variety acts in support of the star of the show. That night we were entertained by dancers, a comedian, a spinner of plates and a magician before the American singing star Guy Mitchell eventually took to the stage to thunderous applause.

Going to an early evening performance at a theatre or cinema was the norm for a top team when playing away from home. The idea behind these trips was to relax the players and, I suppose, at a time when hotel rooms did not have TVs, to dispel boredom. There was also the idea that a night out together galvanised team spirit and togetherness. Such trips remained part of the pre-match routine for a team playing away right up to the early 1970s, when there was a complete revision of what was best for players in terms of preparation for a game, and the ubiquity of television took variety acts and, audiences, away from theatres.

After the theatre we took tea and toast in the hotel lounge, another ritual of away trips, before taking to our rooms at 10pm I was sharing a room with right-back Cec Coldwell but I slept fitfully. My mind wouldn't rest. I lay in bed thinking about the game, what I would do, what I might do. I tried to sleep and cursed myself for not being able to as I knew I needed a good night's rest. I eventually dozed off around half-one, but was up and about before seven the next morning. I just couldn't wait for the game – my doorway to opportunity.

As we players changed in the dressing room Reg Freeman came and sat next to me. In keeping with daily training, Reg had hardly said a word to me since we had assembled at Bramall Lane on the Friday morning.

'This is your big chance, Alan,' Reg said, as if I needed any reminding. 'Just go out and play your normal game.'

That was it as far as words from Reg went. He gave me no instructions about what he required from me at corners, goal-kicks, or distributing the ball when I had gained possession. No advice as to how he wanted me to organise our defence. Reg's lack of advice was par for the course as far as managers of this era were concerned. I remember once having a conversation with Jack Charlton about his debut for Leeds United against Doncaster Rovers in the very same season I made my Football League debut. The Leeds manager was the great Raich Carter of Sunderland, Derby County and England fame. According to Jack, Raich had never spoken to him at any point from him joining Leeds in 1952. Minutes before taking to the pitch, Jack was in a quandary as to what exactly his manager wanted him to do at centre-half. As the Leeds players left the dressing room, Jack turned to Raich. 'What do you want me to do, boss?' asked Jack. 'I want you to see how fast their centre-forward can limp,' replied Raich.

A sonorous noise from 52,000 Geordies assailed my ears as I ran down the tunnel and out into the Tyneside sunshine. I had never played in front of such a large crowd before, but rather than being overawed I felt good about it. Of course I had butterflies in my stomach but the worst part had been the twenty minutes or so prior to taking to the pitch. Now I was out there, fielding shots from my teammates in the pre-match kick-in, although I was many miles from home and in front of 50,000 partisan Geordies, I felt strangely at home. I felt I was in my rightful place in life – keeping goal and for Sheffield United.

Newcastle had a formidable side. Their team included one of my boyhood heroes, the great Ronnie Simpson, in goal. Casting my mind back to my debut, who would have thought, thirteen years later and coming up to thirty-eight years of age, Ronnie would be keeping goal for Celtic when they defeated Inter Milan to become the first British team to win the European Cup? What's more, in the first fifteen minutes of that final, Ronnie's heroics in goal kept Celtic in the game. I can't recall if Joe Shaw won the toss but I do remember having to change ends before the game got underway. When this happens, goalkeepers always shake hands and wish one another good luck as they pass each other. As I reached the centre circle on my way to the Gallowgate End of the ground, Ronnie shook my hand firmly.

'Know it's your debut. Good luck, son, give it your all and don't let your mind wander to the crowd. Always concentrate on the game and you'll be fine,' Ronnie said.

I thanked him, wished him luck and carried on my way. As a young debutant, Ronnie's kind words meant much to me and were typical of the man. In addition to Ronnie, the Newcastle team also included Bobby Cowell, Alf McMichael, Bob Stokoe, Vic Keeble, George Hannah and the aptly named Jimmy Scoular, without doubt the hardest player I ever encountered in my entire career in the game. Jimmy served in the submarines during the war and was to football what Brian Close was to cricket: a dedicated, determined, combative and talented player who never knew the meaning of fear. Jimmy was as hard as teak. When the going got tough he would remain as unmoved as a rock in a raging sea. With his balding head, a neck that could dent an axe and a mouth like a pair of pants whose elastic had perished, he cut an imposing and frightening figure on a pitch.

The star of the Newcastle team was Jackie Milburn, affectionately referred to by Magpie fans as 'Wor Jackie' and, when his fame spread globally, 'World Wor One'. Jackie's beginnings with Newcastle could have come straight from the pages of a *Boy's Own* story. In 1943 he wrote to the club for a trial. He turned up with borrowed boots and his lunch of a pie and bottle of pop in a brown paper bag. The trial match took the form of Stripes v Blues. Jackie sat out the first half. Come half-time the Stripes were losing 3–0. In the second half Jackie played centre-forward for the Stripes and scored six goals, Newcastle manager, Stan Seymour, signed him straight away. Days later, Seymour played him in a wartime Northern League match at Hull City in which Jackie scored five. After the game a delighted and astounded Seymour said to Jackie, 'You're some goal-scorer, eleven goals in two games!' 'One and a half,' Jackie reminded him. It is the stuff of legend.

Jackie was, and still is, a Tyneside legend whose goals and rampages in opposing penalty boxes contributed in no small way to Newcastle's three post-war FA Cup victories (1951, 1952 and 1955). In 1951 he scored in every round of the FA Cup, including both goals in the Final against Blackpool. He was a spectacular centre-forward who used his exceptional speed, powerful shot and thundering heading of the ball to great effect, scoring 200 goals in his eleven seasons with Newcastle, making him Newcastle's all-time greatest goal-scorer in League and Cup matches (Alan Shearer scored seven more should you include European games).

It is unthinkable now but following a Newcastle win, when the players received their wages and win bonus, the club always gave them an extra bonus of a packet of twenty cigarettes. The majority of Newcastle players didn't smoke, but Jackie did, so they gave their cigarettes to him. Off the pitch Jackie always seemed to have a fag on the go, and sadly this may well have contributed to his death from lung cancer at the relatively young age of 64.

As great a goal-scorer as he was, Jackie Milburn didn't score against me on my debut, though Bobby Mitchell did. A hard low drive on the turn which came through a thicket of legs and I didn't see it until the last moment. That equalled matters, for a fine effort from Jimmy Hagan had put us in the lead. In the second half we gave as good as we got and with some fifteen minutes remaining, Jack Cross met a cross, and steered the ball past Simpson. It was a lead we were to preserve, though I was kept a tad busy in those last ten minutes as Newcastle threw everything at us bar the proverbial sink. In the final minutes, I managed to make a point-blank save from George Hannah and, diving to my right, finger-tipped a bullet header from 'Wor Jackie' around the post. When the final whistle blew I was so happy I nearly jumped over the main grandstand.

I left the pitch to hearty back-slapping and congratulations from my teammates. I think I shook hands with every Newcastle player and twice with the referee, whilst both Ronnie Simpson and Jackie Milburn made a point of saying how well I had done. With adrenalin coursing through my body I tried to spot Dad and Brenda in the crowd but among some 52,000 souls it was, of course, hopeless. I knew they would be as excited and delighted as I was, though. I nearly didn't make it down the tunnel – it wasn't built for people ten feet tall.

When a team plays away, the journey home is always a more hectic affair than the journey to your destination, particularly in the 1950s when teams invariably travelled by train. The dressing room was buoyant but we had no time to relax and savour our first victory of the season. It was a mad rush to change, bath, put on our suits, eat some sandwiches, run upstairs for a quick drink with the Newcastle lads before boarding the coach that would take us the half mile to Central station.

In those days players heard results from other games on the wireless that was in the dressing room, or, failing that, by word of mouth from the backroom staff or directors. Naturally we only heard a few results; the way we players obtained the full classified results and football news of the day was to buy a football paper at a station on our way home. We were at York when we bought a local evening football paper. The paper boys who operated at the stations knew which trains were due and located themselves on the platform, knowing that they could sell anything up to fifty papers at one go when a train came in. That night at York our party must have bought nigh on twenty football papers from the paper lad. That done, we all sat back to digest every detail during the final leg of our homeward journey. In the middle pages of the paper was a small report, probably from a press agency, of our game at Newcastle. I didn't get a mention until the final paragraph when it said, 'As the home side went in search of an equaliser, Sheffield United owed much to debutant keeper Hodgkinson who first denied Hannah, then Milburn, to ensure the Blades enjoyed their first win of the season'. That was one for the scrapbook.

With today's saturation coverage of football by television and radio, the internet, mobile phones with apps and what have you, one area of the game which has all but died is the Saturday evening football paper. In the past twenty years up and down the country 'Green 'Uns','Pinks' and 'Buffs' have disappeared from the shelves of newsagents, the victims of an ever expanding and more personalised media. In the fifties Britain boasted nigh on a hundred Saturday evening football papers. Now there are less than twenty in existence, and some of those such as 'The Pink' (Manchester) have moved from a Saturday night to a Sunday in the hope of enjoying a longer shelf life.

Without saying 'a star is born' the newspapers were in praise of my efforts at St James's Park. All agreed I had made a good debut, whilst both the *Sunday Mirror* and *Sheffield Star* went as far as to say I was 'set for a promising career in the game'. Well, another game at least.

On the Monday following my debut, we entertained Manchester City, though to be more precise, City entertained a 29,000 Bramall Lane crowd as all the enterprising football came from them. We turned in a poor performance and without doubt Manchester City were full value for their 2–0 success. If there was a crumb of comfort to be had for yours truly, it was in the thought that I had again played okay. Needless to say, Reg Freeman was not happy with the result or the performance against City. Reg made three changes to the team for our next game, at home to West Bromwich Albion. It was a boost to my confidence that I was not one of them.

The predictions of some newspapers that Sheffield United were in for a 'long hard season' gained further credence when West Brom left Bramall Lane with smiles on their faces, a 2–1 win under their belts and consequently two points in the bag. Two successive home defeats on top of the home draw on the opening day of the season did not bode well. 'The natives are restless,' Joe Shaw reflected one morning during training. Little wonder, we were sitting just above the relegation places in Division One.

Our next trip was to Cardiff City, who were one place above us in the League table. Cardiff boasted in their ranks Trevor Ford, a true legend of Welsh football and one of the most prolific centre-forwards of the post-war era.

Trevor was an aggressive and bustling centre-forward, a noted charger of goalkeepers, especially young ones he sensed were averse to being rocketed through the back of the net with a meaty shoulder. He looked as if he should have been cast in bronze, a big man from the waist up with a chest in keeping. People trod carefully around Trevor, as if the road to his door was peppered with eggshells. Nothing distracted Trevor Ford from doing what he was was paid to do, which was to fill the net with footballs and, if necessary, the opposing goalkeeper too. As much as I respected Trevor, I was of the mind he wasn't going to make chips out of me. Formidable as Trevor was, I relished the opportunity of playing against one of the true stars of fifties football. As a young rookie goalkeeper, I was aware that how I dealt with Trevor Ford would go some way to demonstrating my timbre as a keeper to my teammates.

In our dressing room before the game, Joe Shaw told me not to be intimidated by Ford. 'Give as good as you get,' he told me, 'and don't buckle.' I announced to the dressing room that no one had any cause for concern and not to worry about me.

'I'll come out and give Ford what for, don't you worry,' I boldly announced.

I looked about the room and my teammates were giving me the sort of look that Captain Oates received when he said he was going for a walk.

The *Daily Mirror* described our game against Cardiff City as a 'highly contested and very physical encounter'. Believe me, in an era when referees were far more lenient towards physical play, for a newspaper to mark out a game out as being 'very physical' placed it a little short of the Battle of Waterloo in terms of combativeness.

There was a cauldron simmering just beneath the surface from the kick-off as the match unfolded in vigour and excitement. Joe Shaw was having a titanic struggle with Ford, neither of them giving an inch. When Cardiff's Derek Sullivan lofted balls into my penalty box, I never hesitated as I ran and jumped to punch clear. In doing so I invariably found myself colliding with what seemed like a fridge-freezer swung from the jib of a crane but was, in fact, Trevor Ford bent on earning every penny of his fifteen quid. It proved to be a match of gleaming steel, mostly of the broadsword which, I have to say, was used with impunity by both teams and allowed to be used by a referee whose vocabulary seemed confined to but two words – 'Play on!'

Come the final whistle, with the score-line pegged at 1–1, all the aggression and volatility that had beset the match immediately appeared to evaporate into the ether. Players shook hands and invited one another to participate in a quick beer, before boots clattered down the tunnel to a hot bath to ease their aching limbs. As I walked off the pitch, Trevor Ford shook my hand heartily and told me how well I had done. He then asked me how many games I had 'under my belt'. I told him, this was my third.

'Third!' exclaimed Trevor with some surprise. 'You've got a heart as big as a bucket, boy. Learn from every game and you'll do all right. Good luck, boy.'

Having had words of encouragement from Jackie Milburn and now Trevor Ford meant a lot to me. I felt I was growing in confidence with every game and I was convinced I had what it took to play regular First Division football. In football, however, as in life, when one door opens, another is liable to slam in your face. As I was to learn, it is how you react to such disappointment that is the mark of you.

United's next game was a tall order, against Arsenal at Highbury. Arsenal were among the pacesetters at the top of Division One, we knew it wasn't going to be easy and we were spot on in that assumption. On the morning of the game I looked out my hotel bedroom window and watched the rain pepper it, flatten out and slide down the pane in a thick wave like melted gelatine. It was mid-September, too early for that type of rain. Such wet conditions can make life perilous for a goalkeeper. The ball, when slippery and wet, is like a bar of soap, very difficult to get a good grip of when coming at speed, particularly off a greasy surface. Such conditions, of course, are the same for both goalkeepers. In Jack Kelsey, Arsenal had a goalkeeper with some three years' experience of playing top-class football. Jack was making a name for himself in the game as a very fine goalkeeper, one who had recently established himself as the regular number one for Wales. Jack was indeed a very good goal-keeper, and I wondered if he had learned any special techniques for playing in extremely wet weather. Then the penny dropped: even if he had, he wouldn't share them with me – well, not before the game anyway.

Arsenal was to English football what Middlesex believed them-selves to be to English county cricket, namely a cut above the rest. It was the first time I had ever been to Highbury and to my teenage eyes it was vastly superior to any other ground I had ever visited in my fledgeling career. On arrival, rather than entering through a play-ers' entrance, we were ushered through a marble-floored 'Entrance Hall', the *pièce de résistance* of which was a Jacob Epstein bust in bronze of legendary Arsenal manager Herbert Chapman. The old boy doing the ushering was wearing a double-breasted dark serge uniform; on the shoulders of the jacket were mounted gold-frilled epaulettes that looked for all the world like hideous spiders set to pounce. The Commissionaire, as I later discovered was his job title, was a large man with a chin you could balance a piano on and one which looked as if someone had tried. Even when he gave us his best smile his eyes were as hard as the marble on the floor and, when he said 'Good afternoon', he somehow made it sound like, 'Who let this rabble in?'

Behind the imposing entrance hall were five storeys containing offices, lounges for guests and players, the boardroom, a gym, and, uniquely for the 1950s, a four-star restaurant and heated dressing rooms. The players' lounge was something to see. The pile on the carpet was so deep I just about managed to walk across without the aid of snow shoes. Dotted around the room were large comfortable easy chairs and sofas that looked like they cost little more than an entire Third Division team. On the far side of the room, underneath a large frosted window, was an equally large oak table that shone like a lake with the early morning sun on it. On this oak table was a silver salver containing a variety of sandwiches whose fillings didn't appear to be of the ham and cheese variety; a silver condiment set, a silver vase of flowers, a silver ink-well, a silver writing set and a silver framed photograph of the Queen. For a football club with no current trophies, it seemed like a lot of silver.

When we went out to inspect the pitch I found myself marvelling at Highbury's East Stand, with its clean straight lines and the two tiers of seating leading down to the paddock terracing. Highbury's art deco style set the stadium apart from any other ground in the country, Wembley included. The weather was of the kind that makes people who don't drink know how a hangover feels. The rain was incessant and, as it fell, moved around a thin grey mist that hung in the atmosphere like an unwanted guest at a party.

The pitch squeezed like a sponge when I pressed my foot down on it and sent little popping bubbles to the surface at either side of my shoes. It was going to be as greasy as a chip pan. Fielding low shots on that type of pitch, ones which shot up off the surface like ricocheting bullets, would be a lottery for a goalkeeper. As we stood with the rain anointing the shoulders of our gabardine macs, the ground was silent, but I knew that in two hours, irrespective of how much rain fell, that would change.

The rain had eased off to a light drizzle when we took to the pitch to polite applause from a 52,000-strong crowd. When Arsenal emerged the crowd roared their approval. To my great disappointment they were doing so again some six minutes into the game. Wearing the number nine for Arsenal that day was another great

British centre-forward, Tommy Lawton. Tommy had rocketed on to the English football scene in the 1930s when, on his debut for Burnley four days after his seventeenth birthday, he became the youngest player ever to score a hat-trick in the Football League. Tommy was transferred to Everton and was given the arduous, many would say, impossible, task of replacing Dixie Dean. Tommy was not as prolific a goal-scorer as Dean (but then again, who was?), but he proved potent in the penalty box and his goals helped him win a League Championship medal in 1939. He was the top goal-scorer (337 goals in major matches) in wartime football when he appeared for a variety of clubs and also scored 24 goals in 23 war-time internationals. He signed for Chelsea in 1945 and two years later shocked everyone by signing for Notts County, who were then in the Third Division North. To put this into perspective, it would be the equivalent of Wayne Rooney leaving Manchester United for, well, Notts County.

Tommy left Chelsea because of the maximum wage, which in the late 1940s was £12. Notts County agreed to pay Tommy the maximum wage he was earning at Chelsea but also offered him the carrot of a 'dolly job', which was a job a footballer supposedly had outside of football. A dolly was usually arranged with a company owned by a director of the football club, or else a close business associate of his. In the case of Tommy, in addition to him playing for Notts County, he was employed as a consultant to an engineering firm owned by one of the County directors at a wage of £14 a week, which more than doubled his weekly income. Tommy knew as much about engineering as I do quantum physics and I doubt if he ever set foot in the company. It was simply a ruse to get around the maximum wage. Tommy wasn't alone in this. When Trevor Ford played for Aston Villa after every match he had to go and play the Villa manager or a director at snooker for a wager of £5. Trevor was no John Parrot but he never lost at snooker. Tommy was transferred from County to Brentford where, in addition to his football, he also worked as an advisor to a firm of architects. Seemingly, when that company had drained Tommy of every ounce of Norman Foster that was in him, he moved back to top-flight football with Arsenal.

Tommy Lawton had passed the tipping moment in his career but he was still a formidable opponent. With little over six minutes of the game gone, he rose to head a corner back to Alex Forbes, who dutifully dispatched the ball past me and a knot of my teammates. Just before half-time Tommy ensured he would not be the toast of the evening in the pubs along the Ecclesall Road when he made the ball slither across the sodden pitch and nicely into the path of Doug Lishman, who did a fine impersonation of Alex Forbes some thirty minutes earlier.

In the second half Arsenal added two more without riposte, their third, a stinging drive from Derek Tapscott that I had covered only for the ball to rear up when it momentarily skidded on the surface before its trajectory took it over my left shoulder as I dived to my right. As I had suspected from the start, it was that type of pitch.

Leaving St Pancras station for Sheffield we made for a downcast lot, me particularly so. A director had spoken to someone at Bramall Lane and been told Ted Burgin had played a blinder for the reserves. I had conceded four, although I felt three of the goals were not directly down to me. Either way, I feared my tenure as the United's number one was far from a racing certainty, and so it was to prove.

I found myself back with the reserves for the following game. Reg Freeman never offered me any explanation, Ted Burgin was reinstated for the next first-team game, at home to Cardiff City, and I doubt if Reg spoke as much as two words to Ted either. United lost 3–1 against Cardiff, but there was to be no immediate recall for me.

I was called upon to play eleven first-team games that season. United enjoyed a much better second half to the season and finished just below halfway in the League; another two points would have given us a top ten finish which, given our bleak beginning to the campaign, was some turnaround. Obviously I would have liked to have been the regular number one, but as 1954–55 drew to a close, I took stock of my situation. I was still only eighteen when the season came to an end. I reminded myself I had been playing non-League football two years ago and now I was facing the likes of Jackie Milburn and Tommy Lawton, albeit on an intermittent basis. Still, I was of the mind I had made excellent progress. Though aware I had one hell of a lot to learn, in my heart of hearts I believed I could play First Division football on a regular basis. There was only one tiny little snag, and that came one bright summer morning in the form of a brown envelope through the letterbox.

Whilst Sheffield United could get by in the First Division without yours truly, my country, seemingly, was not so well set. According to the contents of the brown envelope, Queen and country required my services and who was I to deny them such? The letter informing me of the National Service did say my conscription to the armed services would be dependent on me passing a medical; however, given I was a professional footballer I took this to be a formality. It was.

During the summer of 1955 tragedy befell Reg Freeman who died suddenly of a heart attack. His replacement was the former Everton, Arsenal and England wing-half Joe Mercer who, at the time of his appointment as United manager, was running the family grocery business in Wallasey on Merseyside. When a new manager is appointed every player thinks of it as a new start not only for the manager but also for himself. The player hopes the new manager will see things in his play the old manager didn't see. He also hopes he will undergo a renaissance under the new manager and produce the type of performances he always knew he was capable of. Perhaps the new manager will introduce a system of play that brings out the best in the player. Initially, a new manager always brings hope. Of course it is never long before the manager sets out his stall and begins to impose his own culture on the club and the players. Usually then, certain players get the message they do not 'feature in the future plans'. I had every reason to believe I did have a future at Sheffield United but I wasn't going to feature in any plan of Joe Mercer's, not for nigh on two years at any rate.

National Service was first introduced to Great Britain in 1916 to bolster the perpetually decreasing ranks on the Western Front – cannon fodder, as well we know. It was scrapped in 1920 and re-introduced in 1939 when we faced the might of Nazi Germany. In 1957, Harold Macmillan announced National Service was to be scrapped and the last conscripts were called up early in 1960.

I was assigned to the Royal Signals Corps for my two-year stint and sent to Catterick Camp in North Yorkshire for my basic training. National Service was a bit like the internet, in as much as it scooped up and displayed the very best and worst. There were some terrific and talented young lads from all walks of life in the army due to National Service, but there were also the toe-rags, rogues, nutcases, villains and gangsters. The army, of course, has no prejudice. We all received the same treatment. You can imagine.

In terms of history and tradition the Royal Signals Corps is a relatively young regiment. As I learned during my first week, the Royal Signals began life in 1920 as the 'C' Telegraph troop of the Royal Engineers, whose principal role was to provide visual and telegraph signalling and communications in the battlefield and, in time, to wherever the British army found itself throughout the world.

In my first few weeks with the Royal Signals I saw rookie recruits change irrevocably. One young guy, whose self-advertised claim to fame was that he was the 'hardest bloke in Bradford', went to pieces like a clay pigeon. Another who back-answered and refused to carry out orders from a drill sergeant was frogmarched off to the glasshouse. When he came out two weeks later I saw him sitting on the edge of his bed, looking like a piece of driftwood carved by Barbara Hepworth to look like a man. The often-shouted mantra was, 'We'll make a man of you, lad,' and with many they did – with some, however, they only succeeded in creating a monster, and with others, simply shadows.

One day a sergeant major with a beer-barrel chest came into our barracks and marched purposefully towards the end of the room where I was seated on my bed. When he reached me he stopped so I jumped to my feet and saluted. He returned the salute. After which we looked at each other for a second that to me seemed long enough for an oak tree to grow to maturity. He took an intake of breath that almost hurt my eardrums and asked me to confirm my name and number, which I did without managing to squeak. The sergeant major told me I was to be assigned to a six-month course to learn Morse Code as I had 'displayed initiative and intelligence'. His next words were not so much an order as a majestic chorale to my ears. I was told there was to be a football match between the Royal Signals and another regiment and that I was to play in goal for the Signals. With that, I was told to pack my kitbag and follow him, which I did, at a pace marginally slower than if we were both competing in the one hundred metres.

My six months with the Morse communication boys was far different to my basic training. Although the army treated everyone the same during basic training, after they had assessed your worth you were assigned to duties they felt were in keeping with your intellect and capabilities. There were no toe-rags, nutters or gangsters among the Morse boys; on the contrary, many were former top secondary modern, technical or grammar school boys.

During 1955–56, my army leave coincided with weekends, which allowed me to not only get home to my family and Brenda, but also to play for Sheffield United. I played some five matches for the reserves and, to my delight, new manager Joe Mercer selected me four times for the first team. They were not the best of games: I felt I was trying to prevent water from draining through a sieve. Sheffield United had a glum season, finishing rock bottom of Division One behind Huddersfield Town, who joined us in relegation by virtue of having a slightly inferior goal difference to Aston Villa, both teams having finished on 35 points. Relegation in his first season was an ignominious start to Joe Mercer's managerial career, though many had seen it coming. Undaunted, Joe set about dismantling one Sheffield United team and building another, although still without me for a while.

After communications with the Royal Signals, I spent most of my second and final year of National Service as a regimental policeman, much of it on guard duty, in the guardroom or 'glasshouse' as the military jails were known. This, of course, brought me back into contact with the rogues, the rabid and the gangsters, all those who couldn't cope with being given orders or the discipline of army life. Though my role was passive, for whatever reason, some of the inmates directed their resentment my way and threatened to get even with me when their National Service was over.

I can recall a particularly mean-looking Scouser saying to me, 'I know you play for Sheffield United. Just wait till you come to Liverpool. See what I'll do to you.' Neither he nor anybody else who issued threats ever did carry them out.

I learned much in the army: one of the things I learned was, if you were good at sport, you were called upon to play as much of your particular sport as you would be if you were a full-time professional. I kept goal for the Royal Signals Regimental team, which included my Sheffield United teammate Graham Shaw, Area Command and the Army. The Army team played against not only the Navy and Royal Air Force, but also English, Scottish and Irish FA Representative teams, England 'B' and a Football League Representative XI. These latter games drew very healthy attendances: as the Army team we played and beat Rangers before an Ibrox crowd of over 48,000; there were over 34,000 at St James's Park for an Army v FA XI match, whilst a healthy 19,500 turned up for a game against the Navy at Ipswich Town.

With due respect, you can't imagine the Army Representative football team commanding such attendances these days but, at a time of National Service, people would flock to see the Army, Navy or RAF play as their teams included some of the very best young footballers in Great Britain, and for the good citizens of, say, Carlisle, this was the only way they could see Duncan Edwards or Bobby Charlton in the flesh.

I also travelled to Continental Europe for the first time courtesy of the Army football team. We played a match against a French FA XI at the ground of Racing Paris FC before setting off on a tour that took us to Holland where we beat Sparta Rotterdam, Belgium and Germany. Whilst in Germany, we played Cologne and, to my utter delight, Hertha Berlin in the Olympic Stadium. I couldn't get over the fact I had played football in the very same stadium in which the famous Jesse Owens had created Olympic history and in so doing courted the wrath of the Nazi hierarchy, including Hitler himself.

As young as we were, the Army team would, I am sure, have held its own in the First Division. My teammates included the great Duncan Edwards, Bobby Charlton, Eddie Coleman (all Manchester United), Jimmy Armfield (Blackpool, who is still to be heard on BBC Radio 5 Live), Stan Anderson (Sunderland, the only player to have captained all three major North East clubs), Phil Woosnam (West Ham United, who was to play a major role in establishing football in the USA), Dave Mackay (then of Hearts and later Spurs and Derby County), Maurice Setters (then of Exeter City, later his clubs were to include West Bromwich Albion and Manchester United), Dave Dunmore (Arsenal), Trevor Smith (Birmingham City) and my Sheffield United teammate, Graham Shaw.

One game that particularly stands out in the memory was a 3–1 victory against an FA XI at St James's Park. Over 44,000 were present to see us beat a team that included Colin McDonald (Burnley), Peter Sillett (Chelsea), Ronnie Clayton (Blackburn Rovers), Vic Keeble (Newcastle United), Don Revie (Manchester City), Denis Wilshaw (Wolves) and Jimmy Murray (Wolves). I felt I played particularly well that night, executing a number of saves when the scoreline was 2–1 before Bobby Charlton put the game out of the reach of the FA XI. England manager Walter Winterbottom and his FA Selection Committee members seemingly also felt I had played well, because in late September 1956 I received a letter that couldn't have surprised me more if it had contained a cheque for a million pounds. I had to read the later twice to convince myself it wasn't a wind-up perpetrated by my mates in Signals – I had been selected for the England Under-23 international against Denmark.

Henry Rose devoted most of his column in the *Daily Express* to previewing the match. I flushed just a tad when I saw the headline – 'Army 'Keeper Wins Under-23 Cap'. This was followed by a sub-heading given to Rose by someone at Sheffield United, which read, 'Greatest ever, says his club'. No pressure then.

The article is dotted with excruciating puns: 'this private's progress', 'marching towards a great career in the game', 'nothing uniform about his selection' – you've read such articles... According to Rose, my selection for the England Under-23 team was toasted with pints in the NAAFI at Catterick. Even if that was true I knew it didn't mean anything, they'd have toasted my grandmother's new shoes in there if it meant them having another pint. Rose makes much of me having been at 'Worksop Town in the Midlands League less than three years ago' and, though I am about to make my debut for England Under-23s, rather than speculate as to how I may fare at that level, dives straight in by suggesting I am 'within driving distance of a full England cap'. The most striking aspect to the article, however, is when Rose refers to me as being, 'almost 5 foot 7 inches tall'. Even for the time I was not the tallest of goalkeepers, but five-seven was three inches off the mark. In this respect Rose epitomised the cigar-chomping sports writer of the day: rarely would they let the facts get in the way of a good story.

An unknown source at Sheffield United – the quote is simply attributed to 'his club' – is quoted as saying, 'Hodgkinson will turn out to be the greatest goalkeeper this country has ever seen.' I smarted when I read that. Even at nineteen years of age I saw it as a possible millstone around my neck; the sort of quote from an unattributed source that, should a player go through a particularly bad spell of form, will come back to haunt him, as badly as if the player had said it himself.

The England Under-23 team was a relatively new concept, the game in Denmark being only the fifth fixture, the first having taken place in 1954 against Italy in Bologna after which there had been a twelve-month hiatus until England Under-23s met their Italian counterparts again at Stamford Bridge. The concept of an England Under-23 team was the brainchild of England manager Walter Winterbottom, the purpose of which was to groom future full England players. The idea had grown in popularity and come 1956 England were playing four or five such games a season.

England Under-23 home matches nearly always took place in the provinces, at such grounds as St James's Park (Newcastle), Roker Park (Sunderland), Carrow Road (Norwich City), Ashton Gate (Bristol City), Home Park (Plymouth Argyle), The Dell (Southampton) and Hillsborough (Sheffield Wednesday). The idea was to bring international football to a city or town that would not normally stage that level of representative football. To have such an honour bestowed upon it, the local football club had to be well supported, as this more or less guaranteed a healthy attendance for the England Under-23 fixture. Just to be sure, the FA selection committee would often include in the England team a player from the local club, which always put an extra few thousand on the gate. This explains why there are one or two players of the time who enjoyed journeyman careers but, among their personal memorabilia, can boast an England Under-23 cap awarded for a home game.

You can play away from home in England among unfamiliar surroundings, yet they never look as unfamiliar and alien to you as your surroundings when you play abroad. I have always felt this wherever I have played throughout the world and I remember first being aware of this prior to the England Under-23 game against Denmark in Copenhagen. The stadium that hosted the game was flanked by flats some five storeys high and what looked to me like office blocks of similar height. When you look at the surroundings of a ground and see unfamiliar styles of house, office, street lighting and particularly church, it emphasises you are indeed a long way from home turf. Our National Anthem never sounds the same when played, as it was in those days, by a band either, and this difference was more pronounced the further from England you went. In South America for example, prior to the 1962 World Cup the military bands before our matches against Ecuador and Colombia somehow contrived to give our National Anthem a mariachi feel.

Denmark were duly beaten 3–0 and I was to keep my place for England Under-23's next game the following month, a goalless draw against France at Ashton Gate. My fellow Signals serviceman and Sheffield United teammate Graham Shaw played at left-back in this game, his partner on the right flank being West Brom's Don Howe. The match was noteworthy for featuring the first official substitute of any England representative match when Doncaster Rovers' Alick Jeffrey was replaced in the second half by Colin Booth (Wolves). Though substitutes were not allowed in Football League matches until 1965–66, they had been part and parcel of continental football since the 1930s. FIFA allowed substitutes for international matches at all levels, but England had never previously taken advantage. The first substitutes to feature in a full England game happened when we visited Mexico in April 1959. Warren Bradley (Manchester United) replaced Doug Holden (Bolton Wanderers) and minutes later Ron Flowers came on for Wilf McGuinness (Manchester United).

In February 1957, I kept goal for England Under-23s against Scotland at Ibrox. A game which the posters around Glasgow and the match programme proudly announced would take place 'Under Floodlights'. Again, Graham Shaw was included in the England team as was Alan Finney (Sheffield Wednesday) and a fantastic young left-winger, David Pegg (Manchester United). This game also marked the first appearance in an England shirt of a young centre-forward from Middlesbrough by the name of Brian Clough – much more of whom later. Included in the Scotland side were Alex Young and Dave Mackay (both Hearts), Eric Caldow (Rangers) and an amateur who, in keeping with Queen's Park tradition, appeared on the team sheet and in the match programme under the initials of his first names followed by his surname – 'W.G.M. Glen (Queen's Park)' which, to me, lent him the dusty formality of a Victorian cricketer. Curiously no player from Celtic featured for Scotland. Another very healthy attendance of 42,897 saw a 1–1 draw. Jack Dyson (Manchester City) scored for England whilst the Scotland goal came from the penalty spot courtesy of Hearts' Billy Crawford. It was hard-hit penalty, driven low and to my right. I remember thumping the ground with frustration when it went in because I got the fingertips of my right hand to the ball but only managed sufficient leverage to push it into the inside side netting.

A couple of weeks after appearing for England Under-23s at Ibrox, I completed my National Service, was de-mobbed and immediately returned to Sheffield United. On my first day back in the fold I noticed how much had changed under Joe Mercer's management. For a start he was out on the training ground taking the training. Secondly, he supervised the coaching sessions. Third, there was such a thing as coaching sessions. Reg Freeman was a lovely man whose management belonged to the pre-war days; Joe Mercer was what today you'd call a 'hands-on manager'. There were new faces around the training ground and some of the old faces, if they hadn't moved on, sported the sort of expression which suggested they knew they were about to.

On that very first morning back Joe Mercer took me to one side. After welcoming me back to full-time football and a little conversation about my time in the Signals, he asked me if I was match fit and 'up for the big challenge at this club'. I answered him in the affirmative on both counts.

'Good, I've been waiting for you to be demobbed,' he told me, 'From now on, you are my number one goalkeeper. I'll have Ted in after training and let him know the score.'

There were seventeen games left of the 1956–57 season but I very much felt I was beginning a new season. I reasoned Joe Mercer must have had every confidence in me to instate me as the regular number one and the fact that he had such confidence in my ability spurred me to repay his belief in me.

United enjoyed an unbeaten run of eight matches, the pick of which was a resounding 6–0 victory at Port Vale. I felt for their keeper, John Poole; the regular Vale goalkeeper, Ray King, was injured and John came into the team for his first game of the season. As we left the field John was inconsolable but, remembering how a few words from Jackie Milburn and Trevor Ford had meant so much to me, I made a point of talking to him over a beer after the game. I told him not to shoulder the blame. We'd been on fire and on such form we would have put most Second Division sides to the sword. I told John not to think too much about the game but to concentrate on how he was going to react to it. Little over a year later, John was Vale's first choice goalkeeper, which told me he had reacted to that mauling in a very positive and determined way. That's what a goalkeeper has to do when he concedes a bagful of goals. Of course he has to reflect on what he did wrong, so he can devise ways not to repeat those mistakes, but the key thing is not to reflect too much and for too long. Get a heavy defeat out of the system as quickly as possible by planning and preparing to ensure that in the next match your confidence is high.

The 6–0 victory at Vale Park elevated United into the upper echelons of Division Two, but I knew it was too late in the season to pose any threat to leaders Leicester City and second-placed Nottingham Forest, both of whom gained promotion. During the Vale game I tweaked a hamstring, nothing serious, but in the dressing room after the match I asked the United phsyio, Alf Willie, to take a look at it as a precautionary measure. As Alf examined my leg he told me one of the FA Selection Committee had been at the game.

'He'd have been here to have a look at Joe [Shaw],' I replied. 'Besides, they have to be seen to attend matches other than those at their own club, otherwise they get it in the ear.'

'That's as maybe,' said Alf. 'But the same old boy was also at Bury and our home game against Huddersfield.'

There are very good players who, to the surprise of many, are never called upon to play for England, even though the consensus is that they are eminently capable of playing at international level. Other players are awarded one, or, at best, a handful of caps that appear meagre reward for their undoubted talent. Sometimes it is simply down to the fact that the player in question was unfortunate to be competing for a position in the England team currently held by a truly world-class player. Colin Todd (Derby County) up against Bobby Moore, for example, or any one of around ten of us goalkeepers and Gordon Banks. There are numerous Stoke City supporters of a certain age who still can't understand why centre-half Denis Smith was never selected for England, likewise Sheffield United supporters and Joe Shaw.

Following our victory of Port Vale I received an envelope through the post bearing the three lions motif of the Football Association. The England Under-23 team were due to embark on a continental tour in three weeks, immediately after the domestic season ended. I was hoping to be selected and though I had kept goal for the Under-23s in their recent three matches knew my selection was far from certain. Bolton's Eddie Hopkinson, Gordon Clayton (Manchester United) and Tony Macedo (Fulham) were but three other goal-keepers in contention for the two places in the touring squad.

As soon as I laid eyes on the envelope I knew it was good news. The FA never wrote to players to inform them they had been dropped from the squad. I tore open the envelope and as I read its contents my face must have turned as white as the paper that contained the words, 'You have been selected as goalkeeper for England versus Scotland, Home International Championship, Wembley Stadium, 6 April 1957.'

I was standing in the hall, on one wall of which hung a large brass-framed mirror. I heard my mother call, 'Is that you, Alan?' I managed to reply in a voice the size of one of those silver balls you see on wedding cakes. My mother came into the hall to see what was the matter.

'Alan, are you all right?' she asked.

I handed my mother the letter. She read as much as I had done before looking up at me. She looked shocked. Brenda emerged from the kitchen. Mother handed her the letter. Brenda looked shocked. I looked at myself in the mirror. I looked shocked. My legs felt as weak as fruit tea and I waited for my pulse to come down into the low hundreds before I spoke.

'I can't believe it,' was all I managed.

Brenda shrieked with joy and threw her arms around me. My mother stood with tears glazing her eyes.

I really couldn't believe it. Three months out of the army. Just under four years after keeping goal for Worksop Town in the

Midland League I was now about to make my England debut, at Wembley, in the most prestigious match in the international calendar. I was suddenly aware I was laughing. It was nervous, uncontrollable, high-pitched laughter.

| CHAPTER THREE |

'There is a tide in the affairs of man,
Which taken at the flood, leads on to fortune and success.'

Julius Caesar

The letter from the FA told me to report to the England team hotel in Hendon, North London, on the afternoon of Monday 1 April. I recognised, of course, the significance of the date and hoped it would not prove ominous.

Letters from the FA tended to be rather curt, the same being true of those sent to the Scottish lads by their respective Football Association. When Jimmy Greaves was first called up for England, his letter from the FA began, 'Dear Greaves'. Jimmy simply thought a typist had erroneously omitted the 'Mr' part of the letter until, that is, he received his second letter. Jimmy felt the tone of such letters was suggestive of how the FA perceived footballers, as being little more than minions and menials in service. Jimmy saw the tenet and tone of the letters he received from the FA as being like something from the pages of Dickens, so much so, he would always complete the reply slip confirming his availability by writing, 'Greaves is willing'. At the time, I always wondered if anyone within the FA was familiar with *David Copperfield* and would have recognised the impish, ironic humour of Jimmy's replies.

My Sheffield United teammates were delighted for me. To a man they congratulated me on my call-up and wished me good luck. Joe Mercer was also pleased. Joe, of course, had played many times for England. He told me it was like taking medicine – not particularly pleasurable to begin with but much better to stomach the more games you played.

'You're working hard at your game and being rewarded for that,' Joe told me. 'You're progressing all the time. Being selected for England is great. I'm pleased for you but, remember, in football the great thing is not where you are at any given time, but in what direction you're moving. You're going in the right direction, Alan, just be sure to continue that way.'

Wise words that I have never forgotten.

The press too were fully behind my call-up, which surprised me somewhat given my rise to full international status had been meteoric to say the least. Ted Ditchburn of Spurs had kept goal for England in their previous international, a 5–2 win over Denmark in a World Cup qualifying match that was distinguished by a hat-trick from young Tommy Taylor and two spectacular goals from his Manchester United teammate Duncan Edwards. The success of Taylor and Edwards, along with two other young players, Ronnie Clayton of Blackburn Rovers and Jeff Hall of Birmingham City, perhaps paved the way for my call-up. Three and half years after England had been humiliated by Hungary and, by the same token, English football had been placed in true perspective in global terms, Walter Winterbottom was placing faith in youth. Walter wanted to create England teams in four-year cycles with a view to winning or, at least, doing well in the World Cup. Walter was still hampered by the fact that the England team were chosen by a committee of FA selectors, but ever since Hungary, Walter had exerted his influence over the committee without ever being able to wrench from them selection of the team.

Walter's first eye-opening experience of the FA International Selection Committee had taken place some weeks after he had been appointed as England's first full-time manager. Walter's 'Road to Damascus' moment happened in, of all places, the Victoria Station Hotel in Sheffield in 1946. In addition to Walter, also present were the Chairman of the International Selection Committee and eight other members of the FA.

According to Walter, after a 'very good lunch', they all sat around the dining table putting forward nominations for each position for Walter's second game in charge, at home to the Republic of Ireland.

There were five players nominated for the position of goalkeeper. The list was reduced by a process of votes until it was down to the final two and a straight majority vote.

Walter was fascinated by the whole rigmarole, and when it was over and Frank Swift (Manchester City) had been selected he asked: 'How many of the Committee have actually seen these goalkeepers play this season?'

The reply astonished and perplexed Walter: 'None'.

At the time, selection for the England team was much the same as it had been for decades. Selection was not based on pure ability or merit alone. Quite often a player would be awarded an England cap in recognition of his services to the game. As Walter told me, prior to his first game in charge, against Northern Ireland, one of the selection committee put forward the name of a player adding, 'It really is time we gave this deserving player a cap, he's a really good sort.'

It was that sort of attitude that Walter had continually battled against. His frustration intensified in 1950 when Arsenal's Leslie Compton was selected for an England debut against Wales at the age of 38. Arguing the case for another centre-half who Walter felt truly merited an England call-up, he was told by one committee member, 'But this Compton, he's a gentleman through and through, it's only right we recognise that and give him a chance.'

Water was not in agreement, but the committee had their way as committees tend to do. The FA International Selection Committee was the bane of Walter's life and every player knew this to be so. Arguably the best summing-up of their worth was made by no less than the great Stanley Matthews who for all his awesome talent had, throughout his lengthy career, suffered more than most from the Quixotic policies of the International Selection Committee.

'I've visited nigh on every country in the world,' said Stan. 'In those countries I have walked through numerous cities and in countless parks, and have yet to see a statue to a committee.'

Walter could see the selection system needed to be overhauled rather than simply refined. What helped his cause was his establishment of the England Under-23 team whose remit was to develop players to full international status. Also, Walter managed to persuade the powers that be to use matches involving the Football

League XI as a means to honour players with representative appearances. Which left him with the main task to create an England team fit to represent the nation in the World Cup.

In every problem there is a gift. The gift may not immediately make itself known to you, but it is there all the same and, in time, even the most problematic of situations will produce a positive. Such was the case for Walter following England's heavy defeats by Hungary in 1953. The stark reality that England was no longer a world power in football was hammered home by a brilliant Hungary team. In the wake of England's first home defeat at Wembley by foreign opposition and the 7–1 thrashing inflicted on them by Hungary in Budapest some months later, it was clearly evident that England, once the masters of world football, were now merely pupils. The double mauling at the hands of Hungary was widely considered to be a disaster at the time; however, in every problem there is a gift. The FA International committee were 'bewitched, bothered and bewildered' as to what should be done to re-establish England as a force again in world football, which played into the hands of Walter Winterbottom.

In the wake of the Hungary defeats, Walter slowly but surely managed to exert his influence over the selection committee and, come 1957, had persuaded them to go along with his policy of selecting youth with a view to creating a team capable of doing England proud in the World Cup, the finals of which were to take place the following year in Sweden. Hence the selection of Tommy Taylor, Duncan Edwards, Jeff Hall, Ronnie Clayton and yours truly for England.

Ted Ditchburn was a very good and experienced goalkeeper, likewise Bert Williams of Wolves, both of whom had superseded Gil Merrick of Birmingham City in the England team. Walter, however, wanted to create an England team for the future and so Ted and Bert were, to his mind, the wrong age. I, seemingly, fitted the bill. In truth, I didn't have a great deal of top-level experience and was, of course, playing Second Division football with Sheffield United. This mattered not one iota to Walter, who saw me as part of his policy of developing an England team that would mature together, and be ready in four years' time to make an impact in the World Cup. As evidence of this, in addition to myself, Derek Kevan

(West Bromwich Albion), Tommy Thompson (Preston North End) and my Sheffield United teammate Colin Grainger were also due to make their England debuts in a team that also included Roger Byrne (Manchester United), Jeff Hall, Ronnie Clayton and the teenage sensation, Duncan Edwards. With over half the team suggesting youth, Walter Winterbottom added a degree of balance and much needed experience at international level by also including skipper Billy Wright (Wolves) and two truly world-class players in Stan Matthews (Blackpool) and Tom Finney (Preston).

The inclusion of Wright, Matthews and Finney not withstanding, it was still a very bold selection on the part of Walter. More to the point, it was testimony to his ability to persuade and cajole the International Selection Committee into supporting his policy of youth with a view to future World Cups. The annual encounter between England and Scotland was still the biggest and most important fixture in the international calendar. Somehow I can't imagine the England set-up of today selecting, for a game seen as being of vital importance, four debutants and four young players whose collective international appearances did not constitute double figures. Credit to Walter Winterbottom.

The letter from the FA instructed me to report to the Hendon Hall Hotel at 5pm on the Monday preceding the game on Saturday 6 April. Players made their own way to and from international matches so I simply booked a return train ticket from Sheffield to St Pancras. Today the notion of players making their own way to and from international games on public transport is unthinkable. When the England team returned from the 2010 World Cup in South Africa, for example, a fleet of Mercedes cars awaited them at Heathrow, one for each player in the squad, which then duly took them to their respective homes. In 1957 it was very different. On arrival in London I, along with all the other England players from provincial clubs, travelled to Hendon on the Tube. The FA letter informed me to send my 'second-class' rail and London Underground ticket to their finance office and I would be 'reimbursed in due course provided travel expenses were deemed appropriate'.

A couple of days after having received my dream letter from the FA, I received another important-looking piece of correspondence in the post. On opening the envelope I discovered a letter from the Chamber of the Lord Mayor of Sheffield, together with a card bearing the city crest and detailing an invitation in faultless copper-plate handwriting. The letter bestowed upon me (their words not mine) the 'hearty congratulations and best wishes' of the Lord and Lady Mayoress of Sheffield on my selection for the England foot-ball team. Seemingly the city's councillors were also delighted for me. The invitation informed me I had been invited to partake of coffee with the Mayor and Lady Mayoress at 9.30am on the morn-ing of Monday 1 April, the day I was due to travel down to London to meet up with the England squad. The invitation went on to say following coffee, the Mayor and Lady Mayoress had organised a special occasion to celebrate my England selection at which they would be delighted should I also be able to attend.

Working on the principle it would not be much of a celebration of my England selection should I not attend and, after enquiring at the City's Town Hall how long my presence would be required and being told 'no more than an hour', I worked out I would still have enough time to catch my train to London. I found the Basildon Bond letter paper in the sideboard and duly penned a reply saying I would be delighted to accept their kind invitation, perplexed as to what the 'special occasion' would actually entail.

There was only one worry. The invitation informed me I would be partaking of coffee with the Mayor and his wife. I am not partic-ularly fussy when it comes to food or beverages but the only drink I have never taken to is coffee. I had never met any dignitaries before. As far as I was concerned the Lord Mayor and Lady Mayoress of Sheffield had the status of Earls or Baronets; to my mind, they inhabited a world far removed from my experience. I hoped my dis-like of coffee would not produce a social faux pas, one that would cause embarrassment to both parties. I posted my acceptance pray-ing tea would also be available.

It was one of those shooting-green mornings you get in early April. The wretched winter weather was over. The hills in the dis-tance had taken on the look of verdant green. The cherry blossoms were in bloom and the gents' outfitters that sold worsted overcoats and Burberry macs were advertising their annual sales. At the time I had a suit for every day of the week and I was wearing it when I presented myself at the Lord Mayor's Chamber.

The Chamber was set deep within the ambitious gesture of the Victorians that is the Sheffield Town Hall and Civic Offices, where some elected and unelected folk had worked unstintingly to the benefit of the city, whilst others had been known to walk around its maze of corridors without making any more progress than a maggot in a fisherman's bait box. I was escorted to a large wooden double door that wouldn't have looked out of place at Hampton Court in terms of age or size. When one half of it opened, I stepped into a large, square, cool room that had all the restful atmosphere of an old Methodist chapel and something of the same smell. Dotted about the room were heavy carved chairs with plush red-cushioned seats; a large dark oak table that looked as if it could comfortably sit sixty for dinner and some; while on wood-panelled walls hung oil paintings of past Mayors in ceremonial robes draped with gold chain, their faces sporting thin white moustaches. On the far wall to my right, a landscape oil of Sheffield viewed from a hill recorded an elevated view of the city just as the Industrial Revolution was seemingly getting under way. On the left, a stained glass window about the size of a tennis court shed every colour of the prism dancing across floorboards you could have skated across in stockinged feet. It was an old musty, fusty, narrow-minded room, as quiet as a minister's study, the sort of room that didn't look as if anyone ever worked in it or would ever want to.

The Mayor was a small, round, avuncular man with a cheery face and voice to match. He seemed to be of friendly and humorous disposition, but something about him suggested to me he'd held a lot of noses to the grindstone in his time. The Lady Mayoress was taller, larger, with a rotund face covered in sufficient make-up to keep Max Factor's profits ticking over nicely and chins that lay on top of one another like slices of processed cheese. She had blue-rinse hair set in a ruthless perm and her eyelashes were twin miracles of mascara. When she welcomed me her voice had a blustering, hard quality to it and sounded as if it would never tolerate any nonsense.

Introductions over, a woman dressed in a blue overall entered the room pushing a metal trolley containing cups and saucers, a pot of coffee and all the usual trappings that go with the drinking of coffee. There was no tea.

I gingerly sipped miniscule amounts of coffee as we passed a pleasant enough fifteen minutes. I was told His Worship and his wife saw my selection as a 'feather in the cap for the city'. For my part I informed them I felt it a great honour to be selected to represent my country and would do my very best not let down the good folk of Sheffield. As the minutes ticked by like hours I fielded questions about Stanley Matthews and Tom Finney, players I had yet to meet, whilst the Lord Mayor said he would offer me a cigarette as he 'liked the occasional one', only they brought on the asthma of his good lady wife. I put him at ease by thanking him and saying I didn't smoke anyway. He looked a tad disappointed.

I'd managed to decrease the coffee in my cup a couple of millimetres when the doors to Ben Hur's temple opened again and a tall, thin, silver-haired man of around sixty entered and informed His Worship the car was ready. The Lady Mayoress snorted and said she hoped it wasn't the Daimler as she had ridden in it before and it had brought on her asthma. The old boy with the silver hair bowed about a centimetre. He didn't scowl but he looked about as happy as a man in a starched collar ever looks.

'Well, Mr Odgkinsun, shall we depart to our, ehm, special hoecasion, to celebrate your Hinternational status?' said the Mayor, and he duly extended a chubby little hand in the direction of the towering doors.

The Lady Mayoress's asthma was spared. It wasn't the Daimler. An old black Rolls Royce with headlamps the size of Royal Doulton dinner plates awaited us. On seeing us descending the Town Hall steps the driver leapt out of the car, scuttled around to the pavement side and opened the rear door. I followed the Lady Mayoress on to a cool, leather back seat and sat feeling very self-conscious between the pair of them. The driver closed the door of the Rolls Royce as if he were closing the lid of a jewellery box. That done, he returned to his own seat for a journey that lasted all of four hundred yards.

We drew up outside the Odeon cinema. It would have been as quick to walk and would have made more sense to do so. As we ascended the steps of the Odeon I thought, 'This is going to be some occasion.' The Odeon seated 1,500 people and though I did not expect the auditorium to be anywhere near full to capacity, for the 'special occasion' to be held in such a vast hall I imagined a decent crowd of the great and good of the city to be present. The cinema manager and a young usherette welcomed us with no less reverence than if they had been welcoming the Queen of Sheba to King Solomon's pied à terre. We three followed in their footsteps, up the carpeted stairs towards the main auditorium, in so doing, I ran through my mind a few words of gratitude should I be called upon to speak, which I was certain I would be.

On reaching doors leading to the auditorium stalls, the cinema manager and usherette stood to either side, extended a hand and swung the doors open as if beckoning us to enter another dimension.

'After you, Mr 'Odgkinson, tis your special day,' intoned the Mayor.

I checked my tie was straight, took a deep intake of breath and strode into the vastness of the Odeon cinema auditorium. The sight that greeted me turned the shape of my mouth into an O. The place was completely and utterly deserted.

I was so taken aback I stopped dead in my tracks, but the genial Mayor extended a chubby hand again and indicated I should carry on walking down the aisle. When we reached a point about half-way, the chubby hand got to work again, pointing to a row of seats.

'I think about 'ere will do very nicely.'

The three of us parked ourselves in the middle of a row of seats and with the cinema lights still up, his Worship the Mayor revealed to me the purpose of our visit.

'My good lady and I wanted to mark your selection for the England football team by doing something special for you,' said the Mayor with not a little enthusiasm, 'but what could be done to honour one of our own sons of the city on such an horse-spicous hoe-cassion as playing for 'is country? What form could this special occasion take?'

Before I could mount a guess, he told me.

'We 'ave arranged for you to see, with us, a film of Saturday's Grand National 'orse race. Now what about that? Surprised?'

I certainly was. I couldn't have been more surprised if he'd suddenly produced evidence that proved Elvis Presley was the illegitimate son of Mother Teresa. In truth, I had no idea as to what the 'special occasion' to celebrate my England call-up would entail but, should I have been asked to guess, watching a film of the previous Saturday's Grand National would have been pretty low on the list.

The cinema lights dimmed, the big screen flickered into life and I found myself watching horses and riders in the Aintree parade ring. I settled back in my chair, crossed my legs and hoped that the action wouldn't bring on her Ladyship's asthma.

Little over twelve minutes later we were bidding our farewells. Once again the Lord Mayor and Lady Mayoress wished me luck, reiterating my selection had helped put Sheffield 'on the map' and said they would be in touch on my return to hear all about my big day. I thanked them for their hospitality, and the coffee, picked up my grip bag and headed for Sheffield Midland station. I never did hear from them again.

Of all the ceremonies and situations my football career has presented me with, sitting in a deserted cinema at ten on a Monday morning watching a re-run of the Grand National is, without doubt, the most bizarre. I did, however, appreciate the time and trouble taken by His Worship and his good lady and I did, in a curious way, feel honoured to have been invited to what they obviously saw as a rare treat. Even in 1957, the number of homes in the UK which possessed a television set was in the minority, at the time Mum and Dad didn't own one, so it was somewhat of a treat to see a major sporting occasion as opposed to hearing it on radio or reading about it in my newspaper.

The England squad trained at the Bank of England ground. I don't know about the others but I certainly needed that week to get to know my teammates. Although I had some thirty First Division games to my name I was meeting the likes of Stanley Matthews, Tom Finney and the Manchester United lads for the first time.

Having a week to prepare for the Scotland game enabled us not only to become familiar with the system Walter Winterbottom had devised but also with one another as people and teammates. To my delight, Stanley Matthews turned out to be exactly as his public persona painted him to be. He was genial, friendly, ever ready to offer advice, witty, dignified and a gentleman to the core, a man of unyielding integrity; likewise Tom Finney.

It was only under Walter Winterbottom that the England squad had been assembled for a week before an international. Prior to

Walter, England players had got together the day before a game, or, at best, if the game was taking place on a Saturday, Thursday afternoon. Walter had persuaded both the FA and Football League he needed at least a week with the players prior to an international, and it is to his credit that he managed to persuade the 'Blazer Brigade' of the FA and dinosaurs of the Football League to comply. Even so, on the day of the England-Scotland game a full programme of League fixtures was to take place as was the norm when England played at a weekend. The Football League, in particular, were loath to release players for England matches, an attitude that still prevailed well into the 1960s when that old dreadnought of an official, Alan Hardaker, was Secretary of the Football League.

In 1966, the West Ham United manager, Ron Greenwood, telephoned Hardaker a fortnight or so before an England match to ask if West Ham could postpone their League match of the same day as Bobby Moore, Geoff Hurst and Martin Peters – the hub of the West Ham team – were on international duty.

'Postpone? Postpone your League match just because you're missing three players?' growled Hardaker down the phone. 'What the bloody hell do you think you have a reserve team for?'

On the Friday, a match was arranged with a Bank of England team. It was nothing more than a kick-about for us England players, though I learned such a game always took place as a 'thank you' to the Bank for allowing England to use their facilities. The result was a foregone conclusion though I suspect the result mattered not one jot to the employees of the Bank. Their reward was an opportunity to play against England, albeit our team comprised players playing in unaccustomed positions, such as Billy Wright at centre-forward and Bobby Charlton at right-back. Bobby at right-back surprised me as Bobby used to love to play in goal at any given opportunity. You find that, particularly with centre-forwards. In kick-abouts they can't wait to play goal, whereas goalkeepers usually love to have a go at playing centre-forward. As no one volunteered to go between the posts, I took up my normal position against the Bank. In truth, I could have played upfront and our team without a goalkeeper as I think I touched the ball twice in the entire game.

With play concentrated in the opposing half of the field my attention was drawn to three beautiful young blonde women who had taken up a position at the side of the pitch. I recognised them immediately, it was the Beverley Sisters.

The Beverley Sisters hailed from Bethnal Green, and were the daughters of George Chiney and Victoria Miles who, under the name of Coram and Miles, had been a highly successful variety act. The Beverley sisters comprise Joy, the eldest, and her twin sisters, Hazel and Babs. I use the present tense as they still occasionally perform today and have very strong links with the Burma Star Association. The Beverley Sisters had enjoyed a string of hits in the 50s and had been the first UK female group to make it into the US Top Ten. To see them at the England training ground was a thrill for a young player such as myself. I suppose the modern day equivalent would be seeing The Saturdays or Girls Aloud roll up to watch you play football. The Beverley Sisters may have lacked the sassy sexuality of Diana Dors but they were, without doubt, absolute stunners. To me the Beverley Sisters appeared as remote as Saturn, as fresh and clear as a mountain stream and as attainable as the winning jackpot on the pools. Somebody would land it but I knew it would never be me. Likewise a date with one of the Beverley Sisters, not that that bothered me. I was spoken for and very happy to be so.

When the kick-about game was over, the reason for the Beverleys' attendance immediately became apparent. Billy Wright made a beeline for Joy and the pair of them proceeded to walk arm-in-arm towards the changing room with Hazel and Babs in their wake followed by ten England footballers with their tongues on their chins. It was obvious to me Billy and Joy had a thing going, though it also came as something of a surprise. I had no idea for there had been no such inference in the newspapers, which was also surprising, as their pairing was the 1957 equivalent of Posh and Becks.

Back in the changing room, the England trainer, Harold Shepherdson, sat next to me after my shower.

'You obviously clocked Billy and Joy Beverley,' said Harold.

I nodded and told him, 'Yes'.

'Thing is, keep it to yourself, Alan. The other lads know about it, only Billy and Joy don't want it made public. Well, not yet anyway, until they see how things go. So, keep it in the family, eh?' said Harold.

I told him I wouldn't breathe a word.

'Their private life is their private life. Nothing to do with me,' I told him.

'Good lad,' said Harold, patting the side of his nose with the forefinger of his right hand as he rose to attend to other players.

It is testimony to how private lives were respected that the news of Billy and Joy's romance did not break in the media until a year later when they themselves announced they were to be married. Their relationship was common knowledge to England players, as I discovered, yet no one breached the confidence placed in them. Today, with social media and Twitter, not only does it appear impossible to keep private lives private, to my mind it would appear many people, including people in the public eye such as footballers, don't wish to. Such people have a cavalier attitude to their private lives and thus make themselves vulnerable by willingly divulging information about themselves and making public their musings and personal opinions on almost anything. This penchant to reveal personal information and opinions is ambiguous to say the least, especially regarding top footballers, who often complain about press intrusion and have made themselves inaccessible to the ordinary supporter.

England versus Scotland was the most looked forward to and important fixture in the football calendar. The publicity surrounding the annual clash of the auld enemy, was billed as 'The greatest football match of the year' and, in so doing, for once, football was not given to hyperbole. I understood the kudos and significance to players and supporters alike, of the oldest international fixture in the history of football. This game, however, had taken on extra significance south of the border, for it was seen as a measure of how far England and Walter Winterbottom had developed in the quest to modernise.

I had been a spectator at Wembley that grey November afternoon back in 1953, a witness to the twilight of the gods as England succumbed to foreign opposition at home for the very first time. England had been beaten 2–0 by the Republic of Ireland at Goodison Park in 1949, but the fact the game was staged at Everton and the Republic team contained nine players who had plied their trade in English football since their mid-teens curiously blurred the fact that

England had lost to a foreign team. Hungary at Wembley, however, was a totally different proposition.

Against Hungary, even though the game was played at Wembley, England found themselves strangers in a strange world. The marked difference between the two teams was even apparent as they took to the pitch. I remember looking on with both interest and amusement as the Hungary team, led by Ferenc Puskas, marched out onto Wembley's greensward in lightweight V-necked cherry shirts, shorts that were indeed shorts, thin cotton socks, unobtrusive shin-pads and boots the likes of which I had never seen before – low cut, lightweight with the white laces wrapped around the top and sole only, rather than being also threaded through the loop on the heel as was de rigueur in British football and had been so for as long as anyone could remember. England, by comparison, looked archaic in their heavy white cotton shirts with buttoned fronts and collar, baggy dark blue shorts that looked as if they could have provided sail for an East India-bound clipper, heavy woollen socks which offered the impression they were stuffed with six quires of a pulp fiction magazine and heavy boots with bulging toe-caps. The only part of the England players that was visible below the upper neck was their hands and the white knobble of their kneecaps.

It was not simply the contrasting kit that marked the teams apart. Hungary wasted no time in demonstrating their superior skills, tactics and technical nous. England found themselves chasing flitting and elusive cherry ghosts amidst the mists of Wembley. Outpaced, out-thought, outmanoeuvred and, for large sections of the game, totally outplayed, England were 2–4 down at half-time. It was obvious they had no answer to playmaker Puskas, the deep-lying striker Hidegkuti or the cavalier Cibor. Hungary's third goal, from Puskas, was something to see. A diagonal pass from Hungary's left to right looked as if it was going out for a goal-kick, but Puskas was on the ball in a flash a yard or so from Gil Merrick's left-hand post. Puskas was facing the goal-line and there seemed no danger as Billy Wright came roaring in with a slide tackle. What happened then was the stuff of legend. Puskas suddenly dragged the ball back with the sole of his left boot as Wright tackled fresh air. Puskas then swivelled and fired a low drive that beat Merrick all ends up at his near post. In terms of skill in the heat of battle I had never before seen the like. Writing in *The Times* the next day, Geoffrey Green said of Billy's futile lunge, 'Wright rushed in like a fireman arriving to the wrong fire.'

The second half was only minutes old when the past was dead and buried forever. A venomous rising drive from Bozsik made it five and, minutes later, Hidegkuti brought his personal contribution to a hat-trick with a volley from a lobbed pass from Puskas. Hungary couldn't have spelled it out more clearly if they had then raised eight placards bearing the letters C-U-R-T-A-I-N-S. From thereon it was pure exhibition stuff from them, with a penalty converted by Alf Ramsey being merely consolation to England and giving the final score-line of 6–3 an air of respectability.

I remember trooping out of Wembley with my pals and feeling very dejected at having seen England so soundly beaten. In truth, like the majority of the 100,000 present that afternoon, the true magnitude of the defeat didn't register with me. Minutes after the final whistle I certainly didn't see the defeat as a watershed for English football. Like so many truly seminal moments in sport, true perspective and gravitas only comes with the considered reflection of inquest, and 'inquest' was apposite for the rumination that was to follow.

Within the framework of English football at the time, England had fielded a decent team, albeit Preston's Tom Finney had been unavailable. England's 2–3–5 formation, the 'W' formation as it was called, had been the norm for decades. That day, Hungary played 4–2–4, a formation few, if any of us, had ever heard of let alone witnessed. The 'W' formation to which every British team had adhered for decades was, to all intents and purposes, consigned to history, certainly at the top level of the game. Hungary had come along with a new formation, a new way to play the game, albeit the Switzerland team of the 1930s had adopted a similar formation. There was an argument for saying, rather than having been given a harsh lesson that the 'W' formation was now superseded, British football in general had been playing the wrong formation for years. Whatever, the message was, England and British football had to awake to a new future or, like sandcastles on a beach, be washed away by a tidal wave of new ideas. Even today, should I fall into conversation with an old timer who tries to put forward the

argument that a team playing the old 'W' formation would beat
any team adopting 4–4–2 or 4–5–1, I will make reference to that
England-Hungary game of so many years ago and tell him or her,
it's all right to take fancy as a companion but we must follow reason
and practicality as our guide.

The inquest into England's double humiliation at the hands of
Hungary called for a complete modernisation of the game. For
some players, it also spelled the end of their international careers:
Alf Ramsey, Bill Eckersley, Harry Johnston, Stan Mortenson and
debutants Ernie Taylor and George Robb were never to play for
England again. In the wake of the defeats, strips and kit changed;
lighter, more practical strips and boots were adopted. Moreover,
teams began to experiment with new formations; for example,
Manchester City enjoyed success with the 'Revie Plan', where Don
Revie played as a deep-lying schemer in much the same way as
Puskas had done. Whereas, in 1954, Blackpool adopted a variation
of 4–4–2 with Stan Matthews and Bill Perry on either flank, Stan
Mortenson and Alan Brown upfront and Jackie Mudie and Ernie
Taylor in what we would now refer to as centre of midfield.

That times were so very different then can be evinced by the fact
that Walter Winterbottom had presided over England teams that
had suffered the most humiliating defeats in the history of English
football, there having also been the 1–0 defeat by the USA in the
1950 World Cup, yet few in the press had called for his head.

This had much to do with the fact that the press and football
supporters in general understood what Walter was trying to do
and that he would be doing it a hell of a lot quicker if he wasn't
having to battle with an archaic FA to get his ideas implemented.
Even after the Hungary defeats, many FA officials were still doing
fine impersonations of ostriches with their heads thrust deep in the
sand. There was a body of opinion among some in the FA, and
this was certainly more true of the Football League, that overseas
football didn't matter, what was all important was the domestic League programme. A myopic view evidenced when the 1955
League Champions, Chelsea, entered the newly formed European
Cup and were drawn against Djurgardens of Sweden only to with-
draw under pressure from the FA and Football League. The following season both bodies placed similar pressure upon the champions

Manchester United. However, United manager Matt Busby was a visionary and made of sterner stuff. To their complete and utter consternation, the FA and Football League were defied by Matt because he envisaged what the future of football was going to be.

Walter Winterbottom gave countless interviews after the Hungary defeats in which he was at pains to point out English football had fallen behind the times in terms of tactics, technique, training and coaching. Though Walter did get stick from some quarters of the press, the venom of the media was mainly directed at an antiquated FA. Slowly but surely a gentle revolution occurred as the majority in the FA accepted they had to listen not only to Walter but also to the players and press. Walter was given more time with England players to prepare for matches. Appearance money for international games was increased from £30 to £50, at a time of the maximum wage for Football League players, which was the equivalent of two weeks' wages.

The press continued to lobby the FA, insisting they had to listen to professional opinion. Walter was given leave to not only pursue his dream of an England Under-23 team, but also an England Youth team which he believed would provide the full England team with continuity and a stronger foundation. In addition to being manager of the England and England Under-23 teams, Walter was also appointed the FA's first Director of Coaching and instigated the FA coaching schools at Lilleshall, the end product of which was the award of an FA Coaching Badge, a qualification that was to be recognised and respected worldwide. Walter's Lilleshall coaching schools provided British football with a network of coaching not only for Football League clubs but at all levels of the game. Walter's diplomacy and good-natured enthusiasm wore down his critics, laying down the foundation for more sophisticated schemes for developing and improving players from grass roots to international level.

Walter Winterbottom can take unadulterated credit for having raised standards of performance throughout English football. The one thing the FA did not relinquish, however, was their selection of the England team. Albeit, come the late 1950s, Walter had persuaded enough on the International Selection Committee that, rather than they alone selecting the England team, his remit should be as an adviser to them. A situation that was far from ideal as far as Walter was concerned but one he believed was progress, of sorts.

Walter announced to the press he had a list of thirty players who were going to form his initial squad for the 1958 World Cup Finals, should England qualify. He was at pains to point out the door was open to any player not on the list who might prove worthy of international football in that time. The list was by no means conclusive but word was that Walter wasn't thinking of tinkering with it too much. That pleased me no end, because my name was on it.

Previewing the England-Scotland match in the *Daily Mirror*, Peter Wilson wrote, 'This Saturday's clash of the auld enemy takes on even greater significance for England and their manager Walter Winterbottom. "Girls we love for what they are; young men for what they promise to be," said the German writer Goethe. The likes of Hodgkinson, Edwards, Hall, Byrne and Grainger promise much. We shall have a clearer idea of how far such promise will be fulfilled come a quarter to five on Saturday. Walter Winterbottom, who instigated and has presided over a deft revolution of English football these past four years, will see England's encounter with a skilful and resolute Scotland as the litmus test to the chemistry he has created.'

Wilson's words were echoed by other top footballer writers. On reading the likes, I was left in no uncertain terms that we would be very much under the microscope against Scotland. The game was seen as a barometer of how far England had progressed since the watershed of 1953. Incidentally, I wonder how long it has been since Goethe has merited a mention in the *Daily Mirror*, and in the sports pages at that?

On the Saturday we took an early lunch of boiled ham and salad at our Hendon hotel – cometh the day, cometh the ham. After which we travelled by coach to Wembley. The journey is not far; in the distance, to the north, you could see Wembley's twin towers from various parts of Hendon High Street. To ensure there were no hold-ups, however, our coach enjoyed the escort of a police motorcycle rider. It was little things such as that which emphasised to me the importance and significance of such a football match. The game may well have been seen as a gauge as to how far England had progressed since Hungary, but for the majority, the key importance to a clash between England and Scotland was, as it had always been, national pride at stake. My stomach was doing cartwheels on that short journey but I knew, once I was crossed that white line, the nerves would disappear and my concentration would be total.

As our coach approached Wembley the magnitude of the fixture became clearly apparent to me. The roads and streets were jam-packed with supporters – mainly of Scotland. Almost anywhere you go in this world, you will find a Scot, maybe not in the Dalai Lama's temple, or on the Communist Party Central Committee of the People's Republic of China, but most places. As our coach travelled towards Wembley's twin towers I was left to wonder if so many of them had ever been gathered together at one time in a non-native city as there were on this day.

There must have been some 60,000 Scots, and they appeared to have taken over Wembley with their high spirits and genial disposition. It was like an invasion from across the border. As our coach wound its way through the throng, the mass of tartan-bonneted, flag-waving Scots gave the impression of an army of occupation. With banners unfurled, bagpipes – yes bagpipes – skirling, trumpets and klaxons hooting, rattles swirling and harsh voices howling they completely overran Wembley. There was a moment when our coach slowed to almost a halt, providing a group of merry Scots with an opportunity to let us know just exactly what they thought of the England team. Fists banged on coach windows and we were treated to a torrent of good-humoured joshing.

'Ye's are gonna get it today. Ya bloody Sassenach nancies.'

'Hey, Hodgkinson, yor gonna need a doctor for that bad back o' yors. It's gonna break from ye pickin' the ball oot o' the net so many times.'

'The best thing that can be said for England is, it inner Ireland.'

'Hey, what's the difference 'tween Englishmen and toast? Ye can make soldiers outta toast!'

I can't remember any of them using expletives. I could be wrong, but I can't recall any rich language reaching my ears. The rivalry was intense but it was a good humoured and in the right spirit, even though many looked to have handsomely bolstered the profits of Tennent's, Teacher's and Haig.

Crowds of drinkers had spilled out of the pubs and onto the pavements, adding to an excited atmosphere that was teetering on the precipice of chaos. Even from the relative peace and safety of our coach it was evident the streets were ringing with joshing, cackling, strident, roaring, raucous voices. Every pub we passed, our coach was the signal for the crowd of drinkers to stream forward to give us what for. I had never seen anything like it, ever, and thanked the stars I wasn't an England supporter trying to make my way up to Wembley through their number.

Again I was reminded how far I had come in such a relatively short period of time, in little under four years, from Worksop Town against Grantham to this. Everybody has one thing they can do better than anybody else, usually it's the ability to read their own handwriting, but on that coach journey to Wembley I felt that perhaps, just perhaps, my vocation in life might be goalkeeping.

As the two teams assembled in the whitewashed Wembley tunnel, I took up a place behind skipper Billy Wright as per my instructions. Opposite me, behind the Scotland captain, George Young, was their keeper, Tommy Younger. We shook hands and wished one another all the best before a shrill blast from the referee's whistle indicated we should march forward. From the relative gloom of the tunnel I stepped out into glorious sunshine and a sonorous noise from the 100,000 fans. Wembley was full to the topmost layer. The crowd, in those days mainly out in the open, roared their approval and I immediately felt a tingle in the back of my neck.

The teams that day are indelibly in the mind, so much so that I can recite them now without recourse to reference books. We lined up as follows:

ENGLAND

Yours truly; Jeff Hall (Birmingham City), Roger Byrne (Manchester United); Ronnie Clayton (Blackburn Rovers), Billy Wright (Wolverhampton Wanderers – captain), Duncan Edwards (Manchester United); Stan Matthews (Blackpool), Tommy Thompson, Tom Finney (both Preston North End), Derek Kevan (West Bromwich Albion) and Colin Grainger (Sheffield United).

SCOTLAND

Tommy Younger (Liverpool); Eric Caldow (Rangers), John Hewie (Charlton Athletic); Ian McColl (Rangers), George Young (Rangers – captain), Tommy Docherty (Preston North End); Bobby Collins, Willie Fernie (both Celtic), Hughie Reilly (Hibernian), Jackie Mudie (Blackpool) and Tommy Ring (Clyde).

Referee: Mr P. Roomer (Holland)

The ceremony of introductions and presentations over, I jogged to the far goal area for the kick-in that preceded any game, whether it be at Worksop or Wembley. Billy Wright, brandishing a pennant bearing the motif of the three lions, made his way to the centre circle for the ritual of the tossing of the coin. That done, Billy informed us, 'As we are' and less than a minute later, at last, the battle was joined.

The game was less than a minute old when Jeff Hall played a pass through the middle of the park only for it be intercepted by the advancing John Hewie. The Scotland left-back played the ball down the centre and deep into the England half of the field where Tommy Ring raced forward with the ball intermittently kissing his right boot.

Jeff Hall's misplaced pass had caught us pushing forward. As the England back-line quickly tried to reform, Ring continued his advance down the middle. At the time there was a public infor-mation film regularly shown on television, the topic of which was courtesy on the roads. The film adopted a comic approach to what had then become a serious problem with the sudden plethora of cars on the roads. Two drivers were seen being ultra-courteous in their endeavour to allow the other right way. 'After you,' said Driver One leaning from his window. 'No, after you,' replied Driver Two. 'No, sir, I really must insist, after you,' intoned Driver One. 'And I insist, after you,' replied Driver Two. Billy Wright and Ronnie Clayton did something of an impersonation of those two well-meaning though misguided drivers. As Tommy Ring advanced they left it to one another to close down the Clyde winger. In the event, neither of them moved towards Ring who happily continued his advance, straight between the pair of them and into the wide open space that existed between me and the England back four.

As soon as I had seen Tommy Ring advance towards Billy Wright and Ronnie Clayton I too had advanced, some four paces. On seeing Ring breach our rearguard I was hot-footing it forward to a point a yard or so from the penalty spot. Tommy was a winger, left-footed. As he continued his advance he veered to his right. I was certain he was shaping for a shot across me aiming for the left-hand corner of my goal. I moved slightly to my left, only, as I did so, Tommy fired off a cracking low drive with his right boot that seared across the turf to my right. I adjusted my position and got down as quickly as I could. I wasn't quite quick enough. I extended my right arm. There must have been only a fag paper's width between the lower part of my arm and the ball but enough for it continue its low trajectory before bulging the base of the net. The vast majority of supporters on Wembley's towering terraces immediately erupted. I looked up from my prostrate position to see Tommy Ring wheeling away shouting, 'Yes! Yes! Yes!!'

I felt as if a lead load had suddenly been thrust into my stomach. I happened to glance up at the giant Wembley scoreboard at the far end of the pitch. The score still read 0–0, the pointers of the clock appeared not to have moved. They read three o'clock. Less than a minute gone and we were a goal down. As play resumed my mind was still occupied with that goal. Bloody hell, I thought to myself, I can see it now: 'Alan Hodgkinson, his first touch of the ball on his England debut was to pick it out of the net.'

I told myself that fact was something I was going to have to live with, forever. Then, whilst my teammates went in search of an immediate equaliser at the other end of the pitch, I collected my thoughts and told myself I had to think positively. In truth the goal was not down to any error of mine. Nevertheless I had conceded – the goal was officially timed at 59 seconds. I told myself, or rather convinced myself, I would not be judged on that early goal alone. I recalled what Joe Mercer had told me when he offered his congratulations to me on the occasion of my England call-up. It is not where you are at any given time in football that matters, but where you are going. At this given time I felt as low as a cafeteria tray, but I told myself I had 89 minutes, more or less, to erase the memory of that early goal. I convinced myself it was what I was to do in the remainder of the game and, in the future, that would determine my worth as a goalkeeper, not the conceding of an early goal on my England debut, as galling as I felt that to be.

'One goal. They're sure as hell not going to put another past me this afternoon,' I kept repeating to myself.

England continued to pressurise Scotland for most of the remainder of the first half but the Scotland defence, well marshalled by the giant Rangers centre-half, George Young, remained resolute. Stan Matthews had the better of John Hewie, but when the England forwards managed to get on the end of Stan's good work, they found Tommy Younger in inspired form. Midway through the first half, Younger produced a superb save when diving to his left to hold a fire-cracker of a shot from, of all people, left-back Jeff Hall, who appeared hell-bent on making amends for his earlier error.

Minutes later Scotland responded with menace. Tommy Docherty, who was having an imperious game in midfield, played in Willie Fernie and the Celtic inside-forward fired a shot low to my right. I managed to get down and push it away. In getting down to a low shot, if a goalkeeper feels he can't hold the ball, what he must do is angle it away from advancing opposing forwards. This I managed to do by pushing the ball wide to my right. The ball was picked up by Billy Wright who, in turning with it, only succeeded in turning into Bobby Collins. The tenacious Collins whipped the ball off Billy's toe and immediately played it square to Hughie Reilly who dispatched a thumping drive from just inside our penalty area that was heading for the top left of my goal. Having taken to my feet I took to my toes and flung myself through the air to my left and managed to fingertip the ball over the bar. I heard the vast majority of Wembley cry, 'Go-awwww!'

That double save served to boost my confidence. Nothing could erase the early goal, but I felt I had done something to tip the balance back in my favour. Minutes before the break, I was called into action again to first deny Tommy Docherty then a bullet of a header from Hughie Reilly. Following the half-time whistle, as I made the long walk down the pitch towards the tunnel at the far end of Wembley, I felt a whole lot better about things.

In talking to the players there were times when Walter Winterbottom sounded more like an Oxford don than a football manager and his half-time talk was such a time. Apart from emphasising Billy Wright and Ronnie Clayton should be tighter, Walter told us to continue to play the way we had been. 'In so doing, a break will materialise which, I have no doubt, the forwards will capitalise upon.'

Walter turned his attention to the quality of the crosses. He was of the opinion, and rightly so, that crossing the ball into the 'heart of their penalty box' was a mistake as George Young was winning almost everything in the air.

'George is not the most mobile, he doesn't like to wander,' said Walter and he pointed to Colin Grainger. 'Colin, you're a fine crosser of a ball but I haven't seen you demonstrate that to great effect, as yet. All the telling crosses and pull-backs have come from Stanley, here.

'I want you to get the ball into their penalty area, the earlier the better, and I want you to avoid the central area. Hit them deep to the far post.'

Walter then turned his attention to Derek Kevan and told him he wanted him to drop off Young, arrive late into the area and at the far post expecting Colin Grainger to deliver.

Everyone nodded. The shrill of the buzzer ended the half-time talk and we took to our feet once more. As I was leaving the dressing room, Walter came up to me.

'Well done, Alan, young man. You've kept us in this,' said Walter.

I can't remember if I replied or not, there isn't much you can say when a manager pays you a compliment like that. You just take it. Walter's words did, however, serve to bolster my confidence even more.

Minutes after the re-start, Colin Grainger shot past Eric Caldow and just when I thought he might be heading for the exit at the far end of the ground, he whipped the ball to the far post. The ball flew over George Young and Tommy Younger and, frustratingly, also past the advancing Derek Kevan, who had only just mistimed his run but sufficiently so as not to make contact.

Fifteen minutes later, Duncan Edwards took out a knot of Scotland players with a perfectly judged pass that slowed as Colin Grainger advanced upon it. Colin swept past Caldow only to then check back. Switching the ball from his left to his right, Colin then crossed the ball to the far post. On this occasion Derek Kevan had timed his run almost to perfection. Derek still had something to do to reach the ball, but he launched himself forward and connected with the ball with the meat of his forehead to send a thunderous diving header past the flaying left arm of Tommy Younger. England supporters may well have been in the minority, there were some 40,000 present that day, but for the first time that afternoon they made as much noise as the Scots had done in the first minute of the game.

These days when I am asked what influence a manager can have on the proceedings of a game, more often than not I find myself recalling Walter Winterbottom's instructions to Colin Grainger and Derek Kevan. Our equaliser was the direct result of an observation and instruction from Walter. If in us levelling the game Walter derived any degree of satisfaction from that, he didn't show it. As I jumped for joy, I glanced across at the England bench. Walter was sitting impassively as ever.

If our equaliser rattled Scotland they didn't show it. On the contrary, following Derek's super diving header, Scotland placed us under a prolonged period of pressure. Prompted by Bobby Collins, Jackie Mudie and Tommy Docherty, of whom the latter was getting through a tremendous amount of work with seemingly little discomfort, Scotland drew on bruised pride and their attacks acquired increasing shape and fluidity. Deciding this was not a time for the finer points of the game, England defenders hacked and whacked the ball to all corners of Wembley, but still the Scots continued to pour forward.

During a concerted period of pressure I was relieved to see a header from Willie Fernie clip the top of my crossbar. Moments later, I found myself leaping with Hughie Reilly, Jackie Mudie and Billy Wright to meet an in-swinging cross from Tommy Docherty. All four bodies clashed. In so doing, I spilled the ball. As I hit the ground, to my horror, I saw Bobby Collins advancing on the loose ball which was some three yards from my goal-line. Instinctively, I immediately threw my body towards the ball. Not only did I manage to block Bobby's effort, to my great relief I also somehow managed to hold on to the ball. The response of the massed ranks of Scotland supporters was to make a noise that sounded like 60,000 bicycle tyres being simultaneously deflated.

Having repelled a series of attacks from Scotland, we then enjoyed a bout of pressure, only to find the Scotland defence in a similarly uncharitable mood. Back came Scotland in a second half that was proving topsy-turvy in terms of territorial possession. In one such Scotland attack a lofted ball from Tommy Docherty was met on the half-volley by Jackie Mudie, whose shot rose only to then dip sharply. I leapt into the air, extended a hand and managed to tip the ball over the crossbar to the safety of the curious semi-circle of sand situated behind either goal at Wembley, the purpose of which no one ever knew.

There was only three minutes remaining when Duncan Edwards, the seventeen-year-old wonder, powered his way through the middle of the Scotland half of the field. When Duncan was twenty-five yards from goal, he took one touch of the ball to steady himself, then let rip with a screaming low drive that swept past all and sundry – including the diving Tommy Younger. The ball cannoned off the stanchion in the left of Younger's goal. I skipped and danced around my penalty area with joy – not of the Beverley Sisters fame. Again I glanced across to the England bench. Walter Winterbottom was sitting as calm as an oyster, displaying no more emotion than if he had just seen his mother try on a hat.

Some three minutes later I again allowed myself a little jump for joy as the final whistle sounded.

As I shook the hands of the Scotland players as I left the pitch, I felt pretty pleased at my England debut. It had been a nightmare of a start but we had won. I felt I had done enough in the game to justify my selection and, possibly, played sufficiently well to negate the fact that my first touch on my debut was to pick the ball out of the net. Possibly, even well enough to have contributed in some small way to victory. Walter Winterbottom thought I'd had a good game and told me so, and, when the Sunday newspapers hit the streets of London around ten that night, the consensus was I had played well and enjoyed a good debut. I slept the sleep of the just that night.

Walter Winterbottom later gave a sober assessment of England's victory, which he described as 'A pleasing result and performance that bodes well for the continuation of progress.'

Scotland had every reason to feel they should have achieved something from the game. In truth Scotland had placed us under considerable pressure at various times during the ninety minutes and, on the balance of play, were worthy of a draw. I felt the two teams were well matched, not a great deal between them. In the end, however, it had taken something special and out of the ordinary by a young player who himself was special and out of the ordinary to separate the two teams. That's football.

As a footnote to my England debut, may I advance us some nine months to December of 1957. It was mid-December and, having trained with Sheffield United in the morning, I had decided to pop into the city centre to do some Christmas shopping. I was walking through Coles department store, which even then had been acquired by Selfridges, when I found myself in the books department. I happened to look at the Christmas annuals as I passed them and there, to my utter astonishment, was the *Charles Buchan Football Annual*, on the cover of which, in full colour, was yours truly, airborne having just tipped Jackie Mudie's dipping shot over the crossbar. At the time I was Sheffield United's regular number one and was a regular member of the England squad. On seeing myself, however, on the cover of a football annual that I knew would form a part of thousands of Christmas stockings, I felt for the first time that I had truly arrived in the game I truly loved.

CHAPTER FOUR

A month after having made my England debut I returned to Wembley for a World Cup qualifying match against the Republic of Ireland. Walter Winterbottom made three changes to the team which had defeated Scotland. Manchester United's Tommy Taylor replaced Tom Finney at centre-forward, with Tom switching to the left wing in preference to Colin Grainger. John Atyeo of Second Division Bristol City took over the number eight shirt from Tommy Thompson, whilst Johnny Haynes of Fulham came in for Derek Kevan.

The choice of John Atyeo raised a few eyebrows in the press. John was a big, burly centre forward, one not without skill, who had never played in the top flight. His goal-scoring record that season of 23 League goals in 40 matches was decent enough, but certain quarters of the press questioned whether it was good enough to earn him an England call-up ahead of the likes of Derek Kevan, Bobby Smith (Spurs), Albert Quixhall (Sheffield Wednesday) and Peter Broadbent (Wolves), whose goal-scoring exploits were of similar stature but in the First Division.

The commonly asked question was, 'Could Big John score goals in the First Division, let alone at international level?'

In the event John Ayteo and Tommy Taylor proved Walter right, not that there was ever a doubt about Tommy's ability. Taylor notched his second successive hat-trick for England and two goals from John Atyeo gave us a comfortable 5–1 victory. What was unusual about the game was all the goals came in the first half. With such a lead Billy Wright and the lads simply 'played out' the second half and, apart from a low, stinging shot from Jenson, I spent almost the entire forty minutes watching them do it.

A week later I was on World Cup duty again against Denmark in Copenhagen. Walter decided to stick with the eleven who had so comfortably beaten the Republic – and it paid off. Tommy Taylor helped himself to another couple of goals, taking his haul to ten in four matches. One wonders what the media of today would make of such a goal scoring record by an England player? Probably call for him to be knighted. John Atyeo justified his inclusion by chipping in with a goal as did Johnny Haynes. The game was not as plain sailing as the 4-1 score-line might suggest. John Jenson had given Denmark the lead in the twenty-fifth minute, and in truth it was not until the final fifteen minutes that we seized the initiative when our fitness told over a Denmark team who comprised, in the majority, part-time players.

Though he was not aware of it at the time, the victory over Denmark marked the swansong of Stanley Matthews in an England shirt. Stan had enjoyed an England career of some longevity, twenty-two years, but with qualification to the World Cup Finals now almost certain, Walter, and perhaps the FA Selection Committee too, decided to pursue the policy of youth. Stan was forty-two and, although he had enjoyed a good game in Copenhagen, the notion of a forty-three-year-old winger in the World Cup Finals was not one Walter felt was in the best interests of the England team.

Not many know this but Stan was actually named in the team to play the Republic of Ireland in England's next and final World Cup qualifying match. Having been told by an FA official he was playing, in the next breath he was informed that should England qualify for the World Cup Finals, as expected, he wouldn't feature in the plans. A few days later Stan telephoned Walter Winterbottom to inform him he had picked up a niggling injury and 'regrettably would be unavailable for the Republic game'. Stan's place went to David Pegg of Manchester United; sadly, it was to be David's only cap for, like Duncan Edwards, Tommy Taylor and Roger Byrne, he was to perish in the Munich air disaster.

Stan was more than simply a footballer. He was a true legend of football and a fine ambassador of the game across the globe. At his peak, which I would say was from the late 1930s to the early 1950s, managers strove to find ways to limit the mayhem and panic he was capable of creating among defenders. Stan's forte was an art one seldom sees today, that of dribbling. For a dribbling player he was very direct, almost unpredictable. He revolutionised wing play in the 1930s by taking the ball up to the full-back; prior to Stan, wingers had always waited for the full-back to come on to them before trying to beat them.

Four days after victory in Denmark I travelled with the England party to Dublin for our final World Cup qualifying game against the Republic. With Stan Matthews now out of the equation, that Swiss Army knife of a player, Tom Finney, switched from the left to right wing, with David Pegg assuming the number eleven shirt.

Although we had beaten the Republic very comfortably at Wembley, no one expected our game against the Republic at a packed Dalymount Park to be easy – and it wasn't. The Republic then, as now, tend to be a totally different proposition on their own turf. So it proved.

Within the first two minutes I was called upon to prevent first Arsenal's Joe Haverty, then Liam 'Billy' Whelan (Manchester United), giving the Republic an early lead. The second effort, a blistering low drive from the edge of my penalty area, came through a thicket of legs. I only saw it at the last moment but, somehow, managed to react quickly enough to fingertip the ball wide and to safety.

The initial onslaught from the Republic had the Dalymount faithful in a suitable state of disequilibrium and they roared their approval as the Irish team continued in similar vein. In the fourth minute Aston Villa's Pat Saward swept past Billy Wright before playing the ball back into the path of my Sheffield United teammate Alf Ringstead, who showed no compassion or camaraderie by rocketing it high into the roof of my net. If there had been, at the time, modern technology of the kind to have constructed a roof on the Dalymount Park stadium, it would have been raised a foot or so by human voices alone.

England's response was swift and sure. We took the game to the Republic only to find goalkeeper Tommy Godwin (Bournemouth), Pat Saward (Aston Villa) and centre-half Charlie Hurley (Millwall) in imperious form. The young Hurley in particular belied his tender years by marshalling his defenders well and winning everything in the air. It was an outstanding performance that would soon earn him a transfer to First Division Sunderland. For England, Duncan Edwards, another teenager, was our outstanding player. As strong as Hercules and as imperious as Caesar, Duncan worked tirelessly to tilt the scales in England's favour; arguably, never had the 'boy man' intervened more cleverly, used the ball more wisely and run into space to make himself available more astutely than against the Republic.

I was by no means a spectator in the game. Minutes before half-time, the Republic broke from the confines of the penalty area and I had to act smartly to palm away a low drive from Alf Ringstead. As I walked from the pitch at half-time I thanked my lucky stars I'd managed to save Alf's second effort. He had already scored past me with his first. I knew once the pair of us were back in training at Sheffield United and enjoying the dressing-room banter and joshing, the fact he had scored past me would only merit a few thousand mentions.

Prompted by Edwards, we probed and prodded rather than parted a resolute Republic rearguard. The home side were still dangerous on the break and after some seventy minutes had elapsed a long ball out of defence by Noel Cantwell (West Ham) was latched onto by the lonesome figure of 'Billy' Whelan who was lurking with intent. Whelan showed everyone a clean pair of heels but, anticipating his run, I had come quickly and far off my line. As Whelan hastened hare-like into my penalty area I forced him right and, never taking my eyes off the ball, swept down at his feet to steal it from him. I remember clutching that ball to my chest as if it had been a baby in danger, thinking to myself, 'If he'd put that away, it would be all over.'

There was only a minute to go for it all to be over when the tireless Duncan Edwards robbed Pat Saward and sent Tom Finney on perhaps one last exploration of the nether reaches of the right wing. Tom rounded Cantwell, arched around the ball and sent over a peach of a centre which found the forehead of John Atyeo. The ball seared past Godwin with such celerity he thought it imprudent to move and stood crestfallen as big John turned away arms aloft.

Writing in the *Empire News*, David Jack said of England's game in Dublin, 'England may have won the home match 4-1, but it was an uninspiring win. In Dublin (1-1) Duncan Edwards, Roger Byrne, Johnny Haynes and Alan Hodgkinson were the only players deserving of bouquets, though Tom Finney and Tommy Taylor enjoyed brief spells of success. England's progress continues – just – but, for the gallant Irish, this draw was also a moral victory.'

The draw was enough. England qualified for the World Cup Finals in Sweden; what's more, to my utter delight, so too did Scotland, Wales and Northern Ireland. It was the first time the four home nations had ever qualified together for the finals of a World Cup and, sadly, to date, still the only occasion on which this has happened.

Stan Matthews was not the only British football legend destined not to be going to the World Cup Finals. The Scottish FA Selection Committee had omitted Rangers' centre-half George Young from the team that played their final qualifying match against Spain in Madrid. George had taken the news with all the effortless composure of a corpse in a morgue but, inside, he was devastated at the thought he would not to be going to Sweden. Mel Gibson could have cast George Young in *Braveheart*. He was a big man with a chest no wider than a petrol tanker and wore the fresh and ruddy complexion of a rude man of the open. He had 53 caps to his name during a period when fewer internationals were played than today. For many, the thought of a Scotland team without granite-like George in the heart of defence was unthinkable, an opinion shared wholeheartedly by George himself. As had been the case with Stan Matthews and England, George was a victim of a desire on the part of the Scottish FA Selection Committee to arrive in Sweden with a team which contained, ironically, young blood in its veins.

That game against the Republic in Ireland was to be my last for England. England did not play another match until the October of that year, some five months later, by which time Walter and the selection committee were to prefer Bolton's Eddie Hopkinson. Of course, at the time I had no idea.

The 1956–57 season ended on a very happy note for me. I was the England goalkeeper and, as with England under Walter Winterbottom, Sheffield United under Joe Mercer were also making progress. We finished in seventh place in Division Two, albeit the improvement coming too late to challenge promoted Leicester City and Nottingham Forest.

The FA Cup Final of 1957 between Aston Villa and Manchester United exemplified the changes that had taken place in English football since the Hungary humiliations of four years previously. When the two teams emerged from the Wembley tunnel they both did so wearing V-neck short-sleeved shirts made of a light cotton fabric; shorts were indeed short and again made of light cotton, as were their socks. The majority of players who participated in this final also wore the new, lighter type of boot as manufactured by Lawrence, Valsport, Puma and Gola. These boots still came above the ankle but were made from a combination of synthetic material and leather which made them considerably lighter than the traditional boot.

Thousands of youngsters had taken to wearing the Co-operative Society football boot, or the Co-op boot as it was commonly known. These boots were manufactured at the Co-op's 'Goliath' boot and shoe factory in Heckmondwike, in West Yorkshire, and the reason they sold in their thousands was down to the fact that Stan Matthews promoted them. As I have said, Stan was the first footballer to really exploit his commercial potential. The deal he struck with the Co-op involved him making personal appearances at their stores throughout the country where he would distribute photographs of himself bearing the Co-op football boot logo. Should a boy purchase a pair of boots, Stan would sign the photograph for the lad as a souvenir. When Stan made a personal appearance he would be besieged by hundreds of schoolboys. It must have been chaotic at times, but these boys had an opportunity to meet and talk with a world-class footballer in their home town, be it Lincoln or Leicester, and there is much to be said for such accessibility to stardom.

These promotional trips would often take place on a Saturday morning in the town or city in which Blackpool had an away game. It is unthinkable that a top player of today would be allowed to leave the team hotel of a Saturday morning before a game in this way, but Stan had persuaded Blackpool manager Joe Smith that such a visit would not affect his performance – and it never did.

The summer break was indeed a break from football, particularly for supporters who, after having seen the FA Cup Final which had been broadcast on BBC television, were starved of football until the pre-season friendly matches began at the beginning of August.

When I reported back for pre-season training with Sheffield United in readiness for 1957–58, an air of expectancy seemed to have gripped the club and it was all down to manager Joe Mercer.

Out on the training field, the first thing you noticed about Joe was his bandy legs. Those celebrated brackets first arrived in 1931 when the teenage Mercer, talented son of a Wirral footballing family (both his father and grandfather had made a career in the game prior to World War One) signed for Everton. The equally famous grin took a little longer to establish, but when it emerged it was there to stay.

Joe had been through the mill as a footballer. After fifteen years with Everton, the club with whom he had grown up, they believed him to be finished and decided to discard him after the war. He joined Arsenal at the age of thirty-one where he proceeded to bask in his own personal Indian summer. His qualities of leadership saw Joe become Arsenal captain whereupon, in 1953, he led them to the League Championship. The following season, on a spring afternoon at Highbury, playing against Liverpool, he sustained a very bad leg break. He insisted he would play again, but sadly, a little over a year later, he had to accept the inevitable.

Joe took to working in the family grocery business in Wallesey and was boning bacon when he received the telephone call from Sheffield United's wonderfully named chairman Senior Aitken. It transpired Aitken had telephoned one or two people in the game asking if they could recommend a successor to Reg Freeman. It was Aitken's call to Manchester United manager Matt Busby that brought Joe's name into the frame. Having received such a recommendation, Senior Aitken wasted no time in contacting Joe and inviting him to Bramall Lane for an interview.

South Yorkshire bluntness and a barrage of questions from Aitken and his fellow directors did not find Joe wanting. Joe was offered the job there and then, but he informed Aitken that he would take it on one condition:

'I and I alone run team affairs, sign and get rid of players as I think fit, and introduce my own ideas for training and coaching,' said Joe.

'That sounds to me like four conditions, at least,' replied the extrovert Aitken, 'but take it as read that is what'll happen. I knows nowt about football and footballers, and these sitting either side of me know a bloody sight less.'

Joe could have had easier starts to football management. In truth Sheffield United had been struggling and our supporters were sceptical. Joe, as I have indicated, arrived too late to save the club from relegation but he outlined his plan to create a team built on youth which would eventually return Sheffield United to the top flight. Myself being one of those young players.

Whilst my appearances had been intermittent due to National Service, Joe also had to contend with a catalogue of injuries. In 1956–57, whilst I was still in the army and not knowing the season would end with me as first-choice keeper not only for United, but also England, Joe played three different goalkeepers, seven different full-backs and nineteen different forwards in an era when, injuries apart, there was little variation to first-team selections on a week-to-week basis.

Should there have been such a thing as Human Resources at the club in those days they would have been working overtime. Joe Mercer rang the changes in personnel, players came and players went with the regularity of an army drum roll. Joe had been told by the board if he wanted to bring in new players he would have to generate money himself, which is precisely what he did. The most notable exits were those of Colin Grainger, who was sold to Sunderland, and Jim Iley to Tottenham Hotspur for combined fees of £67,000, a not inconsiderable sum of money at the time. Joe also managed to collect small fees for several outgoing players, most notably centre-half Malcolm Barrass, who joined non-League Wigan Athletic as their player-manager, and Ronnie Waldock, who was transferred to Scunthorpe United.

In Joe's first six months in charge, fourteen professionals left the club. Joe had his critics as some of the exiting players were firm old favourites of fans, but he took the brickbats on his considerable chin and kept smiling. No manager likes to tell a player he is no longer needed but Joe knew the job had to be done. As he said at the time, 'Releasing players is a hell of a lot less painful than the need to release them.' To counter the mass exit, Joe signed three players who were to give sterling service to Sheffield United and promoted others from the reserve and youth teams.

Derek Pace joined from Aston Villa and was to prove himself a fine penalty-box predator. In nigh on 300 games for Sheffield United, Derek's average was to be a goal every other game.

Billy Hodgson was signed from St Johnstone and his performances in some 180 games for the club were to make a mockery of the £4,000 Joe had paid for his services. Billy was what in those days was termed a 'tanner ball player', or, as they were known in Scotland, 'tanna baw players'. The term was used in England only in terms of Scottish players and was, by and large, very complimentary; it meant the player in question possessed an array of ball-playing skills with which he was so adept he could perform them on a 'tanner', which was a sixpence (2.5p) slightly smaller in circumference than the current one-pence coin. I say the term was largely complimentary for there were some quarters of Glasgow where the term was used to describe a player who possessed amazing ball skills but little else.

Following his policy to give youth a chance, as 1957–58 got underway Joe told right-half and local lad Brian Richardson and left-half Gerry Summers that they 'featured very prominently' in his plans for the first team. With Brian and Gerry joining Graham Shaw, Billy Russell, Billy Hodgson and myself, the team was beginning to take on a more youthful look.

I mentioned how, when returning from National Service, I had been taken aback to see Joe Mercer not only taking training but coaching sessions too. There had never been such a thing as coaching under Reg Freeman, but Joe was very keen that all players be coached. So keen, that when first-team training finished at lunchtime, it would not be unusual to see him working with the youth team players on our training ground just up the road from Bramall Lane. That sort of thing did not go unnoticed and uncommented upon by the players. Reg Freeman was a lovely feller, but he hadn't even got involved with the first-team players out on the training field, never mind the reserves and youth teams.

Joe Mercer epitomised the 'revolution' that was taking place, if not exactly apace, in English football at the time. He talked tactics and would hold 'talk-ins' (as he referred to them) where he would discuss the 'organisation' of the team, particularly the defence. Regarding tactics, British football began after World War Two where it had stood in the 1930s; attack was based on the 'W' formation, which saw both inside-forwards holding back a shade behind the centre-forward and the two wingers. The inside-forwards linked with the two wing-halves, behind which was deployed the centre-half and the two full-backs. For decades, despite the role of the defensive centre-half, match programmes had depicted two full-backs, three half-backs and five forwards when illustrating team line-ups.

Following the 'education' meted out by Hungary, an inside-forward dropped into midfield playing between or just in front of his two wing-halves at the heels of the other four forwards. The preference was to have one creative, ball-playing wing-half who would link up with this deep-lying inside-forward to provide a creative 'engine room' for the team, in much the same way as Hidegkuti had linked with Bozsik for Hungary. The role of the other wing-half was primarily that of a ball winner.

It was this system of play that Joe Mercer introduced to Sheffield United. Billy Hodgson dropped off to link with the creative and youthful Gerry Summers. To complement playmaker Gerry Summers, the tough-tackling ball winner was usually the equally youthful Brian Richardson, whom Joe had also promoted from the ranks. I should imagine Joe opted for younger players because it was easier to have young players adopt and adapt to his system rather than seasoned old pros who might be resistant to new ideas – and, it has to be said, a much greater work-rate.

Joe's penchant for organisation saw us affect a totally different ploy as far as the defence was concerned. Joe introduced us to the 'sweeper' system. Joe Shaw was nominated to 'sweep' behind our two full-backs and either Brian Richardson or Tommy Hoyland, depending on who was given a shirt.

I appreciate all this may appear common enough now, but in 1957–58, it was radical and revolutionary stuff. Of course, no system can work unless you have the players capable of making it work. Joe had moved on a dozen and more players, signed two and promoted others from the junior ranks. That the system did work to our benefit and good effect says much, not only of Joe Mercer's tactical nous but also his ability to spot players who could put his ideas into practice.

'Practice' being the apposite word. We spent countless hours out on the training ground perfecting this system and trying variations of it, until Joe was satisfied it was as good as it was going to get. What is more, Joe had the reserves, youth and colt teams play the same system so that players promoted through the ranks could slip seamlessly into the team they had been elevated to. There were occasions when, after a couple of hours of practising the system, our enthusiasm would wane. Joe would always sense this and say, 'I know, boys. But it has to be done so we are prepared for whatever come Saturday. Remember, lads, fail to prepare and you should prepare to fail.'

The proof is in the pudding, so to speak. We began 1957–58 with a 1–0 victory over Notts County before a sun-kissed crowd of 21,000 at Bramall Lane. Any thoughts that this heralded a new dawn for the club were soon diminished when, the following Wednesday evening, we suffered a 3–1 defeat at Charlton Athletic. There followed a 2–2 draw at Lincoln City and a 3–0 home defeat in the return with Charlton Athletic. It was far from the start I, or anybody else connected with the club, had hoped for. The press and supporters were underwhelmed with this new-look Sheffield United, but if Joe Mercer had any qualms he didn't show them; not even when he met the press in the 'Games room' after the Charlton home defeat. When Joe eventually emerged, Ernest Jackson, our first-team trainer and Joe's right-hand man, asked if the press had given him a hard time.

'Nah,' replied Joe with characteristic wit, 'it was so quiet in there you could've almost heard an atom bomb go off.'

The next twenty matches vindicated Joe. We lost only four of those games and, come early December, Sheffield United were handily placed in the top six of Division Two. December, however, proved an uncharitable month. We suffered three successive defeats at the hands of Leyton Orient, Notts County and Blackburn Rovers, the latter being on Christmas Day.

It was traditional for there to be a full Football League programme on Christmas Day, albeit this festive fixture would be abolished within another year. It was a time when values and mores were somewhat different. The football match was predominantly attended by males and it was considered part of the working man's holiday that there should be a football match as a part of his festive entertainment. Roles within the home were well defined and had changed little since the beginning of the century, in so much as it was considered the role of women to prepare Christmas dinner and entertain children, whilst the husband and older sons left her 'in peace' for a couple of hours while they went off to support their local team. I can just imagine what the vast majority of women would have to say today should their husband say, 'Okay, love, I'll leave you in peace to get on with the Christmas dinner and look after the children, I'm off to the match.' I'm even wincing as I write this...

The Football League always organised what we players termed 'double-headers' at Christmas, where a club would play the same opposition home and away on Christmas Day and Boxing Day. Having lost to a Peter Dobing goal at Blackburn Rovers on Christmas Day we redressed the balance and got back to winning ways with a 4–2 victory over the same opposition on Boxing Day. It was always curious to players and supporters alike that rarely did one team win both Christmas fixtures; invariably one would be lost, the other won. No one ever truly explained why this curious phenomenom should be so; perhaps the 'spirit' Christmas played its part. The attendance for the Christmas Day game at Ewood Park was a healthy 25,283, whereas for the return on Boxing Day Sheffield United enjoyed their highest of the season when over 26,000 forsook their family and fireplaces. Things were looking up.

When the fixtures for a new season are published in July, the vast majority of supporters will look to see who their team face in the opening two matches to assess the likelihood of their club getting off to a good start; the final game of the season (just in case a promotion or relegation battle goes to the wire) and the one over the festive period. That aspect of the game has never changed. Christmas games have always had a special magic to them. As a player you detected more cigar smoke than usual drifting down from the terraces. There were always supporters who would turn up on their favourite terrace brandishing a fifty-box of cigarettes as opposed to the normal twenty or ten. Hip flasks would flicker and glitter like humming bird's wings under the illumination of the floodlights. There was a more pronounced atmosphere of bonhomie and conviviality around the ground than on a normal match day. What's more, there would be many more spectators too as, apart from FA Cup matches, most clubs would enjoy their biggest attendance of the season. As a player you were always conscious of the latter. You always went out to win, but the desire was more pronounced at

Christmas before a big crowd, because what you didn't want was to turn in a poor performance that would make the casual supporter not wish to return for at least another year.

Another aspect to the Christmas game was that, for many, it marked time. Supporters would readily recall even a mediocre Christmas match whereas such a game in, say, October or March would be forgotten. Even today, many fans nurse the memories of a festive game like a hot water bottle. In so doing, they are able to recall what they were doing in life at that time, who they were dating, married to, or what stage of development their children had reached. Christmas games serve to act as signposts to our past, they are stations on our way, and, I feel, it is as true now as ever it was.

For any club not directly involved in, or merely on the periphery of chasing honours or promotion, the FA Cup presented an opportunity for glory, for turning a journeyman season into a highly memorable one. Invariably, clubs would enjoy another 'bumper' gate for an FA Cup tie, irrespective of the opposition. The FA Cup had glamour, real history and tradition. The back story of the competition was awash with legend and folklore – players and supporters loved it. It is one of the sadder aspects of the modern game that many clubs and managers do not give the respect and credence to the FA Cup that its long history merits. Until the formation of the Premier League and the establishment of what are now, ostensibly, European Leagues, a manager would always field his strongest team in FA Cup matches. The FA Cup mattered, and greatly so, as it presented journeyman players with the opportunity to become celebrities.

The FA Cup pushed star players and part-time professionals onto centre stage. A good Cup run meant public appearances and an opportunity to make a bit of extra money. There would be reporters and photographers, radio and television, business offers, more autograph hunters than usual, jangling telephones and, of course, more hangers-on. There would be special training, secret plans; players would be whisked away to hide-away hotels to distance themselves from all the aforementioned. There would also be hope, which might even become conviction, that on the day itself they would confound the pundits – and possibly themselves – and upset the natural order of things. We players would be told 'the Cup is a great leveller' and 'Cup football is a one-off' and, as such, different.

Somewhere, inevitably, we would read that the age of the 'giant killer' was over, a piece of stodgy logic we were told was true because of high wages, increased professionalism and the growing gap between big and small. I read that stuff in the late 1950s and I still read it now and, I surmise, players had been reading it for fifty years and more before my career as a player began. The FA Cup has, through deeds of players, teams, managers and supporters, proved such a dogma to be folly. Even today, whilst some clubs appear to pay little more than lip-service to the FA Cup, the competition continues to enchant and thrill players, supporters and football journalists alike, simply because the present will draw from the past as sure as a barman draws off a pint from the barrel. The Cup's tradition and history is something which creeps into the very essence of players and supporters, something which sustains and inspires when the occasion demands. Neither the Champions League nor the Europa League, as thrilling as they are, will ever diminish this.

In the 1957–58 season, with Sheffield United sometimes there but, in the main, thereabouts in the promotion stakes, we were looking to enjoy a good run in the FA Cup. We were gifted a home tie against fellow Second Division Grimsby Town and advanced without too much turmoil by beating the Mariners 5–1.

The draw for the fourth round gave Sheffield United a plum tie, away to Tottenham Hotspur. No one expected United to beat a Spurs team which included Ted Ditchburn in goal, Danny Blanchflower, Maurice Norman, Terry Dyson, Bobby Smith and Terry Medwin – the latter five would go on to figure prominently in the great Spurs double win of two years later. The FA Cup, however, is given to shocks and surprises and Sheffield United effected a number of those that January afternoon by winning 3–0 at White Hart Lane.

Sheffield United fans had followed us in force for this tie, some 5,000 of them had travelled, mainly by train, to White Hart Lane, and I could hear their vociferous voices amongst a crowd of 51,136, particularly after our second goal went in. When the final whistle sounded, we players were in a quandary as to where to go to show our appreciation of the support given by our fans. There was no segregation of fans at the time. Sheffield United supporters had taken to all four sides of White Hart Lane so, having shaken hands and received the congratulations of the Spurs players, we congregated in the centre circle and applauded our supporters, many of whom I noticed wore red and white tissue-paper rosettes, one of the lesser-spotted rituals of the FA Cup and one that seems to have disappeared from the game entirely.

Our surprise win at Spurs galvanised the club and our supporters. A tangible belief descended on and around Sheffield United that Joe Mercer's ideas were indeed right, that the boss knew what he was doing. We players were more perky and energised in training, we were indeed 'this happy breed'. The draw for the fifth round pitched us next against West Bromwich Albion, another good First Division team who included in their ranks my England teammate Derek Kevan, fellow forward Ronnie Allen, Ray Barlow, my fellow teammate from the Army team, Maurice Setters, Don Howe and a young free-scoring inside-forward of whom great things had been predicted – Bobby Robson. Incidentally, Bobby had yet to convert to wing-half and, in 1957–58, ended the season with 24 League goals, more than either Derek Kevan (19) or Ronnie Allen (22).

At the time, however, the minds of everyone connected with football were elsewhere. Prior to our FA Cup tie against West Brom came the news of the Munich Air Disaster. I will not go into detail about this tragic event for it has been well documented elsewhere. Suffice to say, when the news of the tragedy broke, the entire United Kingdom and not just football fans, was stunned. I remember turning on the television (our first and brand new) and as the news was relayed, the grainy black-and-white picture seemed to darken. The normally urbane voice of the newsreader seemed to turn into a lump hammer. I sat stunned as the cruellest and most shocking list ever assembled in football was read. I was totally mortified as I heard the names of my England teammates Tommy Taylor and Roger Byrne among the fatalities. Duncan Edwards too was listed among the seriously injured, which also included Matt Busby. As well we know, Matt was to survive but Duncan, sadly, succumbed. Having listened in stunned silence to this, I turned to see Brenda standing in the kitchen doorway, she had a hand placed across her mouth and was crying. I stood up and put my arms around her to comfort her and found I was crying too. I felt football would never be the same again – I knew Manchester United would never be the same again.

The tie against West Bromwich Albion at Bramall Lane proved a tough and very closely fought encounter, as the 1–1 draw suggests. We had a chance near the end to wrap it up but Derek Pace's half-volley smacked against the foot of Jim Sanders' left-hand post and the replay beckoned. Some quarters of the Sunday press suggested our 'chance' to progress had gone, but we players never felt that way. We had certainly given West Brom a game and for large chunks had dominated proceedings without ever being able to capitalise. When we travelled for the return, we did so with more than simply hope.

The replay at the Hawthorns took place the following Wednesday evening before a crowd of over 40,000. Nagging away at the back of my mind was the thought that man-for-man West Brom had more class. It showed. Within the first ten minutes we were chasing the game, and come half-time, they were nearly out of sight. There was a brief moment when I felt we might get back into the game when Derek Pace pegged them back, but in the end the class of the Baggies told and the 4–1 score-line was well deserved.

It was following this heavy defeat that Joe Mercer demonstrated to us just how good a manager he was. Joe told us the West Brom result was not the mark of us as a team or as individual players. What would mark us was how we reacted to the defeat.

'That's what counts,' I recall Joe saying to us out on the training ground. 'Have you got it in you to immediately bounce back? Do you have mettle and constitution to emerge from the other night as stronger and better players? I believe you have and, if not, you're no good to me.

'We have two tough games coming up, one after the other, Cardiff City at home and Rotherham away. Be the players I believe you to be. Shut that Cup match out of your minds. We didn't play well, which is why we lost, but that's okay, it's the response that counts.

'We have an outside chance of getting in amongst the promotion lot. We're going to go out and win games, that's the most important thing, but there is something else. A footballer's life is a short one, so, from now on, go out with the mind you're going to create your memories too.'

When a player hears his manager talk like that, it makes the hairs on the back of your neck stand on end. You want to give your all – every time you cross the line.

Our reaction to the West Brom defeat and Joe's pep talk was to go out and try to play the opposition off the park. Cardiff City were beaten 3–0, and we followed that with a resounding 6–1 win at Rotherham United. These results were the start of a run of seven consecutive victories in which we scored twenty-five goals and conceded just five.

We came unstuck at Ipswich Town and Liverpool, on each occasion by the only goal of the game, but we rounded off the season with another four victories and a draw in our final game at Fulham. We finished in sixth place in Division Two, a mere five points behind champions West Ham United and four adrift of Blackburn Rovers, who were also promoted. Joe Mercer had made his presence felt at the club; everyone had bought into his ideas on the game and his edict that, as players, we were the architects of our own future.

The cover of this book features me challenging for the ball with Liverpool's Billy Liddell, and the photograph was taken during our 1–0 defeat at Anfield in which Billy scored the goal. Billy is a true Liverpool legend; he signed for Liverpool in 1939 but, due to war service, never made his first-team debut until 1946 at the age of 24. He was tall, upright and strong, and possessed the courage to go in where it hurt. He would chase any lost cause and, as I knew only too well from my experiences of playing against him, no defender could feel comfortable when he had the ball. In the fifties good players did not fade away as quickly as they do now. Billy carried on playing until he was forty, and such was his influence on the pitch when Liverpool were struggling in the mid-fifties, Reds fans often referred to their team as 'Liddellpool'. Billy never reacted or retaliated and was booked only once in a career that encompassed 537 matches in which he scored 229 goals for his beloved Liverpool. A remarkable strike-rate considering he often played on the wing as well as centre-forward. Perhaps the most baffling aspect to Billy Liddell was that throughout his entire career he remained a part-time professional and supplemented his wage from Liverpool by qualifying, then working, as a certified accountant.

Looking back at my sixty years in the game, I recognise I was very fortunate indeed not only to have such a long career in the game I love, but also to have played against and known as true friends some of the greatest players to have graced football. One such player was Billy Liddell. I felt it entirely fitting, when asked to select a photograph for the cover of my book, that it should also feature dear Billy, not only a great player but also one of the true gentlemen of football.

There is a footnote to our game at Liverpool in April 1958. I had not long entered the away team changing room at Anfield when the dressing-room attendant popped his head around the door and informed me, 'Mr Hodgkinson, your friends have arrived in reception to see you.'

Dad and Brenda attended most Sheffield United matches, home and away, but weren't at Anfield on this particular occasion. I was at a loss as to who my 'friends' could be. I walked into the reception area where a steward guided me through the entrance doors. I stepped out on to the pavement and was immediately taken aback. Five of my old army buddies were there to greet me, including two I had 'supervised' in the glasshouse, one of whom had threatened to 'see to' me when I visited Liverpool with Sheffield United. I wasn't concerned and had no need to be. The lads were delighted to see me and full of bonhomie. For my benefit they rattled through what they were now doing in life; five had secured decent jobs whilst the 'scally' who had once threatened me told me he was 'doing this and that'. The frenzied friendly conversation over, they asked if I could obtain them tickets for the game. It was late in the day and a tall order but I told my old pals I would see what I could do.

I returned to our dressing room and managed to secure five tickets that teammates had ordered but, for one reason or another, were not using. Ever mindful Joe Mercer would be calling us to 'get down' (get changed) very soon, I rushed to the Anfield office, obtained the tickets and returned post-haste to my army buddies. To a man they were delighted at the prospect of seeing the game for free. I warmly shook hands with them all and was told, in true Merseyside fashion, they wished me all the best but hoped Liverpool put six past me. As I waved them away, the other lad who had spent some time in the glasshouse took me by the arm.

'He's not so bad,' my old buddy said pointing to the scally. 'It was his idea to contact us all and come down and see you. He's as proud of you as any of us.'

'He could be a right handful in the glasshouse, but I always thought that deep down he was decent enough,' I said.

'Yeah, he was a zebra in prison.'

'A zebra? How'd you mean?' I asked, genuinely not knowing what he was implying.

'Some zebras love to be behind bars,' he said. 'If they take up the right position, they can pretend they're white horses.'

Following Sheffield United's final game of the season against Fulham, I was delighted to receive another of the FA's cordial letters informing me I had been selected to play in goal for the England Under-23s against the full England team. As impersonal as the letter was I was still mighty pleased to receive it. I had started to wonder whether I still figured in Walter Winterbottom's plans for the coming World Cup Finals.

Following England's 1–1 draw against the Republic of Ireland, Walter had opted for Bolton's Eddie Hopkinson in goal for the October Home International against Wales. Eddie was also preferred for the three following games against Northern Ireland, France and Scotland. Although I had been selected in the squads for all of those matches, the newspapers had been full of speculation that Burnley's Colin McDonald was also in contention for the England goalkeeper's jersey. Knowing Walter would only take two goalkeepers to Sweden for the Finals, I was becoming concerned about my place in the England squad.

The idea of an annual game between the full England team and the Under-23s was the brainchild of Walter Winterbottom, and it was played on the eve of the FA Cup Final. The game always drew a healthy crowd and was always played at one of the major London grounds (in this instance, Stamford Bridge). Television was in its infancy; there were only two channels – BBC and ITV – and neither showed very much football. The BBC covered England matches, the FA Cup Final and they showed highlights of the occasional FA Cup tie, but that was about it. The opportunity to see the 'cream' of English players perform in a single match was a rare and great attraction for supporters, which is why the England Under-23 v England matches were always well attended.

The players of both teams assembled at the Hendon Hall Hotel a few days prior to the game, which was to take place on the Friday evening. On the Thursday, the FA held a dinner for officials and players in the Old Hall, a semi-formal affair at which we players had been instructed to wear suit, collar and tie.

On that evening, FA officials sat at the head table like the headmaster and housemasters taking dinner in a public school, with the President of the FA, Sir Stanley Rous, holding court. We players sat across from one another at tables running at right angles from the top table. I was sitting with Peter Broadbent (Wolves) and Maurice Norman (Spurs) either side of me, whilst opposite sat Bobby Robson (West Brom) and, to either side of him, Jimmy Langley (Fulham) and an empty chair.

Sir Stanley Rous tapped a knife against a decanter to achieve order, announced grace and we all stood whilst he dutifully offered a short prayer of thanks for what we were about to receive. With everyone again seated, I sampled some of the red wine that had been placed before me and was on the point of asking Bobby Robson who should be occupying the empty seat when the double doors at the end of the room suddenly flew open. All chatter immediately stopped as everyone turned their eyes towards the doors. What we saw was Brian Clough standing framed in the doorway wearing a blue checked shirt open at the neck, blue jeans and brown winkle-picker shoes. Casually dressed as he was, he was as neat as the first page of writing from a pupil told to 'improve your handwriting' and intent on doing just that.

Brian took his hands from the doors and they swung to and fro behind him like the wings of an albatross tired of flying, before creaking and squeaking to a close. With a face as expressionless as plaster, Brian surveyed the scene. He was obviously aware all eyes were trained on him but remained calm as he glanced up and down the room. Having spotted an empty chair, completely unabashed, he then proceeded to walk up the hall towards the vacant seat.

I glanced back to the top table. Sir Stanley Rous's face went to pieces and the colour of his cheeks were Manchester United red.

No one was speaking. No one dared. I looked across to Walter Winterbottom. He wasn't pulling his hair out or falling to the floor in a fit, but I could see it rattled him. My breathing was so heavy you could have ironed a shirt with it. Ten seconds, which seemed like a solid, slow-moving hour, crawled by until Brian eventually reached the empty seat. Just as he placed a hand on the back of it, Sir Stanley Rous took to his feet.

'Clough!' bellowed Sir Stanley. 'Get back to your room! Do not come back until you are dressed appropriately and displaying due respect to all those who assembled here at the appointed time.'

Brian took his hand off the back of the chair as if removing it from something very nasty. He turned and began to walk back towards the swing-doors. As he reached them Brian turned to look back to Sir Stanley, who was still on his feet. Sir Stanley was giving him a stare that would have frozen a pasty straight from the microwave.

'You may think you're someone, but you're not,' said Sir Stanley. 'I've had bigger men than you for breakfast.'

'Is that right?' asked Brian, his characteristic nasal voice cutting through an atmosphere as taut as piano wire. 'Name two of them.'

Before Sir Stanley could utter another word, Brian swung on the heels of his winkle-pickers, exited the room and left the doors swinging like those of a saloon in a cowboy film.

The whole incident lasted no more than a minute but I felt as if I'd been through a world war. I looked at my empty glass, Peter Broadbent topped it up and I sent that off to look for the first dose.

'Seeing as we've been together all week, there was me wondering what we could possibly find to talk about tonight,' said Peter.

We were all totally gobsmacked. I had never seen anything like it in my time as an England player and told the lads as much.

'Well, he's finished now,' suggested Jimmy Langley. 'Young as he is, he's going nowhere in this game.'

'On the contrary,' I ventured. 'If that's a sample of Cloughie's attitude, he'll go far.'

I still have the match programme of the game. In keeping with such fixtures the programme takes the form of a routine issue from the club concerned, in this instance Chelsea, with insert pages relevant to the England teams. The programme contains match summaries and teams from the final matches of the season of all the Chelsea teams. Glancing through the programme prior to the game, I noticed a young player whose goal-scoring record for Chelsea's youth team beggared belief. In all competitions the lad had scored 142 goals that season. I made a mental note of the name, Jimmy Greaves.

I was kept busy by an England forward line of Brian Douglas, Bobby Robson, Derek Kevan, Johnny Haynes and Tom Finney but felt I gave a good account of myself, the high point being in the second half when I saved a penalty from left-back Jimmy Langley (Fulham). After the game Walter didn't say much, but that he would be announcing his final squad for Sweden the following Wednesday and selected players would be notified accordingly.

I travelled back to Sheffield on Saturday morning full of angst, wondering if I was going to make the final twenty-two for the World Cup. Burnley's Colin McDonald had played for the full England team against the Under-23s and had also given a good account of himself, whereas Eddie Hopkinson had not been available because he was playing for Bolton Wanderers against Manchester United in the FA Cup Final the following day.

Four days later, I was travelling through Sheffield city centre when I happened to see the grill-board of a newspaper seller in the city centre. My heart nigh on leapt into my mouth when I read the headline on the board. Written in thick black pen were the words, 'Hodgkinson in World Cup Squad'.

I continued my journey home as if on silver wings.

| CHAPTER FIVE |

'We are such stuff as dreams are made on.'

The Tempest

The 1959–60 season was prefaced by a major change in the lives of all of us at the club.

I had reported to Bramall Lane early on Christmas morning in readiness for our trip to Grimsby Town. A light powdery covering of snow had fallen for a couple of hours on Christmas Eve night, just enough to give everyone a true feeling of Christmas but not enough to postpone a football match. 'Perfect,' I thought as I pulled into the ground.

As I made my way across the car park, Joe Shaw too was making his way to the players' entrance.

'Summit's up,' said Joe.

I asked what he meant.

'Chairman has called all the players to a meeting in the changing room prior to us travelling. It won't be to wish us "Happy Christmas". Summit's up.'

Joe was spot-on. 'Summit' was up.

With everyone gathered in the changing room, still in our overcoats, the club chairman, Senior Aitken, wasted no time in delivering his news. He told us Joe Mercer had left the club, to take up the vacant position as manager of Aston Villa. I was stunned. I hadn't seen that coming and, judging from the looks on the faces of my teammates, no one else had seen it coming either.

Mr Aitken informed us Archie Clarke, our chief scout was to be in charge of team affairs until a successor to Joe could be found.

Everyone was very disappointed Joe had left, none more so than Senior Aitken, although we all hoped for success for Joe. When the meeting was over, as the senior pro, Cec Coldwell took it upon himself to say something to Mr Aitken.

'It's sad, but I wish you and your fellow directors to know, Mr Chairman, we'll not slacken in our efforts to gain promotion for this club,' said Cec.

'Thank you Cecil, I know you and every player will continue to give their all,' replied Aitken.

'Where do we go from here?' asked Cec, his meaning being in finding a successor to Joe.

'Grimsby,' said Aitken, gathering his coat and gloves, 'when really, Cecil, I feel like going somewhere that has a piano and a bottle of brandy until they throw me out.' We didn't, however, allow the departure of Joe Mercer to affect us unduly and it was soon on with training for the new season.

Training and fitness techniques have changed much over the years. The training and coaching I now undertake with players bears little resemblance to that which I was subjected to. One aspect of training which has not changed, however, is that all the hard work is done pre-season, with perhaps one hard session a month to ensure levels of fitness, strength and stamina are maintained.

The 1959–60 season began for me with pre-season training either at the training ground or at Bramall Lane. When I reported back for duty I was subjected to the routine every player of the day undertook, irrespective of his club. Every player underwent a medical in which he was also weighed. Anyone reporting back with a few extra pounds was given a few extra hours on the training field until the weight was lost. I was always lucky where my weight was concerned. I kept myself fit during the close-season and, for the time, ate healthily on a metabolism that meant I don't gain a couple of extra pounds just by looking at a plate of fish and chips. Others are not so lucky; the metabolism of some players is such that they forever struggle to keep their weight in check, irrespective of how carefully they eat and how hard they train.

Pre-season training at Sheffield United was supervised, in the main, by Ernest Jackson and aided by Alf Willie, though John Harris supervised on a regular basis too, particularly when the season was underway. The average early pre-season training day would begin with a five-mile road run – 'Just to get you warmed up', Ernest Jackson would say. This was followed by a lot of running, then more running in the form of seemingly endless sprints and shuttle runs, before we signed off a session with, just for some variation, a lot more running.

After a week of this, we would mix the running sessions with weights and exercises to build stamina and strength. Push-ups, pull-ups, running on the spot (just in case any of us was feeling withdrawal symptoms), star jumps, lying on your back with your heels six inches off the ground and so on. The latter was always a killer. I can still picture Ernest now, patrolling among us players, eyes ever watchful for any player who, after holding his heels six inches off the ground for two minutes and more, might lower them a millimetre. This exercise was particularly good for strengthening stomach muscles and keeping them trim. Believe me, after twenty minutes of lying on your back, raising heels, holding them for a gradually increased period of time, before lowering for a ten-second rest and constantly repeating the process, your stomach felt as if it had taken a belter of a plexus punch from Henry Cooper. This exercise completed on a daily basis did give you an ironing board stomach but, you were left in no doubt the phrase 'No gain without pain' was absolutely true.

After the first day, every muscle and sinew in your body ached and legs felt as stiff as floorboards. The second session was tedious as it repeated day one, the third more tedious still, for day one was repeated yet again. Come day four, the aches and pains had receded and you thought you had gone through the pain barrier and out the other side, only then to be sent on a five-mile run, the route of which was new to you. The reason for the new route became apparent as you neared completion, for ahead would be one of Sheffield's most notoriously steep hills.

You would spend the morning continually sprinting up the hill, first in groups of four, then in pairs. Having reached the summit you would jog back down (walking was not allowed) in readiness to repeatedly ascend the hill. When this arduous task had been completed seemingly ad infinitum, your quartet would then be set against another foursome in a race to the top, race after race, until your quartet had sprinted against all the other groups. Then, just to introduce another competitive element, Ernest would time you and a teammate sprinting to the brow of the hill. The timing of whoever came second of the pairing would be noted for the next visit, when woe betide anyone who didn't beat their original time.

Having sprinted up the hill for most of the morning, we then had to ascend the hill one last time but with our partner on our back, the process then being reversed. Just as a strident voice from deep within you began to scream, 'No more', Ernest would say, 'Okay, lads, well done, back for a shower and cup of tea', which meant, of course, a five-mile run back to the training ground. It was a gruelling and gruesome introduction to pre-season training – on a hot summer's day, players were known to lose four to five pounds in weight.

The most welcome sight in the world was returning from such a morning of training, entering the dressing room and seeing the large brown metal teapot steaming away like a railway engine on the physio bench. I'd be so thirsty that the first cup of tea hardly touched my lips. I would drink it down and feel like Tom, from *Tom and Jerry*, when he has been riddled with buckshot, taken a drink and water shoots from his body as if he were a sieve. The perspiration would simply pour from me.

After a couple of weeks of this type of fitness training in which work with the ball was limited to small-sided games at the end of each session, training took on a different form and the ball would feature in most of the work we did. This would gradually be built up until Ernest Jackson and John Morris were happy with our levels of fitness, strength and stamina. Then the training sessions would consist mainly of small-sided games, the exception being a Tuesday when, throughout the season, the first team would play the reserves in a full-blown, highly competitive practice match. Oddly, these practice matches were almost invariably won by the reserve team. Anyone who has played at whatever level against teammates in a practice match will know everyone is relaxed and confident about tackling any other player because you know your teammates so well; wingers would get stuck in to tough-tackling defenders such as Brian Richardson or Tommy Hoyland when, invariably, they would not tackle with such vigour and abandon against a 'hard-man' opponent such as John McCue (Stoke City) or Stan Lynn (Aston Villa).

I took part in the daily training with my teammates but I knew that as a goalkeeper in order to develop my personal game I needed a different type of training. Short sprints or running exercises that built stamina were all well and good for wingers such as Billy Russell and Ron Simpson but not much use to me. I decided I needed 'specialist' training. The problem was, as with all the clubs of the day, Sheffield United had no training or coaching programmes for goalkeepers, and as for 'specialist goalkeeping coaches', there were none.

To combat this I devised a series of training programmes of my own. At Bramall Lane there was a large roller at the side of the cricket pitch. I would spend countless hours after normal training kicking or throwing a football at this roller. The ball would bounce off at all manner of angles and I would dive to 'save' the ball. I was conscious of the fact I was not the tallest of goalkeepers, so the exercise with the roller and a football enabled me to improve my reactions and agility.

Quite often, in the afternoon when all the players had gone home, I would gather (they would say 'press-gang') a few youth team players and give them two and six (12.5p) each to stay behind and help me in my personal training. I would have one lad crossing from the right and I would come off my goal-line, leap and collect the ball whilst under pressure from a couple of other young lads. I would ask them to make crosses into the penalty area from various angles on both wings. That done, I would have them taking corners, or free-kicks from a point just beyond the edge of my area. Having practised collecting the ball, I would then punch, making a mental note of the different types of punch and angles required to project the ball to various points outside of the penalty area.

I also had the youth team lads shoot at me in rapid succession from a distance of, say, six to eight yards. I would save or push the ball away, no sooner would my body hit the ground then I would be up on my feet again, side-stepping to save, block or parry the next shot. I discovered 'side-stepping' was essential to improving my technique and development as a goalkeeper. I never turned and sprinted to save a shot at either side of me, I would always side-step, as I discovered it saved a valuable second which could mean the difference between executing a save or conceding a goal. In time it got so I never turned and walked up and down my goal-line, I would always side-step. It became second nature to me, a technique that psychologists now refer to as being 'over-learned'.

I also practised my dead-ball kicking from either corner of my six-yard box and kicking the ball directly from my hands. Regarding the latter I discovered the ball would go further should I make contact with it just before it hit the ground, not at knee height. With the help of youth team players I also practised coming off my line to take the ball off the feet of an advancing forward. Should I persuade enough youngsters to help me, I would divide them into 'attackers' and 'defenders' so I could organise my defenders around me to limit shooting opportunities; also so I could work out which position and angle I should take up dependent on where on the field the attacker with the ball was. I often hear commentators deride an attacker in a veiled way by saying, 'He shot straight at the goalkeeper'; rarely, if ever, do they compliment the goalkeeper for having got his position and angles spot on.

Organising your defenders is an essential skill of a goalkeeper. You organise your teammates in such a way that the opportunities to shoot at goal for the opposition are limited – you 'snuff them out' in other words. Everyone, myself included, loves to see a goalkeeper make a superb save, but, as I have taught countless goalkeepers over the years, including Peter Schmeichel, a save is the last resort of a goalkeeper.

I would conduct my own personal training every single day and, as the years went by, I evolved more and more different ways to improve goalkeeping technique and skills. In those early days there was quite a learning curve and, quite often, there was more than an element of hit-and-miss about what I did; but looking back, that was to be expected as I had no template from which to work, no one to advise me or offer the benefit of their expertise.

The 'corner café' is something that has disappeared from the game. In the fifties and sixties every club had a café situated across the main stand where players would take lunch or simply gather after training to drink coffee, or in my case tea, and put the football world to rights. In the case of Sheffield United this was 'Mrs Crooks' Café'.

Mrs Crooks was a very amiable woman, a mother figure to many of the younger players, who served the sort of fare to make today's club nutritionists pale – egg and chips, sausage, egg and chips, bacon sandwiches and pie and mash – most served with generous helping of bread and butter and washed down with copious amounts of tea. Players would gather around wooden tables covered in blue and white gingham-styled oilcloth and have 'our dinner', as we called it back then, and the talk would be of football gossip.

'They say Villa are in for Alan O'Neill.'

'What? And they let 'Doc' Pace go? Doesn't make sense.'

'Redfern Frogatt's not happy at Wednesday.'

'Well, he ain't getting in regular, is he? Stands to reason, given his age and all.'

'Bristol City, Saturday; I owe their centre-half one, caught me late last year…nearly crippled me, ref never saw it of course.'

'Pretended not to, more the like.'

'He's a right ugly brute.'

'The ref?'

'Bristol's bloody centre-half!'

'Not as ugly as the one I saw you with on Saturday night.'

'Hey, nothing wrong with her. Good-looking lass she is, you couldn't call her ugly.'

'A peeping Tom threw up on her window sill.'

There would be guffaws of laughter. It was footballer's banter, good-humoured, joshing, not deep or insightful, just lightweight and fun, and yet it served to further forge the bond felt between us.

The windows of Mrs Crooks' would be blanketed with steam. Occasionally the blurred figure of a weary-looking woman in a tousled coat and headscarf would pass by carrying her shopping in a raffia bag, or a young mother pushing a hooded pram with large wheels and even larger metal suspension bars shaped to look like the letter 'U' on its side; an older child clinging to her like a jam-smeared limpet. I would hear the bell sound in the nearby St John's School and there would be a daring dash of schoolboys, late yet again, kicking an empty can along the street. In winter, umbrella'd, overcoated, galoshes over shoes, pixie hooded, wearing great python-like scarves, men in cloth caps and mufflers, a Woodbine hanging from one corner of the mouth would pass by…

I would sit listening to the football chat, glimpsing local folk as they went about their day. They were working folk, our supporters, the bedrock support of the club. What is more, such folk were the bedrock of every club in the land, irrespective of its size. Many cobbled together the pence it cost to gain admission to games, but the football match was in the budget of most and they came in the hope of having their harsh working lives sprinkled with a little stardust and seeing odysseys and memories unfold before their very eyes.

That still happens today, of course, but what has changed is the cost. Many of these folk, especially the elderly, have been priced out of modern football; as such, the traditional bedrock support of clubs has been cast aside in favour of making football not simply 'the match' but an 'experience'. Whilst I would never go back to the Spartan grounds of the past, I feel we have paid a high price for stadiums with fine facilities and Premiership players with sublime 'technique'. The traditional bedrock working-class support of football has been supplanted by those with disposable income and the wherewithal to provide the profits that owners, shareholders and Chief Executives crave. The Premiership may be as rich as Croesus, but, somewhat perversely, a high price has been paid for this.

Sheffield United began 1959–60 with a 2–1 win over Derby County in front of a heartening Bramall Lane crowd of 26,000. Four days later, on a sultry Wednesday night in late August, we turned up the heat on Hull City with a convincing 6–0 victory. There followed a 1–1 draw at Plymouth Argyle, a 2–0 success in the return against Hull City and a fine performance to beat our 'bogey' team, Liverpool, when nigh on 30,000 saw us beat Bill Shankly's side 2–1 at Bramall Lane. The following morning when I looked at the Second Division table in my Sunday paper, Sheffield United sat proudly above every other team.

I remember reporting for training on the Monday and Ernest Jackson's words of caution, 'Okay, so we're top. Everyone has only played five games, so don't you lot start strutting about with your big heads on. There's a long way to go and we have a lot of hard work ahead of us.'

That was typical Ernest Jackson, never one to lavish praise on players. Whenever I received news I was selected for the England squad, Ernest would say to me, 'Well done, but don't let it go to your head, Alan, otherwise I'll personally kick you up the back-side.' No matter how well you had played, or how well the team had done, Ernest was always at pains to ensure we always kept our feet firmly planted on terra firma. Ernest had a lot of experience in the game, he knew what a fickle mistress football is, that fortunes could change like a weather vane in a sudden breeze and just one error could be the undoing of a team. Without ever filling us with anxiety he did everything he could to ensure we were on our mettle each and every time we crossed the line.

'Sow a good performance out there on the field and you reap a good habit; sow a good habit and you reap character; sow character and you'll reap success,' Ernest would say.

They were wise words. Football was then, as it is now, about players learning good habits. Ask Sir Alex Ferguson, Martin O'Neill, Ian Holloway or Neil Baker (Crewe Alexandra) and they will bear testimony to the edict, 'Good habits make for good play-ers.' Good habits are something I am at pains to instil in every goal-keeper I coach and teach. When a goalkeeper or any outfield player, practises and learns good skills and techniques, they become easy. When they become easy we take pleasure in performing them, and when they please, a player will perform them frequently and, by frequency of act, they become good habits.

A rich air of confidence pervaded the dressing room before our game with Sunderland. The banter was more excited than usual, there was an expectant and assertive mood which we took onto the pitch, and perhaps, if anything, we tried too hard. The little things that had come off for us against the likes of Hull City and Liverpool didn't bear fruit. Sunderland's towering centre-half, Charlie Hurley, won everything in the air and when we played the ball across the field, their captain Stan Anderson and his counter-part on the left, Jimmy McNab, seemed to anticipate every pass. We lost our early poise and rhythm and Sunderland began to assert themselves. Just before half-time, Sunderland's diminutive Republic of Ireland inside-forward, Ambrose Fogarty, was first to react to a downward header from Hurley following a Sunderland corner and we found ourselves chasing the game. In the second half, Derek Pace freed himself from the shackles of Hurley and, with us now level, I felt we would go on to win. Only, it didn't happen.

A defence-splitting ball from Anderson found Ian Lawther, who made ground down on our left before cutting the ball back to Fogarty and our first defeat of the season was sealed.

When we forlornly entered the dressing room, Ernest Jackson simply shook his head. John Harris, in keeping with the good manager he was, said nothing. John never did say anything to us immediately following a defeat for fear, in the heat of the moment with adrenalin still racing, that words would be said that someone would later regret. In such circumstances John always reserved his comments for Monday morning when everyone had put some distance between themselves and the disappointment of defeat.

Our inconsistent form remained with us up to Christmas; meanwhile Aston Villa, under Joe Mercer, and Cardiff City began to set the pace at the top of Division Two. 1959–60 was the first season in which no matches were scheduled for Christmas Day. The Football League bowed to pressure to allow Christmas Day to be a day of holiday, but it wasn't a holiday for us players, of course, because on Christmas Day morning, having spent just a couple of hours with the family, we set off for Cardiff City.

Our Boxing Day game at promotion-chasing Cardiff didn't make for a happy Christmas. We lost 2–0 at Ninian Park. Two days later, in keeping with the see-saw fortunes of festive matches, we won the return 2–1 before a 30,000 crowd at Bramall Lane.

I remember thinking, 'How come Sunderland can lose six against Ipswich when they looked such a good side when we played them? We hammered Hull, yet they go and achieve a good result against Liverpool. How can this be so?' It then occurred to me that many teams in Division Two were, like Sheffield United, wildly inconsistent. I didn't think Aston Villa or Cardiff City were greatly better than us, but both had managed to put together a sequence of results which had set them apart at the top of the division.

I thought about the reasons for our inconsistency and one conclusion I came to was that Sheffield United were a very youthful team. True, in Joe Shaw and Cec Coldwell we had players of some experience, but many of the players who had featured on a regular basis – Graham Shaw, Gerry Summers, Brian Richardson, Kevin Lewis, Denis Sheils and, of course, myself – were twenty-three or younger. Young players tend to be inconsistent, 'on fire' one game, almost anonymous the next. An experienced pro, however, will never have a bad game. He may, occasionally, perform at a level slightly below par, but he will never have a poor game in which his contribution is marginal. I came to the conclusion our inconsistency, our ability to raise our game for the big occasion but not sustain it, was the prime reason Sheffield United had gained the reputation for being a 'good cup team'.

With half a season under our belts and, consequently, more experience, we began to produce more consistent performances in the New Year. January and February saw us enjoy six consecutive victories, two of them being in the FA Cup, scoring seventeen goals with only one conceded. One of these victories was particularly sweet, a 3–1 victory at Villa Park against Aston Villa, who were sitting astride Division Two.

As 1960 unfolded, the encouraging aspect to our play was that we achieved the level of consistency that had eluded us in the first half of the season and in the two previous seasons. In eighteen League matches we lost but two, at Ipswich and Swansea, won ten and drew six. The season concluded with a five-match unbeaten run but, alas, we were left to rue so many drawn matches. Aston Villa and Cardiff City were the only teams in the division to post defeats in single figures, the only teams to boast in excess of twenty victories (25 and 23 respectively), and were thus worthy of their promotion to the top flight.

It has often been said that winning League titles or promotion is a marathon rather than a sprint. Aston Villa and Cardiff had been the embodiment of this old maxim. From the very start of 1959–60, both had accumulated points on a regular basis, held pole positions from September, and the consistency they had shown and which had eluded all other clubs, Sheffield United included, had secured their elevation. Along with Liverpool we had clung on to their coat-tails but, with but two points for a win in those days, the nine-point gap had proved an insurmountable obstacle. The old 'W' formation may have been superseded but Liverpool had adopted the 'M' formation. Six of their regulars had surnames beginning with 'M', namely: Melia, Moran, Molyneux, Morris, Morrisey and Murdoch.

Our wildly inconsistent form in the first half of the season proved our undoing. However, I felt now we had a more or less settled and more experienced team, so in the following season we could achieve the consistency crucial to gaining promotion. I also knew football never worked like that, things would never happen as one might expect. For example, even should we be consistent the following season, there was always the chance of some club putting together an incredible late run to pip promotion favourites. Or else, some previously unfancied club who had previously inhabited the nether regions of the table would suddenly 'click' and enjoy an outstanding season. In the event, the latter was to prove the case, and the team which caught everybody by surprise was to be one of the most unlikely candidates for Division One – a team that was happy to be known as 'Ramsey's Rustics'.

I felt great disappointment at the fact Sheffield United had failed to gain promotion. Sheffield United finished in fourth place in Division Two, on the same number of points (50) as Liverpool, Bill Shankly's team having a slightly superior goal average, this being a somewhat complicated system used to separate teams finishing on an equal number of points. In the previous four seasons, Sheffield United had respectively finished seventh, sixth, third and fourth by virtue of goal difference. There was a saying afforded to relegated clubs, 'A year down below is good. It provides a sound spring-cleaning.' It had now been four years in Division Two for Sheffield United and a fifth beckoned. There was little doubt we were among the best teams in Division Two, but I also knew that should we again fail to achieve promotion the following season, we would be tagged as one of the Second Division's perennial clubs. No one at United wanted that tag, least of all our supporters, who had remained loyal throughout our recent disappointments, the proof of which lay in an average Bramall Lane crowd of over 25,000, this at a time when one of football's big talking points was falling attendances which had affected nigh on every club in the land.

Once again it was the FA Cup which injected excitement into our season. As previously intimated, Sheffield United had gained something of a reputation for being a 'good cup side' and we again endorsed this epithet with another thrilling sojourn in the oldest football cup competition in the world.

It began with a home tie in the third round against Portsmouth in which we ran out comfortable winners by three goals to nil. When

I was a boy, Portsmouth had been one of the top teams in the country, now they were scrapping for survival at the foot of Division Two, and we put paid to any hopes they had of salvaging what was becoming a troublesome season by scoring three without reply.

When the draw was made for the fourth round, excitement gripped everyone connected with the club – fate dealt us the FA Cup holders, Nottingham Forest, at home. It proved an afternoon to remember. It was a bitterly cold Saturday in late January, one in which coal fires never removed the frost from the rooftops of houses. The gates opened at 12.30, inside a local colliery band was waiting to do its stuff, and the *Sheffield Star* reported, 'A capacity, good-natured crowd waited patiently on a bitterly cold afternoon for the teams. When Nottingham Forest emerged, in their "change strip" of all white with red trim, being the Cup holders, they were applauded and cheered respectfully as royalty might have been.'

If any of our supporters looked to Forest as a team of superior mortals we quickly put paid to such a notion. Derek Pace and Billy Russell caused the Forest defence innumerable problems throughout and Forest, at best, flattered to deceive. Come a quarter to five, the Forest players wearily staggered from the pitch as defeated men stagger away from the field of battle. The final score-line of 3–0 in our favour told only part of the story. I felt we had been the superior team in all quarters, an opinion seemingly shared by the Forest manager, Billy Walker, who in sportingly proffering congratulations to John Harris emitted a sigh like a man relieved from care.

The fifth round pitched us against a Watford team challenging for promotion from Division Four. Watford had accounted for Birmingham City and Southampton amongst others and in Cliff Holton and Dennis Uphill enjoyed the services of two prolific forwards who, between them, would net eighty goals that season. As I expected, Watford proved doughty opponents, but we knew their defence was not the best and although Holton and Uphill were on the mark, we again scored three to take us into the quarter-finals. As a footnote to Watford, over Easter, Cliff Holton became the only player since World War Two to score hat-tricks on successive days, a record he still holds. Cliff notched his first hat-trick against Chester on Good Friday, and on the Saturday he hit another three against Gateshead United.

The draw for the sixth round provided the city with the tie it had hoped and dreamed of: United at home to Sheffield Wednesday. No sooner had the draw been made than our Board of Directors met to make 'special arrangements' for what was going to be a very special cup-tie. The interest in the tie was phenomenal. Applications for tickets far outnumbered the capacity at Bramall Lane, so the board took the bold decision to have a local company erect a temporary stand on the cricket side of the pitch, increasing capacity by some 18,000 to 61,180. Even that was not enough to meet the demand for tickets. It appeared everyone in the city wanted to see what the press had billed as 'The match of the season', one which was to generate then record receipts for United in excess of £9,000.

Our preparation for the tie was as it would be for any normal League match. We trained throughout the week and on the Friday morning, as usual, John Harris called a team meeting in the players' recreation room. We met there because it had a snooker table and John had got into the habit of illustrating certain tactics by using coloured snooker balls (we were always the reds, the opposition, the coloured balls).

Sheffield Wednesday had prospered since their promotion back to the top flight, they were a top-five team and boasted some very fine players. John Fantham was a goal-scoring inside-forward, Keith Ellis was also prolific in front of goal; Alan Finney and Derek Wilkinson were as good a pair of wingers as there was in British football at the time, while Tony Kay and Don Megson (father of Gary), Peter Swan and Tom McAnearney were top-drawer defenders. Wednesday also had a young goalkeeper who was beginning to make a big name for himself in the game, one who had been widely tipped for international honours – Ron Springett.

I had never seen Bramall Lane so packed as on the occasion of our quarter-final tie against Wednesday. My mother and Brenda were among the heaving crowd which was, of course, unsegregated. What's more – and this is another sign of the times – local magistrates had granted seventeen pubs in the vicinity of Bramall Lane an extra two hours' opening time. Even though the game had been sold out within days of tickets going on sale, hundreds of supporters of both teams who would have given their souls for any glimpse of the game had gathered in the streets around Bramall Lane. They were able to live every second of the game, however, because radios in waiting police cars – volume full-up – were relaying the BBC match commentary.

It was generally agreed the match was not a classic. Perhaps there was simply too much at stake for both teams, a place in the semi-finals for sure but, just as importantly, local bragging rights. Wednesday were prepared for us to start with devilish aggression and they were not disappointed. We took the game to our local rivals from the start, and kept up the pressure for ten minutes or so, then, having weathered the storm, Wednesday began to play their way into what was, at times, a scrappy game. John Fantham came in for some close attention but kept getting up off his backside to remind everyone he was a supreme craftsman as well as a goal-scorer. Peter Swan kept 'Doc' Pace in shackles, Billy Russell had the better of the exchanges with Don Megson, and Gerry Summers looked manifestly superior. Nothing we did, however, turned our superiority into goals. Against the run of play, Wednesday took the lead through Derek Wilkinson and when he added a second in the second period, I knew our cup run was over – as opposed to 'run-neth over'. There was a late rally on our part, but nothing to trouble Wednesday and it was to be the blue and white contingent of the city who swept into the pubs that night exuding euphoria.

I was beginning to think thirteen was indeed an unlucky number. The Wednesday cup-tie was Derek Pace's thirteenth Cup appear-ance for United; when Cec Coldwell stepped up for his thirteenth we lost to West Brom, and in the previous season, I made my thir-teenth FA Cup appearance when we lost at Norwich City.

I couldn't wait for the next game to come so I could put the dis-appointment of the Wednesday defeat behind me. It so happened our next fixture was the following Saturday at Leyton Orient. I had never been so pleased to play Leyton Orient; that game, a 1–1 draw, served to eradicate all the disappointment of our derby defeat and get the body rhythms on the upwards curve again.

Though Sheffield United endured a repeat performance in that we again failed to secure promotion, 1959–60 did produce some amaz-ing stories. Burnley won the First Division Championship and did so in a unique way. Burnley clinched the title on the final day of the season, victory over Manchester City elevating Harry Potts' team to the top of Division One, the first occasion on which Burnley had held pole position in the entire season. FA Cup winners Wolves, who were also runners-up to Burnley, scored 106 League goals, the first and, to date only, club to score 100 goals in three successive seasons in the top flight of English football. After being held 2–2 at Fourth Division Crewe Alexandra in the fourth round of the FA Cup, Spurs won the replay 13–2 at White Hart Lane. When the Cheshire side left Crewe station on their way to London for the replay they left from platform 13 and, on their return, alighted at platform 2. Ian St John scored a hat-trick in two-and-a-half-minutes for Motherwell against Hibernian. Also among the goals was Brian Clough. Brian scored all the Football League's goals in their 5–0 defeat of the Irish League to add to his 39 League goals for Middlesbrough, his previous season's tallies being 38 (1956–57), 40 (1957–58) and 43 (1958–59); but, after having made just two international appearances, he was never selected for England again.

*   *   *

Following the disappointment of four 'nearlies' in our quest to gain promotion to Division One, expectations were sky-high at Sheffield United as we prepared to commence 1960–61.

There was next to nothing in the way of comings and goings at the club during the summer break. At the end of the previous season, Sheffield United had sent retained letters to thirty-four professionals and thirty-four families were mightily relieved to receive them. The 'retained' letters were dreaded by all players; they would receive a letter in late April or early May which would inform them whether the club had 'retained their services' or not. A player immediately knew if he had not been retained, as the words informing him of this would always be in red type as opposed to the normal black. Should a player not be retained, he had to try and fix himself up at another club by his own devices. Ostensibly clubs owned players, as a player's contract bound him to the club for life – the 'slavery contract' as I called it. What is more, footballers were subject to a maximum wage of £20 a week. The way I saw it, the slavery contract was a violation of the labour rights as enjoyed by all other UK workers and professional people. What's more, clubs could to get rid of a player for the most tenuous of reasons simply by issuing a 'non-retained' letter with no explanation necessary. Of course, many players who received such letters did so because the club, as advised by the manager, felt the player was not of the quality required. That notwithstanding, there was no period of notice, the player would simply find himself out of work from the day he received the letter, which I believed to be a scandalous state of affairs.

If I sound a little reactive to the way players were treated, that is because my opposition was so great I had been voted as Sheffield United's PFA rep by my fellow players. As such, I had thrown myself wholeheartedly into the growing campaign to have the slavery contract and maximum wage (which the vast majority of pro footballers did not receive) abolished.

My upbringing had much to do with the stance I had taken. I had grown up in a family and in an area where people toiled long and hard in harsh conditions and were paid a pittance for doing so. I had also grown up to believe in the virtue of the 'rights of man', that you should show respect to all fellow men, women and children, and that it was right and proper to stand up for what you believed in.

When I had first joined Sheffield United back in 1953, there was player called Harry Brook. Harry, along with Alf Ringstead, had been the club's top goal-scorer for some four seasons. Harry's wife was due to give birth and he had just finished the season with twenty-plus goals to his name. Harry received his 'not-retained' letter days after the season ended – on the very morning his wife gave birth to twins. I had never forgotten the despicable and pitiless treatment of Harry Brook, just one instance in many of the callous way clubs then treated their employees. Little wonder then I had become, at just twenty-four, not only the union rep at Sheffield United but one of the main PFA activists in the Yorkshire, Derbyshire, Nottinghamshire, Leicestershire and Lincolnshire area.

As the 1960–61 season got underway the efforts of myself and my colleagues for a fair deal would continue to gain momentum. I would chair meetings, canvas players on an individual basis, write letters to fellow union members, Football League, Football Association and media, issue pamphlets, hold interviews with the press, spread the gospel of players' rights and, in so doing, often take flak from certain influential figures in the game. I remained, however, unmoved by such uninformed criticism, resolute in my belief in players' rights. I will later detail how our quest was to end in triumph and what the consequences of our victory were to be, both then and now.

Our pre-season went well but was not without incident. John Harris was adamant Sheffield United would be the fittest and strongest team in Division Two, if not in the whole of the Football League. John had noticed how the majority of goals in a match were scored in the last fifteen minutes, which, although players are supposedly fitter and stronger now, is still the case today. John had the idea that if we were stronger and fitter than any other team we would come out on top in the crucial last period of matches. A not unreasonable theory but it was when his idea was put into practice that the fireworks started.

John appointed a guy called George Smith, an ex-army sergeant-major whose brief was to train us players so we would be as fit, strong and disciplined as the best paratrooper or marine. I think you may be ahead of me on this one. Suffice to say, under the training of George Smith, Sheffield United became known to us players as 'Stalag 17'.

In essence, George Smith was a decent, hard-working guy who had been brought in to the club to do a job and immediately set about to accomplish this with army-like precision. His methods may well have been acceptable in the army, but they found no favour with us footballers. On the contrary, we all took an instant dislike to him and his methods.

George didn't speak to us, he didn't even condescend to shout instructions. He barked orders, always referring to players by their surnames. Our first two sessions with George Smith amounted to us constantly running up and down the terraces holding weights in each hand with a large haversack filled with sand on our backs. Come the third session, Joe Shaw arrived for training with George carrying a sharply pointed metal file. On being told to collect his haversack of sand, to our great amusement, Joe furtively jabbed the sharp end of the file into the haversack. As a consequence, when we began running up and down the terraces with the weights and haversacks, Joe's haversack gradually became lighter as the sand slowly ran out, as if in a scene from the Second World War escape film *The Wooden Horse*. To our immense pleasure, Joe passed the file around, and we all followed suit.

At the end of the session, George Smith discovered the holes in the haversacks and immediately assumed the mental stability of Caligula. George was absolutely livid and completely manic. He shouted and screamed at us, doubted our parentage and issued threats against our person until Joe Shaw, calmly, stepped forward. In short Joe pointed out we were all men and professional foot-ballers at that and did not deserve to be treated as imbeciles, nor did we take kindly to being threatened. The 'discussion' between Joe and George became very heated, but Joe stood toe-to-toe with George and didn't blink. Sensing he had the support of no one and having exchanged words for some five minutes with Joe to no avail, George then turned about and stormed away. Joe too left the scene, heading straight for John Harris's office.

To his credit, John Harris gathered the players around him that day and patiently listened to our complaints, only to then inform us George would not be returning to the club.

'Lads, you try things and sometimes they do not work; this has not worked out as I had hoped,' said John. 'We shall achieve the levels of fitness I feel to be essential, by other means.'

That was John Harris. Always the gentleman, always calm and considered irrespective of the emotion and heat surrounding him. In all the time I knew John, I never once heard him swear, nor did he ever partake of a cigarette or alcohol. He was one of those guys you come across who always appear to be on the same emotional level regardless of what is happening. Good or bad, crisis or cel-ebration, John Harris would remain as unemotional as a cricket.

On 20 August 1960, Carrow Road was bathed in sunshine which mirrored Norwich City's yellow shirts. Norwich City were fresh from promotion from Division Three. Anticipation among their supporters was sky-high and one could not have wished for a bet-ting setting in which to kick off a brand new season. Carrow Road lay flooded in gold-leaf sunshine.

It was Sheffield United's first visit to Carrow Road since our epic FA Cup tie and we knew we would be in for a testing and ardu-ous afternoon. Newly promoted teams always tend to start a new season well. Adrenalin runs extra-high for them, they have the satisfaction of beginning with a blank canvas and no baggage and, invariably, they enjoy the added advantage of being an unknown quantity. Norwich, however, were not entirely unknown to us, nor we to them.

The Sheffield United team that lined up that day was:

Me; Cec Coldwell, Graham Shaw; Brian Richardson, Joe Shaw, Gerry Summers; Billy Russell, Willie Hamilton, Derek 'Doc' Pace, Billy Hodgson and Ron Simpson.

Norwich City included Sandy Kennon in goal, Bryan Thurlow, Terry Allock, Ron Ashman, 'Ollie' Burton, Roy McCrohan, Matt Crowe and Errol Crossan – all but Burton had been in the team which had defeated us in their run to the FA Cup semi-final.

I mention the Sheffield United team in full to highlight, in particular, our defence. It is amazing but, barring the odd enforced alteration due to injury, this defence played unchanged for nigh on eight years and was very much the foundations of the United team in that time.

The score was goalless at half-time, but the deadlock of what was a thrilling end-to-end game was finally broken midway through the second period when Norwich won a corner. Bill Punton swung the ball into our penalty area. I jumped to collect, only for the ball to swerve away from my flaying hands, and there was a rising Terry Allcock to thump it with the meat of his forehead and send the majority of fans into raptures.

Undaunted, we took the game to Norwich. We had Norwich on the back foot for prolonged periods and, just when I was beginning to think all our pressure might come to naught, a cross-field ball from Ron Simpson evaded everyone bar Willie Hamilton who, coasting in at the far post, side-footed the ball home for the equaliser.

His goal at Norwich was to be Willie's only goal of the season for us. Willie was to play some fourteen games for us that season and always did a good job; however, the form of Keith Kettleborough was to ensure Willie would only play a bit part in what would turn out to be one of the most memorable seasons in the history of Sheffield United.

Our satisfaction turned to delight the following Tuesday night when Plymouth Argyle were beaten 3–0 at Bramall Lane. This we followed on the Saturday with a hard-fought single-goal victory over Charlton Athletic, who had been something of a bogey team to us in recent years. The long trip to Devon for the return against Plymouth brought us no reward, and our 2–0 defeat gave us a reality check, but we bounced back to register handsome victories at Leyton Orient (4–1) and at home to Huddersfield Town (3–1). When the first league tables of note appeared in the newspapers, we were enjoying the heady heights of second place.

Though we lost 3–0 at Stoke City, there then followed eight successive victories with eighteen goals scored and only four conceded. Come late October we headed Division Two with the season's surprise package Ipswich Town hot on our heels and Southampton, Norwich, Liverpool and Middlesbrough also keeping up the pace.

During October the one reverse we suffered was in the League Cup, a 3–1 defeat at Bury. This was the inaugural season of the League Cup, a competition introduced by Alan Hardaker, the often bombastic secretary of the Football League. Though Hardaker had been the driving force behind the introduction of the League Cup he had, in fact, borrowed the idea from Scotland, who'd had such a competition since 1945–46. When the draw for the first round of the League Cup was made, the little wooden balls rattled around the velvet bag with no sense of history; nor were there any balls denoting numbers assigned to Arsenal, Tottenham Hotspur, Sheffield Wednesday, Wolves and West Ham United, all of whom had declined to participate.

The League Cup was new and did not enjoy the tradition or venerability of the FA Cup. What's more, this new competition was to be a creature of the night. It was to be played mid-week, under floodlights, and would not enjoy a single ray of sunshine, not even on the occasion of the then two-legged final itself. Many football writers believed the League Cup to be an untidy tournament that would lurch through the season, making way for its elders and betters and earning more money than respect. Though it was destined to become popular and enjoy a truly golden period in the seventies and eighties, a lot of supporters and a number of football journalists and participating clubs didn't take this upstart seriously. I have to say, Sheffield United, for all we had gained the reputation of a 'formidable FA Cup side', was such a club. It is an odd thing, but some clubs never do well in the League Cup. In well over fifty years of the League Cup, United have never been within a hoarse whisper never mind a shout of reaching the final. No Blades fan can explain it. Ask one and he, or she, will tell you it is 'just in the ether'. Sheffield United never do well in the League Cup. It is a fact as solid as day following night and night following day.

December proved not a good month. We travelled to what was a fog-shrouded Anfield five points ahead of Bill Shankly's second-placed team and though a 1–1 half-time score-line reflected an even contest, Liverpool upped the ante in the second half and I sustained a shoulder injury. I should have left the field, but there were no substitutes, so we decided it best I carry on. The injury hampered me but, credit to Liverpool, they were the better team in the second period. The game was still even-steven until the last ten minutes when Alf Harrower contrived to make it a harrowing experience for us, helping himself to a hat-trick to add to Dave Hickson's earlier strike. Though Billy Russell rustled up a couple of goals by way of reply, Liverpool were worthy winners in a game that set the tone for what was to be a miserable festive period for Sheffield United.

My injury was considered serious enough for me to sit out our next game, a 3–2 home defeat against Bristol Rovers, and our following game at Derby County, where our 2–0 defeat provided another setback to our promotion aspirations. My replacement for these matches was Des Thompson who was, without doubt, the most hirsute player I ever encountered. Des's arms were covered in dark hair, his back was a mat of hair and when he raised an arm, it looked as if Tina Turner was tucked up in his armpit. Not for nothing did some players refer to dear Des as 'the gorilla' but, such was his size, never to his face.

John Harris had very good man-management skills but these were sadly lacking where injured players were concerned. When it was obvious I was not going to be fit for the Derby game, John never found it in him to offer any words of consolation; on the contrary, he totally ignored me and never spoke to me until I was pronounced match-fit again. One day, I remarked on the boss's 'cold shoulder' treatment of me to Joe Shaw.

'Oh, he's like that with every player who gets injured,' remarked Joe dismissively. 'Almost as if he sees it as self-inflicted.'

'It's a bit worrying though, the fact the boss blanks me when I pass him in the corridor,' I said.

'It's just his way,' said Joe attempting to put me at ease. 'Ernest Jackson told him your injury was a "bad 'un", the boss told him you were a "malingerer".'

Joe began to laugh at the absurdity of this.

'A malingerer!' I said in astonishment. 'I've missed two games in nigh on five years! And those were when I was on England duty. I dunno, sometimes life can be cruel and unfair.'

'Certainly can,' said Joe, 'what cruel bastard put an "s" in the word "lisp"?'

I was mightily relieved to be passed fit for our next game, at home to Norwich City, not least because John Harris began talking to me again. John behaved as if there had never been a hiatus in our conversation, he simply picked up from where we had left it some two weeks ago.

John wasn't the only manager to shun an injured player. A couple of years later I fell into conversation with Liverpool's Tommy Smith. Tommy told me Bill Shankly was exactly the same, in that he would have nothing to do with a player who had sustained an injury, and as soon as the player was fit again, would act as if nothing had ever happened. Tommy told me the story of Chris Lawler, who had played over 250 consecutive games for Liverpool before succumbing to an injury which ruled him out of Liverpool's next game. When Bob Paisley informed Shankly Chris Lawler couldn't play, he replied, 'Doesn't want to play more the like. Jesus Christ, Bob, I've had my suspicions about the boy for over 200 games now, always knew he'd pull a sickie one day.'

Ron Simpson gave us a first-half lead against Norwich, only for our bête noir, Terry Allcock, to surface again late in the game with a header from an out-swinging corner from Bill Punton – seemingly, we had not learned from the opening day of the season. I was disappointed with the draw, we had exerted enough pressure in the first hour to have warranted a comfortable lead. Our profligacy was to cost us, however, for not only did Norwich equalise, they also had a goal disallowed in the closing minutes when a linesman spotted an infringement. It was one of those where the linesman was the only person on the ground to spot it. Obviously we weren't complaining, though Norwich did.

On Boxing Day we travelled to Roker Park where we again enjoyed a share of the spoils in another 1–1 draw. We travelled back to Sheffield that night, curiously sharing the train with Sunderland, albeit in a different carriage, as we were entertaining them the following day.

There was certainly plenty of reading material in the Sheffield United programme of 1960. For our game against Sunderland, the programme notes, written by our club secretary, Mr Newton, expressed concern that two points won out of the last possible ten was 'not promotion form' and 'gave cause for concern'. If a number of people at the club were concerned about our dip in form, they may well have been addled with anxiety come the end of the return with Sunderland, a game we lost 1–0.

When we travelled to Charlton Athletic for a game on New Year's Eve our midwinter record did not make for good reading: two points from a possible twelve. Our once seven-point lead had evaporated, Ipswich Town were now level with us on thirty-three points and with a game in hand, with Liverpool, Southampton, Norwich and Middlesbrough breathing down our necks.

It is one of football's curiosities that a club will have a bogey team they invariably always lose to. Conversely, there will be a team they always seem to beat. Players and managers come and go over the years, however this one team continues to have the upper hand, and this remains true of the club over which they always seem to have the advantage. For reasons beyond our ken, historically Sheffield United had never fared well at home to Leyton Orient, for example, nor down at the Valley against Charlton Athletic. Since the 1930s, Sheffield United had gained a couple of draws at the Valley, there had been the odd victory but, mostly, Charlton Athletic had won.

John Harris was his usual calm, collected and considered self during the team meeting prior to our game against Charlton. He told us every team, not matter how good, will have a bad spell in a season. He read to us extracts from two match reports which had appeared in the national press in the weeks prior to our dip in form and had praised us for the style and quality of football we played.

Both were of the opinion Sheffield United were a 'good team' play-ing 'entertaining and productive football'.

'A good team doesn't become a bad team overnight,' John told us. 'We are still that good team, perhaps better, because we have learned from the past few weeks. Go out and prove that today.'

John then went around the dressing room, calmly but assur-edly telling every player why he was a good player. He reminded everyone that our poor spell of results had coincided with myself, Graham Shaw and Billy Hodgson being missing at various times due to debilitating injuries, and the 'changing, rather than chopping of the team' had had a disruptive effect.

'We are a good team, the emphasis being on the word "team",' John told us, 'I won't accept less than the best a player is capable of doing, and you lads have the right to expect the best that I can offer you as individuals and a team.

'Take the game to them today,' John said in conclusion. 'All good teams are in some way inspired; be imaginative, be inspirational, be the winners I know you to be.'

John's talk was inspirational in itself. We took the game to Charlton from the start and took the lead through Ron Simpson. Cliff Mason, who had taken the place of the still-injured Billy Hodgson, then doubled our advantage. That Charlton side of Sam Lawrie, John Hewie, Dennis Edwards, Stuart Leary and the young Marvin Hinton (later to make a great name for himself in the Chelsea side of the sixties) were, if anything, doughty fighters. Though Sam Lawrie and Stuart Leary scored to keep the home side in the hunt, Derek Pace added to his season's goal plunder to ensure we always held the advantage.

Our 3–2 victory at the Valley proved the turning point in our season. John Harris's calm, measured and inspirational team talk had reinforced our self-belief, a belief that was to further develop in the ensuing weeks and months.

Sheffield United's rare success at the Valley was the beginning of a run of eleven matches in which we were only to suffer one defeat, at Swansea in mid-March. Thereafter there would be only one other defeat in the League, which we juggled with what was to be a phenomenal run in the FA Cup, one that would make Sheffield United headline news in the press, on television and on radio.

I have never been one of those former players who opine, 'Football was far better in my day.' I am, after all, still working in the game and wouldn't be if I didn't still love football and working with contemporary players. At this time of writing I am in my mid-seventies; the fact that I am still in demand by current managers is not simply because I bring a wealth of experience and considerable enthusiasm, but also because I contribute new ideas about goalkeepers and goalkeeping. It is imperative to constantly analyse the game and to keep coming up with new, practical ideas, for the game is forever changing. It is, and always has been, in a constant state of flux. Sometimes the changes are marked and radical, at other times they are small and contrive to change the game slowly, like raindrops on stone, but change the game does and must. All I will say for football past, compared with now, is that it was very different.

One marked difference is the way a manager, such as John Harris, had in his head what his best eleven was and, given all were fit, he played that eleven, week in, week out. The old maxim, 'Never change a winning team', was adhered to religiously by most managers. As 1961 began to unfold and Sheffield United continued to post good result after good result, the only team changes were those of the enforced nature. No player wants to miss out playing for a winning team. Another old maxim, 'Nothing hurts when you win', was certainly true in this instance. Players who had received a knock treated themselves at home. A kick on the ankle, for example, would result in the discomforted player bathing the ankle in first a bowl of hot water, then a bowl of cold water, and he would do this alternately until the pain and swelling went down sufficiently to allow him to play in the next game. Players only reported to Alf Willie in the physio room when it was absolutely necessary. To do so would result in the injury being reported to John Harris, which could mean sitting out the next match, and no one wanted to do that for fear of losing his place in the team and it being a long time before he regained it. Such was the quality and versatility of fringe first-team players such as Cliff Mason, Johnny Nibloe, Barry Hartle and Keith Kettleborough.

The way managers rotate a squad system today is one of the biggest differences between football then and now. In 2012, I recall sitting watching the day's football news on television. An item appeared about a Bournemouth player who had a broken index finger, the report stating he would be 'out for two to three weeks'. In the past the trainer or physio would have simply taped the injured finger to the next and the player would not have missed a single training session let alone a game. Of course there is a sound argument for saying clubs today take a greater interest in the welfare and well-being of their players than in the past. This is certainly true and I am all for that, but I feel you will get my point.

The profusion of technical, fitness and dietary specialists at clubs nowadays, of which all the top clubs boast, see a part of their remit as ensuring every player is at optimum fitness. No small detail is overlooked. Go to Manchester City's training ground and you will see racks of plastic bottles each bearing the name of a player. Each bottle contains an energy drink created for the 'specific needs' of that player. Gone are the days when players would enter a dressing room prior to or after training and simply grab a cup of tea. The specialist training and fitness 'coaches', dieticians and nutritionists create individual programmes for each and every player. This is done in the quest to ensure nothing has been overlooked to help each player reach the absolute peak of fitness and health. One Premiership team even transports mattresses to away games for use by its players in the hotel bedrooms to ensure they get a good night's sleep. Absolutely nothing is left to chance nowadays, and by that token players have no excuse for having not played well.

Of course, there is an argument for saying, this proliferation of experts have to justify their worth. In 2012, England were well beaten by Sweden. Was the success of Sweden – and any other country you care to name – against England, down to the fact their players had superior personal fitness coaches, dieticians and nutritionists? Of course not. Sweden's handsome victory over England was largely down to the fact they had a better quality of player on show on the night. We are constantly told the technique of today's players is far superior to those of the past, likewise their levels of fitness, strength and stamina. So why is it England fare so badly in major international tournaments ? Why is it the consensus of opinion is, 'England does not have the quality'? It would appear to me, there is something of a dichotomy there.

The squad system, we are told, exists because players play so many games now. In the season to which I now refer, 1960–61, Sheffield United played a total of fifty-six matches and called upon the services of twenty-three players, of which, eight played three games or less. Ostensibly, John Harris relied upon a squad of fifteen players. The number of matches we played compares favourably with that of a top Premiership team of today.

The pitches we played on were also markedly different. Today's pitches are like bowling greens, the ball moves about the pitch far quicker than on the muddied glue-pots we played on in midwinter. This is something one has to take into account when saying the game is quicker now. It is, but this is also enhanced by the fact that lighter footballs are used – just under twelve ounces compared to sixteen ounces – which move about the pitch faster than the heavier balls on the Christmas-pudding pitches of the past.

Another consideration, particularly regarding those Premiership clubs involved in European competition, is travel. I would suggest it is not the sheer of number of games that takes its toll on top players, but the frequency of travelling. Even if a club charters its own airplane, players can still find themselves hanging about at airports for two hours in both directions. Pardon the pun, but this flies in the face of the notion that today's players must be at optimum levels of physical and mental fitness. The 'gurus' work to ensure this is the case, then players hang about airports for hours, fly to the far reaches of Europe and back almost on a weekly basis. Such constant travel, week-in, week-out, is tiring. Add to this, calls upon players for international matches where some players may have to fly to and from South America in mid-week, and pre- and post-season trips to the Far East to generate commercial income: one has to question what effect all this has on the optimum levels of physical and mental fitness. I suggest it is both counter-intuitive and counter-productive.

Come Easter, Sheffield United found ourselves embroiled in a battle for both promotion and the FA Cup, in which we had reached the semi-finals. Games were coming thick and fast, seven within three weeks of March, with another three within the first week of April. Ipswich Town had also hit a rich vein of form. Unbridled by FA Cup commitments, Alf Ramsey's team had posted a terrific set of results and, with the Easter programme beckoning, were top of Division Two with a single-point lead over United. We, in turn, had a three-point advantage over third-placed Liverpool with Bill Shankly's team having a game in hand. The promotion stakes were hotting up and I knew any slip-up on our part would cost us dear.

Liverpool visited Bramall Lane on Easter Saturday and in excess of 30,000 of our supporters turned up to see a 1–1 draw which, given our respective League positions, suited us more than it did Liverpool. Two successive victories on the road, at Portsmouth and Rotherham United, were followed with a 2–1 home victory over Southampton. We then travelled to Derby knowing victory would ensure our promotion to Division One, with two matches still remaining.

Derby County had hit hard times since their heady post-war days. For a number of seasons the club had wandered up and down the middle section of Division Two like some dog that had lost the scent. Attendances had fallen, but on the day we visited the Baseball Ground, Derby's finances received a welcome fillip in the form of some 8,000 United supporters.

If we had any nerves, we didn't show them. Derby County had assumed their position in mid-table and as such their players took to the field without an edge to their game. We, on the other hand, were pumped up, ready to win to secure the prize that had eluded us for some four years. For Derby there was an uncommonly fervent atmosphere inside the Baseball Ground in what for them was a 'fag-end' game to the season. The frenzied atmosphere was the work of Sheffield United supporters who roared their approval as we tore into the home side. I would not go as far as to say Derby County were merely bit players in a promotion production, but through-out the ninety minutes that followed we directed proceedings and, come the final whistle, the final score of 3–1 in our favour flattered the home side. We had completely outplayed them on the day.

The scenes in our dressing room after the game were triumphant and joyous. Most of this Sheffield United team, myself included, had suffered the acute disappointment of four near misses. We heartily supped champagne from our teacups as we relished the prospect of Tottenham Hotspur, Manchester United, Arsenal et al the following season.

Sheffield United went in for a line of exotically named chair-men. Our new incumbent, H. Blacow Yates, along with his fel-low directors, made a very rare appearance in our dressing room to toast our success. John Harris cast caution to the wind and sported a look of quiet satisfaction on his face. In a dressing room that had turned into a place of steam and celebration, the direc-tors struck up cigars the size of rolling pins to add to the general fug. I drank in the atmosphere and my champagne – never had the spoils of victory tasted so sweet. To our further delight, Mr Blacow Yates announced that in recognition of our 'great achieve-ment' each member of the first-team squad would receive a promo-tion bonus. 'Something that will come in handy for a rainy day,' he added. To a man we raised our thick china teacups and toasted him with more champagne.

The newspapers, small and large, handled the story of Sheffield United's promotion with huge and happy relish. The *Telegraph* held nothing back: 'This conclusively, exclusively, was the most important day in the post-war history of Sheffield United.' Whereas the *Yorkshire Post*, using words that have a far different meaning today, said, 'Hang out the red and white bunting! Ring out the joy-bells! Let's go gay. Sheffield United are back where they belong – in Division One.'

When John Harris had taken over the reins from Joe Mercer he had assessed the team, playing strengths, system of play and players that Joe had left him and decided, 'If it ain't broke, don't try and fix it.' However, John had made subtle yet telling changes. For example, we had been in need of a creative, hard-working player who could play at inside-forward or on the wing, so in the New Year he signed Len Allchurch from Swansea, who fitted the bill perfectly.

As I have said, John Harris was not given to emotional outbursts, he didn't raise his voice nor did he go in for heart-thumping moti-vational speeches; what he said, he said quietly and in measured tones. Though he did inspire, he wasn't a great motivator and didn't need to be. He believed in getting a team prepared, so it knew it would have the necessary confidence when it crossed the white line to play good football. One of the many things learned from Hungary's defeats of England and the great Real Madrid team of the time was: collective talent was better than individual talent. John Harris understood this. What is more, he knew how to go about it. I was the only member of the Sheffield United team who was called up for any of the home international squads. We had no star players, but John had moulded us into a team. 'Other teams may have their star player, but no player is better than all of you,' was one of his favoured sayings. He also once told us, 'It's better to have one player working for you than three players working with you.' The team ethic was all-important to John and it was this that formed the bedrock to our success in League and Cup.

John Harris is not often, if ever, quoted, as with some managers of the past such as Bill Shankly, Matt Busby, Don Revie and Bill Nicholson. I guess that is down to the fact he only spoke to the national press when absolutely necessary. Also, having no star players, no Sheffield United player who played for John has ever written a book, until now, so his inspirational words have never been committed to print. He was an intelligent, thoughtful man, capable of inspiring and wise words. Following our victory over Derby County, one of our directors, Dick Wragg, called on John to say a few words. A dressing room that had been chaotic and boisterous suddenly fell as silent as a Minister's study as John stepped forward, a cup of tea in one hand.

'Coming together is a beginning. We achieved that. Keeping together is progress. We achieved that. Working for one another is success, and, lads, we have now achieved that,' said John.

The dressing room erupted. The toast was John Harris.

Our next match was very much a case of 'After the Lord Mayor's show' and resulted in a 3–1 defeat at Bristol Rovers and a reminder from John Harris that we had to be professional at all times and had a responsibility not only to the club but to our supporters to always, but always, give of our best. The curtain came down on a highly successful and satisfying season with a visit from Middlesbrough. We needed no second reminder from John Harris, even though promotion was ours, and we produced a fine performance in front of over 30,000 Blades fans to beat Middlesbrough 4–1. Derek Pace netted twice to bring his season's goal haul in League and Cup to 34, and Len Allcurch and Billy Russell also scored. For once, Brian Clough did not score against me.

We finished the season in second place, and the record of the promoted teams read: (Two points for a win)

Team:	Played:	Won:	Drawn:	Lost:	Goals for:	Goals against:	Points:
Ipswich Town	42	26	7	9	100	55	59
Sheffield Utd	42	26	6	10	81	51	58

Liverpool finished in third place on 52 points, followed by Norwich City (49), Middlesbrough (48) and Sunderland (47).

Like all of my teammates, I was joyous and eagerly anticipating pitting my skills against the likes of Tottenham Hotspur, who had achieved the first 'double' of League and FA Cup in the twentieth century, Manchester United, Arsenal and, of course, our local rivals Sheffield Wednesday, who had themselves enjoyed a great season by finishing runners-up to the great Spurs team. I also felt playing First Division football would improve me as a goalkeeper. I wanted to play against the best at the highest level, and my continual drive to improve my game would be enhanced by playing against the best in English football.

As a footnote to Sheffield United's promotion season I must make mention of the bonus the players received. You will recall our chairman Mr Blacow Yates promised the players a bonus in the form of something for a 'rainy day'. Following our final match against Middlesbrough we embarked upon a short tour of Holland which was a bit of a 'jolly' arranged some months previously. In the way of expenses for this tour, each player received the princely sum of £4.10 shillings (£4.50). I knew we wouldn't be heading for the highlife of Amsterdam.

During this tour, we assembled in Eindhoven in preparation for a game against PSV. It was there that we players were told Mr Blacow Yates would announce the details of our 'bonus' for having won promotion.

As you can imagine, we were all excited at the prospect of banking a bonus.

'I'm going to use it to buy a car,' Billy Hodgson said.

'Knowing what skinflints our board are, it won't be that much,' retorted Joe Shaw.

'Well, however much it is, it'll help go towards a car,' Billy replied.

I had already earmarked my bonus. To our utter delight, Brenda was due to give birth to our first child, a daughter as it turned out, who we named Karen. Brenda and I had agreed to use the money to decorate the spare bedroom as a nursery and buy everything needed for a baby.

When Mr Blacow Yates appeared, we sat in silent anticipation to hear the amount of our hard-earned bonus. Mr Blacow Yates spoke for a few minutes about how we had all done the club proud, how everyone was looking forward to life in Division One and so on. Just when feet began to shuffle, Mr Blacow Yates got on to the matter of our much-anticipated bonus.

'The board promised you all something for a rainy day,' Mr Blacow Yates needlessly reminded us, 'and, so you shall have.'

He then turned to open the dressing room door and ushered in a fellow director.

'As your bonus for taking this club back to Division One, every player will receive...one of these lovely raincoats and one of these stylish and practical barometers,' announced Mr Blacow Yates proudly.

The director who had entered the room held up a belted, grey Burberry-style raincoat with one hand and, with the other, a small wooden-framed barometer for us all to marvel at.

I looked across at Joe Shaw. He was giving Blacow Yates a look that should have stuck eight inches out of his back. A silence as awkward as a man having to tell his brother he's sacking him from the family firm gripped the room. To a man, every player's face was expressionless. Sensing we were underwhelmed, Mr Blacow Yates made a hasty and somewhat edgy retreat.

'Yes, well, er, well done again, lads, I'll have...er...I'll arrange for the raincoats and barometers to be issued later,' said Mr Blacow Yates.

And with that he and his fellow director fled the room.

Gerry Summers turned to Billy Hodgson.

'There you go, Billy, just what you need,' quipped Gerry. 'A barometer to tell you when it's going to be a rainy day and a 'king raincoat to keep you dry when you walk to the ground till you get that car of yours.'

I did receive my raincoat. I think I wore it once, which was one more time than Joe Shaw wore his.

The bonus business apart, nothing could detract from our joy at having won promotion. What is more, I was convinced we had a team good enough to do more than simply 'all right' in Division One. My belief that Sheffield United would do well in the top flight was largely down to the fact that, in addition to winning promotion, we had come within a whisker of winning the FA Cup and in so doing had beaten some choice First Division teams along the way.

Sheffield United's FA Cup journey had begun in the heated atmosphere of Goodison Park. Everton were attracting huge crowds for big matches, well in excess of 60,000 and with two tipping 70,000. Everton had a 'star-studded' team which included Scottish international Alex Parker, Jimmy Gabriel, Brian Labone, Brian Harris, Roy Vernon, Bobby Collins (later of Leeds), Frank Wignall (later of Nottingham Forest) and Billy Bingham, whose goal for Luton in the previous season's FA Cup semi-final had knocked out Norwich City.

Sheffield United enjoyed a tremendous following at Goodison Park, most of whom had paid the 11/6d return fare to travel by train and who roared us on from the first whistle. That day Scunthorpe United came back from 2–1 down to beat Blackpool 6–2 and Sunderland defeated Arsenal 2–0, but our single-goal victory at Everton commanded the headlines in the national press.

Sheffield hosted two fourth-round FA Cup ties simultaneously and they could not have been more contrasting. Sheffield Wednesday hosted Manchester United whilst we entertained Lincoln City. A crowd of 62,000 saw Wednesday and United draw 1–1 at Hillsborough, whereas a healthy 21,000 turned up at Bramall Lane to see two goals from Billy Russell and one from Cliff Mason put an end to any hopes Lincoln may have had of progressing. Lincoln did reply in the second half, through Andy Graver, but that apart, I have to say this was perhaps the quietest game I ever played, such was our dominance.

When a team reaches the fifth round, matters start to hot up. There is a belief, certainly among supporters, that 'This could be our year'. One Blades fan had written to the *Star* to say, 'Three steps to Wembley. Four to Europe.' I guess he meant it too. The FA Cup is full of optimism. That said, when the draw was made and we came out at home to another First Division side, Blackburn Rovers, I felt confident we had what it would take to topple our supposed superiors.

Blackburn arrived at Bramall Lane fresh from a fine victory against Wolverhampton Wanderers which had lifted them into the top five in Division One. Blackburn Rovers were a club with an illustrious past and a promising present. Little wonder, Blackburn had Ronnie Clayton, their captain and once of England, thirty-five times an international, a neat, dark man and a polished and constructive wing-half; and Ally McLeod, who would later go on to manage Scotland in the 1976 World Cup Finals in Argentina. I had the notion that Blackburn, although riding high in Division One, were a club that had become twitchily obsessive about winning something. They had lost to Wolves in the previous season's FA Cup Final but had been called 'unfashionable' for too long and had flattered to deceive too often. Now Blackburn had a good team, probably their best for years, but from the moment Derek Pace gave us the lead, I sensed a certain anxiety in their play, almost as if they were worried their lofty league placing was a false dawn. It was touch and go at times, but in the end I believed we were worthy of our 2–1 success. As we entered the dressing room full of the joys of victory, Joe Shaw cocked a hand to an ear and said, as if in confirmation of his quiet confidence we would put paid to Blackburn, 'What is that I hear calling us from around the corner? Why, it's the quarter-finals!'

I had cause to cast my mind back to my Sheffield United debut when the draw was made for the quarter finals: Newcastle United at St James's Park. This Newcastle team, however, bore no resemblance to the one I had faced on my League debut, which had contained such fine players as Jackie Milburn, Bob Stokoe, George Hannah and the redoubtable Jimmy Scoular. Newcastle were struggling at the troublesome end of Division One. That said, Newcastle boasted one of the finest inside-forwards in the country in Ivor Allchurch, the brother of my United teammate, Len; also a prolific centre-forward in Dick White who, that season, would net twenty-eight goals in a team destined for relegation.

It is the mark of struggling teams that they call upon the services of many players. Newcastle were the epitome of this; I noted they had used thirty-three players in their quest for a winning formula. Such a formula had eluded them and did so the day we paid a visit. To my great satisfaction we left St James's Park having beaten the home side by three goals to one. As we journeyed home, I relished the thought I was about to play in my very first FA Cup semi-final. As a boy I had listened to the radio commentaries of FA Cup Finals. The final was the flagship of the English domestic season, the pinnacle of a player's career. Whoever we were to play – Spurs, Leicester City or Burnley – I knew it would be a big ask, but we were playing extremely well as a team and, as you know, Cup football is all about 'on the day'. I hoped against hope that our 'day' would come at Elland Road on 18 March.

In the event, Sheffield United drew Leicester City. I think we were all happy with the draw. Of the three teams we'd most wanted to avoid Spurs, who were waltzing away at the top of the First Division and were serious contenders to become the first team in the century to achieve the League and Cup double. At the time, Leicester City were a top five First Division team, we knew we would have to be at our optimum to beat them, but we took heart from the fact we had beaten similar teams in Everton and Blackburn Rovers in earlier rounds.

I thought of Leicester as having a particularly fine footballing team. In goal they boasted an excellent keeper who was beginning to make a real name in the game, Gordon Banks. They also had a superbly gifted wing-half in Frank McLintock who would, of course, go on to lead Arsenal to that much coveted League and Cup double. I scanned their team and every player seemed to be top drawer; centre-forward Ken Leek, Colin Appleton, Len Chalmers, Ian King, Richie Norman and Ken Keyworth for example. When I looked up Leicester City's recent results I was left in no doubt this was going to be one tough game for us – they had hammered Manchester United 6–0, beaten Spurs 3–2 at White Hart Lane, beaten Newcastle 5–3 and were fresh from a 3–1 success against Arsenal at Highbury, all within the space of less than four weeks.

A crowd of 52, 095 packed into Elland Road to witness what was a tight goalless draw. Credit to Leicester, they merited the draw for having to play almost the entire game with ten men. Their winger, Len Wills, suffered an injury in the first minute following a tackle from Cec Coldwell and Len had to be stretchered off. There were no substitutes in those days, of course, but Leicester summoned up extra resolve to keep us at bay until, I believed – and still believe – we had won the game in the last minute.

With the game into time added on, Derek Pace hit a superb volley past Gordon Banks. The red and white factions in Elland Road immediately erupted and I ran around my penalty box punching the air with delight. I had a sudden feeling something was not right, then looked up the field to see the celebrations of my teammates had stilled. The referee, Jim Finney from Hereford, was marching across Banksy's penalty area pointing towards the spot where Derek had rifled home and blowing a shrill death-knell to what I believed had been the killer goal.

Jim adjudged Derek to have used an arm to control the ball before volleying past Banksy. He was surrounded by my irate teammates, but was having none of this; he waved away our protestations with a waft of a hand and instructed Banksy to place the ball on the spot where Derek had been, in readiness for a free-kick. My heart sank. Banksy took the dead-ball kick, sending the ball high into the air, and when it began its descent around the halfway line, Jim Finney gave another shrill blast of his whistle to signal the game was over.

Our dressing room was one of deep disappointment as eleven players sat in silence. Later, our feeling of being hard done to was cemented even further when TV coverage of the game seemed to conclusively show Derek Pace had not used his arm to control the ball when scoring. I didn't blame Jim Finney, who was a fine official and top-class referee. Jim gave what he saw. Football is much to do with human error – after all, if there were no mistakes, there would be no goals. Referees always give what they consider to be the right decision, and rather than chastising them for the occasional mistake, albeit a crucial and very cruel one in this instance, I am amazed referees, now as then, make so few errors. Jim Finney had had a superb game, so much so that, up to the point of our disallowed goal, I hadn't noticed him on the pitch – always the sign of a good referee. My sense of objective thinking told me all this at the time, yet it did not lessen my feeling of devastation and, even all these years on, it still riles me to think of Derek's disallowed goal. *C'est la vie, c'est le football.*

The replay was staged at the City Ground, home of Nottingham Forest. Both teams picked up the same script and played out a very similar scenario – a very tight game of few chances that ended goalless after extra time. What, if anything, the two matches had proved was that there was not a fag paper's width between us and Leicester City: two matches, one with an added half-hour, had failed to produce a goal. As we faced a third semi-final game against Leicester, by virtue of which creating a little bit of FA Cup history, I remember saying to Gerry Summers that, given the teams were so evenly matched and balanced, I felt a mistake would be what would separate us in the end. The way Gerry nodded in agreement was strangely ominous.

The second replay was held at St Andrews and, after the two goalless draws that had preceded it, our third encounter was given considerable coverage by the media. 'Who will crack first?' asked the *Daily Express* in previewing the game. It was a question the whole of English football seemed to be eagerly awaiting the answer to.

In the other semi-final, Tottenham Hotspur had cantered to a 3–0 victory over Burnley, so, should we overcome Leicester in the replay, I knew the biggest game in the history of Sheffield United – and that's saying something – awaited us. I sensed the mood among the players was one of quiet confidence. Leicester City had failed to score against us and whilst we had also drawn a blank, in Derek Pace I felt we possessed the player most likely to break the deadlock. Leicester possessed some very fine footballers but, to my mind, lacked the type of player who could turn a game on its head, a striker who, given one moment of freedom, would punish us. As long as we defended as a unit in the way we had in our two previous encounters, I was confident the spoils of victory would be ours.

With less than fifteen minutes on the clock, Jimmy Walsh went down in our penalty area following a tackle from Brian Richardson and my heart sank as I saw the referee point accusingly at the penalty spot. Leicester's centre-half, Ian King, stepped up to take the penalty and appeared to ruck his studs in the turf as he made contact with the ball, which skimmed low across the ground and past my right-hand post to clatter the perimeter wall. Though, let it be said, I went the right way! A tremendous feeling of relief swept through my body and, as play resumed following my goal-kick, I thought to myself, 'This is going to be our night.'

With half-time beckoning and still nothing between the two teams, a long ball from Leicester's left by Jimmy Riley evaded everyone who had suddenly arrived just beyond the edge of the six-yard box. Everyone, that is, bar Hughie Walsh, who, from seemingly out of nowhere, arrived at the far post to head Leicester in front. It was what we used to call a 'good morning goal'. Walsh simply bowed his head as if greeting someone on his way into work and, suddenly, we had all the work to do.

Having found ourselves chasing the tie for the first time in nigh on four hours of football, and with half-time approaching, rather than playing a possession game to allow us to regain our composure and take the verve out of a now uplifted Leicester, we went for the jugular. I happened to look across to the dug-out where, uncharacteristically, John Morris had taken to his feet with Ernest Jackson at his side. John was frantically tapping his wristwatch with the fingers of his other hand whilst Ernest was manically calling to Joe Shaw to pull defenders back. The message was clearly evident to me. They didn't want us to commit so many players to attack with there being only a minute or so to the break.

Len Allchurch played the ball into space just on the left of the Leicester penalty area where Derek Pace was onto the ball with two defenders frantically trying to get goal-side. Derek looked up, cut the ball back, but only to the feet of Frank McLintock who pinged the ball out to the opposite wing. When the ball landed on the grass some three yards in front of Walsh the back-spin put on the ball by Frank held the ball up long enough for the Leicester winger to take it without breaking stride. As Reilly made quick ground down the wing, my mental alarm bells reverberated in my head. With our defenders and midfield desperately trying to get back to provide cover, Reilly drew Cec Coldwell towards him, only to then play a ball of Swiss-watch precision between Cec and Joe Shaw and into the path of the onrushing Ken Leek.

I had quickly come off my line to narrow the angle of the oncoming Leicester centre-forward. Leek, however, took one touch to get the ball under control and with his second drilled it to my right and across my diving body. I didn't get anywhere near it but I knew the ball's final destination as Leek jumped for joy and the blue contingent within the packed City Ground suddenly became wildly animated. There was hardly enough time for the game to restart before the referee sounded his whistle yet again to signal the first act was over.

I sat in the dressing room not sure of my feelings. Disappointment, anger, hope, spirited optimism – I think I felt them all. There had been all to play for, then, within less than five minutes, we found we had a labour of Hercules to undertake. That's football. A game can be turned on its head in a matter of minutes, seconds even. I took some consolation from that, hoping that would apply to us in the second half.

John Harris did not berate anyone. He never mentioned the fact that, with a minute to the break, we had thrown caution to the wind and paid dearly for our reckless play. Had we played out a damage-limitation game for only a few minutes we would have been sitting in that dressing room knowing a single goal would restore parity. Now we needed two. I knew that would be a big ask because Leicester would now be brimming with confidence and the cushion of the two-goal lead would have taken some of the anxiety out of their play. John was obviously aware of this too but simply told everyone to 'keep at it', to 'stick to the game plan' and to try and play Derek Pace in at every opportunity.

We took the game to Leicester in the second half. I knew what the Leicester plan would be. They would play a containing game and hope that, with the clock against us, we would become anxious and possibly make a mistake which they could capitalise on to put the game beyond our reach. This is exactly what happened. We bombarded Leicester but without reward; then, in the sixty-fifth minute, we saw light at the end of the tunnel and, for once, it wasn't a train coming. The referee awarded a penalty kick and Graham Shaw addressed the ball, making a spot-kick that parted the photographers crouched with cameras clicking to the right of the Leicester goal. Graham immediately sank to his knees. As the Leicester fans roared their approval, I joined Joe Shaw in hand-clapping and shouting words of encouragement to my teammates.

'Hey, never mind. Let's keep going! This is far from over!' But it was over.

The dressing room of beaten semi-finalists is one of the worst dressing room atmospheres you can ever experience. There is the 'so near, yet so far' feeling which combines with a desperate feeling of dejection and acute disappointment to leave you empty and hollow. Hardly anyone spoke. Some fifteen minutes after having entered the room, Graham Shaw was still sitting in his strip with his boots on, leaning forward, arms resting on his knees and staring at the floor. Brian Richardson sat with his back slumped against the wall behind him, staring up at the ceiling for a good ten minutes, the cup of tea in his hand untouched. From across the corridor, there was the seemingly constant sound of a door opening then banging shut, jubilant voices filtered into our desolate room from the Leicester dressing room. I heard the sound of champagne corks popping. The contrast in atmosphere of the respective changing rooms was as marked as day and night.

It was the mark of the resolve of this Sheffield United team that just two days later we travelled to Elland Road, scene of our first encounter with Leicester, and beat Leeds United 2–1 to maintain our push for promotion. As John Harris reminded us, we still had a great prize to play for; our fabulous Cup run had been an exciting diversion but we had to be strong enough to put the disappointment of our semi-final defeat behind us and to 'keep the main thing, the main thing'.

'We're physically fit, now we have to show we are mentally fit,' John Harris told us prior to the Leeds game. 'Nothing can stop the team with the right mental attitude from achieving their goal… just as nothing on earth can help the team that has the wrong mental attitude.'

That we were galvanised and displayed the 'right mental attitude' is evidenced by the fact that we did enjoy the glory of promotion to Division One. The arrival of ourselves and Ipswich Town did little, if anything, to enthuse either First Division clubs or the football writers, but, as things were to turn out, both were to be in for one hell of a shock.

| CHAPTER SIX |

'Life every man holds dear:
but the brave man holds honour
far more precious dear than life.'

Troilus and Cressida

Every decade takes two to three years to establish its own identity. This was certainly true of the so-called Swinging Sixties.
In essence, the decade of change did not get underway until 1963
with the emergence of Beatlemania, the Rolling Stones, London as
the hub of modern fashion, the mass popularity of the Mini car,
the Profumo Affair which 'liberated' the press, cutting satire on
television in the form of *That Was The Week That Was* and, in the
USA, Martin Luther King's Freedom March and the abominable
assassination of John Kennedy – to cite but a few of the seminal
events of 1963 alone.

There was, however, a radical change which took place in the
1961–62 season which was to have a telling impact on social change
and which social historians invariably overlook. I am referring
to the fight undertaken by the Professional Footballers Association
to free footballers from the so-called 'slavery contract' and maximum wage. This campaign to secure for footballers labour rights as
enjoyed by every other worker in the UK was a campaign to which I
had given my wholehearted support as a leading PFA union activist.

The suggestion of a maximum wage for players had first been
mooted as long ago as 1891, though the proposals were not undertaken until 1900 when the FA ruled that, from 1901–02, a player's

wages would be restricted to a ceiling of £4 per week (£208 per annum). Over the years various amendments were made. In 1910 the maximum wage was raised to £5 a week, but only for players who had been at a club for four years or more. The figure was raised again to £9 in 1920, again for only those with four years or more service at their club, albeit this was paid throughout the year and not just for the actual football season as had previously been the case. In 1922 the maximum wage was actually reduced to £8 a week, with a lower wage of £6 in the summer, after some clubs had petitioned the FA and Football League citing a fall in annual profits.

The £8 a week maximum wage remained in place for twenty-four years until after World War Two when, in the summer of 1946, a dispute between the Football League and the Players' Union was settled by a National Arbitration Tribunal and a maximum weekly wage was set at £12 (£10 in the summer) and a minimum wage of £6 for full-time professional players.

From when I first signed for Sheffield United in 1953 and throughout the fifties, there had been a long-running dispute between the Professional Footballers Association, so re-named in 1958, and the Football League. Little by little the maximum wage had increased until, in 1958, it was set at £20 a week. The dispute, however, came to a head in 1960.

Following much lobbying by the PFA, in an attempt to stave off further unrest on the part of players, the Football League, with the approval of the FA, offered to raise the maximum wage to £30 a week and increase the signing-on fee to £150. The PFA, led by their chairman, ex-Fulham wing-half, Jimmy Hill, and the secretary, Cliff Lloyd, a solicitor by profession, rejected this proposal. The dispute continued into 1961 because we at the PFA were hell-bent on changing the 'retain and transfer system', the so-called 'slavery contract', which bound a player to a club for life, or until such time as the club decided to get rid of him.

In 1961 I was totally committed to this cause, by which time the disagreement had turned into a 'bitter dispute' with both sides vociferously arguing their case. While acting as the PFA union representative at Sheffield United, I also became actively involved in the broader campaign, informing players in the Yorkshire area of events as they unfolded, addressing players at clubs to put forward the PFA's side of the argument to counter the information, much of it to my mind misinformation, fed to the press by the Football League and various club chairmen.

Without doubt the main protagonist was Jimmy Hill. One man, the right man, could lead and direct his fellow professionals in the right direction, accomplish the necessary goals by intelligent, objective and persuasive argument rather than bombastic hectoring. We at the PFA were fortunate to have such a man in Jimmy Hill. To us PFA members Jimmy was not just our leader, but our hero. Alan Hardaker at the Football League, however, saw Jimmy as his bête noir, a radical, unreasonable activist who was out to 'ruin football'. The powers that be at the Football League, in particular Alan Hardaker, did not see the validity of our campaign. We PFA activists were viewed, as one Football League official told the *Daily Sketch*, as 'audacious upstarts out to upset the applecart'. It was that sort of pompous, anachronistic view that led me and my fellow professionals to believe our campaign was not only right and just but, ultimately, would be successful. In my opinion, like so many men in positions of power in football at the time, Alan Hardaker and his colleagues in the Football League hierarchy were blind to those things that conflicted with their own capacious egos.

I appreciate Jimmy Hill has had his critics over the years, but there is no getting away from it, Jimmy was the driving force and inspiration behind footballers obtaining freedom of contract and a wage in keeping with their worth, an achievement which has since been to the benefit of generation after generation of footballers. Social historians may not think so but, to my mind, Jimmy Hill is a true working-class hero and, as John Lennon said, 'a working-class hero is something to be.'

Sheffield United embarked upon a pre-season tour of Holland prior to commencing business in 1961–62. A 3–1 victory over MVV Maastricht was followed by an emphatic 5–0 victory over DWS Amsterdam. At the time Sheffield Wednesday were also on tour in Holland. Every club felt it essential that their pre-season matches should begin with a series of matches against teams who were not of a similar standard in play, and then gradually they should take on stronger opposition as players achieved match fitness.

Sheffield United's pre-season usually began with a series of public practice matches between players from the club's four teams, which took place on a Saturday afternoon. These public practice matches were held by the vast majority of clubs and were staged under various guises and names depending on the club concerned – Stripes v Plains, Blues v Reds, Possibles v Probables. The first game of the afternoon would last some forty minutes and consist of two teams made up of youth team players, amateurs and trialists. This would be followed by a match between established youth players and reserves. The attendance would gradually increase as the afternoon progressed until there was a healthy crowd for the third and final match between first-team players and those reserves on the fringe of the first team.

One simply can't imagine 12,000 turning up at Sheffield United, or any other club, for a public practice match today, but after the domestic League season concluded in late April, supporters would see no football whatsoever until pre-season matches began in late July, and so the pre-season matches, including public practice matches, were invariably well attended.

The pre-season programme would also include matches for a team formed from the club's reserve and youth teams, which would play games against local semi-pro clubs, as still happens today. Managers often also arranged a friendly against a club from a lower division, even non-League, in which he would field the first team. The reason for this was to boost the finances of the lower division club. Usually the club would have some connection with the manager, such as it was his very first club, or else it would be a local non-League team the Football League club wanted to help out for whatever reason. This type of 'benevolent' match continued into the 1970s.

Sometimes such matches would also take place during the season if the financial plight of a smaller club was acute. In 1976–77, Tommy Docherty, then manager of Manchester United, read in his morning newspaper that Newport County were on the brink of bankruptcy for the sake of some £12,000. Tommy immediately rang the Newport manager, the redoubtable Jimmy Scoular no less, and arranged to bring his star-studded United team to Somerton Park for a friendly, for which Manchester United offered to waive any fee. A crowd of some 15,000 turned up, generating receipts of around £9,000 for the Newport coffers, a little short of what was required to clear the debt but sufficient to satisfy the bank and most of Newport's creditors, and ensure their survival. It was that simple for one member of the football family to help another.

Prior to our opening match of 1961–62 at home to Wolves, John Harris gathered the first team about him on the training ground. It was the Friday before the game. I was grateful the training had been light that week as the weather had been almost tropical. The sun was like a gold sovereign someone had poured petrol on, lit with a match and said, 'Here, hold this why I nip to the loo,' and then put the coin in your hand, and never come back. The heat in Sheffield was so intense it was as if the steel furnaces had been set up on the streets. A white dust heat, thick with the smell of smelting and tinged with the odour of sulphur, hung about the city like an unwanted guest at a party. There was something very un-English about the heat that week.

We sat on the grass of the training field as John Harris, dressed in nylon shirt, woollen tie and beige slacks, prepared us for life in Division One. There was no shelter from the searing heat out there in the training field, my face felt as if a hand had been held against it all day and night. I remembered I had my goalkeeper's cap and put it on to give me some welcome respite from the sun.

John chose his words so what he said acted as a catalyst to thought. That hot, summer morning in August 1961, John entreated us all with one of his most moving and motivational talks. As we sat about him, as disciples may well have done around Jesus, he began by talking of our prospects in Division One, which he believed to be good. He talked about how some quarters of the press had tipped both ourselves and Ipswich Town for an immediate return to Division Two.

'That isn't going to happen,' John told us. 'Whatever cause you decide on there's always someone to tell you you're wrong. We're full of hope and optimism now but, as the season unfolds, we'll encounter problems and these will tempt you into thinking maybe those people who tipped us for relegation are right.

'They're wrong, because as you know, we have a plan, but to follow our plan to the end takes courage when the problems start to crop up and you're tempted to think the critics may be right.

'That's when you need courage, the sort of courage a soldier needs. Let me tell you this, lads: peace has its victories but it takes greater courage than a soldier has to achieve that sort of victory. Same applies to us in the First Division. We have the talent, we have the quality, we have the game-plan...but they are worthless unless you display that special sort of courage. The sort we will need to get something from a game at say, Arsenal, when we find ourselves two-nil down with fifteen minutes to go.

'There'll be games we should win hands down, but for whatever the reason, we'll end up losing. You will be blamed. I will be blamed. I will be told I made a mistake in selecting so-and-so; a mistake by asking "what's-his-name" to play on the left, and so on and so forth.

'If you have anything about you, there are no mistakes in life, lads, only lessons. And football, like life, always gives us a teacher,' continued John to eager ears. 'In life, this includes the bee that stings you, the hot plate straight from the oven. Football's teachers are not me or the coach, they are that moment when their full-back pushed on and you decided not to track back, to leave it to chance, or someone else. When, from the kick-off you left it to others to decide the tempo and impact on the game before making yours.

'Football always provides us with teachers. Think about that.'

We sat in the heat and we did think about that.

'We'll do all right in this division, better than all right. But there will be times when our faith and belief will be tested,' said John, coming across like the lay preacher he was, 'times when we find ourselves chasing a game and running out of ideas. That, lads, is when our real work starts.

'There will be times when results have not been good and we no longer know which way to turn or go. That, lads, is when we know we have begun our real journey...

'Think about football's teachers...call upon the special courage from which peace is made...and we shall be all right in this division, lads. Better than all right!'

A minute or so later I watched as John made his way across the training field towards his car. The armpits of his light blue nylon shirt had turned navy blue. For all the heat, he still had his tie on and hadn't loosened it as much as a millimetre. It was as if he was like some saint of long ago who combined preaching to his flock with penance.

John's talks never failed to make me think deeply. They were more than simply football talks whose intention was a temporary fillip to us players. They did that, but they had more mileage in them. When I went away and thought about what John had said, I found I had a poignant and telling guideline, philosophy even, not only to football but to my life.

The season began in gold-leaf sunshine against old gold-shirted Wolverhampton Wanderers and it began well for everyone connected with Sheffield United. Derek Pace (who else?) scored the first goal of the new season. Derek's effort was quickly followed by one from Ron Flowers to restore parity but, as the second half got underway, I felt we had the edge on Wolves and so it proved. Midway through the second period, Derek Pace headed a cross from Len Allchurch into the path of Billy Hodgson and the canny Scot drilled the ball hard and low past Malcolm Finlayson into the Wolves' goal to get our season off to a cracking start.

In light of the PFA's victory and news that Johnny Haynes of Fulham had become British football's first £100-a-week player, the newspapers had billed 1961–62 as 'The New Dawn'. Frank Butler in the *News of the World* refuted claims that the PFA's victory had resulted in 'The Footballer's Gold Rush' and cited the fact that Stanley Matthews, for all his global fame and years of loyal service to Blackpool in which the club had earned countless thousands playing lucrative friendlies in which he featured, had been offered but £20 a week.

I too was on a basic £20 a week at Sheffield United, which had been the maximum wage and was £10 less than the ceiling limit the Football League had suggested when attempting to keep the maximum wage in place. Johnny Haynes may well have stolen the headlines but, believe me, he was unique in the wage he received. Even players such as those at Spurs and Manchester United were paid nowhere near Haynes' salary.

The big money was still to be earned elsewhere, particularly in Italy. Jimmy Greaves, Denis Law, Joe Baker and Gerry Hitchens had all left British football for the Italian League. Of the four, only Gerry Hitchens was to make a go of it and carve out a meaningful career for himself in Serie 'A', primarily with Inter Milan. Regarding the 'retain and transfer' system, Jimmy Greaves had been a case in point. Jimmy had never wanted to leave Chelsea, or at least London. By his own admission Jimmy is a home boy; he didn't want to leave Essex for Newcastle or Manchester, let alone Milan, which, much against his will, Chelsea had succeeded in selling him to. Jimmy's grief over his enforced move and his desire to return to English football were so great that he was back playing in the First Division for Spurs before 1961–62 had reached the halfway stage.

In the light of the lifting of the maximum wage and abolition of the 'retain and transfer' system, clubs who had renewed or re-negotiated players' contracts were keen to publicise details to demonstrate the club had the players' interests at heart. Whilst we at Sheffield United continued more or less as normal, our neighbours from Owlerton went public with the wage-incentive scheme they had implemented, one we United players could only look across the city at in envy.

Sheffield Wednesday had offered their players a weekly basic pay of £30; first-team appearance money of £10; a crowd bonus of £13 for attendances between 32,000 and 45,000; plus £2 per thousand for attendances in excess of 45,000 with a ceiling crowd bonus payment of £25. Wednesday players were also to receive a £4 bonus for a home or away win, and a £1 bonus for an away draw. Players who were members of any international squad would also receive a weekly bonus of £5 until such time as they were no longer members of a published international squad.

Though Wednesday's Ron Springett had now assumed the England jersey, I, along with Gordon Banks, was being selected for the England squad and, like Gordon at Leicester, never received an 'international bonus' from the club. You may well wonder why a club would concede to pay a player a bonus for being a member of an international squad, but being an international in the sixties carried real kudos. Those pictures of players in football annuals and Charles Buchan's *Football Monthly* proudly stated after their name and that of their club – 'and England', or 'and Scotland', whatever the case might be.

There was still precious little in the way of football on our TV screens. The Football League, in their infinite wisdom, continued to prevent running score-lines and half-time scores from being broadcast on television for fear the announcement of these would affect attendances. Supporters rarely saw players unless they played at their local club, so an international in your team or that of your opponents was always an attraction and added to the gate. Unlike today where the home team keeps the match receipts, less the usual deductions, in the sixties the home club shared the net gate receipts with the opposition so a visiting team that included internationals proved an attraction and would generate a larger revenue for both clubs.

The lifting of the maximum wage may not have heralded a 'new dawn' for the vast majority of players at the time, but wages were to improve in time. I very much felt, however, that Sheffield United *were* experiencing a new dawn.

Our first away trip brought a point from a 1–1 draw at Cardiff City and we continued to chip away at the points as the summer turned into autumn and autumn into winter. As John Harris had predicted, there were lessons to be learned. Chelsea, minus Jimmy Greaves, were struggling at the foot of Division One when we visited Stamford Bridge in September. Their player-coach, Tommy Docherty, however, was beginning to prove just what a master tactician he was. With the score at 1–1 at half-time, a drubbing seemed not to be on the cards. In the second half, however, the game changed dramatically and the final score came in at 6–1 to Chelsea. At the end of the game I found myself saying to myself what I always said when not pleased with my performance, 'Alan, that simply wasn't good enough.'

A fortnight after the Chelsea debacle we were defeated at home by a West Ham United team which contained youngsters Bobby Moore in defence and Geoff Hurst in midfield. Otherwise, our form up to Christmas belied the fact Sheffield United had been widely tipped for a swift return to Division Two. Prior to Christmas we in fact enjoyed some choice victories, none more so than over Sheffield Wednesday at a packed Bramall Lane.

If anyone were to ask me – and I have, on occasion, been asked this – 'What was the best game you ever played for Sheffield United?' I invariably choose a match at Everton in October 1961. It is, of course, impossible to say with any certainty what you consider your best game to have been, because each match has different circumstances and variables to take into account, but for the sake of argument and a preponderance of pondering, I always say Everton at Goodison Park in 1961.

I was, at the time, one of three goalkeepers in the England squad – the others being Ron Springett and Banksy – and was ever-conscious of the fact that playing in the First Division meant I was always in the 'shop window' regarding England selection. We travelled to Everton without Gerry Summers, who had picked up an injury the previous week in our 2–1 success over Ipswich Town. Gerry's place went to Harry Orr – 'Iron' as we used to call him – whilst the also-injured Keith Kettleborough was replaced by a very exciting prospect in Barry Hartle, a Manchester lad John Harris had signed from Watford.

It is a curious thing I should choose the Everton game as my best in Sheffield United colours, as we lost it 1–0 to a Roy Vernon goal. The newspapers were, however, in no doubt the score-line would have been more emphatic if I had not had 'a good day at the office'. The *Sunday Express* who, at the time, could show today's *Independent* a thing or two about word-heavy headlines, led with: 'Hodgkinson Turns On Wonder Show To Stop Vernon'. Whereas *The People* gave me something to live up to with their headline, 'Britain's Best Keeper'.

Writing in the *Express*, Don Hardisty's match report began as follows:

> There was an Englishman, a Scotsman and a Welshman at
> Goodison Park on Saturday… and if this story doesn't have
> a happy ending for all of them, then their respective national
> selectors will live to regret it. Briefly the story went like this –
> the Scot, Alex Young, made the chances; the Welshman, Roy
> Vernon, took them, and the Englishman, Alan Hodgkinson,
> stopped them.
>
>   This triangular clash between three great players at the top
> of their form made this match worthwhile, and judging from the
> applause as the trio walked off together, the 42,000-crowd would
> agree, they are unlucky to be kept out of their national sides.

I don't know how I could possibly have managed this but, according to Hardisty's match report, I 'stopped six searing shots and a point-blank header from Vernon, some of them in fantastic fashion, before foiling two shots from Young in the same confident manner, denied [Bobby] Collins three times, held a thumping header from Jimmy Fell and somehow managed to hold a [Micky] Lill shot at point-blank range before the break.' All that before half-time! Hardisty gives forth with more superlatives in his appraisal of the second half. 'This was goalkeeping at its greatest,' he waxes.

Edgar Turner, writing in *The People*, was equally praising. 'Best goalkeeper in Britain. That's my verdict on Alan Hodgkinson.' Turner resorts to superlatives such as 'wonderful', 'sensational', 'brilliant' and 'tremendous' when describing saves I executed but, like Hardisty, reserved brick-bats for United's attack, which he described on the day as being 'powder-puff'.

On 9 December goals from Ron Simpson and Derek Pace gave us a 2–1 success against Arsenal. It was a result that signalled the beginning of a terrific unbeaten run for United of seventeen games, which eventually came to an end in March at Ipswich Town. Both Sheffield United and Ipswich had confounded the pundits. We had both been tipped for a relegation battle; in the event nothing would be further from the truth. Come the end of February, both Ipswich and ourselves were battling it out with Burnley, Spurs and Everton at the top of Division One, with just four points separating the five clubs. Hot on our heels were West Ham United, playing the type of exquisite football they were to become renowned for under Ron Greenwood. Also to the surprise of the football 'experts' was the position of the two Manchester clubs: United were sixth from bottom with Manchester City two places behind them. Chelsea propped up the table, with Cardiff City and Fulham also immersing themselves in the mire.

For Brenda and me 1961 was our very first Christmas as a family, and we spent it in a very loving way with baby Karen. Of course, I had to work, and my work also provided happiness that festive season. Following Sheffield United's fine victory over Arsenal, December also saw Sheffield United post wins against Wolves (1–0), Nottingham Forest (2–0) and, on Boxing Day, a 2–1 success at the expense of Blackpool.

The Boxing Day game against Blackpool took place at Bramall Lane and was played in typical festive weather. Snow fell across most of Britain on Christmas Day, not heavy, just enough to cover the ground and give everywhere a seasonal look. Heavier snow was to be on the way, however, which would result in many of the games scheduled for 30 December being postponed, including Sheffield United's return holiday fixture at Blackpool. On Boxing Day, though, just about every fixture went ahead as planned.

As I gingerly drove to the ground, descending the seemingly endless hill from Ecclesall to Hunters Bar, into the city and eventually to Bramall Lane, the city of Sheffield lay bandaged before me. The chimney bases of the snow-topped houses looked as if they had been shrouded in cotton wool. The roofs of the houses were ice-cream white as if snow had been shaken manically from whitewash buckets up in the sky. Snow covered the shrubs, hedges and trees of Hunters Bar Park like grandfather moss and whiskered the brick walls of the park. As I took in the winter vista I thought how variable the British climate is. Was it only four months ago I had sat on the training field in blistering heat as John Harris gave the players a pre-season pep-talk? Now the day was iron cold but I knew the game would go ahead.

Sheffield United, like a good many clubs at the time, had a simple answer to frost and snow. Prior to temperatures plummeting, the Bramall Lane pitch would be covered in straw which was applied by the groundsman, the groundstaff and any volunteers they could muster. Once the straw was down, a couple of dozen braziers would be dotted about the pitch. The metal braziers had been made for the club by a local blacksmith, of which there were still many in Sheffield at the time. Once the braziers were filled with coal and set alight they kept the air above and around the pitch relatively warm, certainly warm enough to prevent the pitch from freezing over. The club would employ a couple of old boys to act as night-watchmen, whose job was to ensure the braziers were always topped up with coal. The braziers and straw would be removed by an army of volunteers late on Saturday morning before the referee's pitch inspection. It was a simple solution to cold, frosty weather and it worked. Nowadays, with Health and Safety having reached hitherto unknown levels of lunacy whereby pins cannot be given with Remembrance Day poppies, not only do terraces have to be clear of every morsel of snow and ice in order for a game to get

Me, aged 12, flanked by Dinnington Secondary Modern school team mates John Hepworth and Clive Kerygo on the occasion of us being selected to represent the district.

National Service 1955–57 with the Signals Corps. Here as a military policeman guarding the 'glasshouse'. I am second from left, on my left is Bud Houghton (Lincoln City).

About to collect the ball at Stamford Bridge (1955–56), centre is Chelsea's Roy Bentley. I was on weekend leave from the Army.

Walter Winterbottom welcomes the England players to the Hendon Hall Hotel prior to my England debut v Scotland, April 1957. The first time I met Stan Matthews and Tom Finney.

Billy Wright (curiously, left) and George Young (right) respectively lead-out England and Scotland on the occasion of my full international debut. My first touch of the ball was to pick it out of the net!

Collecting a header from Charlie Hurley, World Cup qualifier v Republic of Ireland, 1957 in Dublin.

Ready to audition for the film 'Escape from Colditz' with Ray Barlow (West Brom) and Stan Matthews. Really arriving at our Copenhagen hotel prior to a World Cup qualifying match v Denmark.

Crystal Palace, FA Cup, January 1959. A snow-covered pitch, snow piled onto the perimeter track and ground frozen due to zero temperature – and V-neck short-sleeved shirts.

Joe Shaw looks on as I punch clear. Prowling is Aston Villa's Gerry Hitchens prior to his move to Inter Milan. Gerry played in Italy for nigh on ten years. He died tragically young, at the age of 48, when playing in a charity match in North Wales.

England World Cup Squad 1962. (Back l to r) Jimmy Armfield, Bobby Robson, Walter Winterbottom, Ron Flowers, Maurice Norman, Don Howe, Stan Anderson, Jimmy Adamson, Harold Shepherdson, Brian Douglas. (Front) John Connelly, Jimmy Greaves, Peter Swan, Gerry Hitchens, Ron Springett, Johnny Haynes, Me, Ray Wilson, Bobby Charlton, Alan Peacock, Bobby Moore, George Eastham, Roger Hunt.

The moment after Everton's Roy Vernon and I collide. Roy and I were among six players helped from the pitch at the end of this game due to injury. Not a single booking.

Norwich City, FA Cup 1962. I'm wearing the corduroy cap I wore throughout my entire career. A decade later they were wearing them in 'Shaft'.

The Sheffield United defence which, injuries apart, remained unchanged for nigh on eight years. (L to R) Graham Shaw, Me, Cec Coldwell. (Front) Gerry Summers, Joe Shaw and Brian Richardson.

England 1962. (Back l to r) Jimmy Armfield, Brian Miller, Bobby Robson, Me, Peter Swan, Ron Flowers, Mick McNeill. (Front) Brian Douglas, Jimmy Greaves, Bobby Smith, Johnny Haynes, Bobby Charlton.

At full stretch to save v Swansea at the Vetch Field.

Joe, Graham Shaw and I try to thwart Jimmy Greaves. Geoffrey Green said of Greavsie, 'He scores goals with all the fuss of someone closing the door of a Rolls Royce'.

With Chelsea's Tony Hateley, Stamford Bridge 1967. Tony was one of the best headers of a ball there has ever been, it was as if he had a boot between his ears.

There are eight techniques for punching the ball – this is one. Sheffield Wednesday's Johnny Fantham arrives for a closer look.

'Derby' day, in aerial combat with Sheffield Wednesday's Gerry Young. Wednesday in the strip their fans never took to.

Sheffield 'derby' with Wednesday's Johnny Fantham (as ever) expecting the unexpected.

Demonstrating what goalkeepers endeavoured to do, as opposed to many nowadays: hold the ball.

On the occasion of my 600th match for Sheffield United. I collected the match programme from every game I played.

Coaching Manchester United 'keepers. On my left is Peter Schmeichel.

With the family. (Back row l to r) Karen Clarke, Nathan Clarke, Leanne Clarke, Jamie Clarke, Hayley Wingrove, Matthew Wingrove, Ash Lowe, Paula Wingrove, Tom Lowe. (Front row) Liz Hodgkinson, Paige Hodgkinson, Brenda Hodgkinson, me, Andrew Hodgkinson.

the go-ahead, so too do walkways leading to the stadium and pavements of neighbouring streets.

Blackpool, in their tangerine shirts, seemed to bring a little of the summer sun to what was a chilly Bramall Lane. It was strange to see a Blackpool team without Stanley Matthews; the 'wizard of dribble' had been transferred to Stoke City, where he was to write a fairy-tale ending to what had been an already incredible story. Blackpool had in their ranks some very fine players: goalkeeper Tony Waiters was one of the best young keepers in the country; Jimmy Armfield was regular choice for England at right-back; Ray Charnley was a prolific goal-scorer, a tall and lean centre-forward who, whenever you got near him, appeared to be all jutting bone; Roy Gratrix was fine pivot, and Des Horne had won numerous honours when with Wolves.

It was one of Blackpool's lesser-known players, Keith Peterson, who struck the first blow when he latched onto a through ball from Armfield and drilled low into the left-hand corner of my goal. Keith was South African by birth and had joined the club from Durban City in curious circumstances. A Preston supporter who had emigrated to South Africa contacted his home-town club to recommend Keith Peterson, suggesting the Deepdale club should invite him over for a month's trial. Preston agreed to 'have a look' at Keith but informed the supporter-cum-scout that Peterson would have to pay his own expenses, including flights and accommodation. Annoyed at the response of his home-town club, the supporter contacted Preston's great rivals, Blackpool, whose manager, Ron Suart, agreed to take Peterson on trial and meet the costs involved. Keith played a number of matches in the Central League for Blackpool reserves and at the end of his month's trial had impressed sufficiently to be offered a two-year contract. Delighted with his new signing, Ron Suart contacted the Preston exile and offered to pay him a £250 'finder's fee'. The Preston supporter thanked Blackpool for their generosity but declined their kind offer, saying, 'My reward is seeing a lad given an opportunity to develop his talent with a top club. I wish for no other reward than the satisfaction of seeing talent rewarded.' I often think about this story when I hear about contemporary agents competing with one another to represent talented schoolboy footballers. Professional football has never been

big on philanthropy, but there were examples of it in the past and
the Peterson story is but one instance of a quality that has seemingly been lost to a game. In the days before the maximum wage,
clubs exploited players, now, in an era when non-League, academy
and even schoolboy footballers have agents, it's just the opposite.

Blackpool's joy at Peterson's goal proved short-lived. Two minutes later, Derek Pace levelled with a rasping drive. In the second
half both teams coped manfully with a pitch that was becoming
increasingly difficult as the temperature dropped. There were some
ten minutes left when Len Allchurch seemingly was of the mind
that enough was enough. Receiving a pass from Gerry Summers,
Len dribbled artfully past oncoming tangerine shirts before scoring
with a sweetly struck shot that never appeared to leave the frozen
ground – it was the sort of goal worthy of deciding any closely contested game and made for a Happy Christmas, for Blades supporters at any rate.

With Sheffield United's unbeaten run of sixteen matches having
come to an end at Ipswich at the beginning of March, the month
proved not a good one for us in that it produced three defeats, a
draw and a single victory. The draw involved us and Everton scoring a goal apiece at Bramall Lane.

Yet again, we had enjoyed a decent run in the Cup, putting paid
to Bury (after a second replay), Peterborough United and Norwich
City – revenge is sweet and, what is more, it's not fattening. Our
FA Cup sojourn came to an end when Burnley came to Bramall
Lane in the quarter-final and progressed thanks to a headed goal
from Ray Pointer seven minutes after half-time. It was another cruel
twist to a game which had dealt us some cruel blows. Graham Shaw
received a deep cut to his head, the consequence of a flailing elbow,
and had to spend the remainder of the game with his head heavily
bandaged. Denis Finnegan, who had replaced the already injured
Joe Shaw, carried on in not a little discomfort having tweaked a
calf muscle when over-stretching to thwart a run by Denis Stevens.

All this preceded a debilitating injury to Gerry Summers. After
only two minutes, Gerry had had the misfortune to pull a thigh
muscle. Gerry went off for treatment but returned later in the first
half and played the rest of the game on the wing. Gerry never lacked
guts, but his injury was so severe that he was, to use another old

football axiom, little more than a passenger. It was a game in which the trainers had been kept busy, but their work was far from done.

Ten minutes from time, with the teams level, Derek Temple threaded the ball through our back four for Roy Vernon to run on to. I had spotted the danger and had come quickly from my line. As Roy raced into my area, he appeared to knock the ball a little too far ahead. I saw this as my opportunity to go down and collect. I hadn't been expecting Roy to momentarily lose control of the ball and it caught me off guard. I didn't go down to smother in my normal fashion and my right shoulder jarred violently against the hard ground.

I managed to get both hands on the ball, then someone appeared on the pitch and hit me square on the forehead with a lump hammer. It was actually Roy Vernon's kneecap that made contact with my forehead as he slid in to try and toe-poke the ball away from me, but it might as well have been a lump hammer, such was the impact and effect.

The combination of our respective momentums and Roy's kneecap coming from one direction and hitting my forehead from the other, produced what Joe Shaw later described as 'one hell of a thud'. The impact was such that, as soon as Roy's kneecap hit me between the eyes I suddenly remembered the purpose of the key on my key ring that, for years had been a mystery to me but, which I had never removed for fear it was in some way important. Still clutching the ball as if it was a crucifix, I took hold of Bramall Lane and spun it around. When I had it revolving to my satisfaction, I then took hold of one of the floodlight pylons and hit myself on the forehead with it. This made me fall to the ground to inspect the length of the grass at close quarters. I lay there, on my side, staring at a few blades of grass wondering how on earth they had managed to survive in a well-trodden penalty area when all their mates had succumbed to trampling boots.

The referee, I shall never forget him, Mr Cooke from Waterbeach in Cambridgeshire, was quickly on the scene. He took one look at me, blew hard on his whistle and signalled with a hand for the trainers to attend – and quickly. Seasoned football followers will know that when a player is genuinely injured he lies still on the pitch, while the player who rolls around is play-acting. I lay there as if I was one of those knights of old laid to rest in one of our more prominent cathedrals.

Ernest Jackson was quickly on the scene, as was Tom Eccleston, the Everton trainer. Roy Vernon was on his feet, manically hopping about on one leg. They ignored him. Again, as a seasoned football follower, you will know that when the opposition trainer is called to assist, it's because it's a potentially very serious injury. Between them, Ernest and Tom Eccleston managed to get me sitting up. Tom supported me from behind as Ernest slapped a cold wet sponge across my face as if I were a boxer being attended to in his corner by his trainer between rounds.

You don't see the cold wet sponge used much by trainers nowadays; as alternative medicine goes, a cold wet sponge had no equal. It was the universal remedy, curative and antidote to any injury. I have seen trainers break the ice formed on the top of the water in their bucket when immersing the 'magic sponge'. When a large sponge heaving with water a fraction of a degree above freezing was ground into your face, the effect was both remarkable and restorative. Invariably players would immediately struggle to their feet, as I did, if only to prevent them being subjected to the heart-stopping shock of the sponge again. Why on earth this universal panacea to football-related injuries has fallen from favour, I shall never know.

Having administered the magic sponge with some gusto, Ernest Jackson then proceeded to undertake the second stage of treatment as administered by all the trainers of the time. He dipped into his bag and produced a bottle of smelling salts. Never has such a miniscule bottle been capable of producing such an enormous and marked effect on human consciousness as smelling salts. The 'salts' were ammonium carbonate and one whiff produced an instantaneous, animating effect on the mucous membranes of the nose and lungs. One snort and your breathing immediately moved up the gears to the higher levels of panting. You were suddenly conscious, in more ways than one, of increased activity in your heart, blood pressure and brain. The world appeared clearer; you were more *compos mentis*. Everyone around you appeared more distinctively defined, your own thoughts more lucid, coherent and comprehensible. The Football Association has advised against the use of smelling salts in the treatment of players – they should try it themselves, they really should.

Having administered the smelling salts, Ernest Jackson then did what all trainers did when treating players suspected of concussion. Adhering to what he believed to be consummate integrated medical care, he began to heartily slap my cheeks with the palms of his hands. That did the trick. Desperate to put an end to round after round of his aversion therapy, I told Ernest I was 'okay', but my shoulder was causing me pain. Ernest pulled my goalkeeper's jersey up around my neck and out came the freezing wet sponge again. When applied to warm skin, the effect was as before, shuddering and a shock to the system.

'There, that'll do you,' said Ernest, packing his delights back into his bag.

It had to.

As the trainers prepared to exit, Roy Vernon asked Tom Eccleston, 'Hey, Tom, what about my knee?'

' 'king run it off,' said Tom, jabbing a thumb in the air to let Roy know the level of his concern as he joined Ernest in departing the scene.

Both sides played out the last ten minutes to a draw and as the 28,000 crowd shuffled off the terraces to the warmth of their hearths, we players, largely content with a share of the spoils, made our way down the tunnel. Gerry Summers hopping on one leg and aided by Cec Coldwell; Mick Meagan limping; Denis Finnegan hobbling; Graham Shaw be-turbaned and teetering, painstakingly sedate; Roy Vernon hurt and faltering, and yours truly swaying groggily. As for the game itself, not a single booking.

After the game, whilst in the plunge bath I felt a little discomfort but it was not until I was home that evening that the shoulder started to pain me in a troublesome way. I reported to Bramall Lane on the Sunday morning and received some treatment, but the prognosis was not good.

Our next match was at Craven Cottage and in the week preceding our visit to Fulham I did little to no training as I continued to receive treatment to my injured shoulder. On the Thursday, John Harris asked me how I was fixed to play. In all honesty I informed John I was fifty-fifty at best. John told me another day's rest would improve my chances of playing as Ernest Jackson had told him my injured shoulder had responded well to treatment.

'I want you to travel,' John told me. 'But to be on the safe side, I am also asking Des Thompson to come down. Bob Widdowson will play for the reserves in place of Des. I have a lad who will play for the Intermediate (Youth) team in place of Bob. But you'll be fit, Alan, I know you will.'

I wasn't so sure, but another twenty-four hours could make a difference.

We took the train down to London to our usual London hotel, the Great Northern. When we checked in it was obvious the hotel was very busy. There was some sort of conference taking place and the bars, restaurant and meeting rooms were heaving with businessmen. Having taken our evening meal at half-five, John Harris informed us players we could go out and catch the early evening showing of the film that was taking the UK by storm, Stephen Sondheim and Leonard Bernstein's *West Side Story*. As we assembled in the hotel foyer, John Harris pulled me to one side. John asked me if I was fit to play against Fulham. I informed him, in all honesty, the shoulder was still uncomfortable.

'Alan, cards on the table, I want you to play tomorrow,' John informed me.

I told him I too wanted to play but the injury was niggling.

John stood looking at me like a man who had waited a long time and come a long way.

'Okay, we'll have to give you a fitness test,' he said.

I agreed that was the sensible thing.

'There's a conference room down this hallway,' said John pointing to a hallway that ran off at a right angle from where we were standing. 'We'll go there.'

'What for, boss?' I enquired.

'Your fitness test. I need to know tonight.'

I was totally taken aback, so much so that I followed John in a state of stupefaction as he made his way to a small conference room. I was still nonplussed when John asked me to remove my shoes and stand in front of a set of closed double doors. I had left the conference room door open when I entered, as I thought we wouldn't be in the room any longer than for him to collect something, but obviously this wasn't to be.

There was a long wooden table at the far end of the room and on it were a dozen or so leather briefcases. John picked one of them up and held it in front of him.

'These belong to some business people. They're in a meeting next door. They won't mind,' he informed me.

I had no idea whatsoever as to his thinking, so I asked him.

'I'm going to give you your fitness test,' he told me.

'In here? What with?' I enquired.

'These,' he said, waggling the briefcase he was holding.

I emitted a strained laugh – it was as taut as piano wire.

'I'll feed, you save. I'll keep them coming,' he said.

Before I could say another word, John hurled the briefcase down the room and I instinctively flung myself to my right, hit the floor like a safe but held the briefcase as if it had been a football. I was immediately on my feet again because John had quickly taken a second briefcase off the table. He hurled briefcase number two low to my left. I went down and held the second briefcase. So we continued, John hurling briefcase after briefcase down the room and me diving to save them. When he'd hurled every briefcase, to my utter astonishment, we repeated the exercise.

'How's the shoulder?' he asked as I lay clutching the last briefcase, my breathing so heavy you could have ironed a shirt with it.

'Seems okay,' I said, taking to my feet.

'Great! You're playing,' John told me, clapping his hands together with joy.

As I turned to gather up some of the briefcases, I happened to glance towards the open door. Three businessmen were standing in the hallway, staring at me, their faces a mixture of astonishment and disbelief. I felt suddenly very self-conscious and embarrassed, as if I had been caught with my pants down at a nuns' garden party.

John and I replaced the briefcases on the table and I then put my shoes on. I attempted an air of nonchalance but failed as I exited the room past the trio of businessmen, who looked like they might have passed comment had their jaws not been on their chests.

'Excellent briefcases,' remarked John, completely unabashed, as he passed the gobsmacked trio. 'You chose well. They'll last you years.'

I have few regrets in football, but one is that when walking down that hallway, I didn't turn around to see the look on the faces of the three stupefied businessmen as John said his piece.

Never in my entire career did I ever have a fitness test as bizarre as the one in the Great Northern Hotel prior to our game at Fulham. What is more, I have never heard of any other player being subjected to anything as outlandish in the way of a fitness test, but that was John Harris. He was an enigma.

Ten minutes into the game, I went down low to save a shot from Fulham's Graham Leggat and felt my shoulder go. It was painful and caused me a lot of discomfort; however, there was no choice but for me to carry on. Fulham took full advantage of my debilitation and stuck five past me, albeit we did score twice. As a consequence of my injury I was side-lined for a couple of weeks and Des Thompson made two rare appearances in goal. When I returned to the fold, John Harris was on speaking terms with me again.

Sheffield United were fourth and flying high, though our eleven-game unbeaten run had come too late for us to concern Ipswich Town or Burnley, for one of which the title seemed bound. Manchester United were evolving into credible challengers for honours, though they struck me as being more of a Cup team than one able to weather the vicissitudes of an eight-month League campaign. United were, however, formidable at home. It would be tough to come away with anything.

When it comes to atmosphere, the crowd at a football match have a more significant role to play than the air, the rain and the sun. Though it was to prove not the happiest of hunting grounds for Sheffield United, one of my favourite venues was Old Trafford for the simple reason every game was played amidst a big match atmosphere, not least because four years after the tragedy of Munich, United were still sitting on a throne of national enthusiasm.

Some players are overawed by a large crowd; when playing away, some even freeze when confronted with a vehemently partisan home crowd. I loved playing in front of a large, yelling, baying, bawling, bellowing crowd, it brought out the best in me. I felt as if my metabolism rose as each swell of sound gushed down from the terraces. A big crowd such as was always experienced at Old Trafford kept my adrenalin pumping. Kept me alert to all possibilities. Kept me on my toes. Kept me in love with football, and made me feel football, just possibly, loved me.

One such match was the one played at Old Trafford on Easter Monday, 1962. In a hard-fought game, with just six minutes to go, Manchester United really piled on the pressure as they fought for an equaliser goal. This was denied them, but the tension didn't end there. With just two minutes to go until the final whistle, Bobby Charlton was awarded a penalty – a penalty which would be the last kick of the game. We were seconds from full time, seconds from a rousing, uproarious, revelrous, ripsnorter of a win at Old Trafford, and now that. Football can be a bloody cruel mistress at times.

I processed 'Bobby Charlton penalty taking' through my mind. Hard hit, bloody hard hit, to the goalkeeper's right. Bobby knew that I knew him from the England get-togethers. He knew that I knew he would hit them to the goalkeeper's right. He was a canny lad in every sense, so he could have hit it to my left. I took a deep breath, puffed out my cheeks and exhaled. I flung myself to my right a split second before Bobby made contact with the ball. I was going the right way in every sense. I was conscious of a loud smacking sound as I managed to get both hands to the ball. The ball ballooned up into the air and I heard a full-throated collective groan sweep down from the terraces. No sooner had I hit the ground than I was on my feet again chasing that ball, but there was no need. Arthur Luty gave a long shrill blast of his whistle and twirled both arms high in the air.

We'd done it. We'd bloody well done it. We'd only gone and won at Old Trafford. Beaten Manchester United on their own holy, hallowed turf in front of over 60,000 of their supporters, none of whom I could see at that moment because I was slowly crumbling to the ground under the sheer weight of all the white-shirted players who descended upon me.

When order was restored I turned to see a red-shirted arm extended towards me, and poking out of the sleeve was a hand. I glanced up. The hand was that of Bobby Charlton.

'Fantastic, Hodgey, well done. Bloody blinder,' Bobby said. I shook his hand and he drew me to him and hugged me.

'Deserved it. See you after for a drink,' Bobby said and I nodded.

I turned to collect my cap and gloves from inside the goal. As I bent down to pick them up, there came the sound of a gigantic pan of bacon and eggs. I raised an arm in acknowledgement of the applause from the United fans in the Stretford End. The sound of bacon and eggs frying got even louder.

Two matches followed our fantastic victory at Old Trafford and the curtain came down on another season. It was a season in which Sheffield United had confounded the football pundits, most of whom had predicted a quick return to Division Two. Rather than it having been a season of struggle, it had been one of success. Sheffield United finished in fifth place which, had it been a few years later, would have gifted us a place in European competition.

In keeping with everyone connected with the club I was delighted with our first season back in the top flight; to have finished in the top five and reached the quarter-finals of the FA Cup was testimony to me that Sheffield United were indeed a top-class side. On a personal note, my performances were rewarded when I was chosen for the England squad for that summer's World Cup Finals in Chile.

I had been a member of the England squad throughout the season without ever being selected for a game. The number-one spot was held by my good friend, Ron Springett, with Banksy emerging as stern competition to us both. There were a number of other goalkeepers whose performances had the press talking of them in terms of the England squad: Tony Waiters (Blackpool), Gordon West (Everton), Peter Bonetti (Chelsea) and Peter Grummitt (Nottingham Forest). Given such hot competition, naturally I was delighted to be one of the two goalkeepers chosen for the World Cup Finals.

Prior to flying down to Chile, I had the honour of being selected to play for an England XI against Notts County at Meadow Lane to celebrate the centenary of the oldest Football League club. A number of other England players bound for Chile also played, as did an exciting young left-winger from Preston North End, Peter Thompson, destined for fame in the great Liverpool team of the sixties. The game ended in a 3–1 victory for the England XI before a Meadow Lane crowd of 21,000. The Notts County goal was scored by their centre-forward. The County winger, Keith Fry, appeared to overhit a cross. Everyone stood back expecting the ball to carry over to the far side of the field and out for a throw-in. It was then that the County centre-forward appeared. Sprinting towards the ball he leapt into the air to a height I had never seen anyone reach.

His forehead made contact with the ball and he bulleted a header past me and into the net. Everyone was slack-jawed and for the same reason. No one could believe the sheer height this lad had reached to head that ball. To this day, I have never seen any player jump so high to head a ball. I made a mental note of the player's name should he ever play First Division football and I had to face him again – Tony Hateley.

As much as Sheffield United confounded the pundits by having a successful season, our impact was nothing compared to that of Ipswich Town, who had been promoted with us the previous season. The Ipswich manager, Alf Ramsey, had worked a minor miracle, guiding his unfancied, unfashionable team to the First Division title in their first season in Division One. Ipswich may not have played the sophisticated football of others whose illustrious names had often appeared on the honours list, but they had proved highly effective.

In the first 'New Deal' season which had produced the first £100-a-week footballer and seen West Ham pay Crystal Palace £65,000 for Johnny Byrne, Spurs £99,000 for Jimmy Greaves from AC Milan and Manchester United £110,000 for Denis Law from Torino, the unsung heroes of Ipswich received £25 a week for winning the Championship. A lesson if ever there was one that the vast majority of footballers do not have to be tempted by astronomical wages and ludicrously lucrative commercial deals in order to give of their best. Of that title-winning team, goalkeeper Roy Bailey (father of Gary, of Manchester United fame), Larry Carberry, John Elsworthy, Jimmy Leadbetter and Ted Phillips had all helped Ipswich gain promotion from Division Three to Two. With the exception of Doug Moran, bought from Falkirk for £12,000, the entire Ipswich Town title-winning team had come up from Division Two. This was very much the case regarding Sheffield United too. In securing fifth place in Division One we had accomplished this feat with the same team that had secured promotion.

Alf Ramsey's football philosophy was not dissimilar to that of John Harris. Both managers were excellent motivators by way of erudition and inspirational speech rather than 'tub thumping'. Both managers were also very good at getting players to believe in themselves and fulfil their potential as individuals whilst knitting as a team – the whole being greater than the sum of its parts. Ramsey and Harris were also very good tacticians who moulded their respective charges into formidable teams. Above all, the success of Ipswich Town proved what a democracy the game was back then. I wonder when, if ever, a team with the suffix of 'Town' will again be crowned champions of England?

Ipswich's amazing feat of winning the First Division Championship, and at the first time of asking, prompted what I think was probably the best quote of the season. The day after Ipswich were crowned champions, Peter Wilson of the *Daily Mirror* secured an interview with the eccentric and lovable Ipswich chairman, John Cobbold.

'Metaphorically speaking,' said Wilson, 'I should imagine this season has been one of wine, women and song for you and your fellow Ipswich directors.'

'I can't remember us doing much singing,' replied Cobbold.

As my fellow Sheffield United players embarked upon their annual holidays with their families, I felt like doing a little celebratory singing of my own as I joined my England teammates on the flight to Chile for the 1962 World Cup Finals.

| CHAPTER SEVEN |

'A sad tale's best for winter,
I have one, of sprites and goblins.'

A Winter's Tale

I had never been to South America before. For me, Chile was unseen, unknown, unexplained and unpredictable. I had by now travelled a bit, but Chile was an entirely different kettle of kedgeree. I knew I wasn't travelling to the ends of the earth, though such is its geographical position, it appeared to me to be as near as damn it.

Chile suggested a totally different terrain, culture and lifestyle to anything I had previously encountered. I wanted to see policemen and soldiers in uniforms that were totally alien to me. Hear music played in a style I had never heard before. Meet people whose lives were totally different to mine and whose lives would never again intersect with mine. Be perplexed by road signs and advertising hoardings. Be alien to everything from the local tipple to fruit and vegetables. I wanted a sense of being on an adventure as well as being at the world's greatest football tournament. I was going to find all that hard to do while cooped up in a village comprising wooden bungalows amidst a copper mine some fifty kilometres from the nearest civilisation.

England were based fifty kilometres from Rancagua in the Liberator region of Chile, in the foothills of the Andes. In 1962 it had a population around 140,000 people and came across to me as being a bit like Middlesbrough, but lacking in Middlesbrough's glamour and elan.

Our base was, putting it mildly, a curious choice for a football team, within a large copper-mining complex owned by the Anglo-American Copper Corporation. We arrived in Chile via Brazil and reached our base not having eaten for nigh on fourteen hours. Our team coach dropped the players off at their assigned wooden bungalows, as if we were package tourists being unloaded at various hotels and apartments along the Algarve. The coach made glacial progress around the complex and I was among the last to be dropped off. As we ravenous players waited a seemingly interminable amount of time before alighting, the strained, grumbling noise from the engine of our ancient bus seemed in danger of being drowned out by that of rumbling stomachs.

Three players were assigned to each bungalow. The first to be dropped off were George Eastham, Bobby Robson and Ray Wilson. They wasted no time in running into their bungalow in search of any food that might have been left for them. As bags were laboriously unloaded from the coach, George Eastham suddenly presented himself at a window heartily munching on an apple. George made a meal of eating the apple in more ways than one. Purposefully adding to our frustrating pangs of hunger, he proceeded to relish each bite which he followed with a loving caress of his stomach with the palm of a hand as if gorging on a meal prepared by Escoffier. As the rest of our party sat gazing out of the bus like starving Victorian urchins staring at gourmandising diners through the window of a plush restaurant, Maurice Norman took to his feet.

'If George doesn't stop with that, he'll be in the High Court again,' said Maurice tetchily, 'testifying to how I nearly killed him.'

Fortunately for George, our coach driver saw that as being the appropriate moment to move on. The Spurs centre-half, Maurice Norman, was normally a quiet, unassuming guy but a colossus, as hard as nails and as strong as an ox. As Jimmy Greaves remarked, 'If Mo and King Kong went up a dark alley to sort an argument, only one would emerge, and it wouldn't be the bloody monkey.'

I was billeted with Stan Anderson (Sunderland) and Don Howe (West Brom) in one of the wooden bungalows that formed a circle within a mining complex, which was, in itself, as large as a small town. A football pitch had been created for our benefit behind what was the mining company's restaurant. It was on this pitch that we were to do all our training and tactical work. The restaurant served decent enough food, which we ate in a room leading off from the mining workers' dining area. A storage shed had been converted into a gymnasium, or perhaps it had been a gymnasium all along, I couldn't tell. Some two hundred metres from our bungalows was the main road into the complex on which large lorries continuously passed to and fro, lumbering and groaning under the weight of their loads. The mining complex boasted the largest cactuses I had ever seen. They grew to some five feet in height but the most formidable thing about them was the spines on the leaves, which were some five centimetres in length and terminated in a point as sharp and sturdy as an ice pick. Beyond the mine the terrain swept steeply upwards to the formidable Andes.

As the base for an international football squad, it was a curious choice of venue to say the very least. Stan, Don and I often wondered which bright spark in the FA had flown to the nether regions of South America, found a copper mine that had wooden bungalows for rent and which was fifty kilometres from the nearest civilisation where we were to play our games, and thought, 'Why, this looks the perfect place to prepare for the World Cup Finals.'

Rancagua, where England were to play all their games, is a decent enough city in a 'Thank you, Lord, for not having made me live here' sort of way. New York had been dubbed 'The city that never sleeps'. We dubbed Rancagua 'The city where the hardware store stays open till half-five on Wednesdays.' The pièce de résistance was the central square known as the Plaza de los Heroes, which was dominated by a fine cathedral flanked by imposing bell towers. I would later be reminded of Rancagua Cathedral when watching Clint Eastwood spaghetti westerns. The surrounding buildings were of the old Spanish colonial style, which offered the impression of a city that had once enjoyed economic prosperity and, thanks to the cultivation of vineyards and fine wine, was destined to enjoy such fruitful economic times in the future. Within a few streets, however, these pleasant and picturesque offices and shops gave way to heartless, grey, concrete, formulaic monstrosities housing apartments from which hung the city's washing. It appeared every day was wash day. Everything seemed old and tired and in need of sprucing up, even the concrete apartment blocks. Litter lined the side streets and the locals seemed quelled, devoid of a genuine spirit of happiness – and money. On the few occasions we were allowed a shopping trip into the city we were besieged by gypsies wanting to sell us all manner of worthless items. It was all we could do to fend them off whilst keeping an eye open for the pickpockets we had been warned about.

These days, Rancagua is prospering again and the city has been smartened up considerably since I was there, which was, after all, over fifty years ago. The copper mine where England stayed has closed and is now a working museum with the obligatory gift shop and cafeteria, so a little of England lives on. Seemingly, it will only be a matter of time before a garden centre opens. Although much has changed for the better in Rancagua, and the litter, monstrous concrete apartment blocks and the copper mining has gone, I am reliably informed the hassling gypsies and pickpockets remain.

Each member of the World Cup squad was issued with a suit, two bri-nylon shirts, which crackled like distant thunder whenever you put one on, an England tie, an England metal lapel badge, a tracksuit, training shorts and socks and two pairs of Adidas football boots, one studded and the other of rubber moulded studs. That was it; if you required anything else you had to provide it yourself. It was a good job Ron Springett and I had packed our own goalkeeping gloves, caps and training jerseys.

A lot was made of the rivalry between Ron and myself for the England goalkeeping jersey. In Sheffield, the arguments as to who was the better goalkeeper and thus worthy of being England's number one galvanised steelworks and factory floors. Apparently, animated discussions took place around pub tables, with United and Wednesday fans citing the goalkeeping virtues of the pair of us. Word got around the city that Ron and I were fierce rivals but nothing was further from the truth. Whilst we were in competition, we were the best of friends and helped one another enormously in our training.

When Walter Winterbottom's squad training sessions were over, Ron and I would 'work' one another on the training pitch, offering advice and passing on tips to each other. Quite often we would engage the help of some of the lads in our personal training sessions. The likes of Jimmy Greaves, Bobby Charlton, Bobby Robson and Bobby Moore were always willing helpers, firing shots at us, practising set-pieces, taking corners and the like. We felt deep gratitude to these lads for the way they were generous with their time until, one afternoon, Jimmy Greaves remarked, 'Well, we might as well come out and help you and Ron, because there's bugger all else to do round here.' I am happy to say that we have remained the best of friends to this day; when Ron retired from football, he returned London to work as a painter and decorator – Michelangelo is hailed as a genius because it took him fourteen years to paint a ceiling, but let me tell you, until he retired Ron could do a hall, stairs and landing in a single day. One of the many gifts football has bestowed upon me is that of lasting friendships, such as the one I enjoy with Ron Springett, and for such friend- ships, I shall forever be grateful to the game I love.

Prior to our first group game against Hungary, we attended a reception party at the British Consulate in Rancagua. I gained the impression that for many of the FA officials who accompanied us – and there were as many as there were players – such functions were the highlight of the tournament. We players wore our England suits and the crackling bri-nylon shirts and 'played the game', making friendly and courteous smalltalk with Consulate officials, British business people who worked in the area and local dignitaries. We were all very conscious that we were representing our coun- try and behaved accordingly, even if one of two officials indulged themselves copiously with the *vino collapso*.

At one point, I was introduced to a British businessman whose work involved the shipping of copper from the mine. Introductions over, I was treated to a diatribe on how the locals, who had helped make him 'a small fortune' and were paid a pittance for the privi- lege of so doing, could not be trusted.

'What's your name again?' he slurred, ten minutes into what passed for conversation.

'Alan Hodgkinson, same as it was ten minutes ago,' I informed him.

The businessman then halted a waiter who was moving around the room with a tray of drinks, grabbed a gin and tonic from his tray and put it to sleep with a single punch. I took that as my cue to make my diplomatic farewell.

A few minutes later my eyes fell on a familiar face, that of George Robledo. George had been in the Newcastle United team I had faced when making my League debut for Sheffield United. I was delighted to see him again and, from the warm welcome he gave me, it was obvious the feeling was mutual. I learned from George that it was he and his brother who had acted as consultants to the FA for our World Cup trip and, it was he who had sourced and recommended the mining complex as a base. I told him I thought it a curious choice. When George told me some hair-raising tales of the hotels in Rancagua, I was left counting my blessings.

As for the football, I wish I could say 1962 was a marvellous World Cup, but it wasn't. Much of the football played was hindered by defensive tactics; only Brazil played consistent, fluent, entertaining and attacking football – it was ever thus. What's more, FIFA's ticket-pricing policy proved way beyond the budgets of locals, which resulted in some very poor attendances.

Walter, as I expected, preferred Ron Springett to me in goal for the opening match against Hungary. England were handicapped from the start by the loss of three players for the whole of the tournament, Peter Swan (Sheffield Wednesday's centre-half), Bobby Robson (West Brom's midfield) and Bobby Smith (Spurs' centre-forward), all due to injuries. On a rain-sodden pitch, two mistakes – one from Ron Springett, the other from Ron Flowers (Wolves) – gifted Hungary two goals, between which Ron Flowers scored from the penalty spot after a Jimmy Greaves effort had been handled on the line.

As well you know, it's important to avoid defeat in your first game in a World Cup and, should you lose, it's vitally important that you bloody well win the second. England's next match was against Argentina, and no one outside the England camp fancied our chances. Gerry Hitchens (Inter Milan) had struggled to get to grips with international football and Walter replaced him with Middlesbrough's Alan Peacock, who was making his international debut. There's an indication of how the game has changed. Bobby Moore and Maurice Norman had made their England debuts in our warm-up match against Peru; the game against Argentina was only their third cap. Alan Peacock was gaining his first. Can you imagine England of today giving international debuts to players in crucial

World Cup matches? Not to mention that such a debut came in a side that contained a couple of players who only had two caps each. I have to say I was a tad disappointed not to get the call against Argentina, as some newspapers had hoped, but I wished Ron well and accepted Walter Winterbottom's decision, most probably that of the Selection Committee, to stick with my rival for the jersey.

England may have lacked experience in certain quarters but the team possessed the quality and football nous to put paid to a technically superior Argentina. Jimmy Greaves and Bobby Charlton were outstanding and both helped themselves to a goal; our other came from Ron Flowers, again from the penalty spot, to give us a 3–1 victory that surprised everyone, not least Argentina themselves.

Following the Argentina victory, I sustained an injury in the most bizarre circumstances. During a practice match I went to retrieve a wayward ball which had been kicked into some scrubland behind my goal. As I ran across the scrub, a searing pain shot through my right foot. I heard somebody scream and was immediately taken aback on realising that someone was me. The pain was unbearable. I manically hopped about, not putting my right foot to the ground for fear I might pass out altogether. Walter, his assistant Jimmy Adamson, and trainer Harold Shepherdson were quickly on the scene. Harold asked what had happened. I didn't know. Wincing and wailing I pointed to my right foot.

Some of the players arrived, carried me back on to the practice pitch and sat me down on the grass. Harold Shepherdson raised my right leg and inspected my boot.

'Bloody hell,' he said. 'Take a look at that.'

They did, and I was treated to a series of 'Ooohs' and 'Aaaahs'.

It transpired I had trodden on one of the pad-like leaves from a giant cactus and a spike had gone straight through the sole of my boot and into the big toe of my right foot. Not without a little difficulty, Harold managed to extract the spike. He then eased my boot off my foot to reveal a sock soaked in blood. Supported on either side by Ron Springett and Bobby Moore, I managed to hop back to the dressing room, where Harold and the team doctor examined my toe, cleaned the wound and dressed it with a toe bandage.

Later that evening during dinner, one of the blazer brigade FA officials came to my side.

'I heard what happened to you today, Hodgkinson, that spike going straight through the sole of your boot. Nasty business,' said the official, a modicum of concern on his face. 'Do you think it will be all right?'

I assured him it would be.

'Jolly good,' he said, perceptibly brightening, 'only you've just been issued with those boots and we haven't brought spares. Good news you'll be able to wear it again.'

I looked about at the players around me. To a man they were holding their napkins to their faces to stifle their laughter.

'That tells you where we players and our well-being are on their priorities,' remarked Bobby Robson when the official had departed, 'somewhere below their concern for 'king boot.'

Jimmy Greaves then told us what had happened to him at Heathrow prior to flying out. Having time on our hands after the check-in, some of the lads went to the cafeteria. Greavsie bought himself a cup of coffee and a little cake and sat down at a table opposite Jimmy Armfield. No sooner had he sat down than Sir Stanley Rous, the secretary of the FA, walked by and, spotting Greavsie about to eat his little cake, took issue with him.

'Greaves, put that cake down,' ordered Rous. 'You will be fed on the plane.'

As Greavsie pointed out, we players would not be 'dining on the plane'. Nor would we be even 'having a meal on the plane'. We were to be 'fed', as if we were little more than workhorses or donkeys.

I was left to ruminate: while I and others had worked tirelessly to change the lot of the professional footballer in our successful campaign to scrap the slavery contract and maximum wage, what we had not, and could not, succeed in doing was change attitudes of those who governed the game.

Walter and the FA Selection Committee kept faith with Ron Springett for our final group game, a dour goalless draw with Bulgaria, which was enough to take England through to the knock-out stage where Brazil lay in wait.

Alan Peacock picked up an injury, so Gerry Hitchens was recalled against Brazil. That apart, I think Walter believed Gerry's experience of playing in Serie A would be better suited against Brazil than that of Alan Peacock, who had played his football in the Second

Division with Middlesbrough. I don't think it would have mattered who Walter and the selectors had chosen to lead the line against Brazil. The Brazilians proved too good for even a spirited England team.

The Brazil game was played in Vina del Mar and proved to be a good game of open, attacking football that went some way to restoring pride to what was turning out to be a disappointing tournament. Pele missed out due to injury but Didi, Zito and Amarildo were always a source of danger. The player who really caught my eye, however, was their brilliant winger, Garrincha. Time and again the player everyone knew as the 'Little Bird' chirped his own sweet song. He fluttered up and down our left flank, only to then leave England players in his wake with his explosive acceleration and amazing ball control. Given his size, the Little Bird was highly effective in the air and it was with a bullet header that he gave Brazil the lead after half an hour following a corner from Zagalo.

Hope sprung, if not eternal, then for a few minutes when Jimmy Greaves hit the post with a header and Gerry Hitchens seized upon the rebound to send both teams off to their half-time drink at level pegging. Minutes after the restart, however, Brazil took the lead in spectacular fashion, and then again, minutes from time, Garrincha sent another viciously swerving shot that swung like a Formula One car cornering before its path was suddenly blocked by the top right-hand corner of the net.

I felt there was no disgrace in England's 3–1 defeat. Had we avoided Brazil we might well have reached the final itself, but it was not to be. Brazil proved far and away the best team in that World Cup and justice was done when they became the first country to retain the trophy by beating Czechoslovakia 3–1 in the final, a fine achievement considering they had been without the injured Pele.

At the time, the *Sunday People*, as it was then known, ran a football gossip column containing supposed news of which club was interested in whatever player. In July, at the very bottom of the column there was a sentence that read, 'Arsenal, looking to sign a top class keeper, are interested in Sheffield United's England international, Alan Hodgkinson.' That was all it said. Whether there was any truth in this, I don't know. I personally didn't hear a thing about a possible move to Arsenal. That said, had there been any concrete interest from Arsenal I don't think I would have left Sheffield United. True, should such a move have occurred, I would have been on a lot more money, but although we were not well paid as far as First Division wages went, I was very happy at Sheffield United, I felt we had a better team than Arsenal, and certainly our final league place was testimony to this belief. I also felt United's prospects for the future were better than those of Arsenal.

The 1962–63 season got underway in not the best fashion for Sheffield United. We lost our opening game 2–1 at Nottingham Forest, only to bounce back to record successive victories against Fulham (2–0) and reigning champions Ipswich Town (2–1). From those balmy days of August we continued to chip away at the points. Come October, when we faced Sheffield Wednesday at Bramall Lane in the first derby of the season, we were handily placed in seventh position in Division One, in which Wolves and Everton were setting the pace and the two Manchester clubs were uncharacteristically occupying bottom four positions.

'Two households, both alike in dignity…from ancient grudge break to new mutiny'

Romeo and Juliet

Of the thirty-four professional players on the books of Sheffield United, twenty-one were from Sheffield or the surrounding area. Sheffield Wednesday had thirty-six professionals, of which twenty-seven were from either Sheffield or South Yorkshire. The number of locally born players on the books was typical of just about every club at the time. Not only did the number of players indigenous to the area cement the identity of a club, it imbued players with a true and devoted sense of loyalty. It also made for cracking, truly passionate derby matches.

Players always want to win a derby match for their supporters; they know how much it means to the supporters of the club to 'put one over' on the local rivals. It is a feeling that is intensified when the player comes from the town or city himself. There is a 'do or die' attitude for local players in the white-hot atmosphere of a derby. I had played in quite a few Sheffield derbies by now with mixed results. Should United lose, I would stagger off the pitch like a defeated soldier staggers from the field of battle. A feeling of melancholy would stay with me for days. On those occasions when we were comfortably beating Wednesday with minutes of the match remaining, it was as if I was watching an autopsy on a man who was still alive.

Finally, 6 October 1962 dawned, and before our game against Wednesday the dressing room was unusually quiet. Tension hung in the air as players donned their strips. Uncharacteristically silent, Brian Richardson went through his pre-match ritual of lathering his legs with whiskey rather than liniment. As always the first to be changed, Cec Coldwell sat next to me staring blankly at the floor on which he repeatedly tapped the studs of his boots. Gerry Summers sat reading the match-day programme.

'Listen to this,' Gerry suddenly blurted and proceeded to read from the programme. 'We are fortunate to possess so capable and so distinguished a defence in which, last but not least, is Alan Hodgkinson,' Gerry read. 'Some of Alan's saves last week at West Ham were out of this world. His brilliance makes it necessary for Ron Springett to be on his toes every time he turns out for England. We are indeed fortunate to possess a goalkeeper of such supreme quality as Alan, whose performances this season have been, as they have in the past – absolutely top class... I see you've been writing the programme notes again, Hodgey.'

It was just what we needed. Every player burst out laughing and the tense atmosphere disappeared into the ether. For any game, in particular a local derby where passions run so high, it is essential for players to take to the field with the right mental attitude and frame of mind. By 'right', I mean one has to achieve that delicate balance between being really up for battle but not too tense or anxious, which leads to a player being impetuous and hot-headed. Gerry Summers was great at sensing when the atmosphere in the dressing room was too tense and would take it upon himself to act as a bit of a safety valve. You need players like Gerry; his importance to our success was not only what he did on the pitch, he also calmed us down and, when the occasion merited, got us going.

With 48,000 fans packed inside Bramall Lane the atmosphere was more than simply frenzied, it was pandemonium bordering on bedlam. Every player wanted to win that first challenge and as the tackles flew there was more than a measure of sedition about the play. Passes were hurried, possession lost, regained, only to be lost again. The Wednesday fans were in uproar when Graham Shaw dumped Derek Wilkinson on his backside, only for United fans to follow suit when Wilkinson left a leg dangling when challenging Graham for the ball a minute later. As both players squared up to one another, the referee, Mr Bullough from Bolton, stepped in between them like a boxing referee between two pugilists ready to carry on after the bell had sounded.

Throughout the opening phase we were committed to attacking Wednesday. With Gerry Summers orchestrating proceedings, Keith Kettleborough jinking with body-swerve and changing rhythms in midfield, and Brian Richardson to support him like some tireless dreadnought, our forwards were prodded and persuaded into unceasing action. So much so, I probably touched the ball no more than three times in the first twenty minutes. Young Barry Hartle was getting through a tremendous amount of work on our left-hand side. On the other flank, Len Allchurch was playing exquisite balls into our opponents' penalty box which their defence dealt with in increasing anxiety. As we laid siege to Ron Springett's goal there was a solid wall of noise and I felt it only a matter of time before the goals tumbled out. We were pummelling Wednesday. There was only one team in it. You will have seen games like this, so you will know what happened. Having been penned into their half for over twenty minutes, Wednesday broke away and scored.

Wednesday had bought David 'Bronco' Layne from Bradford City, where he had scored thirty-six goals the previous season. His nickname came from a character in a popular TV western of the time, but 'Bronco' Layne was Sheffield born and bred, and had joined Bradford City via Rotherham United. He was a very mobile centre-forward, a workhorse with an eye for goal. Peter Swan intercepted a low cross from Len Allchurch, played the ball to Tony Kay, who hit a long ball down our left flank which was latched onto by Derek Wilkinson. As we about-turned and frantically tried to get back to provide cover, Wilkinson made good ground and hit a raking ball that Layne met on the edge of the penalty area and which the striker dispatched past me with some aplomb. I had come off my line and was beyond my penalty spot, upright on my feet, making myself big, which is what a goalkeeper must do in such a circumstance. Layne only needed two touches, one to get the ball under control, the second to drive it low and hard into my bottom right-hand corner.

Having turned the game upside down, Wednesday all but burst every vein to protect their advantage. We laid siege to Ron Springett's goal. Gerry Summers was an inspiration in midfield; 'Doc' Pace, Billy Hodgson and Len Allchurch threatened danger every time Gerry and Keith Kettleborough reached them with pin-point passes. The match quivered on a hair-spring. But Wednesday, as so often over the years, refused to wilt. Minutes before half-time as we buzzed about their penalty area, Peter Swan intercepted a pass from Barry Hartle and sent an 'ale-house' ball hurtling through the air towards the halfway line. As the ball completed its parabola, Layne cushioned it on his chest, laid it wide to the oncoming Tony Kay, who in turn switched play out to the left where the speedy Eddie Holliday had made ground. Holliday spun past Cec Codwell and sprinted forward in such a straight line it appeared he had been released from the traps. Just when it looked like Holliday might be living up to his name and heading off on one, he turned inside. Joe Shaw had been drawn across to combat Holliday, and sensing an opening the Wednesday winger whipped a cross over to my far post. I turned, sprinted but had not enough time to make up the ground. 'Bronco' Layne rose, headed the ball firmly down and past my despairing dive. The disgruntled murmuring of the United fans packed like fags in a packet behind my goal was palpable.

I couldn't believe the score-line as I sat in the dressing room at half-time. For much of the first half, surge after surge of attacks had beaten down the Wednesday defence like waves crashing against a rock. Not only did we have nothing to show in the way of goals for our almost continuous pressure, we were two goals down.

John Harris was unperturbed as ever. He told Barry Hartle he had been holding the ball for too long and that he had to release early for 'Doc' Pace.

'Earlier the better and, if there's nothing on, run at Megson. No defender likes a whippet like you running at him. Get into that box, push the ball past him and go, son.'

John told us to keep playing the way we had been. 'Keep at it,' he told us, 'stick to the plan, keep your shape, a goal will come. Then we'll see what they're made of.'

John then turned his attention to Derek 'Doc' Pace.

'Doc, are you Springett's greatest admirer? You spent the half watching him collect crosses. Get in there! Don't let him come and collect...whack him. He's too good to crumble but clatter him and the next time he goes up he'll have one eye open for you, expecting to be hit. Make it tough for him to catch. He'll punch, and when he does, I want Gerry and Keith just outside that box to pick up those pieces. Now let's get out there and give our supporters something to crow about, because if we don't, it won't be crows, it'll be vultures settling around this ground. You can do it, lads, so go out there and be the team I know you are.'

John concluded by telling Brian Richardson to play deeper in support of Joe Shaw, who had been exposed when Wednesday broke, and called for Joe to stick like glue to 'Bronco' Layne.

'He (Layne) can take a chance all right,' said John, 'but who couldn't with the space he's been enjoying? He's been in more space than Flash Gordon. Get up him, Joe, stay up him, and make sure there ain't yardage between you and Brian (Richardson).'

Minutes after the re-start Tony Kay played the ball to the feet of 'Bronco' Layne. I noticed Joe Shaw gaining a head of steam and making a bee-line for Layne. Joe was looking in the direction of Layne, but his eyes seemed transfixed on some point in the distance beyond the Wednesday player's shoulders. The closer Joe came to Layne, the faster he ran and the more transfixed his eyes became until they eventually bulged from his head like golf balls. When Joe was some two yards from Layne, he took off. Airborne, his right leg jutted forward like Lancelot's lance. As he completed his descent Joe emitted an audible grunt through gritted teeth before his right leg made contact with first the ball then various parts of Layne's anatomy. In TV cartoons, whenever there is a fight, it is depicted by swirling blurs of arms and legs. The immediate effect of Joe's tackle was much the same. 'Bronco' rose into the air as if he was on a highboard and diving into some distant pool below, only there was not a modicum of grace about his movement. Legs splayed behind him, 'Bronco' plummeted forward and carved out his personal niche on the pitch with his chin.

Joe played the ball first but followed through. I had never seen a tackle like it. Such was the force behind Joe's challenge, the ball shot from under 'Bronco' and was still rising when it parted the crowd in the main stand paddock, some twenty yards away, like Moses did the Red Sea. As one the crowd gasped, and this was followed by brief, collective nervous laughter. From the crowd's reaction, two things were obvious to me. One, they too had never seen a tackle like it. Two, they were thanking their lucky stars they weren't on the end of it. Joe's tackle quelled Layne for the rest of the game and set the tone for the remainder. Boadicea might well have been on parade with the knives on her chariot wheels, as some of the football that passed was as raw as uncooked meat. Both sets of supporters, of course, loved it.

Minutes later, Barry Hartle did what John Harris had told him to do. Having received the ball from Gerry Summers, he took to his toes, swept past Don Megson and cut into the Wednesday penalty area. Don was in hot pursuit, lunged at Hartle and made contact with the ball, though which one of Hartle's it was I was too far away to tell. Barry went down and Mr Bullough's right index finger was immediately drawn like a magnet to the penalty spot.

With an army of photographers having positioned themselves behind Springett's goal like a row of seagulls on a harbour wall, Graham Shaw stepped up to take the spot-kick. Amidst suspension bridge tension, Graham remained as cool as an Arctic Roll. He placed the ball on the penalty spot, took five steps back, four forward and, with some aplomb, planted the ball in the bottom right-hand corner. Bramall Lane erupted – the vast majority of it at any rate.

To their credit, Wednesday wouldn't lie down and far from being rattled, proceeded to have their best spell of the game. I had to be on my guard to save from Colin Dobson and, minutes later, was relieved to hold a snapshot on the turn from Derek Wilkinson. Having repelled Wednesday's riposte, we went on the attack again. The thermometer was doing a war dance. With minutes remaining Len Allchurch shot a glorious cross into the Wednesday penalty area to a point around the penalty spot. 'Doc' Pace had timed his run to perfection. Facing Allchurch out on the right, 'Doc' jerked his head so it was in line with his shoulders and deftly flicked the ball beyond Ron Springett and into the far corner of the net. The Blades fans erupted like a volcano and the roof of the stands almost took off in the pandemonium.

Two teams had fashioned a derby match of heroic phases, one not to be forgotten in a month of Sundays. There was no breath left in anyone as the players left the scarred field arm-in-arm. I think we all knew we had done something of which to be proud. I found Ron Springett and as we walked off the pitch clutching our caps and gloves in one hand and, with our other hand, each other, photographers walked backwards before us to capture the moment for posterity. I still occasionally see that photograph on websites or in magazines accompanying articles about what they now, with not a little irony, refer to as 'steel-city derbies'. When seeing that photograph of drained and exhausted Ron Springett and myself, I am forever reminded of what was a truly classic and exhilarating derby.

There have been tremendous Sheffield derbies since, as there had been before, but few to equal the one of October 1962 when so many local players were involved. The game was attended by the French Ambassador who was visiting Sheffield on some trade mission concerning the steel industry. As His Excellency admitted to the *Sheffield Star*, he didn't know much about football, but added, 'I had never heard of a Sheffield derby, but now, having seen such a game, if that is what the British call sport, God help us should they ever go to war.'

On 21 December we travelled to Ipswich Town, only to return empty-handed following a single-goal defeat. We were still handily placed in sixth position in Division One, which I considered no mean achievement for a team that was considered to possess no star players. Our strength was, as I have indicated, the fact that we were very much a team. The whole was greater than the sum of its parts.

I was looking forward to our festive programme. We were due to play a double-header against Manchester City, who were propping up Division One and looking odds-on for relegation. The Ipswich result apart, we had been playing well and I was confident of a maximum return of points from our game at City on Boxing Day and the return at Bramall Lane three days later. Four points would cement our position as a top six team and keep us in touch with

Everton, who were making ground at the top of the division. Should we achieve a double against Manchester City, we were set fair for a sequence of good results as, Wolves apart, we were scheduled for a run of games against teams in the lower half of the table. A consistent run of good results would not only further promote confidence, it would keep us in with a shout for the title. Little did I know, following our game against Ipswich on 21 December, Sheffield United would play just two league matches in the following ten weeks.

The day before Christmas Eve I was driving to the training ground and thinking to myself, 'The past two Christmases have been white Christmases; chances are, this year won't be.' Later that day, I was home with Brenda and baby Karen, placing presents under the Christmas tree, when I happened to look out of the window towards the back garden.

'Brenda, come and look. It's snowing,' I called out. 'Looks like it might be a white Christmas after all.'

As understatements go, it was a humdinger. Not only did it prove to be a white Christmas, it also proved to be a white New Year, a white January and, much to the despair of the nation, a white February too.

When the snow first fell, it was picturesque and romantic. The first snow fell like snow in an Andy Williams Christmas Special and continued to fall, throughout Christmas Eve and into Christmas Day. I managed to get in for training on Christmas morning, when we were told the game at Manchester City had been postponed and we could all go home and enjoy Christmas Day with our families. We required no second telling. The players' cars left the training ground car park like pioneers' covered wagons stampeding to get the choice land in mid-west America.

I've always liked snow as long as it is not too disruptive to life. You go to bed in one type of world and wake up in another. I had never, however, seen snow like this before. It snowed for days on end. There would be a day's respite, then it would snow again. The temperature plummeted. For a few days it would be too cold for snow. Then, the temperature would rise to a few degrees below freezing and it would snow again. This pattern of weather continued during the festive period, into the New Year and, seemingly, endlessly as the new year dragged itself into March.

The roads and streets of Sheffield were silent. The snow came swirling down in great flurries, snow fell on snow. The steps leading up to Sheffield Cathedral became a blanched slope. Huge pointed icicles like those described in a novel by Tolstoy hung from the guttering of houses, shops and factories. The biting wind blew the iced branches of trees and swept them back and forth until they rang like peals of bells. Car tyres and footsteps moved cautiously and silently down the white-walled streets. Buses struggled up the many hills of the city, their tyres wrapped in metal chains to aid their ascent and descent. No home possessed central heating, houses were coal-fired and freezing, numbingly cold. Hoarfrost turned into hard frost. The snow and iced air frosted the windows, chilled front rooms, perished parlours, turned bedrooms into iceboxes and domestic water pipes into solid strands of lead and copper. Many people couldn't use their own loos because the water in toilet cisterns and bowls froze solid. It was not only the countryside but cities too that were dogged by drifts. I awoke one Saturday morning in early January to find I couldn't open the front door due to a six-foot bank of snow which had drifted against the front of our house during a snowstorm in the night.

It was the same all over the United Kingdom. Birmingham became the Baltic, Cirencester turned into Siberia, Cannock into Canada, Southampton the South Pole, Northampton the North Pole; Glasgow was glaciated, Pershore perished and Sheerness shivered. The only sun to be found was in the name of Sunderland. It was, we were told, an even worse winter than the previously record-breaking winter of 1947 which, conversely, was followed by one of the driest and hottest summers on record. The press dubbed the winter of 1962–63 the 'Big Freeze'.

The 'Big Freeze' played havoc with football and sporting fixtures. Only three third-round FA Cup ties out of 32 went ahead on the day they were scheduled. Fourteen of these ties were postponed ten times or more. Having drawn in the FA Cup on 3 January, Blackburn Rovers and Middlesbrough had to wait until 11 March before resuming their third-round tie. On one Saturday in January only four matches took place in England, and only five on 2 February. The following Saturday seven games were staged in England but the entire Scottish programme was wiped out.

Having beaten Spurs 1–0 on 8 December, Bolton Wanderers did not play another game until the end of February. Bolton announced in that time they had to pay out £10,000 in wages and costs without a single penny coming in, they being almost totally reliant, as was every club, on gate revenue. The Bolton directors had to dip into their pockets on a weekly basis to meet the wage bill. Armies of volunteers would clear snow from pitches only for more snow to fall again. Oldham Athletic's Boundary Park pitch was, at one point, under four feet of snow. Two feet of snow fell on Stoke City's Victoria Ground in the space of twenty-four hours.

John Harris had the players help clear snow off the Bramall Lane pitch on several occasions, only for our efforts to stage a game to be frustrated because the pitch was frozen solid underneath. Clubs came up with all manner of ideas to try and beat the 'Big Freeze'. Chelsea hired a tar burner in an attempt to defrost their Stamford Bridge pitch, but it proved futile. Army flame-throwers were used on Blackpool's Bloomfield Road pitch. Leicester City hired a hot-air tent. Birmingham City hired a snow-clearing tractor from Scandinavia, while Wrexham shovelled 80 tons of sand onto the Racecourse Ground. The ice was so thick and permanent at The Shay, home of Halifax Town, that in a desperate attempt to generate some income the club opened it as an ice rink on Saturdays and hundreds of people came to skate on it. The clubs, however, were fighting a losing battle, and the season was extended until the end of May, the final game taking place at Workington Town on 1 June.

The pools companies lost thousands of pounds as week after week the coupons were declared void. To stem the losses the companies united to create the Pools Panel to predict the 'results' of postponed matches, as they do today. When the Pools Panel first sat and passed judgement, the results were the subject of much interest in the press and on TV and radio. One newspaper in Scotland, the *Forfar Dispatch*, actually ran reports of Forfar Athletic games based on the result given by the Pools Panel.

One humorous story concerning the Pools Panel results took place at Chelsea, where Tommy Docherty was the manager. One Friday, the Chelsea player, Frank Upton, came into Tommy's office brandishing his pay packet containing his wage from the previous week.

'You've paid me short in my wages, boss,' said Frank, tongue in cheek.

'Short? How come?' asked the 'Doc'.

'The Pools Panel put us down for a win last Saturday, I haven't received my win bonus.'

'You don't qualify,' said the Doc. 'I didn't pick you.'

Sheffield United played two matches in a little over ten weeks. In mid-January we were involved in a goalless draw against Wolves at Molineux; a month later, we lost 2–0 against West Ham United. In March, the severe winter weather loosened its grip and with the thaw came a hectic period of matches. Sheffield United were involved in nine games in four weeks, three of these being in the FA Cup. Having put paid to Bolton Wanderers and Port Vale we went out of the competition, losing 1–0 at Southampton. Two days later we were back on League duty enjoying a single-goal victory at Birmingham City and, three days after that, played out a goalless draw against Leicester. Games were coming thick and fast as every club played 'catchy up'.

In April we somehow managed to play eight games in less than four weeks. As hectic as our schedule was, we lost but one match in twelve, which included a double at the expense of Manchester City. When our season finally drew to a close in mid-May with a 3–1 defeat by our fierce rivals Sheffield Wednesday, the players were exhausted.

We enjoyed a top ten finish and, but for a margin of a couple of goals, could have finished eighth as Liverpool, Nottingham Forest and ourselves all finished on 44 points. We had established ouselves as a First Division team, a pretty decent one at that. As I have been at pains to say, we were very much a team, working hard and tirelessly for one another, giving our all, for each other and, of course, for the club and its supporters. In my heart of hearts, however, I knew that a team which had not changed its defence in some four years and, over three years, had added just one player via the transfer market, was a team that would not progress much further than our current standing. Today, with the money generated by Premiership membership, that would be good enough for most clubs. Success in the early sixties, however, was gauged by silverware, and, our trophy room carpet was not well trodden.

New players freshen up a team, they provide the competition needed to ensure players always play to their optimum. Sheffield United was the only First Division club not to have bought a player in 1962–63, let alone not to have purchased one in nigh on three years. The club's philosophy was to rely on its excellent youth policy, which was beginning to produce a number of real gems, Barry Hartle being but one. Young players, however, are notoriously inconsistent. They will be on fire one game, anonymous the next. A good team, such as Sheffield United were at the time, can 'carry' one or two youngsters, but I was aware our team was in danger of growing old together, which would mean an influx of youngsters coming into the side. True, all this was some way off as yet, but I did have such thoughts at the time. I was thinking ahead and, somewhat to my concern, it appeared to me the club's directors were not as forward thinking. I knew we'd be all right the following season and, in all probability, for the season after that, but if the current policy were to continue, what then?

As if to compound my view that at least a little investment in the transfer market would have been wise and made a difference to our final League placing, big-spending Everton clinched the title ahead of Spurs. Everton had spent heavily on quality recruits such as goalkeeper Gordon West (from Blackpool), Alex Young (from Hearts), Roy Vernon (from Blackburn Rovers), Jimmy Gabriel (from Dundee), Denis Stevens (from Bolton), Tony Kay (£60,000 from Sheffield Wednesday) and Alex Scott (from Rangers). Those players cost Everton in excess of £250,000, which was an astronomical sum for an English club back then. The press dubbed Everton 'the cheque-book champions'. In nigh on three seasons, Sheffield United's outlay on transfers was nigh on zero. During an end-of-season meeting between us players and Dick Wragg, United's Football Committee Chairman, Joe Shaw mentioned this total lack of investment in new players.

'Well, given no other club has the sort of money Everton have splashed on players, what you lads have to remember is, Everton may have won the title this season, but money doesn't guarantee success.'

'No, Mr Chairman, it doesn't,' I said. 'But in football, you never achieve success without it.'

On the international front, England was looking to the future, four years into the future to be exact, hoping for success in the 1966 World Cup Finals. After sixteen years as England manager, albeit not solely in charge of selection, the FA, as they so deftly put it, 'decided to release Mr Winterbottom of his duties as England manager'. The press conference announcement was delivered by an FA mandarin in a voice as mournful as the dying light in the west. You would have thought a senior member of the royal family had died, such was the morose tone of the announcement. The phrase, 'decided to release Mr Winterbottom of his duties', came across to me as if Walter had been relieved of care the way a terminally injured horse at the Grand National may be 'put out of its misery'. In a way, Walter had been relieved of misery. He would no longer have to deal with the Old Etonian hierarchy at the FA, most of whom appeared to me to have been educated beyond their intelligence.

Walter's final game in charge of England was against Wales at Wembley in November 1962, in which my Sheffield United team-mate Graham Shaw replaced the injured Ray Wilson at left-back. The boys did him proud, scoring four times without reply. There can't be many managers who have been relieved of their duties following a 4–0 win and, to my mind, it was a fitting denouement to Walter's tenure as England supremo.

The squad had chipped in to buy Walter a memento, more a token of thanks and gratitude if anything. Immediately following the victory over Wales, the squad gathered in the dressing room and, on behalf of us all, Jimmy Armfield presented Walter with an inscribed set of cut-glass crystal goblets and a silver salver. We had also bought a case of champagne; Ron Flowers and Jimmy Greaves did the honours and we sang 'For He's a Jolly Good Fellow' along with a toast from Jimmy Armfield to 'Walter Winterbottom, Master Manager'. Walter was deeply moved and thanked us all, not simply for the presentation but for our loyalty and contributions over the years. I was pleased we had clubbed together to buy Walter a token of our appreciation; after sixteen years as England manager (during which time he had also been in charge of the Under-23 team and ran the FA Coaching School), the FA saw fit to buy him nothing.

For the vast majority of his tenure as England manager, Walter Winterbottom was expected to manage our national football team at a time when footballers were treated like slaves, the irony being, the most shackled of them all was Walter himself. Throughout the undignified circus that followed the announcement of his departure, Walter had remained dignified and gentlemanly. It was the mark of the man.

The sports press, of course, had been in a frenzy as to who Walter's successor might be. Multitudinous tongues, like the whispering leaves of a stirred Aspen, bandied several names, the one most mentioned being that of the Burnley captain, Jimmy Adamson, who had been Walter's assistant during the Chile World Cup. The press were not wrong. The job of England manager, however, is not like Mount Olympus, wholly clear and free of clouds. Without making it public, the FA offered the job to Jimmy Adamson but he turned it down, preferring to carry on with his playing career. There was no press conference about the fact Jimmy had turned down the England job, though word spread throughout football that Jimmy had said 'Thanks but no thanks'. Privately the FA were not so much left with egg on their face as having had their cheeks and chests splattered with yolk. As much as I liked Jimmy Adamson, I am glad he didn't become England manager. Jimmy would have hated it because he was too nice a guy. England needed someone who was a master tactician – they talk about being a coach of an international team but, really, there is precious little coaching involved – someone thick-skinned who could handle the press et al, someone who would not make a social faux pas at the cocktail receptions, someone top players respected. Step up, Alf Ramsey of Ipswich Town.

When looking to appoint a new England manager, the FA never goes for someone who is connected with one of the most successful clubs of the day, the exception being Don Revie from Leeds United. True, Ipswich had been League Champions the previous season, but in 1962–63 they were a bottom six club for most of the season and eventually escaped relegation by just four points. It is also amazing to think that a club of the relatively modest stature of Ipswich Town has, in its time, provided two England managers, the other, of course, being Bobby Robson. Manchester United, on the other hand, has never provided an England manager.

Alf Ramsey was determined not to suffer the same treatment as Walter. One of the conditions Alf insisted upon as part of his acceptance of the role was that he, and he alone, would have sole control of the England team, including team selection. Not wishing to have a second rejection, the FA agreed to, as they put it, Alf's 'requests' (demands, as you and I would know them).

Alf's first game in charge was a European Championship qualifying game against France in Paris. I did not receive a telephone call from Alf. This told me my time with England was over. For the past two years I had been number two to Ron Springett, but those days were now over, not least because Ron wouldn't be featuring either. Alf Ramsey's first game in charge saw England lose 5–2 against France in Paris. Uncharacteristically, Ron had something of a personal nightmare against France and Gordon Banks succeeded him, although, as had been the case with me, Ron was to remain a part of the England squad for a number of years – including the 1966 World Cup Finals. Whilst I had been a member of the England squad for some five years without being selected for as much as friendly international against Luxembourg, Ron, however, would play another three internationals when injury prevented Banksy from playing.

My overall reaction to the realisation that my days as an England player were over was one of pragmatism. As I have said, I had been a member of the squad for some five years without playing, so my disappointment was tempered by the notion I wasn't missing out on too much. For me, England had been a great honour, my inclusion in the squad had been the icing on the cake. I wasn't sad because my time with England was over, I was happy because it had happened.

My priority now, as it had always been, was helping Sheffield United develop as a highly rated First Division team. Sometime around the end of 1962–63, Joe Shaw and I gave an interview to a reporter from the *Yorkshire Post* on that very subject and, at one point, were asked how our experience might shape our respective futures. It was not the sort of question we were normally asked by reporters.

'I hope to carry on for another couple of seasons,' said Joe, 'after that, coaching, hopefully, at Sheffield United. I'm coming up to 650 games, I'd like to think in that time I've learned a few things that will be of benefit to younger players.'

'Well, you certainly have the experience and you've always had good judgement,' said the reporter.

'Yes, well, in football, as in life, good judgement comes from experience,' said Joe, 'the downside being, in football, experience invariably comes from bad judgement.'

Rather than asking me a question, the reporter simply turned and looked towards me with a smile that seemed to indicate he wanted me to continue Joe's line of answer.

'Joe's right,' I said, 'and you know how it is in football. If it's good it prompts a barrage of insipid superlatives, if it's bad... it's experience.'

The reporter laughed aloud, slapped a hand on his knee and scribbled my response down in his notebook. I felt his laugh was not so much because he thought my reply particularly witty or poignant; rather, I'd fulfilled his wish to carry on and offer some sort of a punch-line to Joe's line of response. It was clever stuff, not from me or Joe, but on the part of the reporter, who came across as someone who was not simply good at interviewing but also at getting a good response from the interviewee.

When the interview was over, the reporter told us it had been a delight to interview Joe and myself, and our comments were such, he believed it would make a really good, thought-provoking piece for his newspaper. We, in turn, thanked him.

'You asked the sort of questions which made us offer a thoughtful response,' I told him. 'You'll go far.'

It was the first time I'd met Michael Parkinson.

| CHAPTER EIGHT |

'It is not in the stars to hold our destiny
but in ourselves.'

Julius Caesar

'The League Leaders! Yes, that's Sheffield United, and perhaps you will forgive us if we push out our chests just a little further and say that we deserve to be there. Memories have to be long to recall the last occasion on which we occupied this exalted position and we may be open to correction but it is believed to have been in 1925.'

So read the opening lines of the Sheffield United match programme for our game against Arsenal on 2 November 1963. Our season had begun modestly enough, a draw at Blackpool having been followed by a single-goal home defeat at the hands of Blackburn Rovers and a 1–1 draw with Chelsea, again at Bramall Lane. This we turned into three points from a possible eight by securing a 2–2 in the return with Blackburn. Hardly the sort of form to have the football writers and our supporters talking in terms of United being title contenders but, as 1963–64 unfolded, it was a case of dog-eat-dog in the First Division. Bolton Wanderers and Ipswich Town were already in danger of losing touch with other clubs and consequently Division One, but for the majority, no team had managed to put together a decent run of results. Following our faltering start, however, Sheffield United had proved the exception.

We entered the Arsenal game off the back of a fine 2–1 win at Burnley who themselves harboured title aspirations. The Burnley game proved something of a personal triumph for our left-winger

Ron Simpson who scored both goals, the first just eight seconds from the kick-off, which created a new club record for the quickest goal ever scored by a United player. Derek Pace was also continuing to add to his season's goal plunder, a highlight being, prior to our visit to Burnley, his hat-trick in a 3–0 win against Birmingham City. The margin of victory against Birmingham could have been even greater but for an excellent performance from their keeper, Colin Withers, who added to several outstanding saves when he dived to his right to hold onto a penalty from Len Allchurch. There's a little marker as to how football has changed over the years: how many times do you see a goalkeeper hold on to the ball when diving to save a penalty these days? Technique has changed in that respect, more of which later.

One match I readily recall of this period is our 3–3 draw with Tottenham Hotspur. As you may surmise from the score-line it was the sort of game the press described as being a 'fine advertisement for football', and so it was. Tottenham had flair, skill, dynamism and were noted throughout the land for playing expansive, entertaining football. They lived up to such a reputation when visiting Bramall Lane in early October, albeit our penchant for entertaining was also much in evidence. The fortunes of the game went to and fro like a pendulum. With us leading 3–2 and Blades at full throttle, Dave Mackay played the ball into the right-hand channel behind our back four. I took to my toes but he was there already – anticipation and perfectly timed runs being the mark of Jimmy Greaves, as was incisive and decisive finishing. Having darted into space, Jimmy swerved past me and slid the ball into my empty net as easily as a fish emits a bubble. At that very moment the cascade of noise was cut off.

The football writer Geoffrey Green said of Jimmy Greaves, 'He scores goal with all the fuss of someone closing the door of a Rolls Royce.' An apt description of a player who remains, to this day, English football's greatest goal-scorer.

The Arsenal game ended in a 2–2 draw and was memorable for the fact the visitors selected a young amateur to play in goal; Bob Wilson became the first amateur to play a League match for Arsenal since Dutchman Gerry Keiser in the 1930s.

The point earned against Arsenal and a subsequent two points gained from a 1–0 victory at Leicester City kept Sheffield United at the top of Division One ahead of such illustrious company as Manchester United, Spurs, Everton, Arsenal and Liverpool. On the relatively short journey back from Leicester, Brian Richardson remarked, 'Stay clear of injuries and I think we're going to be there or thereabouts.' Most agreed that, all being well, we had a very good chance of lifting the First Division title. In football, however, anything that can go wrong will go wrong – and at the worst possible moment.

When we travelled to lowly Bolton Wanderers in mid-November, our spirits and confidence were high. We had achieved pole position by playing the same seasoned and resolute defence, that of myself, Cec Coldwell, Brian Richardson, Joe Shaw and Gerry Summers. The only change that had been made had been an enforced one, Bernard Shaw coming in at left-back for the injured Graham Shaw. The rest of the team was also much the same as it had been in the previous four years. The only changes to this particular season were young Tony Wagstaff who had, since September, been preferred to Billy Hodgson for the number ten shirt, and Ron Simpson having regained his place on the left wing at the expense of Barry Hartle.

Bolton Wanderers were a tough, physical side but not the team that had won the FA Cup five years previously. They had my old England teammate Eddie Hopkinson in goal, the experienced Les Hartle at right-back, Warwick Rimmer at left-back, a clever and scheming inside-forward in Freddie Hill, Syd Farrimond, who would always do a job and well, and one of the best headers of a ball there has ever been in Wyn Davies. They also had some very promising youngsters, the pick of which were striker Francis Lee and an equally fleet-footed left-winger, Gordon Taylor. The former would go on to find fame with Manchester City; the latter would assume the chairmanship of the PFA.

The Bolton game was not in any way exciting. Both teams prodded and probed to no great effect, there was an inexplicable lacklustre feel to proceedings: the sort of game you might say had nil-nil written all over it. Minutes into the second half, Gordon Taylor played the ball into my penalty area. The ball deflected off Brian Richardson and was falling invitingly at the feet Wyn Davies when I instinctively flung myself towards Bolton's towering centre forward. It was at this moment that Freddie Hill and Joe Shaw thought it opportune to get in on the act. Boots flew, the ball cannoned into my chest and went I know not where, but not in my goal at any rate. Someone, again, I know not who, in attempting to kick the ball laid leather on the side of my head instead, whilst the studs of another boot made a passable impression of treading grapes on the fingers of my right hand.

'You all right, Hodgey?' said Joe's blurred face.

'Last night I dreamed I went to Manderley again.'

'Trainer!'

Ernest Jackson had just retired as trainer but his replacement, the ex-Sheffield United player Harry Latham, was quickly on the scene. Harry had been given the job of first-team trainer as he had attended the recently introduced FA courses for trainers which taught new, more medically sound and exacting methods of treating injured players. Harry duly arrived exuding an air of calm and complete control.

'First thing we do… Joe…Cec…gently help him onto his feet.' Harry instructed.

Joe and Cec gingerly helped me up.

'Okay, stand back, lads, to give him air. But I want you, Joe, to place the palm of a hand across his lower vertebrae to steady him. That's his lower back.'

Joe did as he was instructed whilst Harry delved into his medical bag.

Harry stepped forward, wafted a small tubular thermometer to and fro and, when he was happy he'd wafted it enough, stuck it in the corner of my mouth.

'Keep that in your mouth and look up, Hodgey.'

I looked up to the sky as Harry eyeballed my eyeballs for a few seconds. That done, he made with a 'Hmmm' sound as if processing the information through his newly acquired medical brain.

'My right hand is in a lot of pain, Harry,' I told him as best I could whilst balancing a thermometer in the corner my mouth like a fag.

'All in good time, Hodgey,' Harry said, removing the thermometer.

Harry studied the thermometer, made with the 'Hmmm' sound again and grunted.

'Just as I thought,' he said. 'My diagnosis is mild concussion. I shall treat this first, then look at your hand.'

Harry delved into his bag. From half a bladder of an old football he produced a large sponge dripping with ice-cold water and hit me straight across the face with it. He then waved a bottle of smelling salts under my nose and, that done, proceeded to slap me repeatedly across the cheeks with the palms of his hands.

'These FA courses for trainers are money well spent, Harry,' remarked Joe.

'Yeah, all these new-fangled ways of treating players, bloody marvellous what they can do nowadays,' quipped Cec.

I was still feeling groggy but now I felt physically sick. It was my hand, however, that was really bothering me. A pain shot from my right thumb and first finger up to my shoulder, calling in at my elbow along the way to scream blue murder.

Harry examined the digits of my right hand and told me to wiggle them. I couldn't.

'I think you might have broken your thumb and first finger,' Harry cautiously informed me.

There were no substitutes, of course, so having got me back on my feet and partially back to my senses, Harry proceeded to wrap my thumb, first finger and wrist together, which didn't stop the pain and I am not sure it afforded protection from further damage, but it had to do.

No sooner had Harry completed the running repairs than the firework display struck up again. I didn't feel much like watching. The pitch was wet and tacky but it looked very inviting for a lie down. So I did. As I lay there enjoying the cold, moist earth I heard Harry say, 'Joe, run over to the St John's lads and get them over here with the stretcher.' That sounded like a good idea. A stretcher sounded even more comfortable for a lie down than the tacky ground.

I came back to my senses in the away team dressing room. Harry told me Cec Coldwell had gone in goal. When the lads returned, I was told Bolton had popped one in and won 1–0. A perfect day out.

On our return to Sheffield I was taken to the Northern General for an X-ray.

'It's not as bad as first feared,' the doctor pronounced, holding my X-ray up to a light.

'Well, thank heavens for that,' I replied.

'Oh, the thumb is broken all right, in two places, but the first finger is only dislocated, no break there,' the doctor said, matter of factly.

'And there was I thinking it was going to be bad news.'

John Harris was not going to be speaking to me for some time.

As luck would have it, on the day I was injured at Bolton, Sheffield United's reserve keeper, Bob Widdowson, was also injured in a Central League match. John Harris's only other option was Barry Sheppard, a fifteen-year-old youth team goalkeeper. Des Thompson had left United but had yet to fix himself up with a club, so John Harris subsequently asked Des if he would return to Bramall Lane on a temporary basis.

It was a difficult time for Des to return to the fold. In the ensuing weeks, Cec Coldwell, Gerry Summers, Keith Kettleborough, Derek Pace and Len Allchurch also succumbed to injury at various times. A team that had hardly changed in four years was now being changed on a weekly basis, which didn't help Des. Gerry Summers' injury meant he was to play only a handful of games again that season. The injury to Keith Kettleborough was particularly unfortunate because John Harris had just sold Billy Hodgson to Leicester City for £15,000, and Billy could have assumed Keith's role of schemer as good as buns.

The disruption to the team had an immediate and devastating effect. It is not that the players who came into the side were not up to the job; our young centre-forward, Mick Jones, was to show such excellent form that Derek Pace was unable to regain his place, and John Docherty, Barry Hartle, Len Badger and Reg Matthewson were all capable of playing at the highest level – the problem was, after years of fielding more or less the same team, so many changes imposed over such a short period of time had an adverse effect on the way the team played.

I was out for nigh on two months and in that time Sheffield United failed to win a single game. When I returned to the fold in January for our FA Cup tie with Lincoln City, Sheffield United had not only been toppled from the top of Division One but had slipped down the table below title challengers Liverpool, Manchester United, Everton and Spurs. Things went from bad to worse and, after things had gone from bad to worse, to my great concern the cycle repeated itself. As the New Year progressed and more changes were effected to the team, our form continued to disappoint. Having disposed of Lincoln we then lost 4–0 at Swansea in the fourth round of the FA Cup, and that was immediately followed by a 6–1 defeat at champions elect, Liverpool. There was the odd high point, notably a fine 3–1 win at Arsenal and a thrilling 4–3 win over Wolves, but our sequence of results in the New Year told its own story. Having sat proudly at the top of Division One in mid-November, of our remaining 24 matches we won just seven. Sheffield United's hopes of winning the First Division title did not so much take a nose dive as plummet from a plane at some altitude without a parachute.

I was very disappointed and saddened with our final mid-table placing but adopted a pragmatic attitude. After all, if you were happy every day of your life you wouldn't be human, you'd be a game show host. To this day I believe Sheffield United had a really good opportunity to become champions in 1963–64. But for the sheer number of injuries I am sure we would have continued our fine from through to the business end of the season and, quite possibly, held off the challenges of Liverpool, Manchester United, Everton and Spurs. Champions, of course, must deal with injuries, as they are part and parcel of football. Having for so many years relied on experience to get us results, conversely, it was a lack of experience that proved our undoing.

In 1963–64 and in previous seasons, the likes of Liverpool, Manchester United, Chelsea and even Sheffield Wednesday had bought quality players for hefty fees and built strong squads. When faced with an injury crisis, the policy of Sheffield United was to call upon the fruits of its youth development programme, a highly laudable policy but one not conducive to winning titles. Players such as Mick Jones, Bernard Shaw, Len Badger, Reg Matthewson and Tony Wagstaff were extremely talented and all were destined to become top-class players. They had learned much from John Harris and the United coaching staff, but in football, as Sheffield United learned to their cost that season, players can learn much from being told but far more by finding out for themselves in games – and I say that as a coach myself.

Young players had to be blooded, however, for the inaudible foot of time was beginning to catch up on a number of Sheffield

United stalwarts. Derek Pace had lost a yard off his game and was suffering from a niggling ankle injury. Having found himself playing reserve team football due to the form of his replacement, Mick Jones, Derek joined Notts County the following season, where he scored 15 goals in 29 appearances before finding his troublesome ankle could not cope with the rigours of full-time football. Derek was subsequently persuaded to sign for Walsall, but made only four appearances before finally hanging up his boots for good. Len Allchurch had also come to the end of his career with Sheffield United. Len was only to feature in four matches the following season before joining Stockport County for what was a record fee of £10,000 for the Cheshire club. Len helped Stockport to the Fourth Division title in his second season at Edgely Park before, quite literally, enjoying a swansong by joining Swansea, the club with whom he had begun his career.

Cec Coldwell was to be a 'bit' player in forthcoming seasons, mostly acting as captain-cum-coach to our reserve team, where he played no small part in the development of Tony Currie and Alan Woodward. Like Joe Shaw and, subsequently, Graham Shaw and yours truly, Cec was another player with in excess of 600 games for Sheffield United. He had been signed from local club Norton Woodseats for the princely fee of £10 and was to give nigh on forty years' loyal service to Sheffield United as player, coach and, twice, as caretaker manager. Having devoted the best part of his life to Sheffield United he left the club in 1979 to run a newsagents in Sheffield, then in Cheadle Hulme in Cheshire. Cec died in 2008 at the age of 79. The term 'club legend' is often bandied about now with little regard to its true significance and meaning. Cec Coldwell, however, shall, in every sense of the phrase, always be a true legend of Sheffield United.

Gerry Summers departed for Hull City, from where he returned to his native West Midlands by signing for Walsall. Gerry was a cerebral player, one who thought deeply and intelligently about the game, as was evidenced in the way he played it. Gerry became a successful coach and manager, most notably with Oxford United and Gillingham, the former of whom he managed for seven years, the latter for six-and-a-half. Crewe Alexandra apart, you will rarely, if ever, witness such long tenures of management among lower division clubs these days. I remain best of friends with Gerry, more of whom later, for I was to spend six happy and successful years with him as his right-hand man at Gillingham.

Another player to depart was left-winger Ron Simpson, who at the end of 1963–64 joined Carlisle United, where he was to enjoy his football for a couple of years with a club that was on the up before seeing out his playing days north of the border with Queen of the South.

Every team, even Arsène Wenger's great 'Arsenal Invincibles', or Alex Ferguson's triple-winning side of 1999 has, at most, a life expectancy of two years. Most great teams peak for just a year, as do those merely rated as good. Then a manager must make gradual changes. Sheffield United had been fortunate in that we had done relatively well for some four years. Okay, we hadn't won anything, but given the club had not signed a player of note in the transfer market in more or less the same period of time, I felt we had done well to establish ourselves as a top six side. As a team, however, we had passed the tipping moment and John Harris knew this. Hence he was to pin future hopes on one or two senior pros, of whom I was now considered to be one, and youth. Those youngsters were going to have to learn quickly if Sheffield United was to re-establish itself as a top six side. As John Harris once said to centre-forward Mick Jones, 'You must learn from your mistakes, lessons, as I call them, but, in this game it's imperative you also learn from the mistakes of others, because a footballer's life's too short to make them all yourself.'

Here is a vignette concerning one of our young players at the time, and one serving not only as testimony to how the game has changed but also as to how the attitude and awareness of young players was so different back in the 1960s. Len Badger was an England schoolboy, youth and Under-23 international who had made his first-team debut in 1962–63, and in 1963–64 he made seven appearances at right-back in place of Cec Coldwell. During his seven-match spell in the first team, a football reporter from the *Daily Mirror* approached young Len. The reporter told Len he would like to write an article about him for the *Mirror*, along the lines of 'Sheffield United's rising young star'.

'The fee for the article will be five guineas (£5.25p),' the reporter informed Len.

Len said such an article was fine by him, but that he would have to talk it over with his parents and would let the reporter know of their decision in a day or so.

A couple of days later, the *Mirror* reporter collared Len after training and asked if his parents had agreed to the article being written.

'My mum and dad would love to see an article about me in the *Mirror*,' Len informed him, 'but they say they can't afford the five guineas.'

There was still a place in the game for the loyal club servant who plied his trade for many years at reserve team level. We had such a pro at Bramall Lane in full-back Roy Ridge. As 1963–64 concluded Roy was told he was to have his contract extended, which meant 1964–65 would be Roy's twelfth season at the club, in which time he had made just ten appearances in the first team.

One amazing aspect to 1963–64 was the scores of the First Division fixtures played on Boxing Day. A total of 66 goals were scored in the ten First Division matches that day, and I remember listening in disbelief as the scores were read out on BBC radio's *Sports Report*. Due to the injury sustained in our game at Bolton, I missed Sheffield United's 3–3 draw at Nottingham Forest, seemingly an entertaining match but one that must have paled in comparison to many of the others that day. The rest of the results were as follows:

Blackpool	1–5	Chelsea
Burnley	6–1	Manchester United
Fulham	10–1	Ipswich Town
Leicester	2–0	Everton
Liverpool	6–1	Stoke City
Sheffield Wednesday	3–0	Bolton Wanderers
West Brom	4–4	Spurs
West Ham	2–8	Blackburn Rovers
Wolves	3–3	Aston Villa

I have earlier mentioned the great and eccentric Ipswich Town chairman, John Cobbold. Confronted by a reporter following his team's 10–1 defeat at Craven Cottage, he was asked, 'Do you agree Ipswich Town is now in a state of crisis?'

'Not at all,' replied Cobbold in his characteristically flamboyant fashion. 'A state of crisis at Ipswich Town would be the boardroom running out of gin.'

I mentioned earlier how rare it was for a team to win both home and away matches against the same opposition over the Christmas period. Two days later, Ipswich met Fulham in the return fixture at Portman Road and won 4–1; likewise, having lost 6–1 at Turf Moor, the following day Manchester United beat Burnley 5–0 at Old Trafford, whilst West Ham made amends for their 8–2 home defeat at the hands of Blackburn Rovers by winning 3–1 at Ewood Park, and Stoke City, hammered 6–1 at Anfield, triumphed 3–1 at home to Liverpool.

*   *   *

Football reflects society, an axiom that was particularly evident in 1964–65, when the decade that was to be dubbed the Swinging Sixties was truly underway. New fashions in clothes, and hairstyles, innovative British pop and rock music, new and more liberal mores, radical ideas in politics and writing, cutting-edge television programmes, the wider availability and affordability of consumer white goods, exciting new ideas in home styling – all those and more combined to irrevocably change British society.

It was a time of joyous and despairing licence. It was a crazy time – at times mad, at other times ugly, beautiful and licentious, but it tasted of the future. Young people were living for the moment, believing anything was possible. It was free, it was innovative, it was dangerous and... it was nothing like the life I was living. Nor, should I imagine, that of the vast majority of teenagers or people in their twenties.

Our second daughter, Paula, was born in 1965. With two children and the fact I earned my living as a professional footballer, the excesses of the swinging sixties passed me by. Many of the changes that took place in the game were small but, collectively, they gave indication of a game that was moving into another age. The style of strips changed. The V-neck short-sleeved shirts that had been de rigueur in the late fifties and early sixties went out of fashion. Clubs began to favour shirts with round collars and long sleeves as manufactured by Uwin and Bukta. Shorts were made of nylon and worn longer. The mantra was to have kit made as light as possible so as not to hamper speed. Socks made of spun nylon or Terylene were lighter. Boots were also much lighter, the low-cut Adidas 'Europa' boot with the trademark three white stripes became a common sight at every level of the game, as did the Puma Form-Strip, the boot which, according to the manufacturer, 'offers lightness and speed without loss of ruggedness'. Lighter shin-guards made of durable and tough plastic with a foam backing replaced those made of leather, whose padding was reinforced with strips of bamboo. Goalkeepers' gloves changed too. Though I preferred not to wear gloves, I bought my first pair of Adidas gloves, the fingers of which dimpled with black rubber nodules for extra grip. Players chewed Dextrosol glucose tablets, 99 per cent pure glucose which, according to the advertising, 'enables glucose to pass straight through your bloodstream with immediate energy to your muscles.' In training players were often to be seen in winter wearing Millington track-suits with ribbed waist and cuffs and their distinctive tapered legs, at the bottom of which was a band of elastic to slip under your foot so the tracksuit trouser always appeared shaped to your legs.

We kicked off 1964–65 at Spurs, which was always a ground I liked to visit as there was always a big match atmosphere. In those days when you came up the steps into what was a short tunnel, hanging on the tunnel wall above and behind you there was always a small banner which read 'Up The Spurs'. There were a number of architectural aspects to White Hart Lane which marked it out from other grounds. The press box was situated on the roof of the impressive East Stand, and on top of the press box was a copper cockerel perched on a ball. Jimmy Greaves once told me the cock-erel became the club motif because fighting cockerels used to wear spurs, as did Harry Hotspur.

It wasn't long before the cockerel on top of White Hart Lane's East Stand was crowing and, need it be said, it was Jimmy Greaves who opened the scoring in characteristic fashion. Latching on to a ball from Alan Mullery, Jimmy swept past me and stroked the ball into the net with all the nonchalance of a man dialling his own telephone number. Frank Saul later added a second to send the vast majority of the 46,000 crowd happily home to their hearths.

When you entered the dressing room after a game at Spurs, on a table in the centre of the room there would be tea, a crate of lemonade and a selection of sandwiches and snacks. Once you had tucked into those there was just enough time to join the Spurs lads for a quick drink in the players' lounge before boarding the coach that would take us to St Pancras and the early evening train back to Sheffield. Having played host to the opposition, many of the Spurs players would then pop across the road to the White Hart pub for a drink with football journalists and supporters. One can't imagine such a scenario ever happening these days, but players were more accessible to football writers and supporters back then and no one ever thought such a social gathering to be untoward. This is just another example of how the game has changed over the years. In the sixties, footballers were still 'working-class heroes'; what's more, when they went home they did so to homes in areas in which their supporters lived. After a game it was a case of the kings and pawns returning to the same box and, as a top-flight footballer, I was happy at that.

The following Wednesday night, we lost by a single goal at home to Stoke City. The portents were not good, but just when our supporters were beginning to think the club policy of pinning hopes on youth was folly, we suddenly clicked. Following what had been a pretty abject performance against Stoke City, we enjoyed an unbeaten run of seven matches, five of which resulted in victories with two drawn. After losing to Stoke we desperately needed a fillip and achieved it when we went to Hillsborough and beat Wednesday in the derby. Only five of United's old guard were on duty that day: myself, Graham Shaw, Brian Richardson, Joe Shaw and Keith Kettleborough. Whilst delighted to have won the derby, when I looked at our line-up in the match programme, I was reminded how much had changed in twelve months. Sheffield United was not so much a club in transition as one that had already entered a new era.

What was particularly encouraging about the victory over Sheffield Wednesday was the performance of our two young strikers, Mick Jones and Alan Birchenall – with the latter scoring in each half to give us a 2–0 victory and our first success of the season. I was excited by the pairing of Jones and Birchenall up front; though both young, they were tall and powerful strikers who caused opposing defences a lot of problems both on the ground and in the air. The Wednesday game seemed to be something of a turning point for them: not only did they really 'click' for the first time, their respective performances also saw them grow in confidence. The plan was to play the ball to them early and for them to play off each other. Mick Jones was particularly good at leading the line, and Birchy very good at getting in behind defenders and on the end of passes played through by Keith Kettleborough or Barry Hartle.

In late September a 3–1 win against Birmingham City in which Birchy netted twice and Mick Jones scored our other goal saw Sheffield United elevated to fourth place. 'Can this be maintained?' asked the *Sheffield Star*. I think you may be ahead of me here.

Following the Birmingham game a virus swept around Bramall Lane. Four days after beating Birmingham we travelled to Plymouth Argyle for a League Cup tie. John Harris counted his blessings there was no reserve game that night, as he had to leave behind fifteen players who were either ill or injured. Among those taken ill were Cec Coldwell, Graham and Joe Shaw, Brian Richardson, Keith Kettleborough and John Docherty. Ironically, having waited so long for a first-team opportunity, Roy Ridge was also taken ill and, disappointed at having missed his big chance, would subsequently soon depart on a 'free'. We travelled by coach to Plymouth and as I looked about the bus and saw fresh-faced youngsters such as Len Badger, Bernard Shaw, Tony Wagstaff, Ken Mallender, Reg Matthewson, Alan Woodward, Denis Finnigan and, of course, Birchenall and Jones, I felt as if I'd boarded a coach for a FA Youth Cup tie. It was a long trip to Plymouth and even longer journey back, seeing as we lost 2–1.

Only four victories were recorded from our next twenty League matches. We would play exceptionally well and win a game, such as Aston Villa 4–2, which would make me think we were about to turn the corner, only to then turn in a below-par performance in our next match.

Our double fixture at Christmas saw us play Manchester United. I began this book by recalling the goal from George Best by which Manchester United won the Boxing Day meeting at Bramall Lane. Two days later, we travelled to Old Trafford with bookies tipping the game as a 'home banker', but in fact we produced a very good performance to earn a point from a 1–1 draw. Again I thought the Old Trafford performance was the beginning of a turn in our fortunes but, when facing Sheffield Wednesday at home in our following game, we contrived to end up on the wrong end of a 3–2 score-line. Our League form was poor and the FA Cup provided our fans with little to cheer, as we exited in Round Four, beaten 2–0 at home by Aston Villa.

Following the Villa game we managed to put together a decent run, winning four and drawing two of our next six matches; it was a little run of form that, in the event, would save our bacon. That six-game run culminated in a superb 3–0 victory over Liverpool; there were eight games remaining, and we lost seven of those, the only respite being a drab goalless draw at Nottingham Forest. Had it not been for that run of six games in February and early March, we would have run out of road as far as the First Division was concerned. As it was we finished 1964–65 fourth from bottom in Division One, five points ahead of relegated Wolves, who joined basement club Birmingham City in availing themselves of the delights of Carlisle United, Bury and Coventry City the following season.

Our performances in 1964–65 had been wildly inconsistent. In October we had lost 4–0 at Blackburn Rovers; the following game we beat high-flying Arsenal 4–0, only to then lose 4–1 at Leeds United. Such pendulum form goes hand-in-hand with a team containing so many youngsters. By and large, Mick Jones and Alan Birchenall proved an exception. Though there were occasions when it seemed neither was on the pitch, they both hit double figures sharing twenty-nine League and Cup goals, which is an exceptional strike rate for a teenage pairing up front. Alan Woodward, was only 18 but had established himself on the right wing and chipped in with seven goals. Rather than being concerned about our future prospects, as many Blades seemed to be if the letters in the 'Green 'Un' were anything to go by, I harboured high hopes for a very rosy future. As the youngsters gained in experience, I felt the results would come. I sensed the most difficult season, one of considerable transition at the club, was now behind us and, from now on, each season would see continuous improvement. In football, as in life, the best way to predict the future is to create it, and I felt we possessed sufficient quality to do this.

No club had shown such fluctuating form. Our periods of success were interspersed with spells when nothing seemed to go right, the prime example being in the closing stages when, after those six matches without defeat, we took only one point from our last eight games, scoring just two goals and conceding seventeen. The run-in to the season was a period when we had also been denied the services of Joe Shaw due to injury. While both Ken Mallender and Denis Finnigan, who deputised for Joe, showed considerable promise, they lacked Joe's vast experience which had stood us in good stead for so many years. Given Mick Jones and Alan Birchenall had done well for us, we had only 50 goals to our credit, our lowest tally in memory and the lowest aggregate in the top two divisions.

Manchester United were crowned champions. We had lost to Matt Busby's team by a single piece of brilliance from George Best when playing them at Bramall Lane and had secured a well-deserved point at Old Trafford in the return. Liverpool had been soundly beaten, as had Arsenal (4–0), and that told me we had it in us to not only compete with but beat the best. Every footballer is born to win, but to be a winner you must plan to win, prepare to win, expect to win and play consistently well. It was the latter we were lacking. Football is a tough and unforgiving learning curve, and experience is what you gain by not having it when you need it.

Of course, one never stops learning in football. After sixty years in the game, I still learn every day. Mick Jones was nineteen, as was Alan Birchenall, even after a season in the First Division in which they had learned much, so I was prepared for them to continue to make mistakes. I had been in the game long enough to know that the experience you gain as a nineteen-year-old is useful for only as long as you are nineteen because when you are twenty you make twenty-year-old mistakes, and so it goes on. A professional footballer will make less mistakes as the years go by, but he will still make mistakes nonetheless, only different ones, because the game is organic, forever changing and developing and thus presenting you with new challenges to counter and problems to solve. If you are a good, quality pro you learn from experience not to repeat mistakes. In this regard, Crewe Alexandra's assistant manager, Neil Baker, holds to a tough maxim. Quite simply, if he finds he has to tell a player the same things three times, he gets rid of him, because that player isn't learning.

No sooner had 1964–65 ended than a meeting was called to inform us players of the details concerning our close-season tour. Burgeoning air traffic had contrived to make not only Europe but the world 'shrink'. Clubs were broadening their horizons in terms of where they travelled to for close-season tours. For the first time North America and Australasia became close-season destinations for many clubs. These tours to such continents were seen as 'spreading the gospel of football' and were usually sponsored by airlines who wanted to promote travel to such countries as Australia, Canada and Singapore. I was excited about our close-season tour because, rather than touring the continent, as Sheffield United had done in the past, we were off to Canada and New Zealand.

Players always enjoyed close-season tours. The football was played in a relatively relaxed atmosphere with the pressure off. There was also the novelty of playing against an unfamiliar opposition. If you have anything about you, you always learn from playing against foreign teams. You are invariably exposed to new techniques you might later incorporate in your own personal game. You are often exposed to new tactics, set-pieces or even different methods of training. Football apart, close-season tours also provided players with an opportunity to see another part of the world and, best of all, at the expense of the club.

Players like close-season tours and this one was to take us to parts of the world unbeknown to us. Canada and New Zealand suggested different cultures and customs tempered by Englishness, the sort of countries a footballer likes just fine. Besides which, Canada and New Zealand would make a welcome change from Holland and Belgium, which had been our regular destinations in past tours.

The players gathered with great anticipation in the players' lounge at Bramall Lane for a meeting presided over by John Harris and Mr Newton, the club secretary. Mr Newton outlined the travel arrangements, then John Harris took to the floor to offer details of the touring squad. Quite a few of the club's promising youngsters were to accompany us. The first jaw-dropper John Harris delivered was that the tour would involve us playing sixteen matches in little over four weeks.

'Bloody hell, boss,' intoned Cec Coldwell, 'that's a third of a season.'

I suddenly saw the reason for such a large touring squad. This was not a close-season tour, it was going to be an endurance test.

'So, who are we going to be playing against?' I asked.

'Blackpool for a start. They've signed up to tour Canada and New Zealand as well. We'll play one match in Canada, against them. Then we fly down to New Zealand.'

Canada appeared to me to be a long way to go to play a single game. I could only assume both clubs had been promised a hefty fee from someone in Canada for playing, otherwise why travel all that way for single match?

'So, that means we're playing fifteen games in New Zealand,' I said.

'Not quite. The tour ends with us flying home via Hong Kong where we'll play a Hong Kong Select XI,' said John.

'Okay, boss,' I said, 'so we're playing fourteen matches in New Zealand.'

'Correct,' confirmed John.

'Against who?'

'Good-quality opposition, so we will have to be on our toes.'

'This "good-quality opposition", do we know them?' I asked, pressing the issue.

'Yes, Alan, you know of them.'

It seemed hard work to get from him who we would be playing, but a little light was now being shed. It was far off and coming very slowly, and it was a very little light, about half a firefly's worth.

'Come on, boss, who exactly will we be playing?' asked Joe Shaw encouragingly.

'Well, Blackpool.'

We waited for John to continue. It would be an exaggeration to say we were all on tenterhooks but we did have a vested interest.

'And? Who else?' asked Joe.

John stood there looking a mite uncomfortable.

'Well, that's it. Blackpool,' John said rather sheepishly.

I was gobsmacked and so too were all my teammates.

'You're telling us, we're playing Blackpool fourteen times on the trot?' balked Joe.

'Fifteen,' I interjected, 'if you include the Canada game.'

'Yes, but it'll be all right. We'll mix and match the team. Keep it fresh,' John replied, looking somewhat relieved the cat was finally out of the bag.

I don't know for sure, but I should think Blackpool and ourselves created some sort of football record that summer – and a bizarre record at that – of playing against the same opposition for fifteen consecutive games. When the day of departure came, I had the sneaking feeling that we and the Blackpool lads would know all there was to know about each other come the end of the tour.

From what I saw of Canada, or, more to the point, Edmonton, I liked it. A vast country of open spaces, with breath-taking scenery that leaves you in awe of nature. As for the game against Blackpool, a 4–4 draw meant that down in New Zealand, both teams had everything to play for… fourteen times.

When we arrived in New Zealand, Joe Shaw and I got together over a beer with Blackpool's Jimmy Armfield and Dave Durie. We discussed the unique and preposterous situation facing both teams. The long and short of it was, we agreed to contrive a situation whereby the outcome of the fourteen matches would be equal in the way of victories, defeats and draws. Should one team race into a lead concerning victories, 'exhibition' football would be played by that team until parity was restored. Both parties agreed to play entertaining football and provide plenty of goals for the entertainment of the New Zealand football fan, whoever he was.

Both parties travelled about New Zealand together; they say familiarity breeds contempt, and while it would be a gross exaggeration to say that as the tour unfolded the two teams bore contempt for one another, they did, however, take on an increasingly competitive edge. I thought matches would become stale as we played more and more, and players would begin to simply go through the motions, but in fact the tour produced a number of personal battles, such as Joe Shaw against Ray Charnley and Barry Hartle against Jimmy Armfield – scores which were settled from one game to the next. When the number of matches reached double figures, however, things had settled down and some fun line-ups were named,

Joe Shaw playing centre-forward and Keith Kettleborough at full-back, whereas Blackpool named Jimmy Armfield on the wing and Ray Charnley at right-back. Curiously these unorthodox line-ups served to revitalise the competitive nature of the games as players in unaccustomed positions appeared intent on showing every-one they could play there. The games were always full of goals, score-lines such as 4–3 and 5–4 being commonplace as both teams adhered to the agreement to entertain.

I sat out a few matches to give Bob Widdowson some games. Come the final game, in terms of matches won, we led Blackpool 7–6. The night before the match, Joe and I had a chat with Jimmy Armfield and Dave Durie, during which Jimmy reminded me of the agreement that the tour should end with both teams having the same number of victories.

'Don't forget to tell your lads, Hodgey, it's our game tomorrow,' Jim reminded me when we eventually bade our farewells.

On the day of the game, John Harris decided to name a starting line-up which included a lot of youngsters such as David Monks, Mick Heaton, Mick Ash, Tommy Fenoughty, Barry Wagstaff (brother of Tony) and Charlie Bell, who had only played the odd match and made a few appearances as a substitute. The young-sters were obviously out to impress John Harris as to their first-team credentials because they played as if it were an FA Cup Final. Blackpool, expecting an easy game of it, found themselves 4–0 down at half-time. As we left the pitch at the interval, a very miffed Jimmy Armfield grabbed me.

'Hey, Hodgey, what's going on? Thought we had an agreement?' said Jim. ' I told my lads to play the exhibition stuff because the game was ours. You're playing it like a cup tie! What's going on?'

I explained to Jim the likes of Joe, Keith Kettleborough, Brian Richardson and myself were trying to take it easy but the kids must be out to impress the gaffer.

'Well, in the second half, make sure they know what's what,' Jim said.

As second-half come-backs go there has never been anything to beat it. I contrived to miss every shot Blackpool had on target, whilst Joe Shaw tottered around in defence like a camel heading for an oasis after a 400-mile hike through the Sahara. Our defence welcomed

Blackpool, offered them right of way, before folding like a concertina. The final score – Sheffield United 4, Blackpool 5 – was surely unique in the annals of football in that everyone went away happy.

I was happy too as we headed home from Hong Kong where, incidentally, I heard one of the best ad-lib jokes I've ever heard, as cracked by Joe Shaw. During our time in Hong Kong, our guide took us on a tour of a factory which manufactured Chinese typewriters. When we returned to our hotel, Cec Coldwell, who had not opted to go on the tour, asked Joe what the factory was like. 'Place was full of characters,' quipped Joe.

As enjoyable as the tour of Canada and New Zealand was, I couldn't wait to be home to see Brenda and the girls; I had missed them more than I ever thought possible. I was also looking forward with some optimism to 1965–66. I felt Sheffield United would be in for a much better season, and England was hosting the World Cup.

CHAPTER NINE

'We know what we are,
but not what we may be.'

Hamlet

The 1965–66 season began with a major change to the domestic game. The FA sanctioned the Football League's proposal to allow substitutes for injured players, bringing our football in line with that of the rest of the world.

The season kicked off on 21 August, and the player whose name would go down in the history of English football as being the first ever substitute in a League match was that of Keith Peacock of Charlton Athletic. Keith replaced injured goalkeeper Mike Rose during Charlton's game at Bolton Wanderers, with John Hewie taking over in goal and Keith assuming Hewie's outfield position.

Initially the rule legislated for substitutes to replace only injured players. Within weeks, however, managers were introducing the substitute for tactical and other reasons, which is why one often saw a substituted player feigning a limp when being replaced. Keith Peacock will be forever remembered as the first substitute in English football, but another less vaunted name also made a little history where substitutions are concerned.

The first substitute to come on and score in a League match was Bobby Knox, who netted for Barrow against Wrexham on the opening day of 1965–66. Not content with making this little bit of football history, in December Knox also became the first substitute to come on and save a penalty in a League match, his first act after coming on to replace injured keeper Ken Mulholland in Barrow's 1–0 victory at Doncaster Rovers – a case of opportunity Knox.

There was a new face in our dressing room, that of winger Gil Reece who joined us from Newport County for £15,000 and was only John Harris's fourth transfer signing in five-and-a-half years at the club. Gil proved a more than useful acquisition but the modest outlay said much about the drive and ambition of the United board. To place it into perspective, around the same time, Bury paid £11,000 for Burnley's centre-forward Ray Pointer, and Swindon £17,000 for Middlesbrough centre-half Mel Nurse. I didn't expect Sheffield United to pay the sort of fees for players the likes of Spurs and Everton were paying, but £15,000 was the level at which Second and Third Division clubs were happily paying.

Footballers are eternally optimistic; irrespective of the circumstances, you take to the field hoping to win. I was always optimistic too; however, where winning trophies was concerned such optimism was tempered with reason. That said, I knew we had a decent First Division team and, given a share of luck (which one always needs to win cups), I felt a trophy was not beyond our capabilities.

Sheffield United began 1965–66 in a most satisfactory fashion. A 1–0 win at home to Aston Villa was followed in the midweek with a superb single-goal victory at Anfield against Liverpool. Hopes were high when we travelled to Sunderland for what was to be the Wearsiders' first home match of the season. Sunderland were managed by Ian McColl, who had resigned as manager of Scotland to take over at Roker Park.

Sunderland had begun their season with two away fixtures. On the opening day they had lost to a late goal at Leeds United after playing most of the second half with ten men. (Winger George Mulhall had been sent off for swearing at a linesman, who he had taken umbrage with for not drawing to the attention of the referee what he believed to have been a very late and high challenge from Leeds' Billy Bremner. Those of you old enough to remember the Leeds United of the late sixties may well now be thinking, 'Mulhall probably had a case.') Following defeat at Leeds, Sunderland had another away match in which they secured their first point thanks to a 1–1 draw at West Ham United. Our visit to Roker Park presented Sunderland supporters with their first opportunity to see

Jim Baxter, and they turned out in some force to see his home League debut, nigh on 45,000 of them.

One of the heartening aspects to playing at Roker Park in the sixties was the reception given to opponents as they took to the field. As we came along the corridor from the dressing room, like all other visiting teams, we were halted at the entrance to the tunnel. The announcer on the public address system then said, 'Ladies and gentlemen, boys and girls, please give a warm Wearside welcome to our visitors today…Sheffield United.' We then received the signal to advance and ran out into Roker Park to generous and warm applause.

In the Premiership and Football League today, opposing teams walk onto the field side by side. The governing bodies' public projection of this is that two teams walking out alongside one another alludes to sporting behaviour and conveys to supporters a sense of occasion whilst also emphasising the gladiatorial nature of the contest to come. The true reason behind having teams walk out side by side, however, you'll not be surprised to know had more to do with image and money. The powers that be had become disconcerted by many opposition teams, especially the likes of Manchester United and Chelsea, being roundly booed by home supporters when they took to the field. This, it was considered, was not good for the image of football on television. The powers that be have, for some years now, manipulated football to suit the image they wish to project, and the teams taking to the field alongside one another is but one example of this.

As there was a colour clash, Sheffield United wore our 'change' strip against Sunderland, that of white shirts, black shorts and white socks with two red hoops at the top of the socks. In the past the only time a team wore a change of strip was on the occasion of a colour clash, but nowadays you see Liverpool wearing their change strip when playing at Queens Park Rangers, likewise Chelsea at Norwich City. Tradition in the form of the club strip is very important to supporters; it emphasises identity and connection, amongst other things. Teams were as readily identifiable by their change strip as they were by their normal one. Now clubs will wear a change of kit when there is no necessity to do so and, again, it is all for reasons of money.

There was gold-leaf sunshine in an aqua-blue sky over Roker Park and one might have been forgiven for thinking that when Jim Baxter was born, above him a star danced. David Munks had the unenviable job of marking Baxter that day; credit to David, he was to recover from the experience. Jim Baxter appeared to glide around the pitch conducting proceedings with all the aplomb of Sir Malcolm Sargent whilst adopting a raffish air. Come half-time, with Sunderland leading 2–1, we were still very much in the game. Yours truly had been called upon to make a succession of saves, whilst a fine headed goal from Mick Jones drew polite applause from the home crowd. In the second half, however, Baxter upped the ante, playing thirty-yard passes of such exquisite weight and direction to John O'Hare and George Herd they landed like snow-flakes on the toes of their boots. Throughout the final forty-five minutes, Baxter slid, stroked, swerved, chipped and drove passes with a watchmaker's feel for weight and precision. Like all great players, he always appeared to have time when on the ball, and on this day, Jim appeared to create enough time to make his own coal.

Jim Baxter scored twice and made Sunderland's other two goals for fellow Scots George Herd and Jimmy McNab. When the ref-eree, Mr Cooke from Blackburn, sounded the final whistle, Roker Park reverberated to the repetitive chant of 'Bax-ter, cha cha cha!'

Without exception, every newspaper waxed lyrical in praise of Baxter's performance that day. Those newspapers who afforded a mark out of ten for individual performance all awarded him ten out of ten. I left Roker Park knowing I had seen one of football's most gifted players produce a superlative performance. Baxter said he had wanted to create a big impression on the Sunderland fans. He certainly did that. They fell in love with him and felt, at long last, they had in their ranks a world-class player, the equal of Raich Carter of the 1930s.

Arguably, no club has experienced more false dawns than Sunderland, and the amazing performance of Jim Baxter proved just another in what has been a long legacy of false dawns for the North East club. Jim was never to repeat that performance in Sunderland colours. In his time with Sunderland he would show flashes of his genius but, as time went by, these became rarer. In the end, Sunderland did a good bit of business. Having bought

Jim for £90,000 in 1968, they persuaded Nottingham Forest to pay £100,000 for him.

Jim Baxter died of pancreatic cancer in 2001, and evidence of the esteem in which he is held as a footballer was provided by the fact his funeral took place in Glasgow Cathedral and among the mourners were those from both Rangers and Celtic – fitting as Jim abhorred sectarianism and two of his best friends were Jimmy Johnstone and Billy McNeill of Celtic. Jim's ashes are buried at Ibrox and there is a statue erected in his memory in his home town of Hill-of-Beath; appropriately, it depicts Jim in characteristic gliding fashion with the ball at his favourite left foot.

Following our defeat at Sunderland or, more to the point, by Jim Baxter, we surprised the pundits by losing only one of our next eleven matches. There were some choice performances too, a 5–3 victory over West Ham United, a draw against FA Cup holders Liverpool to follow our earlier 1–0 win over Bill Shankly's side, and a single-goal victory in the derby against Sheffield Wednesday courtesy of a goal from Alan Birchenall. This excellent run carried Sheffield United to the top of Division One. I was hopeful we could maintain such form, but the realist in me told me such a young team was going to find it hard to carry on winning and stay ahead of the likes of Liverpool, Leeds and Manchester United.

It was during this spell that Len Allchurch left the club for Stockport County for a fee of £5,000. I was sorry to see Len go as he had done us a very good job, but he had featured in only four League matches in the past year and so it was in his best interests to move on. A few weeks after Len left the club, John Docherty was sold to Brentford for £10,000. In the January, Keith Kettleborough also exited, to Newcastle United for £22,000. Annual transfer income: £37,000. Annual transfer outlay: £15,000. Mr Micawber would have been pleased but, from what I heard from our supporters, they were less than enamoured.

Our eleven-match unbeaten run came to an end with a 2–0 defeat at Burnley at the end of October. It was in this week I was reminded of Brian Clough's 'performance' at the England Under-23 dinner, when I had suggested to Jim Langley that Cloughie would go far in the game. Brian still had a long way to go but he had secured a foot on the management ladder by being appointed as manager of Hartlepool United. I sent him a Good Luck card, to which he replied: 'Dear Alan, thank you for your kind wishes of good luck – having assessed matters here, I'm going to need it. Love, Brian.'

The festive period brought us no cheer. A Spurs side, minus Jimmy Greaves who missed almost the entire season due to hepatitis, completed the double over us, from which time results can be best described as fitful. We received a blow when we lost Alan Birchenall to injury, who went on to miss nigh on half the season, and it is to the credit of Mick Jones that without his partner he continued to produce excellent performances and score twenty-one League goals.

Easter saw us in a double-header with Blackpool, in between which was sandwiched a visit to Everton. I always enjoyed playing at Goodison Park; in addition to a big-match atmosphere I was always given a warm reception by the home fans. When I took to the pitch with my United teammates and ran into the penalty area, be it the Gladys Street or Park End, the home supporters would always give me a generous round of applause. I also received a similar reception at Anfield and Roker Park but, for some reason, the one at Goodison was always very warm.

Now, you cannot imagine the following ever happening nowadays, more's the pity. I had, on previous visits to Goodison Park, taken onto the field with me a spare goalkeeper's jersey and did so on our Easter visit. I always warmed up prior to taking to the field and during the pre-match kick-in would go behind my goal and select a lad from the crowd to join me in goal. I would put him in the spare goalkeeper's jersey which, of course, was far too big for him. That done, I would position the lad next to me and instruct him to keep goal on his side whilst I looked after the other half. Mick Jones, Alan Woodward and Tony Wagstaff would play along by firing a few shots at us; of course, I would let their shots into the net, whereas when they shot at the stand-in young goalkeeper they would do so in a tame fashion so he could save the ball. When this happened the lad's face always beamed with pleasure, and when the little display was over and the jersey returned to me, the whole of Goodison Park would erupt into applause. I did this on the odd occasion at Anfield and again the reaction was extremely positive, but it was at Goodison where it seemed to go down the best.

Nowadays it is a criminal offence to encroach onto a football pitch and I understand the reasons why. I do find it sad, however, that inviting a lad from the crowd to join me in the pre-match kick-in, or Banksy posing for a photograph for someone who had leapt from behind the goal, are gestures to supporters that belong to another age. John Harris never thought it 'unprofessional' of me to do this, in fact he never, at any time, commented on it. As for such frivolity being detrimental to my concentration and ability to produce an optimum performance, that Easter Saturday we beat Everton 3–1 and I saved a penalty. Football has never been richer than now; conversely, in many ways, it is also so much the poorer.

In April we entertained Manchester United at Bramall Lane and enjoyed a deserved 3–1 victory. Mick Jones was outstanding that day and, according to the newspapers, I did okay too. The day prior to United's visit, Sheffield was in the news as it was the venue for an extraordinary meeting of the FA Disciplinary Committee. They were sitting in judgement on Leeds United's Billy Bremner, who had shocked and enraged the FA and football press alike by having acquired four bookings during the season so far. Such a dubious distinction would pass without comment these days, but in the sixties, when not just referees but everyone connected with the game viewed football differently, to collect four bookings was not only rare but it was suggestive of devious deeds indeed. As Jimmy Greaves once said of the era, 'There was a time when I got to thinking the only way a player could be sent off was if he took a gun onto the pitch and shot somebody.' Billy was banned for seven days and fined £100, but readers of a certain age will know such punishment changed Billy Bremner not one iota.

Of all the teams I ever played against, Don Revie's Leeds United was singularly the most devious and dirty in an age when football was played in a far more physical way. I used to glance about our coach as we travelled to Elland Road, look at the faces of our young players and think to myself, 'We're 2–0 down already.' No matter how many times Joe Shaw and I told the younger players not to be intimidated, most of them were. Hardly surprising if you are a nineteen-year-old and you're kicked and verbally threatened by a member of the opposition – in the tunnel prior to the start of the game.

Credit to Don Revie, he turned a moribund club into a magnificent one, a team that had been treading water for so long its limbs were lifeless into one of the major forces in Europe. Revie taught Leeds how to win before they entertained but, outside the city boundaries, Leeds were, at best, respected, invariably despised, but never at any time loved. Whereas Liverpool, Manchester United, Spurs and, lest we forget, Celtic aroused admiration and adoration for their cavalier approach to football, Leeds were cynical when deftness would have served them better, dour although to dazzle was well within their capabilities and, in an age when most teams adhered to magnanimity, they contrived to be mean-spirited.

Leeds adopted a policy for corners whereby Jack Charlton would stand on the goal-line in front of the goalkeeper so that the keepers were prevented from reaching the ball. Such a tactic was not against the rules, but it was considered not in the spirit of the game. Having put up with Jack blocking my line of vision for a few games I decided upon a counter-tactic. When Jack stood on the goal-line for a corner, instead of standing behind him I would retreat to my far post. When the in-swinging corner was delivered I would sprint forward to get a fist on the ball and, as I took off, allow a knee to slam into his back. Jack put up with this for some time before he, or Don Revie, decided to change tack and have corners delivered to a point just beyond my six-yard box where Jack could attack them from the edge of the penalty area.

In subsequent years whenever I met Jack and asked how he was he would say, 'Fine, Hodgey, except for my back. I have trouble with it, and it's all because of you and your bloody knees thudding into it all those years ago.'

Leeds didn't simply court controversy – they created it. In the late sixties I don't think there was a team who didn't have an issue with them. Even teams such as West Ham United, Leicester City and Spurs, sides not noted for robustness and overt physical play, found themselves toe-to-toe with Leeds players. In 1965, Leeds' match at Everton erupted and referee Ken Stokes took the players off the field for ten minutes until tempers calmed. One can only imagine the reaction of the media should that happen today.

Football is as much about mental fitness as it is skill, technique and physical fitness. As the senior pros, Joe Shaw and I always stood up to Leeds and their antics. It would be a gross exaggeration to say our younger players were meat and drink to Leeds, but our inexperience was exploited by what was after all a very good Leeds team. Football then, as now, was not wholly about exquisite skill and technique. West Ham United had gained a reputation for playing purist football, Everton too were a skilled team, and Sheffield United were not too far behind in those stakes. We always went out to win but, hand on heart, we always went out to entertain. In the likes of Alan Woodward, Mick Jones, Alan Birchenall, Gil Reece, Tony Wagstaff, Len Badger and Joe, we had players who could really 'play'; expansive and entertaining football was well within our capabilities.

I never blanched at having to play Leeds; for me their style of play was as much a part of football as was the more stylish approach of West Ham United, Manchester United and Spurs. You can't play the purist teams every week. Football produces all manner of teams and styles. Sometimes you have to roll up your sleeves and get stuck in and get on with it. While football has changed much over the years it has continued to produce teams of contrasting styles: take the Wimbledon and Watford teams of the 1980s as opposed to the Glen Hoddle-inspired Spurs team of the time, or, more recently, Arsène Wenger's Arsenal and Tony Pulis's Stoke City.

In March 1966 we made the very short journey to Hillsborough and came away with a point from an exciting 2–2 draw. Birchy, who had missed fifteen matches due to injury, led the Wednesday defence a merry dance; his strike partnership with Mick Jones was arguably one of the best in English football at the time and, given time together, I felt it would prove to be the best. I did wonder, though, how the club might react should a big club come knocking for their services. I knew if Sheffield United was to continue to progress, we had to hold on to our best young players. Should we not do that, I sensed the road ahead would be rocky to say the least.

Our neighbours Sheffield Wednesday reached the FA Cup Final in 1966, and in so doing created a little bit of FA Cup history, as did their opponents – Harry Catterick's Everton. Wednesday become only the second team of the twentieth century to reach Wembley having not played a cup tie at home – the other instance being that of Birmingham City in 1956. For their part, Everton were the first team since the extended format of the FA Cup to reach the final without conceding a goal. I was pleased for Wednesday, particularly my good pals Ron Springett and John Fantham, but unfortunately for Wednesday, after they established a 2–0 lead, Everton fought back to win 3–2 in what proved to be one of the most enthralling and entertaining finals in the history of the Cup.

Of course, no mention of 1966 would be complete without mentioning the World Cup tournament itself. Like everyone else I was delighted for England and their success. For weeks afterwards people were still pinching themselves, especially the sceptics who had said such a feat was beyond Alf Ramsey's team. Perhaps England did not possess the scintillating flair of Portugal and Hungary but, in the final analysis, Bobby Moore and the lads were the best prepared on the field, with the best temperament, based on a functional plan to which every player contributed to the full. Also England had a fine defence and, further to that, they built up to a peak. The timing was all good.

The nation rejoiced at England's success and, in the sporting sense, we were not to witness such a truly collective feeling of national joy and celebration until the success of the 2012 Olympics, albeit this had a very British feel to it and rightly so. The 1966 World Cup Final was the first to be beamed 'live' around the world courtesy of the Early Bird communications satellite. Millions of people watched the match live across Europe, as did football fans in North and Central America and the Middle East.

Credit to Alf Ramsey: three years earlier, when he had been appointed manager, he had made what seemed a dangerous comment: 'England will win the World Cup'. Every following year, and sometimes game by game, he stuck to his guns. The success of Alf Ramsey's team was widely seen as the beginning of a new era for English football, but I didn't see it that way. I saw England's success as the end to an era that had begun way back in 1953 with those two humiliating defeats against Hungary.

England's success was the culmination of all that had happened in the drive to modernise English football following the wake-up call of 1953. The numerous FA coaching courses at Lilleshall and the subsequent emergence of qualified coaches at clubs and, as a consequence, new and varied tactical formations and a greater emphasis on skill and technique all played their part. From having realised the football world had left it behind, for over a decade England had worked hard to develop its football – which, in 1966, saw England crowned World Champions.

One thing that England's success did for me was to emphasise the importance of coaching. You can't put in what God left out but, without doubt, given a player has talent, skill and the ability to learn, the period of transition for English football which I had actively been a part of from the start, told me the value of coaching. This was the first time in my career I began to think about the possibility of coaching goalkeeping. There were, as I have said, no goalkeeper coaches at that time. The likes of Gordon Banks, Ron Springett, Peter Bonetti, Gordon West, Tony Waiters, Peter Grummitt, Jimmy Montgomery and Alex Stepney were all self-taught. The fact that no such coaching course for goalkeepers existed in the world I saw as being to my advantage. I had it in mind that, sometime in the future, I might devise my own.

For Sheffield United supporters – and players – a familiar name was missing from our team sheet. Joe Shaw had decided to retire. Joe's replacement was Reg Matthewson, who had come through the ranks and established himself with some credit in the heart of defence. Graham Shaw was still on the books but was destined only to make one League appearance in 1966–67, so I was the last of the old guard and, as far as the first team was concerned, very much the senior pro.

At the start of 1966–67, Sheffield United had thirty-nine full-time professionals on the books, of which thirty-three were products of the club's youth policy. We knew who we were at Sheffield United and what sort of club it was. We were a club that relied heavily on its youth policy to counter a lack of investment. The transfer market was not to be indulged, moreover, but only visited very occasionally over the years. We were not the best team in the First Division, but by the same token we were far from being the worst. We were a mid-table First Division team who lived in hope of greater achievement, and there were some eighty other clubs in the Football League who would have loved to enjoy such a standing.

Sheffield United was widely acclaimed as having a superb youth policy, as evidenced by only two of the thirty-nine professionals having joined from other professional clubs. Our shortcomings were quickly exposed. The first four matches of 1966–67 saw four defeats. The opening day brought a crushing 4–0 defeat at Burnley, a game in which the home side's Gordon Harris helped himself to a hat-trick. It was not a good day out for youngster Frank Barlow, who had the unenviable task of marking Harris that day. We eventually got a win under our belts in early September when an Alan Birchenall goal gave us a 1–0 victory at Fulham – curiously, the team that beat Fulham was the same that had succumbed to Burnley on the opening day, the only difference being positional, with Frank Barlow having moved across to the left of midfield, swapping with Barry Wagstaff.

Sometimes only a slight adjustment to a team, such as a positional change, can have a marked effect on the performance of a side. It takes a good manager to spot it and effect the subtle change, and John Harris was such a manager. He would never wield the axe after a poor performance, or, as had been the case, four successive defeats. John knew his players and had faith in their ability to turn things around. Come hell or high water he always fielded what he believed to be his best eleven; the rotating squad systems of today would be anathema to him.

Victory at Fulham was followed by a fine 2–1 win against Spurs at Bramall Lane, the Spurs goal coming from the penalty spot from, of course, Jimmy Greaves. The Spurs game was played in brilliant sunshine and I donned my cap in the second half to shade my eyes from the glaring sun, which was always a source of amusement to our supporters. Most keepers of the day had taken to wearing a baseball cap when need arose, but my cap was an old corduroy one which had become something of a legend in its own right. I'd bought it in a shop in Rotherham when I signed for United from Worksop in 1953, and it was dour brown in colour and, come 1966–67, full of holes, but I steadfastly refused to consign it to the bin in favour of more modern headwear. I was often asked by players and fans why I didn't buy a new cap, but I couldn't bear the thought of parting with it. I had taken it onto the pitch with me in every game I had played and would continue to do so. I would insert my gloves, a stick of chewing gum and perhaps some tape inside the cap before folding it and taking it onto the pitch with me.

I didn't wear gloves often and the ones I had were blue and five sizes too small. I'd inherited them during our tour of New Zealand and Hong Kong. In our final match against a Hong Select XI, the opposition goalkeeper was a local lad who had such a fine game that I presented him with a pair of my gloves in appreciation of his efforts. A little later he came into our dressing room and reciprocated by presenting me with his gloves. He wasn't the tallest of lads and his gloves were too small for me to wear, but I carried them with me onto the pitch in every match since. I am not by definition superstitious, but mainly for sentimental reasons as with the cap, those tiny gloves became a part of my kit. Mark Schwartzer (Middlesbrough, Fulham and Australia) continued to wear the shin-pads he had bought when seven years old; Jimmy Montgomery (Sunderland) always wore a rugby-type shirt under his goalkeeping jersey, and Gordon West (Everton) always took the same small towel onto the pitch in case he had occasion to wipe his hands. For whatever reason, I never felt comfortable if I did not take to the pitch with my customary goalkeeping paraphernalia and, in my experience, most goalkeepers are like that.

Results throughout September and October gave rise to genuine optimism. Having got off the mark with the win at Fulham we lost but one of our following fourteen matches, that one reverse being a 3–0 defeat at Stoke City. The run of good results saw a return to right-back for Cec Coldwell who stepped up from his role of reserve team captain-cum-coach to fill in for the injured Len Badger. Mick Jones was proving to be one of the finest centre-forwards in the game: during this run he netted in five consecutive matches and even at the age of twenty was proving to be a twenty-goals-a-season striker.

One amusing aspect to the season occurred in late October when Newcastle United, who had endured a poor campaign thus far, announced in a press conference that every player on their books was available for transfer.

'Every player?' asked the football writer Bob Cass.

'Every player,' confirmed a Newcastle director.

'But you only signed Wyn Davies from Bolton three days ago and he's yet to play a game,' said Cass.

'Yes, well, every player bar Wyn Davies, obviously we're not looking to sell him because we've just bought him,' replied the flustered director who then, seemingly, also had second thoughts about Newcastle's rising young star. 'Not Wyn Davies ... or Alan Suddick.'

'So, every player is available bar Davies and Suddick, is that what you're saying?' pressed Cass, looking for confirmation.

'Yes,' replied the director.

The following week Newcastle sold Alan Suddick to Blackpool for £60,000.

A winless streak of eight matches (of which four were drawn) came to an end on Boxing Day with a thrilling 2–1 win over Manchester United, courtesy of goals from our lethal strike duo of Jones and Birchenall in front of a healthy attendance of nigh on 43,000. The press was particularly kind to me this day. 'A superlative display by home keeper Alan Hodgkinson kept Best, Law, Charlton et al at bay,' said the *Daily Mirror*, adding, 'proof, if ever it were needed, that John Harris has a top-class keeper in the England veteran.'

I had never been referred to as a veteran before, I was thirty years of age and, in goalkeeping terms, still had plenty of years left in me at the highest level. It made me think, though. I didn't have any firm plans as to what I might do in retirement. I couldn't bear the thought of not continuing in the game and began think again about a second career as a coach, as I had been helping the development of Bob Widdowson and Barry Shepherd. To my mind, however, there was time enough for that yet.

In January we got into our stride and played some really good and entertaining football during a seven-match unbeaten run which included six victories, two of them in the FA Cup at the expense of Charlton Athletic and Fulham. The only goal of the game at Charlton came from Mick Jones and it meant we entered the fourth round for the tenth successive season. Hopes of a good run in the Cup came to an end at Stamford Bridge when we were beaten 2–0 by what was a very good Chelsea team, destined to make it to the final that year. I often used to cast my mind back to the game I had played for an England XI against Notts County to commemorate the centenary of the Meadow Lane club. I had made a mental note of the County centre-forward that night whose ability to leap to great heights and power headers at goal was incredible. At Stamford

Bridge that day, Tony Hateley showed he had lost none of his aerial prowess, leaping high above our defenders to head Chelsea in front. After the game I remarked to Len Badger, 'That Hateley, it's as if he has a boot between his ears instead of a head.'

'Well,' replied Len, ' he's the only player I've ever seen come back down to earth after having headed a ball and have snow on his head.'

That was Tony. If only he could have played half as well with the ball at his feet as he did with it at his head, he would have been a world beater.

Bramall Lane enjoyed another bumper gate, of 44,000 for the derby against Sheffield Wednesday. It was strange to face a Wednesday team without my old pal Ron Springett in goal. Peter Wicks had taken Ron's place and was beaten by a second-half goal from Bill Punton who, by his own admission, didn't score many. 'I think my last was in 65,' quipped Bill after the game. 'That's 1865.' The derby match preceded what was to be a unique transfer when, later in the year, Ron left Sheffield Wednesday for Queens Park Rangers, swapping clubs with his brother, Peter, also a goalkeeper.

Fluctuating form carried us through to the end of a season in which we found ourselves if not enjoying, then somewhat satisfied with a top ten finish. Manchester United were crowned champions while our old adversaries Aston Villa and Blackpool were destined for Second Division football the following season. Mick Jones, Alan Birchenall and winger Alan Woodward all hit double figures where goals were concerned. All things considered it had been a decent enough season and, with the youngsters having grown and gained in experience, I felt Sheffield United's future prospects were good.

1967 was the so-called 'summer of love'. It was also one which began with Celtic becoming the first British team to win the European Cup, beating the tactically superior but dour and star-studded Inter Milan with a scintillating performance of attacking football. As Hugh McIlvanney wrote, 'Jock Stein must be the best manager in the world, who else could have won the European Cup with a Glasgow and District XI?'

A novelty for me was occasionally being able to watch myself on BBC's *Match of the Day*. It offered me an opportunity to observe myself as a goalkeeper and, of course, to observe the performances

of other goalkeepers, giving me my first real opportunity to formu-
late ideas about the coaching of goalkeepers and what was required
to improve performance.

Sheffield United always welcomed the *MOTD* cameras in those
early days of the programme, which was not always the case with
some clubs; Everton and Burnley refused to allow highlights of
their respective matches to be shown for fear it would affect attendances. The emergence of *MOTD* meant many top clubs, Sheffield
United included, erected permanent staging for cameras and commentary. When the match appeared on our television screens it
had been edited down to some forty minutes of football, but even
this afforded me with the opportunity to observe and assess other
goalkeepers at my leisure. In those days, of course, we didn't have
domestic video players, but even seeing other goalkeepers in action
and at close quarters for forty or so minutes got my brain ticking. I would make notes in a notebook of what I perceived as their
strengths and weaknesses as well as the idiosyncratic style of each
keeper. My education as a goalkeeping coach had begun.

The 1966–67 season concluded with Sheffield United embark-
ing upon our most ambitious and exotic close-season tour as yet.
We flew off to Bolivia, from where we travelled down to Chile,
thankfully not staying at the Anglo-American mining complex.
One match that stays in the memory is a 3–1 victory over Santa
Cruz in La Paz, which is the highest capital in the world. At such
an altitude the thin air took some getting used to, but it was not
simply our lungs that had to adapt. I found the ball travelled very
much faster through the thin air when struck, which served to
keep me on my toes. On our return a reporter from the *Star* asked
show he thought the South American tour had gone and concluded
by asking Cec if he had any tips for travellers.

'Yes,' he said. 'Never go abroad. It's a bloody awful place.'

| CHAPTER TEN |

'There is some ill a-brewing towards my rest,
For I did dream of money-bags tonight.'

The Merchant of Venice

Our first four matches of 1967–68 gave little indication of what was to befall Sheffield United in the new season. An opening day defeat at home to Nottingham Forest (1–3) was an early wake-up call but the resolve of the team was such that we immediately bounced back, achieving draws at Stoke City and Coventry City before winning the return against Stoke by the only goal of the game.

It was an unremarkable start to the new campaign, but one that was in keeping with Sheffield United of recent years. Given the players we had, I was convinced we would be in for another top ten finish, and that belief was not diminished by the fact we contrived to lose our next four League matches, which included a 1–0 defeat to Sheffield Wednesday in the derby. In the previous seasons we had flattered to deceive; a run of good results would be followed by a run of results that were not so good, and because such a pattern had invariably continued to repeat itself I saw no reason why anything different should be the case this season.

In Mick Jones and Alan Birchenall we still possessed a young strike force that was the envy of most other First Division clubs and, given their progress, I could only see us continuing to improve. What was a tad concerning to me, however, was our conceding of fourteen, which was very unlike us. John Harris was always reluctant to wield the axe, but he was now thinking in terms of changes in defence. It was around this time a football reporter from the *Star* asked one of the directors if there was any truth in a rumour circulating that Sheffield United were about to part with one of their bright young stars. I'd heard this, but no one had mentioned anything in the dressing room so I thought it was, indeed, simply a rumour.

The United director denied it in no uncertain terms, expressing his annoyance that the reporter had listened to such 'scurrilous rumours' and generally rubbishing the story. Such had been the director's vehement dismissal of the story that my thoughts turned to Lady Macbeth's outburst at the suggestion she and her husband might have anything to do with Duncan's murder, and the subsequent response: 'The lady doth protest too much, methinks.'

We had been well beaten (5–2) by a very good Manchester City team at Maine Road in mid-September and in the week that followed, John had us playing a full-scale match against the reserves with, somewhat ominously, Mick Hill as a striker for the first team. We were due to play Newcastle United at Bramall Lane on the Saturday, and the day before, as usual, we reported for a light training session at the training ground. The first thing we noticed was that Mick Jones wasn't with us, which set tongues wagging.

Later that morning Mick wandered into the changing room and told us, 'I'm off.' I had thought as much. I asked, 'Where to?'

'Leeds,' replied Mick.

'How much?'

'Hundred grand.'

'You going to do all right out of that, Mick?'

'I think so, Alan,' he replied.

Mick Jones was a superb young striker but, on the face of it, not your archetypical Leeds United player. Mick was tall, strong and powerfully built, but he was quiet and didn't have a bad bone his body. This, however, was a Leeds United team that was changing. Leeds had learned how to win now, it appeared, and they were beginning to change their policy by learning how to entertain into the bargain. Mick Jones would be just the type of striker who could help them do that.

I couldn't blame Mick for moving. He was on £40 a week with us; Leeds were going to pay him nigh on three times that. Leeds was also one of the top clubs of the time, always challenging for the title and the FA Cup and now regularly in European competition. He would have been a fool not to go and he was certainly anything but a fool.

I knew we were going to miss Mick and what he gave us. In addition to the goals he scored, he was a fine leader of the line and his work on the ground was matched by his prowess in the air. He was a good target man and could, when circumstances required it, hold the ball as well as any striker of the day. He wasn't a robust striker but his style of play was a constant irritant to opposing defenders and his strength enabled him to make individual runs into opposing penalty boxes with the ball at his feet. Irrespective of the shabby tactics meted out to him, he never paled, he simply got on with his job of leading the attack, quietly and to great effect. He was a top-quality striker and though there were a number of them about at the time, they cost big money, hence the £100,000 Leeds had paid for his services.

Following the departure of Mick Jones, Mick Hill stepped up from the reserves to take his place. Mick was a decent lad and an amiable character but, as Mick Mills of Ipswich Town was later to say, suffered somewhat from 'taking his off-the-field lifestyle onto the pitch with him'. In all fairness Mick Hill did a decent job, but he wasn't of the quality of Mick Jones – very few strikers were.

The day after Mick Jones told us he was leaving, we got back to winning ways with a 2–1 victory over Newcastle United, the Newcastle goal coming from Wyn Davies, who appeared to leap higher than the floodlight pylon to head the Tynesiders' consolation.

Victories home and away were becoming difficult, a solitary victory against Leeds United of all teams being our only success in the nine matches which followed the victory over Newcastle in September. Mick Jones was not included in the Leeds line-up at Bramall Lane, and ironically it was his replacement, Mick Hill, who got the only goal of the game. In the same week, Joe Shaw left his post as manager of our reserve team to take over the reins at York City. Joe had his work cut out when he arrived at Bootham Crescent, as York were rock-bottom of Division Four. Life at Bramall Lane wouldn't be the same without Joe, I had never known a time when he hadn't been at the club. After twenty-one years of loyal service it must have been quite a wrench for him to leave, but come the end of the season he had managed to lift York off the bottom, albeit they still had to apply for re-election, successfully as it turned out.

Although we had not been achieving good results, the defence was now looking much more solid – two goals conceded in four matches was proof of that, but we were also finding goals hard to come by. Our supporters were becoming increasingly agitated and through the letters column in the Green 'Un were demanding the board backed John Harris in the transfer market. Following a goalless draw at home to Leicester City at the end of November, the club paid £30,000 for the services of Colin Addison from Arsenal.

Colin was a very good player, a cerebral footballer who thought deeply about the game and had some great ideas as to how it should be played. He was a seasoned pro and, as such, never had a bad game in all his time at United, but his best days were behind him. Colin was a Somerset lad who had grown up in York and signed for the club when he left school, and from there he had joined first Forest then Arsenal.

I thought Colin would be the perfect foil for Alan Birchenall, but the day after Colin arrived, Birchy was missing from training and I feared the worst. It transpired Birchy had travelled to London for talks with Chelsea, for whom he signed for the fee of £100,000. When Birchy came back to clear out his locker I managed to catch him, told him I was very sorry to see him go but understood and wished him the best of luck.

'Thanks, Hodgey, but I somehow think you and the rest of the guys are going to be the ones who're going to need the luck.'

I had the terrible feeling he was right.

Alan was also a big loss to Sheffield United. Apart from his ability as a striker or to play in an attacking midfield role, both of which he accomplished to great effect, he was the type of player who you often hear described as being 'great in the dressing room'. Alan was a larger than life character, always ready with a witticism or a put-down line, a player who could handle himself on the pitch in more ways than one. With his platinum blond hair cut mod-style, he was often the target for what cricketers call 'sledging' by certain opponents. In the game against Leeds United,

Birchy had a memorable exchange of words with their firebrand captain Billy Bremner.

'Is that a gun in your shorts or are ye just pleased to see me ye long-haired Nancy boy?' said Billy with characteristic antagonism.

'No, it's 'king gun,' replied Birchy, quick as a flash.

Alan not only gave as good as he got, but because he was quick thinking and witty he invariably came out on top in verbal battles. When he was with Leicester City Alan responded to a match report saying he was asleep when presented with a chance at goal, by taking to the pitch at the following home game wearing a dressing gown over his strip. Now, who wouldn't pay good money to see that? When one hears people say, 'There aren't the great characters in the game anymore,' it's to players such as Birchy they are referring.

The sales of Mick Jones and Birchy told me much. Sheffield United's involvement in the transfer market had been minimal over the years but the sale of our two prize assets suggested to me we had become a 'selling club'. When Birchy was sold we were mid-table in Division One; no sooner had he followed Mick Jones out of the door than the slide began. We desperately needed someone to a partner Colin Addison, or play just in front of him. The answer came in the form of Willie Carlin.

Again, Willie was a tremendous lad and a very good player. A scouser who had begun his career with Liverpool, Willie had moved on to Halifax Town, then Carlisle United, where he gained a reputation as a goal-scorer during the Cumbrian club's promotion to Division Two (now the Championship). There were a number of itinerant centre-forwards at the time – Frank Large, Hughie McIlmoyle and Frank Lord being but three well-travelled strikers – and I would put Willie amongst their number. Willie might have done Sheffield United a good job but he never really got the chance. He had been at the club for less than a year when he was on the move again. His other clubs included Derby County, whom he helped establish as a First Division club under Brian Clough, Notts County, Leicester City and Cardiff City.

A young midfield player joined us from Watford, too. Tony Currie was to become a massive hit with United supporters; he was a very skilful, cultured and extrovert attacking midfield player who arrived from Vicarage Road for £26,000 and, after some six years at Bramall Lane, would later be sold to Leeds for £250,000. To off-set the £30,000 paid for Willie Carlin, Reg Matthewson was sold to Fulham for the same figure. A number of fringe players also left for a total sum of £8,000. Income from transfers: £238,000. Outlay for transfers: £86,000.

So £152,000 was a very hefty profit from transfers in a single season, but what happened to that money, I don't know. What I do know is, it wasn't paid to players in increased wages (in 1968 we had eventually usurped Leicester as the poorest paid players in the First Division), nor on ground improvements to benefit our supporters.

Colin Addison and Willie Carlin were good players but they weren't a match for Jones and Birchy as a spearhead attack that rifled in the goals. That said, over the festive period and into the New Year we enjoyed results that bore no hint of the trouble to come. During this period we lost but three of fourteen matches; the pick of which was a 4–1 win over Southampton, a 3–2 victory over Spurs, wins at Wolves and Fulham and FA Cup victories at the expense of Watford, Blackpool and West Ham. It was in the 3–2 victory over Spurs that Tony Currie made his debut and immediately endeared himself to our supporters by marking the occasion with a fine headed goal. Our next game was at Leicester City and on the Thursday when John Harris announced the team, Tony surprised everyone by raising a hand and saying, 'Sorry, boss, but I can't play on Saturday.'

'Why not?' asked John.

'I'm getting married,' replied Tony, who had not thought fit to mention this the previous week when he had signed for the club.

It was our old adversaries, Leeds United, who put paid to our FA Cup hopes in what was a hard and closely fought tie at a packed Elland Road. The Leeds cup-tie was particularly galling. Having competed with Leeds for the entire game and missed a couple of chances ourselves which Mick and Birchy might, or might not, have put away, minutes from time we stupidly gave the ball away in mid-field and Leeds broke away to score. We more or less had set it up for them really. Up to that point we had battled hard and played sufficiently well that Leeds created only a handful of chances and, what shots they did have on target, I dealt with. Having worked so hard, concentrated totally and given our all, to then 'gift' Leeds a late goal knocked the stuffing out of us – for a couple of days.

After the FA Cup loss at Leeds we found ourselves just below mid-table – but there was no panic, no alarm bells ringing, everything seemed fine. Whilst the teams around us began to pick up points we didn't, but for a surprise and remarkable 2–1 win over Liverpool at Anfield and a 1–1 draw in the return. We suffered five defeats in our final seven League matches. On the face of it, given we hadn't been embroiled in a relegation dogfight, it didn't seem catastrophic. As had been the case for the majority of the season, no team turned us over. We would play well enough, we would battle, there would not be much between us and, say, Everton or Manchester United, only for us then to make an error which proved telling and cost us dear. We were, however, sucked into the battle to avoid the drop in the closing stages of the season. Our final game was at home to West Ham United. For Sheffield United it was a must-win game. We didn't win it. What's more, we lost it. Coventry City, Sheffield Wednesday and Stoke City had meanwhile managed to put a couple of results together at the death and eased themselves out of the mire into which we slowly slid.

Victory on the final day of the season against West Ham would have lifted us to fourth from bottom above Coventry, who would have been relegated, and our neighbours Sheffield Wednesday. In the event we accumulated 32 points (there being two points for a win), a point behind Coventry, and dropped into Division Two. The *Sunday Mirror* said, 'After looking comfortable in mid-table for much of the season, everyone must be shocked and surprised at Sheffield United's relegation.' If people were, believe me, they weren't half as shocked and surprised as everyone connected with the club. Our relegation had a devastating effect on everyone, no one more so than yours truly.

There are basically three ways in which a team can be relegated. There is the club that is rooted to the foot of the table for the entire season, who can't buy a win for love nor money, and which is favoured by all the other clubs because matches against this sort of team are seen as points in the bag. It is also because their permanent basement position means there are, in essence, only two relegation places left for the other teams to fall into.

Then there is the team who spends the entire season in the bottom five or six scrapping with the other teams down in the basement.

One week they move up a place, only to move down again the following week, and so it goes on. The entire season is fraught with anxiety and a desperate need to acquire points from the other clubs in the dogfight. Games against the top clubs are, more or less, written off in terms of gaining points. This sort of relegation fight is bloody and messy and usually goes to the wire.

Finally, there is the team who are coasting along, no real worries or cause for concern, and are suddenly caught with their pants down when they hit a poor run at the same time the teams below them enjoy a points surge. From the relative security of mid- to lower table they are sucked into a vortex and, like fluff in an emptying sink, are sucked down the plughole. That was Sheffield United in 1968.

As for the reasons for relegation, apart from the obvious one that the team didn't do well enough, it varies from club to club. Had Sheffield United not sold Jones and Birchenall, I am convinced we would have been all right. That was the albatross around our neck, but there were other telling factors too. Some of the players (and I emphasise 'some') who a few years before had shown enormous promise and potential, had simply not developed into main-frame First Division players. I am talking here of players with a few years' first-team experience under their belts. They had developed into good pros and decent players, but decent is not good enough for the First Division where only top quality will suffice. These players would do a fine job in the Second Division (Championship equivalent) but had their shortcomings exposed in the top flight.

Relegation hit everyone very hard, John Harris in particular. As manager John felt he was responsible for our demise. It is said that he tendered his resignation but the board were split on accepting it. In the event John agreed to 'go upstairs' and take on the role of General Manager. I was very sorry to see him step aside, he was good manager and had done much for Sheffield United since taking over from Joe Mercer in 1959. I would miss his inspirational speeches, whereas I felt the press might be looking forward to a manager who spoke to them rather more often than John tended to do. The board went in search of John's successor.

It was 1968, and what Sheffield United needed was a vibrant, enthusiastic, modern manager full of great ideas, one who could communicate such ideas to the players; a manager who knew the strengths and weaknesses of players and how to get the best out of them individually and as a team. Someone who would instil confidence, make everyday training exciting, fun and rewarding and who would bring in players better than those we had. A manager who would breeze into Bramall Lane, assess what had to be done, get on and do it with the total support and respect of the players; a manager who could inspire. That's the type of manager Sheffield United needed – they gave us Arthur Rowley.

In concluding 1967–68, I refer back to the summer of 1967, for it was then that the United Board granted me a Testimonial in recognition of my fifteen years with the club. Back in August of 1967, a Testimonial Committee had been set up comprising prominent United supporters and myself. Throughout the year I, along with teammates, had attended a variety of fundraising activities, such as a sporting dinner, Players v Supporters quiz nights, Pie'n'Pea Suppers, and the like. The culmination to my Testimonial year was a game in 1968 between the current United and Sheffield Wednesday sides which was to be preceded by a match comprising two halves of twenty minutes between former United and Wednesday players – they would all be referred to as 'legends' now.

I was grateful to the board for offering the club's facilities for our use, particularly for the Testimonial match itself. Following our relegation, I feared there might be a disappointing crowd on the night, but the turnout of Blades supporters – and a good number of Wednesday fans too – was such that I felt humbled and close to tears. A crowd of 19,700 turned up to see what was, for me, a terrific and very emotional night.

The game between former United and Wednesday players brought a host of former teammates and opponents back to Bramall Lane and, judging from the reaction of the crowd, appeared to go down as well as the main match between United and Wednesday.

I was deeply touched by all who gave up their time to support and participate. Eddie Burgin, Cec Coldwell, Brian Richardson (then at Rochdale), Tommy Hoyland, Joe Shaw, Gerry Summers (first-team coach at Wolves), Jimmy Hagan, Doc Pace and Billy Hodgson all returned to offer their services. Included in the Wednesday Veterans' team were Peter Johnson, Norman Curtis, Jimmy McAnnearney,

Redfern Froggatt, Alan Finney (then at Rotherham United), Keith Ellis and Albert Broadbent. As is often the case with this type of match there were plenty of goals, the final score-line being 5–4 to United, not that it mattered.

Given it was a Testimonial, the main game was a keenly contested affair which, if my memory serves me right, ended 2–2. Come the end of the night I was fighting back the tears as United and Wednesday players formed a guard of honour and applauded me from the field accompanied by generous applause from the 19,700 supporters present.

Two days later, the club secretary, Mr Newton, asked to see me. As soon as I stepped into his office I knew something was wrong. Mr Newton was the type of man who knew better than anyone the affairs of the club. Everyone respected Mr Newton. He was organised, very good at his job, always in control of everything (not least his emotions) and a man of unyielding integrity. He went about his work with quiet but total efficiency and did so with a face that held the effortless composure of a corpse in a morgue. This day, however, Mr Newton was far from his usual self, in fact he was totally distraught. He told me to take a seat. I took a seat. I would need it.

Mr Newton sat there with a pained expression on his face, wringing his hands in angst.

'Alan,' he said, almost close to tears, 'I don't know how to tell you this. I really don't.'

For a split second the thought occurred to me that he was about to tell me the club were about to get rid of me. This I dismissed as soon as the thought popped into my head. I was still under contract and, in such circumstances, it was always John Harris who told players they were through the door.

'Well, give it a try,' I said encouragingly.

He didn't appear encouraged.

'It's gone,' he said, his words tumbled out of a mouth that sounded as dry as parchment, 'All of it. And we don't know where. There's been a hell of a panic on I can tell you. There's no trace. It's gone. All of it.'

I didn't know what he was referring to, but something told me that when I did find out, I wasn't going to like it. Not one little bit.

'What are we talking about here, Mr Newton?' I asked.

He played a tattoo with his fingers on the arms of his chair, then flung his hands in the air as if reacting to a 'stick-up'.

'The money. Your money. From your Testimonial night. It's gone, all of it. We bagged it up. It was kept safe. This morning we go to bank it and it's gone.'

'Stolen?' I managed to squeak, hoping I could disbelieve my ears.

He shrugged his shoulders.

Through Mr Newton's window I could see it was a nice day outside. The sun was shining. The sky was blue. A gentle breeze was blowing. I sat there saying nothing, my forehead prickling with adrenalin, a muscle tightening like a sheepshank knot in my chest, my guts resting somewhere just above my knees and my legs feeling as weak as fruit tea. That apart, I was fine, just fine.

An internal investigation was launched but the money, some £7,000 in total, was never recovered. Who had taken the money? No one knew and I never did find out. Had the money been stolen by someone from outside the club? Joe Shaw thought it unlikely because of the way the club had been at pains to keep the matter 'private' for fear the image of Sheffield United would be forever tarnished should the story of my missing Testimonial money be made public.

Cec wondered why the board had not offered to reimburse me, even in part.

'They could afford a couple of grand at least, easy,' Cec suggested.

Joe suggested re-staging my Testimonial match. I told him that could never happen because the club would then have to offer the reason for a second match.

'Yeah, well, bloody well let the people of Sheffield know. You know them as well as I do, Alan,' said Joe. 'Should they find out what has happened to you, they'd be enraged, rally to your cause. Wednesday fans as well. They'd tear that board apart.'

That is what I feared. I had been at the club for fifteen years and I loved Sheffield United. I couldn't bear the thought of the club shamed, its name dragged through the gutter. I accepted I would never see any of my Testimonial money. I never did.

✻ ✻ ✻

The 1968–69 season saw Sheffield United back in Division Two with Arthur Rowley as manager; well, at least he was there. On his first day at the club Arthur was pictured in the press wearing a Bukta tracksuit and holding a ball. He must have borrowed that tracksuit because I can't recall him wearing it again. John Harris had promoted John Short from youth team manager to assistant manager and it was to be John who did all the training, coaching and everything else. Arthur Rowley was a decent guy but not, in my estimation, a football manager. I wondered how on earth he had lasted ten years as manager of Shrewsbury Town if the way he managed Sheffield United was anything to go by.

John Short was a grand lad. Gateshead born, he had begun his playing career at Leeds United in the 1930s before being transferred after the war to Millwall, for whom he made some 250 appearances throughout the fifties. It was John who really ran team affairs that season. When individual players wanted to discuss something with Arthur, so elusive did he prove to be that he became known as 'The Scarlet Pimpernel'.

Arthur had been a prolific goal-scorer in his time; his 433 League goals still stands as a record, albeit he scored the vast majority in the lower divisions. He had been a barnstorming centre-forward and, even in his management days, had a formidable physique, more like that of a British heavyweight boxer than a football manager. In the time that he was manager of Shrewsbury the team had shuttled up and down Division Three, but in 1967–68 they had missed out on promotion by a single point. I assume it was on the strength of this that the United board believed he was the man to guide us back to Division One.

One of the first things Arthur told the press was that he would make signings to strengthen the team for our 'promotion push'. Alan Woodward asked me one day who I thought Arthur might be signing.

'No idea,' I told Alan in all honesty, 'but you can bet your bottom dollar he'll go back to his old club and sign someone from there.'

Arthur did go back to Shrewsbury Town, to sign defender Ted Hemsley. Ted proved to be a good signing and made the position of left-back his own. Ted was also one of what was rapidly becoming a rare breed of sportsman in that he was also a county cricketer with Worcestershire. The United scouts got to work scouring the country for players who could help United's quest for promotion and who could be acquired at bargain fees. In this respect the scouts did a good job. In October, with Sheffield United tenth in Division Two, Eddie Colquhoun was signed from West Bromwich Albion to bolster a defence that had conceded twenty-one goals in the previous ten matches. Eddie went on to become something of a 'cult' figure at Bramall Lane, making 416 appearances for the club, during which time he was also capped by Scotland.

Another arrival was John Tudor from Coventry City. John was a striker who was most effective when playing just behind a target man. John produced some excellent performances for United before being sold to Newcastle United, where he was to form a prolific pairing up front with Malcolm McDonald. When his playing days came to an end, John emigrated to the USA, where he subsequently coached a number of college teams in Minnesota.

David Powell was signed from Wrexham and made twenty-seven appearances in defence in 1968–69. He would, I am sure, have gone on to enjoy many more seasons in the game but for the fact he was dogged by injuries. He left United for Cardiff City, where he spent a year before his career was cut short through injury.

In my opinion, Arthur Rowley's heart was never in the job of manager from the start. As I have said, he left the day-to-day training and coaching to John Short and even team talks were often left to John. What Arthur did have great enthusiasm for, however, was horse racing – which was not a prerequisite for the role of a football manager. In these days before 24/7 television and radio news, most footballers bought a newspaper on their way to morning training in order to read match reports of the previous night's games and the latest football news. The majority of players bought the *Mirror*, *Sun*, *Express* and *Mail*, a couple of us the *Guardian* or *Telegraph*. The only paper I ever saw Arthur Rowley with was the *Racing Post*; he bought it every day and seemed to spend most of his time at the club studying it.

Arthur's obsession with horse racing became something of a joke with the players. One morning, during a practice game supervised by John Short, of course, Len Badger hit a long pass up-field to reserve team player Mick Harmston who had, for some weeks, been trying to tell anyone who might listen he was worthy of an outing with the first team. Len's over-hit pass cleared Mick and ran out of play, prompting Mick to turn to Len and say, 'Bloody hell, Len, I'm not a racehorse.'

'If you were, the boss would not only know who you are, but everything about you,' replied Len to guffaws of laughter.

Prior to home matches, we players had got into the habit of visiting the players' lounge to watch either the BBC or ITV football preview programme. One Saturday lunchtime, prior to a home game the players had assembled in the home-team dressing room when Gil Reece entered, told us he had just passed the players' lounge and noticed two televisions had been set up in the room, seemingly so we could watch both football preview programmes at the same time.

'That's ludicrous,' I ventured. 'How's that going to work? We can't watch two different channels at the same time.'

We decided to wander up to the lounge to find out. When we entered the lounge, the reason for the two televisions was immediately apparent. On one TV set was a race from Wincanton; on the other, a race from Towcester. Arthur Rowley was seated before both TV sets, his head going from side to side as if watching a centre court match at Wimbledon as he watched both races simultaneously unfold. Suddenly aware of our presence behind him, with a waft of an arm Arthur indicated we should quietly take our seats behind him, never at any time taking his eyes off the two screens.

So obsessed was Arthur with the horses, during a match he would often leave his seat in the dugout to find a television screening a race on which he had placed a bet. In March, we played Charlton Athletic at the Valley. At the end of the game, Arthur entered what was a subdued dressing room.

'Hey, come on, boys, cheer up. Okay, we missed a few chances but a point here is a good result,' said Arthur, who then slurped some tea from a cup and exited the room.

I looked around the dressing room at what were still glum faces.

'Tell you what, lads,' I said, 'let's not spoil his day by telling him we lost.'

We had indeed lost, 2–1. Arthur had obviously missed Charlton's winning goal, most probably because he had sneaked off to watch a race on television.

Sheffield United finished 1968–69 in ninth position in Division Two. It had not been the season we had hoped for and, seemingly, not the season the directors had hoped for either. Following our final match of the season, a one-goal defeat at Oxford United, Arthur Rowley left the club. The board didn't have to look far for Arthur's replacement, they simply went upstairs and asked John Harris to take over again. I wasn't alone in being very happy at this.

1969–70 proved a better season for Sheffield United, in that we improved our standing in Division Two and, come the season's end, everyone felt we had a team that could clinch promotion the following season.

1969–70 got underway on 9 August, the earliest ever start to a new football season. What is more, the season began well for us, two goals from Alan Woodward and one from Gil Reece giving us a 3–0 victory over Middlesbrough. What was disappointing was the Bramall Lane attendance of 14,707. Some 5,000 less than for my Testimonial. The low attendance for an opening day of the season match was put down to the season's early start and the fact that many people were away on holiday. Whilst this was most certainly a factor, there was another more telling reason.

Following England's World Cup success, English football at all levels had slavishly copied Alf Ramsey's 'wingless wonders', playing either a 4–3–3 or 4–4–2 formation. Defences had become more organised, play was not so cavalier. Instead of the mantra being 'score goals', as it had been prior to 1966, the emphasis now was on not conceding them. This wasn't Alf Ramsey's fault. Alf had played a system he felt could win the World Cup and was proved right in this, but that was for the World Cup in 1966. Due to the success of Alf's system – not original by any stretch of the imagination – managers at all levels of football copied it because they thought this was the way to achieve success. After all, what better example could there be to follow than that of the World Champions?

Comparatively, the football post-1966 was not as cavalier and adventurous as pre-1966. There were still fantastic and exciting games but, in general, the football was nowhere near as adventurous. Many games evolved into a battle for midfield dominance. The game still had its great and gifted entertainers – George Best, Bobby Charlton, Jimmy Greaves and Charlie Cooke (Chelsea) to name but four. There were also connoisseur's delights in the likes of Bobby Moore, Dave Mackay, Colin Harvey (Everton), Colin Bell (Manchester City) and Johnny Giles (Leeds). However, there is no getting away from it, as the seventies dawned there was a more cynical aspect to the game.

Goals are what lovers of football like to see. Well-organised defences and an emphasis on not conceding goals rather than scoring them had resulted in far fewer goals being scored post-1966. This was the main factor for the fall in attendances.

We all know what Disraeli said about statistics. However, the following indicate how in the post-1966 era far fewer goals were scored in comparison to the beginning of the 1960s, which is why I previously said England's victory marked the end of an era rather than it being the beginning of a new dawn for English football.

GOALS SCORED IN THE FIRST DIVISION

Year	Goals scored
1960	1790
1961	1725
1962	1724
1968	1398
1969	1203
1970	1211
1971	1089

That is just the First Division, but the pattern was repeated throughout the Football League, which resulted in some 2,800 fewer goals being scored in 1970–71 than in 1960–61. That's a lot of goals in anybody's book. Did the powers that be ever think, 'Is this the way we want football to be going? Is this what supporters want to see?' I think you know the answer to that one.

Football had changed much since 1966. There is nothing wrong in that. It is right that the game continues to change; if not it would be sterile. Many of the changes effected in the late sixties and the start of the seventies, however, were not conducive to the open, entertaining and attacking football supporters like to see. There were now many other ways than a football match for people to enjoy their leisure time. When football should have been thinking of ways to become more attractive and entertaining, it was moving in the opposite direction. What the supporters thought about that could be gauged by the 14,000 attendance for Sheffield United's opening match of 1969–70, or the 20,000 who, on the same day, watched Sunderland against Coventry City, the Wearsiders' lowest attendance for an opening day fixture since 1914–15, the season when football was suspended due to the war.

Christmas was, as always, a hectic period. A full programme of fixtures took place on 20, 26 and 27 December, with the third round of the FA Cup taking place a few days later. In keeping with every team of the day, Sheffield United fielded the same team for each of these games, the only change being an enforced one for our match against Watford when Geoff Salmons replaced the injured John Tudor.

Players would always rather play than train, and I was no exception where this was concerned. Four matches in the space of eleven days meant training sessions were brief and lighter than usual, just enough to keep everyone at the optimum level of fitness. Players didn't need any more than this, the games kept you fit. It was unthinkable for a manager to explain away a bad performance by telling the press players were 'tired'. As a footballer you were expected to cope with a lot of games over the festive holiday, the same as you were at Easter, when three matches would be played over four days.

Given far fewer goals were being scored in 1969–70 than at the start of the sixties, another new factor was that, the way some teams played, having a striker who rattled in thirty-plus goals per season was not critical to success. Goals were being shared among a team, as some teams playing 4–4–2 relied on collective responsibility where goals were concerned. Sheffield United no longer had a player like 'Doc' Pace, but we did not suffer for that. In 1969–70,

Alan Woodward ended the season as United's leading goal-scorer with 18 League goals, but Gil Reece, John Tudor and Tony Currie also notched double figures, with Colin Addison not far behind.

Things were a lot better under John Harris, not least because every player from youth team to first team knew John took an interest in him. John, as I previously said, liked a settled team and was not one to chop and change the side. Arthur Rowley had called upon the services of twenty-eight players during his season in charge. In 1969–70, John Harris used eighteen players, of which Phil Cliff, Graeme Crawford, Ian Mackenzie and David Staniforth played just the single game. This more settled team produced better performances and results. Sheffield United finished the season sixth in Division Two, four points behind promoted Blackpool who, in turn, finished runners-up to champions Huddersfield Town.

I previously mentioned that defences were now better organised and ours was no exception. During games it was my job, as it had always been, to organise the United defence, to keep the number of shooting opportunities for the opposition to a minimum. We conceded just ten goals at home all season, twenty-eight away from home. In terms of goals conceded at home, it was the least in the entire Football League. In addition to organising the United defence, at the risk of sounding immodest, I felt I had played well throughout the season. The *Daily Express* seemingly thought so; in their report of our final match, a 5–1 win over Oxford United, Desmond Hackett wrote, 'This match was by no means the walkover for Sheffield United the result may suggest. Oxford too had their chances and, had it not been for a series of outstanding saves from Alan Hodgkinson, this match could well have produced one of the season's more bizarre score-lines. Hodgkinson capped what has been another superb season for the former England man with another fine display of the goalkeeper's art.'

By the very nature of the job, goalkeepers tend to enjoy longer careers than outfield players. As we approached 1970–71, I was now thirty-four years of age but felt I had at least three more years in me. My enthusiasm for playing and for football had not diminished one iota from the day I had started my career at Bramall Lane. If anything, as we prepared for 1970–71 my enthusiasm had an even greater edge to it, for I believed Sheffield United had a team capable of winning promotion back to the First Division. The thought of returning to the top flight imbued me with a greater enthusiasm for playing. I worked harder in pre-season than I could ever remember, determined to produce the sort of performances throughout the season that would help United secure their goal of First Division football. At thirty-four I knew I was up to the job, no problem.

One day Brenda asked how I thought the coming season would go.

'To be honest, love, I think we'll win promotion and I'll get a chance to play in the First Division again before I retire,' I replied.

I was to be proved correct in one of those predictions.

1970–71 was a season noted for Arsenal winning the double and Charlie George lying on his back on the Wembley turf after he scored the winning goal in the FA Cup Final against Liverpool; Matt Busby resuming as manager of Manchester United, replacing Wilf McGuinness; Colchester United causing one of the biggest FA Cup upsets in years by defeating Leeds United, and John Hope joining Sheffield United from Newcastle United. Now I am well aware you will be thinking that last item had little effect on the season – it's true, but it was to have a monumental effect on the career of yours truly.

On the opening day of the season what you like to avoid is a team who has just been promoted. Newly promoted sides invariably play like they have the devil in them; they're pumped up with adrenalin, keen to do well, high on confidence and are, to the opposition, a somewhat unknown quantity. Irrespective of how they will fare in the remainder of the season, newly promoted teams invariably win or, at least, avoid defeat in their first match in a higher division. It's another of those aspects of what Danny Blanchflower called 'the heart of the game', matters organic to football that no amount of money or influence from the more 'business-minded' who run football now can ever alter.

Sheffield United opened 1970–71 with a visit to newly promoted Orient, who had won the Third Division Championship the previous season. A crowd of 15,584 (how Barry Hearn would love to see such a crowd at Orient for a League match these days) saw the home side triumph with goals from Mark Lazarus (2) and David Harper. For the latter it proved to be his only goal in his only appearance for Orient that season, as sadly the former Swindon Town defender was forced to retire from the game through injury. As if to bear out what I have said about newly promoted teams, following their flying start against Sheffield United, Orient thereafter struggled and only just managed to avoid relegation. We, on the other hand, put that early disappointment behind us and went from strength to strength.

We lost only one of our next eighteen League matches, which included a 5–1 win at Portsmouth and a 3–2 derby success against Wednesday in front of a 40,000 crowd at Bramall Lane. During this run we also caused something of a shock when we beat Leeds United 1–0 in the League Cup, our goal coming from Tony Currie, who was the outstanding player on the night amidst such illustrious company as Billy Bremner, Norman Hunter, Eddie Gray, Peter Lorimer, Allan Clarke and, of course, Mick Jones. Our interest in the League Cup ended in Round Three when we were beaten 2–1 at Spurs, but it took a late deflected goal from Martin Chivers to see us off. You need luck to win cups. Spurs had their luck against us that night as we hit the woodwork twice, but Bill Nicholson's side took full advantage of their good fortune and went on to win the League Cup.

In January we travelled to Bolton Wanderers off the back of successive home wins against Portsmouth and table-topping Leicester City. Sheffield United were third in the table and embroiled in a battle for promotion with Leicester City, Carlisle United and Cardiff City. Even though we lost 2–1 at Bolton, no alarm bells rang, it was seen as a setback, nothing more. I knew we would put the disappointment of defeat at Burnden Park behind us and bounce back.

Cec Coldwell was now first-team coach and supervised training with John Short. John Harris joined us only occasionally, so I thought nothing was untoward when I didn't see John on the training field in the week following our defeat at Bolton. We had no match the following Saturday as we had been knocked out of the FA Cup. The first hint I had that something was afoot occurred the following week when John Tudor didn't train with us on the Wednesday. John had been fine the day before, so experience told me that he might well be on his way.

The news broke on 27 January that Sheffield United had bought Trevor Hockey for £40,000 from Birmingham City and 'sold' John

Tudor to Newcastle United. 'Sold' being something of a misnomer for, as far as John's move was concerned, to the best of my knowledge no money changed hands. John went to St James's Park in exchange for two Newcastle fringe players, defender David Ford (a Sheffield lad) and goalkeeper John Hope.

John Harris named all three new recruits in the squad for our following game at Oxford United. Now John Harris rarely, if ever, sat next to a player on the team coach. So when John came down the aisle of the coach, and sat next to me, I immediately sensed a problem. A feeling swept over me similar to that when someone says, 'We need to talk.'

John appeared nervous and edgy. He didn't look at me. His eyes gazed out of the coach window, seemingly transfixed on some point in the distance.

'I'm going to play him tomorrow,' said John, still gazing out of the coach window.

I felt a prick of adrenalin on my forehead. My stomach seemed to swish to and fro like a washing machine.

'Well, it's your decision and your prerogative, boss,' I eventually managed to say. 'I appreciate it must have been a very difficult decision for you; difficult for you to sit here now. As I say, it's your decision and I must respect it.'

John seemed to lose interest in whatever it was outside that had held his attention. He turned and looked at me.

'Yes, Alan, it is my decision and far from an easy one, so, thanks for your understanding; and … thank you for affording this awkward moment some dignity.'

He patted my arm with his hand, took to his feet and returned to his seat at the front of the coach, no doubt relieved his onerous task was over.

A solid, slow-moving hour crawled by. No one spoke to me, not that it would have made one iota of difference. I glanced about the coach. Some players were quietly engaged in a game of cards, some were reading, some catching a nap, a couple idly looking out of the window at the passing countryside. When a teammate is dropped from the side, or told he can leave the club, players behave like water-buffalo when one of the herd has been hunted to the ground by a pride of lions. They accept the tragedy as part of the cycle of life, turn their backs on the carnage, seek solace in the thought it wasn't them, never at any time thinking one day the inevitable will come when such a fate will befall them.

I was never selected for a League match again that season. Come the end of the season, the popping champagne corks had a slightly hollow sound for me. I was absolutely delighted Sheffield United had gained promotion back to Division One and I joined in the celebrations, but foremost in my mind was what the future might hold for me.

Sheffield United were promoted along with champions Leicester City.

I spent the summer wondering what on earth to do. I'd played well over half of the games during our promotion season and, as a result, received my commemorative promotion winners' medal. I knew, however, I was now John Harris's second-choice keeper. I was thirty-five but still fit, still in love with the game, still keen provide excellent cover between the sticks for United. I knew I was up to playing First Division football for another two years at least. The thought crossed my mind I might play for the reserves and wait for an opportunity with the first team and grasp it. I dismissed that idea. At thirty-five I didn't want to be playing Central League football.

As part of Sheffield United's pre-season programme of friendly matches we played a local derby at Chesterfield. John selected me for this game, I made up my mind it was to be my last for Sheffield United. A couple of days after the Chesterfield game, I went to see John Harris and told him, at my age, I didn't want to be a cover goalkeeper.

'So, what you're saying is, this is the end for you, Alan?' said John.

'There's never really such a thing as an ending, is there, boss?' I said in the manner he often used when speaking to the players, 'It's just a place where you end one chapter in your life only to begin another.'

John smiled at this. He wished me luck.

I had played 652 matches for Sheffield United, won five full England caps and seven at Under-23 level. My first game had been a friendly, against Clyde; my last, a friendly against Chesterfield. I had made my Football League debut against Newcastle United;

now my time as a player with Sheffield United had come to an end because of the arrival of someone from Newcastle United. I felt as Edmund did in *King Lear*, that the wheel had come full circle.

I had plenty of offers. Clubs such as Bolton Wanderers, Hull City, Rotherham United, Doncaster Rovers, Barnsley, York City and Mansfield Town all enquired, but I didn't want to step down. I had played my part in helping Sheffield United back into the First Division and wanted to end my playing days at the top, so to speak. I was, as I have said, still fit and could have joined another club but I didn't want to. I had, in my time, seen players drop down the leagues and carry on playing because playing football is all they could do. As the seasons rolled by they would drop another standard until the time came when they weren't so much over the hill as specks on the horizon. I didn't want that. I felt I had a lot more to offer the game than playing, albeit I loved playing.

I did listen to the offers that came my way, but turned them down in favour of an offer made to me by John Harris. With Cec Coldwell now first-team trainer and coach, John informed me he needed a reserve team trainer-coach and asked if I would be interested. I was.

I was a man with a plan. I decided I would work as trainer-coach of the reserves, at the same time taking my FA coaching badges. In truth, I would have liked to continue to play for Sheffield United in the First Division; that would have been the perfect scenario for me. Being happy in life, however, doesn't mean everything has to be perfect. Happiness is more about you being able to look at your life beyond its imperfections. I was happy enough to stay at Bramall Lane as reserve team trainer-coach and actually looking forward to my new role at the club as one of John Harris's coaching staff. I was also happy my character was such that I had not kicked up a fuss and stormed off in a strop at losing my first-team place. My career as a player with Sheffield United had ended happily enough, and good endings make for good beginnings.

| CHAPTER ELEVEN |

'The very substance of the ambitious
is merely the shadows of a dream.'

Hamlet

In football, as in life, people tend to forget what you said, in many cases people will even forget what you did, but they never forget how you made them feel. I was made aware of this once my playing days were over. Numerous people, and not simply Sheffield United supporters, approached me and told me how excited or happy I had made them feel during my time at the club, something which never failed to instil in me a combination of humility and gratification. I would be told how a certain save had been the talk of the steelworks or brewery for the following week. It was only when I gave up playing that I truly realised the important role football and footballers played in the lives of some people. For some, their weekend would be made or broken, their mood enlightened or diminished, according to how a certain player played and their club had fared. A save, such as the last-minute penalty save I had made against Manchester United at Old Trafford, according to one Blades supporter, 'put me on cloud seven for a week'.

During their playing days not many footballers realise what they do creates mood and, later, memories for supporters. One hears talk of footballers being role models to the young; the fact that what a footballer does may dictate mood and create memories is the biggest responsibility of all. Having given up playing, I was going to miss that.

I had only been in the job of reserve team trainer-coach for some two months when John Harris asked if I would return to playing. I had no hesitation in saying, 'Thanks but no thanks.' I was now pursuing a career as a coach, or rather, as I saw it, on a brand new journey in life. A return to playing at the age of thirty-five was possible for a goalkeeper, but I felt it would be a retrograde step, so I respectfully declined John's offer. Besides which I had started the FA courses at Lilleshall that I hoped would lead to me becoming a fully qualified FA coach. Such were the demands of the latter stages of this award, you couldn't play First Division football at the same time.

I enjoyed over four years as United's reserve team coach-trainer (I had, by now, managed to convince the club the term 'coach' was more important than that of 'trainer'). In that time I guided the United youngsters to success in two international youth tournaments in Cyprus and played a role in the development of youngsters such as Micky Speight, Steve Cammock, Keith Edwards, Simon Stainrod and goalkeeper Tom Alister, all of whom went on to enjoy fruitful careers in the game.

After over four years of running a reserve team, however, you begin to ask yourself, 'Is this as far as I am going? Is this what I want to be doing for the rest of my career?' You live in hope your talent has not gone unnoticed, that one day the telephone will ring.

It was the autumn of 1975. My old pal Gerry Summers was manager of Oxford United. For seven years Gerry had kept a Third Division team in the Second Division, whilst at the same time having to sell his best players to balance the books; such as Welsh international Dave Roberts and Scotland's Hugh Curran. It was early October when I heard Gerry had been given the sack. A few days later, Ken Furphy, who had succeeded John Harris at Sheffield United (who again had gone 'upstairs'), became another managerial casualty.

Ken Furphy's successor was Jimmy Sirrel, who joined Sheffield United from Notts County. In so doing Jimmy created a little piece of football history. Jimmy was not under contract to County at the time. The Sheffield United board wanted Jimmy to take charge as soon as possible. Jimmy, however, didn't want to leave Notts County in the lurch, so an amazing agreement was reached between the respective boards. Until such time as Notts County found a successor, it was agreed Jimmy would manage both Sheffield United and Notts County simultaneously. Unbelievably, Jimmy worked alternate days at each club, being there for United matches on a Saturday. Jimmy did this for over three weeks until Notts County appointed Ron Fenton as his successor.

One always fears for one's job when a new manager is appointed. I was considered by many to be a fixture at Bramall Lane, but I knew my thirty-three years with the club would matter not one jot to a new manager who wished to appoint his own backroom staff.

In addition to wondering if I would be kept on by Jimmy Sirrel, I had the feeling I was beginning to tread water at Sheffield United. I had begun to ask myself: 'Is this as far as I am going? Is this what I want to be doing for the rest of my career?' 'I hope my talent has not gone unnoticed,' when the telephone rang.

The voice on the other end of the line was that of Gerry Summers.

'How do you fancy moving the family down to Gillingham?' asked Gerry.

Not the sort of thing you are asked every day, if at all. Gerry told me he had been appointed manager of Gillingham in succession to Len Ashurst and that he wanted me with him as his assistant.

'You'd be assistant manager but also share the coaching with me. It's a three-year contract with a club that has good potential,' Gerry informed me. 'We'll have a free hand. No interference from the board. Chairman is a lovely fella ... a Doctor Grossmark, and one of the other directors is the ITV football commentator Brian Moore. What do you say, Alan?'

I said, 'Yes.'

In the autumn of 1975, Brenda and I bundled Karen and Paula into the back of the car and, for the first time in our lives, uprooted and left South Yorkshire. With a smile on my face and a heart full of hope, I set off for Gillingham. And it isn't often you read that.

There used to be a question that did the rounds whereby one was asked to name five famous Belgians... It should have been replaced by, 'Can you name anyone famous who originates from Gillingham?' This is an altogether tougher question. To the best of my knowledge there has been no one born in Gillingham who went on to enjoy popular fame. No, you'd be hard pressed to come up with famous people from Gillingham, likewise any notable exploits of its football club.

For as long as anyone could remember Gillingham had wandered up and down the Third and Fourth Divisions like a dog that had lost the scent. Gillingham was a bit of football backwater and Gerry and I were not foolish enough to think we were going to turn that on its head. We did, however, have a plan to take the club forward. The 'headlines' of our plan were to make season-on-season progress in the League, whilst developing an excellent and productive youth system that would produce not only good footballers but ones who thought deeply about the game. By and large, in six years at Gillingham, this is what happened.

Gillingham did make steady progress under Gerry and myself. To headline the seasons in Division Three, we guided Gillingham to tenth (1974–75), fourteenth (1975–76), twelfth (1976–77), seventh (1977–78) and fourth (1978–79), only to then experience something of a backlash to the disappointment felt at having narrowly missed out on promotion by finishing sixteenth in 1979–80.

We built a team in the traditional way, with a strong spine. Ron Hillyard was as good a goalkeeper as one gets in Division Three; we had a strong, dominating centre-half in Dave Shipperley whom we would later replace with a young Geordie by the name of Steve Bruce.

Up front we enjoyed the services of the Republic of Ireland international Damian Richardson and Ken Price, a lad we had picked up for a song from Southend United, both of whom scored plenty of goals season after season.

I think it fair to say the club made progress under Gerry and myself. In 1978–79 we had, according to supporters, the best Gillingham side for many a year. For much of the season we had been embroiled in a battle for promotion with Shrewsbury Town, Graham Taylor's Watford and John Toshack's Swansea. With four matches remaining we were looking good for promotion but defeat at Swindon was followed by a draw with Colchester United. Whilst we dropped points our rivals continued to win. Two victories in our final two matches of the season, at home to Exeter City and away at Chesterfield, proved to no avail. Gillingham missed out on promotion by a single point.

A mid-table finish in 1980–81 prompted the Board to seek a new management team they hoped would provide the extra impetus to secure promotion to Division Two. It was the first, and would prove to be the only time, I was given the sack. There was no animosity, no acrimony, no back-biting on the part of anyone. Gillingham wasn't that sort of club, Gerry and I not those sorts of people. Given another season I felt Gerry and I could have guided the club to promotion, but it wasn't to be.

We left the club in very good shape, the squad was strong and a number of the young players we had introduced were developing into fine footballers. Two youngsters in particular had displayed the sort of deep thinking we had been at pains to instil into all the players. I was convinced they would go on to enjoy fruitful careers in the game when their own playing days were over and, I am happy say, Steve Bruce and Micky Adams did exactly that.

Gerry Summers and I left Gillingham in 1981. After a journey that had its ups and downs but in which much good was accomplished, we moved on in life. During my time at Gillingham, Brenda gave birth to a baby boy. Andrew was born in 1977 and with three children to bring up, Brenda and I were very conscious that what I needed in order to sustain and maintain the family was a more secure job, not one where we might move to another part of the country only for me to lose my job after twelve months on the whim of some club director. I was a fully qualified FA coach but in all my time at Gillingham had been constantly studying goalkeepers and goalkeeping. I had created programmes for the coaching and training of goalkeepers according to age, standard and experience. During my time with Gillingham I had also conducted a series of goalkeeping sessions for the FA. It occurred to me that there was no one in the world who had made such a detailed study of goalkeeping and devised coaching programmes that could be adapted to the individual needs of goalkeepers. In 1981 there was not one club in Europe that employed a specialist goalkeeping coach, because there wasn't such a thing. 'Well,' I thought to myself, 'there is now.'

Brenda and I decided to buy a home in a village not far from Rugby, because it is only a matter of a few miles from both the M6 and M1. My plan was to contact as many football clubs as I could, offering my services as a goalkeeping coach. I didn't expect any club to get back and offer me a full-time post; rather I was looking to work one, hopefully two days at two or three clubs in order to make a living.

I had a blank canvas. I had the ideas, but more importantly I felt I had the expertise, knowledge, understanding and ability to communicate. I had no idea whatsoever how managers would react to someone offering their services as a specialist goalkeeper, but there was only one way to find out. I compiled a CV, a document outlining what I could offer in the way of coaching and the benefits thereof, sent these off with a covering letter and waited.

I didn't have to wait long. The first club responded within a couple of days. Dave Sexton, the coach at Coventry City, was handed my correspondence by his manager, Gordon Milne. Dave informed me my name and work was known to him and that the idea of a specialist goalkeeping coach would prove extremely beneficial to him. Coventry had three goalkeepers, Jim Blyth, Les Sealey and Steve Murcott, and he felt they would benefit greatly from specialist coaching. I subsequently met with Dave, Gordon Milne, his assistant Ron Wylie, Jim, Les and Steve, and it was arranged I would visit the club twice a week.

A couple of days after my initial contact with Dave Sexton I received a call from Graham Taylor at Watford. A similar agreement was put into place whereby I was to provide specialist coaching and training for Watford's senior keepers, Steve Sherwood and Eric Steele, along with their younger goalkeepers. The following season, I managed to complete a full week of work as goalkeeping coach when Billy McNeill contracted me to work with, among others, Joe Corrigan and Alex Williams at Manchester City.

So, with a mixture of the haphazard, opportunistic and pragmatic, I carved out a career as football's first specialist goalkeeping coach. Apart from a plan of wanting to coach goalkeepers, I 'fell' from one job to another. I got on extremely well with Graham Taylor, who realised the value and importance of a good goalkeeper to a team. In addition to being manager of Watford, Graham was appointed as coach to the England Under-18 team. No sooner did Graham assume this role than he asked me to coach the England Under-18 goalkeepers, Frazer Digby (Manchester United) and Perry Suckling, who I already knew through my work at Coventry City.

The work I did with Frazer Digby and Perry Suckling went down well with not only Graham Taylor but also England manager Bobby Robson. Bobby subsequently asked me to do some work with his Under-21 goalkeepers, Gary Bailey (Manchester United) and Alan Knight (Portsmouth). In turn this resulted in Bobby asking me to work with Peter Shilton and Ray Clemence. I was hoping to hear from Bobby Robson that my role of coach to the England goalkeepers might become something of a more permanent nature, albeit part-time, when life took me on another path.

It so happened England Under-18s played Scotland Under-18s and it was following this game that the Scottish FA's Director of Coaching, Andy Roxburgh, approached me and asked if I would conduct a coaching course for a number of young Scottish goalkeepers. Andy Roxburgh assembled twenty promising young Scottish goalkeepers (you never thought you would see those words in the same sentence) at the Scottish FA Training Centre in Largs. Among those who attended the week-long course were youngsters such as Campbell Money, Brian Gunn, Gordon Marshall and Alan Main, all of whom would develop into top-class goalkeepers. The course was considered a great success, so much so that Andy outlined his plans for me to hold further sessions on a regular basis.

In 1986, Andy Roxburgh was appointed manager of Scotland as successor to Jock Stein, who had tragically died moments after guiding following Scotland to victory over Wales in a World Cup qualifying match. Andy wanted to assemble 'an experienced backroom staff of proven expertise at the highest level' (his words not mine). Within a week of his appointment as Scotland manager, Andy called me and told me he wanted me to be international football's first specialist goalkeeping coach. I had no hesitation in accepting.

The appointment of a specialist goalkeeping coach to an international team made headlines in the sporting press throughout the world. I conducted numerous interviews for all aspects of the media and, by and large, my appointment and the idea of a specialist goalkeeping coach got a very positive reaction.

I was delighted to be working with Andy Roxburgh, whom I considered not only to be one of the top coaches in the world, but also a man with a constant flow of great, refreshing and practical ideas about football. Though I had no way of knowing it at the time,

Andy Roxburgh would play a key role in my development as a goal-keeper coach and set the standards for goalkeeping coaching.

International squads only come together for matches, which, finals of major tournaments apart, is some half-a-dozen times a year. My appointment as Scotland goalkeeping coach was on a permanent basis, but due to the nature of international football, it was going to be part-time employment. Though delighted to be working with Andy Roxburgh and Scotland, I needed to find additional work if I was to sustain the family.

I read somewhere that when Alexander Graham Bell first took his invention of the telephone to a Patents office they turned it down. 'Don't telegraph us, we'll telegraph you.' The telephone proved my lifeline to managers. I was keen to pick up work in addition to my job with Scotland, and word was circulating among managers that I could offer coaching for goalkeepers which resulted in a marked improvement in performance and their understanding of goalkeeping. One of the many calls I received was from Steve Coppell, who was beginning to make a name for himself as a young manager of great promise at Crystal Palace. Steve told me he was very keen for me to do some work with his goalkeepers at Selhurst Park but would have to get back to me on this. I took that to mean Steve had to okay the finance with his chairman.

The following day I had just settled into a hot, relaxing bath when the modern version of Archimedes principle was put into practice ... the telephone rang. It was Oldham Athletic manager Joe Royle. Joe told me he had a goalkeeper, Andy Goram, who he believed had the potential to be a top-class keeper should he receive the right coaching. Would I be interested in working for Oldham?

'You're the man, Hodgey. In fact you're the only man,' said Joe, 'I want you to come here and work with Andy, turn him into that top-class keeper.'

I was upfront with Joe. I informed him I was waiting for Steve Coppell to get back to me, in addition to which there was the work with Watford, Coventry and Scotland, plus a number of other clubs such as Everton and Manchester City wanted my services.

'Fair enough,' said Joe, 'but there's nothing stopping you working here with Andy when time allows. In the meantime, how about having a look at the lad?'

I agreed to come and take a look at Andy Goram who, Joe informed me, was returning from an injury and would, in a couple of days, be having an outing with the reserves.

I drove up to Boundary Park and received a warm welcome from Joe, who waxed lyrical about the talents of Andy. Superlatives tumbled from Joe's lips; so gushing was he in his praise of Andy, I couldn't wait for the reserve team game to start so I could see him in action.

I sat in the directors' box with Joe behind me. Oldham reserves were playing Coventry City in a Central League Division One match. There can't have been more than 250 people present but they didn't have to wait long to see a goal. One minute, in fact, at the Oldham end.

Four minutes later, the scant crowd saw their second goal, again at the Oldham end.

'He's not normally like this,' Joe assured me.

Two minutes later it was 3–0.

'Honest to God, Hodgey, he's not normally like this,' rasped Joe.

Another two minutes, another goal. I was beginning to shift uncomfortably in my seat. So too was Joe, who again tapped me on the shoulder.

'I tell you, he's not normally like this,' protested Joe.

After twenty-five minutes, a fifth goal went in…at the Oldham end.

'What's going on?' cried Joe, coming across now as being very irritated. 'He's not normally like this.'

Five minutes later it was 6–0.

'Six-nil! After half an hour! I don't know what to say, Hodgey,' said Joe, throwing both arms in the air in exasperation.

'Tell me he's not normally like this,' I said. 'If you tell me it often enough, I just might believe you.'

Joe sunk lower into his seat and his blue Oldham training coat. The final score was 8–0. When the final whistle blew I turned to Joe. I told him I would have no problem working with Andy, I had seen enough of him to know Joe was correct in his analysis. Oldham fielded a very young side against what was an experienced Coventry City reserve team. True, Andy conceded six goals in the first half-hour, but most of those were not his fault. What's more, having conceded six in the first third of the match he demonstrated not only his talent but also his resolve and mental strength by only conceding a further two. Believe me, but for him it would have been double figures.

Andy's performance told me he had the hallmarks of a top-class goalkeeper. The problem was, I was now receiving so many requests from managers to work with their respective goalkeepers it would be nigh on a year before my diary allowed me to work with Andy Goram.

Ten months on, I arrived at Oldham to begin my coaching of Andy. We didn't get off to the best of starts. Andy came across as many a club chairman had done when confronted by a manager who wished to appoint a specialist goalkeeping coach – at best, sceptical, at worst, dismissive. I sensed he felt the training session I had created for him was rather pointless, so I took the time to explain why we had to work in the way I was suggesting. At one point, in frustration, Andy kicked the ball across the training field. I stopped the session there and then.

'Go and get the ball, Andy.'

Andy stood staring at me.

'Not asking, Andy, I'm telling you. Go and get that ball and don't walk…you run…there and back.'

Andy continued to stand staring at me. I walked towards him.

'Listen!' I said through gritted teeth, 'I'm not driving a hundred and twenty miles here, and then back, to mess about with you. You either show me some respect and a better attitude to learning, or I'm finished here…and you can pick that one up with Joe.'

'I've got plenty of clubs who want me to work with their keep-ers. With respect, bigger clubs than this one…so, you either show a keenness to become the goalkeeper Joe and I know you can be… or I'm out of here.'

To his credit Andy apologised, retrieved the ball and, from such an inauspicious start, our working relationship and friendship went from strength to strength. Such was the improvement in Andy he was transferred to Hibernian and from there to Rangers. Not only did he become Roxburgh's first-choice goalkeeper for Scotland, but Andy was ultimately acknowledged as being one of the best goalkeepers in the world. He was also voted the Scottish Football

Writers Footballer of the Year and no one was more deserving of such an accolade.

After such a dodgy start with me, Andy worked tirelessly to improve his game, and his dedication and efforts paid off handsomely. We also became good friends and, I am happy to say, have remained so. Andy Goram remains, to my mind, the greatest Scottish goalkeeper there has ever been and a truly world-class one at that. He's also something of a rarity in that he is one of only two people to have represented Scotland at both football and cricket.

May I take you back to 1986, when clubs are ringing me. I am waiting for Steve Coppell to get back to me when I receive a call from the newly appointed manager at Manchester United, Alex Ferguson. Alex tells me he has heard about my coaching work and that he would like me to be a part of his coaching staff and work to improve the performance and technique of his goalkeepers. I have no hesitation in saying yes.

When Alex Ferguson was appointed manager of Manchester United in November 1986, he was told he was 'inheriting a fortune' in terms of players. Two days later, Alex lost his first match, to Oxford United, a team which, under the management of Maurice Evans and Ray Graydon, was just about holding its own in the First Division.

On that day Alex was under no illusion about the task which confronted him. He saw with his own eyes that, contrary to popular belief, United were not overladen with quality.

It was a few weeks after the Oxford United debacle I received the call from Alex asking if I would join his coaching staff. Alex told me he reckoned it would take three years to build a United team good enough to win a major trophy. Uncharacteristically, he had underestimated the task.

It was to be five years before United beat Crystal Palace in a replayed FA Cup Final to lift their first major trophy under Ferguson's charge. The following year they clinched the European Cup Winners Cup with a 2–1 victory over Barcelona. The edifice of achievement associated with the forthright Glaswegian has seen many a substantial brick added to it since.

When Alex asked if I would consider the job as goalkeeper coach at Old Trafford, I was still waiting for Steve Coppell to get back to me. At the time Steve was a young, up-and-coming manager for whom I had a lot of respect. Alex had only been at Old Trafford for seven weeks and was not so much finding his feet as making his mark, but I didn't think twice about saying yes to him. When Steve did call back and offer me work, I had to decline his kind offer. Given I was a freelance goalkeeping coach, I was now signed up to work with Scotland and also Manchester United, and there are, after all, only so many days in a week.

Even before he bought his first tin of Duraglit at Old Trafford, I considered Alex Ferguson to be an exceptional manager. His success with Aberdeen was proof of that. Anyone who accomplished the remarkable feat of elbowing Rangers and Celtic off centre-stage in Scotland for more than a decade, and convincing a provincial team they are better than a big city one, had to be a very special manager indeed.

There are few managers whose kudos in the game is so great they have towered over the considerable achievements of their team, but Alex is such a man. He has an unrivalled affinity for football and football people but is as happy discussing politics or history. His interests are wide-ranging but his time is dedicated to United and football.

Alex works extraordinary hours. During my eight years at United, he took training every morning, stayed on for special coaching of individuals, was interminably on the telephone in his office, at the training ground or at home, talking to football people, to managers, agents, contacts, journalists, absorbing the current news of the game.

There has been recurring talk among those who do not know Alex that he is a tough, dour, uncompassionate man. I never found that – quite the opposite in fact. He doesn't suffer fools gladly, if at all, and is scathing of those who don't attempt to aspire to the high standards he sets for individuals and the club, but he is eminently likeable and sociable, a witty man, with a caring compassion for mankind, especially those who labour long and hard for little reward.

Like Busby, Stein, Shankly and Paisley before him, Alex is the unpretentious embodiment of the 'old school' of football men, steeped in working-class ethics and ethos. He's done very well for himself, and deservedly so, but there has never been the remotest danger of him being contaminated by the materialism that infects so many of those who have found wealth and prosperity through football. For all his success, despite what some football journalists may think, he remains as down to earth as a conducting rod, and still capable of conveying an electric charge of frightening power.

I have always found him to be fair, willing to give people a chance. From his predecessor Ron Atkinson, Alex inherited the mercurial talents of Bryan Robson, Norman Whiteside and Paul McGrath. Each was an outstanding player, but the trio were lovers of the treatment room and had fallen into the habit of meeting up for drink in the afternoon at a hotel in the Altrincham area. There was a hardened drinking culture in the club at the time among certain players, and Robson, Whiteside and McGrath were its keenest advocates. Alex was having none of that. In time, Norman Whiteside set sail for Everton, whilst Paul McGrath was sold to Aston Villa.

Bryan Robson stayed, because Alex knew he was an outstanding player who fitted his plans for the team. He also knew that Bryan's fierce desire to succeed and turn in match-winning performances meant he never drank to the eexcessive levels of McGrath and Whiteside. Alex was very impressed by Bryan Robson's motivation, commitment, technical ability, stamina, selfless workrate and desire to win. He has since told me, of all the players he has worked with, he would place Bryan Robson in the top three. Given the players Alex has had under his charge at Old Trafford over the years, that is praise indeed.

Their relationship was a curious mixture of mutual respect, exasperation and disagreement coupled with a desire to please and deliver success. Alex once said in frustration, 'No player has ever given me so much trouble.' Robson in chastened mood agreed that no player could have. In spite of that I always felt Alex and Bryan engaged with one another well. For all their occasional differences, Bryan Robson was, as Alex put it, 'reachable'. I never sensed Alex felt that way about Paul McGrath.

'We have three goalkeepers, (Chris) Turner, (Gary) Bailey and (Gary) Walsh,' Alex told me. 'Bailey's talking of going back to South Africa. Of the other two, Turner's by far the better, but neither are what I need.'

'What do you need?' I asked.

'Well, I was hoping you would tell me, Alan.'

Gary Bailey, as Alex had predicted, returned to his home country to host the South African equivalent of *Match of the Day*. Chris Turner moved on, Gary Walsh stayed, but was joined by Jim Leighton, who Alex knew from his days at Aberdeen. In 1990, they were joined by veteran Les Sealey and the young Australian goalkeeper, Mark Bosnich.

Most managers would have been happy enough with such a stable of goalkeepers, but not Alex. I had told him how, in 1967, when Stoke City manager Tony Waddington signed Gordon Banks from Leicester City for a then world record fee for a goalkeeper of £65,000, the Stoke City board had balked at the money. 'Waddo' justified paying that amount by telling his directors, 'He will save us at least 20 goals a season. Just think of how many more matches we'll win with him doing that.'

Alex told me that was the type of goalkeeper he wanted at United. Every scout was charged with finding him, and, as goalkeeping coach, I too was assigned to be part of that quest.

In 1991, four years after Alex had joined United, I went to see a Danish League match between Brondby and Odense. We'd heard good things about the Brondby goalkeeper and so I went to check on him myself. Within ten minutes of watching the game I knew this goalkeeper was special.

At 6 foot 4, weighing sixteen-and-a-half stone and with his mop of blond hair, Peter Schmeichel made for an imposing and unmistakable figure on the pitch. If you want to know how good a goalkeeper is, you judge him not by how many saves he makes during the course of a game, but by how few. Executing a save is the last resort of a top-class goalkeeper. A top-notch keeper will organise his defence and work out his positioning and angles to deny the opposition opportunities to shoot at goal. From the start, it was evident to me Schmeichel was not only a top-class goalkeeper but had all the hallmarks of being world class.

I noticed he was extremely vociferous in condemning mistakes by his defenders. Alex was beginning to introduce some young and talented players such as Ryan Giggs and Lee Sharpe, followed by David Beckham, Paul Scholes and Nicky Butt. A goalkeeper with a formidable personality who berates youngsters can be detrimental. He puts them on edge, and hinders play because they are afraid of making a mistake. Part of my work with Peter was to temper his desire to openly castigate players who made an error.

Watching Schmeichel for the first time, I knew I had found the goalkeeper Alex had been looking for. I became more and more anxious as the game progressed because I convinced myself that a representative from another top club would be there to sign Schmeichel before we had a chance. No sooner had the final whistle sounded than I was making my way to the Brondby manager's office.

I quickly discovered that Peter Schmeichel was available and for what price. He had an agent, the Norwegian, Rune Hauge. Having established our interest, I rang Alex.

'He's the one,' I told him. 'He will win the Premiership for you.'

'How much are they asking?' enquired Alex.

'Five hundred thousand, believe me, he'll be the bargain of the century.'

Alex asked me if I was 'absolutely sure' about 'the Schmeichel boy' as he called him. I told him I was. What's more, I was convinced Peter Schmeichel would have no problem adjusting to the rigours of English football, which is often a problem for goalkeepers coming into our game from overseas.

The rest is history and of the most glorious kind. Peter Schmeichel developed not only into a world-class goalkeeper but, to my mind, along with Gordon Banks and Lev Yashin, one of the top three goalkeepers there has ever been. Peter always trained hard under me and hated losing goals, even if it was just me kicking the ball at him. He had a huge presence in the goal and there weren't many strikers who were not intimidated by him. His technique, talent, confidence and consistent form also served to make many strikers doubt whether they could score when presented with a chance to beat him. That is a quality very few goalkeepers possess, and it only comes from being consistently at the top of your game for a number of years. A goalkeeper reaches his peak a little later than an outfield player; for a goalkeeper that's around twenty-eight to thirty-two years of age, but, and it's a big BUT, in order to reach that peak he must have been playing consistently for some seven to eight years. As was the case with Peter Schmeichel and keepers such as David Seaman, Andy Goram, Ray Clemence, Pat Jennings, you name them. A goalkeeper will not reach his peak at around twenty-eight having spent most of the previous four or five seasons sitting on a bench. It is something I told Alex Ferguson and, judging how he sticks with young, highly talented but developing goalkeepers, he has never forgotten.

I am often asked to suggest one thing that has made Alex one of the greatest, if not the greatest, manager British football has ever known. My answer often varies, from his ability to get the most from his players, and tactical nous, to his understanding that effective leadership and effective football management are two entirely different things. Alex, more than anyone, appreciates good leadership is putting the first things first, whereas good management is carrying them out. Sounds simple enough, difficult to do in practice, but Alex effectively accomplishes this. He also understands that leadership is action not position, and the key to successful football management is having the power of your convictions, and the key to failure is trying to please everybody.

The one thing I would say marks Alex from other managers is his ability to move with the times and adjust to the ever-increasing demands of a game which is constantly in a state of flux. Football has changed irrevocably since Alex first took charge of Manchester United in 1986, yet for over a quarter of a century he has remained at the top. His ability not only to adapt but innovate is exceptional. To my mind no other manager is better than Alex at effectively operating the squad system. If I was to be asked to cite one thing which had contributed most to Sir Alex's success at United and which makes him stand out from all other managers, it would be his deft, canny and highly effective operation of the squad system. No other manager, including José Mourinho, Roberto Mancini or Arsène Wenger, is more adept at this.

I think I can best sum up what sort of man Sir Alex Ferguson is by jumping ahead to 2011. In 2011, whilst with Oxford United, I helped arrange for Oxford to train at Manchester United's Carrington training ground during a stopover on our way to play Morecambe. As the Oxford United team bus drove towards the main gate, one of our party drew my attention to a large purpose-made banner hanging above the entrance of the training ground. On it were the words, 'Welcome to the Master – Hodgey – the Goalkeeping Guru'.

When not working with Scotland I divided my time, coaching the goalkeepers at Manchester United, Sheffield Wednesday, Oldham and Millwall. Goalkeepers need someone who understands them, understands their specific role in the team, the trials and tribulations they endure which are different to those of an outfield player. Even a great manager such as Alex Ferguson would say, 'When there's a problem with my back four I know what to tell them, same with my midfield and strikers, but not my goalkeepers.'

Often my work with goalkeepers has to do with counselling and building confidence. Prior to the arrival of Peter Schmeichel at United, Jim Leighton had been number one for a number of seasons. Part of my job was to rebuild Jim's morale after the 1990 FA Cup Final, when Alex replaced him with Les Sealey for the FA Cup Final replay against Crystal Palace. Jim is a good guy but his self-esteem and confidence had taken a big hit; I knew he would, in time, return to being the top-class keeper we all knew him to be, though. When Reading wanted to take him on loan, Jim rang to ask my advice. I got out of the bath and told him to go and play. The bench was no good for him; in order to overcome his demons he had to get out there and play. To his credit, Jim did just that.

I was keen to have UEFA adopt my ideas for a UEFA-approved Goalkeeping Award, and in this Andy Roxbrough was extremely helpful to me. It was something of a chicken and egg situation in that I was the first specialist goalkeeping coach in the world, so who was there to approve my suggested UEFA Goalkeeping Coaching Award scheme? In the end it was approved by Andy and the UEFA Technical Committee. The course involved practical elements as well as theoretical ones, which were broken down into various sections according to age and ability. It began with youngsters aged eight and extended upwards, to the final coaching award which was applicable to working with goalkeepers of Premiership to international class.

The dedicated coach tells; the good coach explains; the superior coach teaches by example, but the great coach will do all the aforementioned and, above all, inspire. That was the tenet of my UEFA-approved goalkeeping coaching, and it still applies to this day.

In recent years I have been saddened by the fact that Scotland had failed to qualify for the finals of a major international tournament. As part of the Scotland coaching staff I felt very proud to be part of a Scotland team that qualified for the finals of four major tournaments – the 1990 World Cup and 1992 European Championships (under Andy Roxburgh), and the 1996 European Championships and 1998 World Cup (under Craig Brown).

Andy Roxburgh and Craig Brown, although different in their approach to management, were both very good managers as far as Scotland was concerned. Andy, the more technical of the pair, had a gift for making problems appear so interesting and solutions appear so simple yet constructive that everyone was champing at the bit to deal with them. Andy is also very good at man-management; he knows that in order to create a team you have to treat everyone as an individual. A football team, including backroom staff, comprises all manner of individuals.

Think of your own work situation. It is rare indeed that you get on like a house on fire with everyone you work with. The same applies to football. In the main players do get on with one another because there is a common cause they are committed to. They will support and battle for one another on the pitch. If they are the best of friends, then great, if not, the very least you ask is for them to have respect for one another as footballers. Andy and I were fortunate in having Scotland squads containing players who got on with one another. Even before I was introduced to the players, I would have respect for them. The way you see players is the way you treat them, and the way you treat them is the way they often become. I have always adhered to this and Andy has too. We treated the Scotland players with respect and we led and taught to inspire. How well we succeeded in this can, I believe, be evidenced by the fact that Scotland qualified for the finals of the World Cup and the European Championships.

For some Scottish FA officials and football writers this, seemingly, was not enough. In Italia 90, though Scotland beat Sweden and lost by a late goal to Brazil, Andy came in for criticism for having lost to Costa Rica, a single-goal defeat which put us on the plane home.

In Euro 92 in Sweden, Scotland enjoyed a far better tournament than England. We were unlucky to lose to Germany after matching them for much of the game, likewise against Holland, whereas we completely outplayed the CIS (USSR), winning 3–0. Of course I was keen for Scotland's goalkeeper to do well, but Andy Goram did more than that. He was the only British player to feature in *L'Equipe*'s 'Squad of the Tournament'. Andy outshone goalkeepers such as Kahrin (CIS), Illgner (Germany) and Chris Woods and was named along with another of my 'pupils' – Peter Schmeichel.

Whilst manifestly lesser talents have since led Scotland to the brink of international football oblivion, I find it incredible that a manager who led the nation to the finals of two major international tournaments and instigated innovative coaching schemes from grass-roots to the canopy of the football tree, came in for as much criticism from certain quarters as Andy did towards the end of his reign. Throughout it all, Andy remained dignified and calm until the day came when he felt his talents would be better employed elsewhere – and then UEFA snapped him up.

When Andy Roxburgh moved on, I remained goalkeeper coach for Scotland under Craig Brown. Again, there was to be the finals of both a World Cup and European Championships to enjoy, finals in which Scotland did very well.

Scotland had the honour of playing in the opening match of the 1998 Finals against Brazil. We raised a few eyebrows when, prior to the game, we all appeared for the ritual of the pre-match pitch inspection wearing kilts. This drew much applause and many a wolf whistle from the crowd, but we were as ready for battle as William Wallace ever was. As for the game itself, what we didn't want to happen, happened. We conceded an early goal when Cesar headed home at the near post past Jim Leighton. Jim was not to blame, there were two Scotland players on Cesar and he shouldn't have been able to get his head on the ball, let alone turn and direct it into the roof of the net. John Collins equalised from the spot and just when I felt we had the measure of Brazil, they scored a killer goal. With fifteen minutes to go, a shot cannoned off one of our defenders, hit Tommy Boyd and deflected past Jim Leighton. Not for the first time in my career I was left to wonder why underdogs rarely enjoy such good fortune when playing a top team.

There followed a draw against Norway and a defeat against Morocco. It was not a good World Cup for Scotland; then again, when has Scotland ever enjoyed a good World Cup? Scotland's achievement was in having qualified yet again for the finals.

I served as goalkeeping coach to Scotland for 202 international matches, combining my work for the SFA with coaching the goal-keepers of Manchester United (for nigh on eight years), Sheffield Wednesday, Millwall and Oldham before moving north to serve Rangers under Walter Smith and then Dick Advocaat.

Whilst Brenda continued to run the family home near Rugby, I moved into a flat in Glasgow. Glasgow, as you know, is a city of great culture whose influence has spread across the world, though, in my experience, only three phrases of Glaswegian origin are in common usage south of the border: 'whisky', 'Auld Firm' and 'Partick Thistle nil'.

I thought I had worked at some big clubs but nothing, not even Manchester United at the time, compared to Rangers. The tradi-tion and history of the club is readily apparent the moment you set foot inside Ibrox. Paintings of former chairmen and managers adorn the walls, as do photographs of the legendary players to have worn the famous blue shirt. I joined Rangers under the manage-ment of Walter Smith, who succeeded Graeme Souness to whom Walter had been assistant manager. In addition to myself, Walter also appointed Archie Knox from Manchester United as assistant manager. The success roll had begun to gather momentum; Graeme Souness had established Rangers back at the top, and Walter was to continue the good work which would result in nine consecutive League Championship titles.

I joined Rangers at the start of Walter's first full season in charge (1991–92) and one of his first signings proved to be an old pal of mine, Andy Goram. Other signings to follow included Alexei Mikhailichenko, Stuart McCall, David Robertson and Paul Rideout.

Andy Goram had emerged as one of the top goalkeepers in Britain and would develop further to become one of the best in the world. Often in 'Old Firm' derby matches, especially at Parkhead, it seemed as if only Andy stood between Celtic and victory. So often did Andy deny Celtic, Tommy Burns said, 'You can put on my gravestone that Andy Goram broke my heart.'

Rangers is a way of life for many of the club's supporters and the devotion continues beyond that. At the Rangers training ground

I once asked the groundsman why little patches of scorched grass occasionally appeared at various points around the training field.

'Oh, aye, those,' said the groundsman casually, 'people break into the ground at night to spread on the pitch the ashes of a relative who's been cremated earlier that day.'

This story made the hairs rise on the back of my neck, for there had been a time when I felt I might have been reduced to ashes. Following the 1992 European Championship Finals in Sweden, I had one of those once-in-a-lifetime experiences that make you re-evaluate everything.

I held a coaching session at the Rangers training ground, it was a bitterly cold day and I didn't feel well. On my return to Ibrox, Walter Smith even commented on my ashen appearance, which I attributed to the onset of flu. It was coming up to Christmas and the following day I returned home to spend a few days with the family. I saw my doctor, Dr Hunter, who, having examined me, immediately referred me to a specialist. 'Not flu, then,' I thought.

The specialist, Dr Bessi, gave me an ECG test and I was then admitted to hospital. I thought I was going home, but Dr Bessi stopped me in my tracks when he said, 'You need a major operation. How you have not dropped dead on a football pitch, I do not know.' When you are told something on the lines of that, it has a very sobering effect on the mind. Like most people, I am a firm supporter of the National Health system up to a point. The point being when a member of your family requires a major operation and quickly, and you're told there is a ten- to twelve-month waiting list. I asked if I could go private, Dr Bessi told me how much. If I hadn't had a heart attack I nearly had one then. I informed him we would find the money. My conscience was clear. The way I saw it, me going private freed a bed and operation for someone in need using the National Health Service.

I underwent a quadruple bypass under the supervision of a surgeon by the name of Dr Dimitri, to whom I owe my life.

Not long after, I was in the wars again when, during my recuperation period at home, I haemorrhaged when suffering a burst ulcer. I collapsed and was rushed to a specialist hospital in Birmingham, where I received a transfusion of eight pints of blood, which, as you know, rather than being Hancock's armful, is a body full. I had lost so much blood the doctors had trouble locating a vein in which to provide me with the transfusion. As they did so, I felt myself drifting.

What I am about to relate now I could never have imagined happening to anyone, let alone me, quite simply because I didn't believe such a thing was possible. As I lay on the hospital bed I was suddenly overcome with a great sense of serenity. I could hear footsteps running. I felt my 'inner self' begin to rise out of my physical body. I saw myself looking down at myself lying on the hospital bed and was overcome with a desire to float away, only I resisted this urge and seemed to struggle to return to my physical self. Slowly, I sensed myself descending back into my physical body.

When I regained consciousness the image of what I can only describe as an out-of-body experience was clearly ingrained in my mind. I related it to the surgeon, who informed me the running footsteps were those of nurses running up and down the corridor ferrying transfusions of blood. It was the strangest experience of my life. Was I on the point of dying? Who knows? What this experience did for me, however, was to instil in me the notion that death was not to be feared, that it is merely a bridging point to some other life.

*　　*　　*

In 1992–93, Rangers won the domestic treble and came within a match of reaching the European (Champions League) Cup final. Rangers were defeated by Marseilles, who went on to win the competition but were stripped of the title when found guilty of match fixing.

In 1994–95, Walter paid £2.7 million for Basile Boli from Marseilles and £2.4 million for Brian Laudrup. The former did not prove to be anything like as good a signing as everyone hoped; the latter would have been a bargain at three times the price.

Basile Boli never adjusted to Scottish life, living in Glasgow or the rigours and physical nature of Scottish football. He nigh on froze stiff in the tunnel when confronted with the bedlam and noise of his first Old Firm match. Basile never got the humour either, such as Andy Goram asking him to call his pals back in Marseilles to find out the results of the matches in the forthcoming round of the European Cup.

Basile did, however, possess a sense of humour himself. Walter Smith was something of a stickler for dress as far as the players were concerned. He wanted players to arrive at the club looking smart, even on training days. One day Walter took Basile to task for having arrived for training wearing a tatty T-shirt, ripped jeans and loafers with no socks. Walter tore a strip off Basile, sent him home and told him the next day he must report to training looking 'very smart or else'. The following morning I was sitting in Walter's office at the training ground going through training schedules with him and Archie Knox when there was a knock at the door. One of the coaching staff, Alex Penny, popped his head around the door and told Walter, Basile Boli was outside wanting to know, 'Is this smart enough?' Alex flung the door back to reveal Basile dressed in a formal dinner suit complete with black bow tie, black top hat, spats (where did he find those?), walking cane and a monocle pressed against one eye.

In 1995–96 Gazza arrived from Lazio. The Rangers board were looking for the club's domination of domestic football to be repeated in Europe. Paul Gascoigne was the hottest football property in Europe at the time, and for Rangers to secure his signature was a real statement of intent.

I will not go into the problems Gazza has endured over the years, for they have been well documented elsewhere; suffice it to say, he was an immensely gifted footballer with sublime skills. One of Gazza's first matches for Rangers was against Celtic and he endeared himself to the Blues fans by running almost the length of the pitch before scoring what was an incredible individual goal. There were occasions when Gazza's naivety, moreover his inability to recognise the impact his actions may have on many people, got him into hot water, the instance of him mimicking the playing of a flute, for example. There were also times when some harmless fun on his part was treated far too sternly by football's authorities. When referee Dougie Smith dropped his yellow card only for Gazza to pick it up and pretend to book the referee: years before, that would have been laughed off, but the authorities came down on him. Yet another instance of football's governing bodies using a guillotine to cure dandruff.

The 1997–98 season proved to be trophy-less for Rangers, and it was also Walter's last in charge. Seemingly the disappointment of one trophy-less season together with Rangers not securing a historic ten League Championship titles in a row was too much for some people. Walter was succeeded by Dick Advocaat, the first non-Scot to manage Rangers.

Reminders that only optimum success would be tolerated were all around the club for Dick to see – no pressure then. One such reminder took the form of a poster made to look like a school report, with ticks alongside the seasons in which Rangers had won their titles under Graeme and Walter. Above this list, in large type-face, was the headline: 'Nine Out of Ten…Must Do Better!'

I had never worked for a manager who was such a stickler for dis-cipline and standards as Dick Advocaat. By no stretch of the imagi-nation could one describe Alex Ferguson as ever running a loose ship, but Alex was Bohemian in his approach to running a club in comparison to Dick. When eating meals the players and coaching staff had to take their seats and no one was allowed to touch any-thing, let alone eat a bread roll, before Dick arrived. Once present he would survey the scene and, happy all was in order, would then say 'grace', after which he would say, 'Gentlemen, you may com-mence dining.'

Rangers' chairman, David White, was reported as saying, 'For every five pounds Celtic spend, we will spend ten,' a quote that would come back to haunt the club. The board wanted Dick to repeat Rangers' domestic success in Europe. Dick was given resources no other Rangers manager had ever enjoyed, and that's saying something, as Graeme Souness hardly had to penny-pinch.

The sense of superiority and arrogance of some (and I emphasise the word 'some') in the club for a time penetrated Dick Advocaat. Following Rangers' achievement of winning the domestic treble, when receiving the Manager of the Year award, rather than being gracious and dignified, Dick simply said 'Thank you' and 'See you next year'. Dick had spent £36 million on players – in a single sea-son. Players such as Claudio Reyna and Michael Mols delighted the fans, Tore Andre Flo less so, unfortunately, and this substantial investment did not produce the success in Europe the board hoped for. What is more, the massive debt run up during Dick Advocaat's tenure sowed the seeds for the financial meltdown the club would later endure.

I moved on a little after the club opened its new £14 million training centre at Auchenhowie. I wondered if the new groundsman would have problems with scorch marks on the pitch...

I enjoyed my time with Rangers, particularly as I had seen Andy Goram mature and develop from a stroppy young lad of promise into a truly world-class goalkeeper, and also because Rangers is truly one of the biggest clubs in the world – I don't care what some may say; in football, people want to work at the really big clubs.

I didn't have any truck with the religious elements for which Rangers is infamous. My time at Rangers was when, publicly at least, a more tolerant attitude was displayed. For the 'imports' such as English and overseas players and staff, religion and politics was never, at any time, an issue. I did, however, detect an undercurrent of Protestant superiority among some connected with the club – and on occasion this was not so much an undercurrent as a visible wave.

Rangers is a club high on history and tradition, and the club's phenomenal success over the decades has provided it with its dilemma. The club's success and tradition are so intricately interwoven that some fear any change to traditional ideology might be to the detriment of future success. Rangers is a club that has stumbled much in recent years, but that's no bad thing; even when you stumble, you still move forward.

| CHAPTER TWELVE |

'Oh, this learning, what a thing it is …
How it may change us and for better.'

The Taming of the Shrew

I hold, so I am told, a unique standing regarding the history of Anglo-Scottish football. This unique status is, apparently, because I am the only person to have participated in the historic 'Auld Enemy' fixture as a member of both international camps: as a goal-keeper for England, and a coach with Scotland.

England versus Scotland is the oldest international football fix-ture in history of the game. The first, a drab goalless draw in 1872 in Glasgow, was merely a dud fuse to what subsequently proved to be the most combustible of international encounters.

It was during the Finals of Euro 96 when, as a coach to Craig Brown with the Scotland team, I came up against my home coun-try, managed by Terry Venables. The home side for each game was determined by the group draw. Scotland came out of the hat first for this Group A game. As this particular match had been scheduled for Wembley irrespective of the two participating teams, Scotland was in the unprecedented position of playing a 'home' game against England at Wembley. As an Englishman and former England inter-national and now a member of the Scotland coaching staff, I felt as if I had been invited to a dinner party by a friend who had scribbled on the invitation, 'Come dine with us and brace yourself.'

We English feel passionate about a game between England and Scotland, whether it's football or rugby. We want to beat the auld enemy for the sheer delight of bragging rights to our Scottish friends and workmates for a day or two. For the Scots, however, the feelings go much, much deeper. They are fundamental to their very essence and being. That much-maligned Scottish goalkeeper, Frank Haffey, who had the misfortune to keep goal for Scotland on their blackest day against England, a 9–3 defeat at Wembley in 1961, attempted to play down the significance of the demolition during the post-match buffet. Having been berated by teammate Dave Mackay for whistling a merry tune whilst selecting food for his plate, Frank turned to Dave, Denis Law, Ian St John and Billy McNeill to ask if they were going to join him in chatting to the England players. Frank received a stony silence.

'Awa' with you, it's only a football match,' said Frank. 'It's not as if we lost a war or anything like that.'

The jaws of his teammates dropped to their chests, in the case of Mackay to a very proud and considerable chest.

'We Scots were hammered by the English at Culloden,' added Frank, 'and that was a battle.'

'Aye,' replied Mackay with characteristic grittiness, 'and after Culloden we Scots didn't make small talk with the English over sandwiches, and we're bloody well not going to do it now.'

Don't ask Denis Law about England winning the World Cup in 1966. He didn't bother to watch the game, preferring instead to play a round of golf with fellow Scot Paddy Crerand on a deserted club course in Altrincham. The following day, during a phone call to Billy McNeill, the Celtic centre-back berated Law for knowing England had beaten West Germany. Up to that point McNeill had managed to avoid discovering the outcome of the Final, not through any jealousy, simply because the very notion of England as World Champions induced too much angst and frustration for him to bear. Not even the Biblical Jacob, fobbed off with Leah after seven years, could be more downcast than a Scottish football fan faced with the prospect of an English success in a major international tournament. North of the border they count their blessings such an occurrence has been singular.

Before the English FA in their wisdom put an end to the annual England-Scotland match, Scots lived for the fixture. Any game that could bring a die-hard Rangers supporter to full-throttle support of a Celtic player, and vice versa, has to be very, very special indeed.

Played annually and alternately at Wembley and Hampden, the match could not have had more contrasting venues. Before Hampden had the soul wrenched from its Alp-like terraces in the name of Health and Safety and progress, it regularly accommodated 135,000 fans for a visit by England, on occasion in excess of 147,000. Of these, all but a couple of hundred would be fervent Scots of all persuasions. In those days Hampden was grey, grime ingrained and grubby – football writer David Lacey memorably wrote of his first visit in 1965, 'Hampden is the only ground in the world which looks the same in colour as it does in black and white.' Perhaps, but Hampden was always a fervent cauldron of tartan tribalism.

Wembley has never truly been the bastion of yeoman-esque English support. Like London itself, the crowd for an England game has always been cosmopolitan. Regular attendees are joined by chance ticket-holders, the internationally curious, groups having a day out in the capital whose number will include at least one who has not the faintest interest in football but who has tagged along simply for 'the beer and a good time'; the football agents, business associates of football agents and business associates of the business associates of football agents; fathers accompanied by sons or daughters so that they can say at some point in the future, 'When you were young, I took you to Wembley'; supporters of a particular team, there to see one of their own club players perform in an England shirt; members of County FAs; supporters of non-League teams there to discover what a big game is all about; winners of competitions run by companies like Coca-Cola, Mars and Gillette; and, more and more these days, the corporate guests of investment bankers and financiers whose enthusiasm for the game can be gauged by the swathe of centre-stand empty seats that signals the start of the second half of any big game at Wembley.

Everything changes at Wembley, however, when Scotland visit, which may well explain why the fixture rarely happens now. For such a game, the ambivalent, cosmopolitan crowd is replaced by legions of tartan-bonneted, often ginger-wigged Scottish supporters brandishing yellow flags on which red lions roar rampant:

Wembley is soaked in Scotland. In 1961, after England's 9–3 victory, rather than leaving the pitch to a tumultuous appreciation of their efforts from a Wembley packed with England supporters, I recall Johnny Haynes et al making the long walk back to the dressing rooms to guarded applause from around 15,000 England supporters scattered about the terraces and stands, the remaining 85,000 Scots having long since left to drown their sorrows courtesy of Messrs Bell and Teacher. Once they're returned north of the border, however, such an apocalyptic event will be granted legendary status. Whatever the outcome was, never ask a Scottish supporter for their thoughts on these games if you have anything else to do that day.

For both teams this was a second Group A game and the pressure applied on both sides to produce a victory was intense. Whilst Scotland had gained a creditable goalless draw against the much-fancied Dutch in our opening match, England flattered to deceive when drawing 1–1 against a Swiss team that was full of energy but deficient in skill.

Craig Brown had selected a Scotland team that included in Andy Goram the one goalkeeper in the United Kingdom equal to England's David Seaman, to my mind. Also in the Scotland team were Gordon Durie, Stuart McCall, Tommy Boyd, Stuart McKimmie, Colin Calderwood, Colin Hendry, Jon Spencer and Gary McAllister. Seated behind me on the substitute bench was the legendary and prolific Rangers striker Ally McCoist. Included in Terry Venables' England team were Alan Shearer, Gary Neville, Stuart Pearce, Paul Ince, Tony Adams, Teddy Sheringham and the enigmatic Paul Gascoigne, at the peak of his imperialistic pomp as a footballer.

In the build-up to the game I had conducted dozens of interviews, every one of which questioned whether I was suffering divided loyalties. I was not. On this occasion I remained true to the country who had given me an opportunity to coach at international level. I was approaching 150 games with Scotland and had an excellent working relationship with the players and, at the time, with manager Craig Brown. The countless hours I had spent with Andy Goram had created a special bond between us: more than simply the 'goalkeepers' union', I felt we understood one another. I was wholeheartedly with Scotland.

Such was the number of Scottish supporters among the capacity crowd of 77,000, and the brilliance of their tartan bonnets and red and yellow flags, that the normally vivid green of the Cumberland turf seemed pale by comparison. The plan was to keep the game tight for the first twenty minutes, not concede an early goal, have McCall police Gascoigne, let McAllister deal with Ince and, close down quickly on Neville and Pearce to stop them rampaging forward; and last but not least, get in quickly at the England full-backs and Ince to stop them giving the ball to Gascoigne. Starved of the ball, we felt he would become frustrated.

At the risk of sounding immodest, I felt we were tactically superior to England. This was certainly the case in what proved to be a very tight first half, during which Andy Goram was never called upon to entertain the crowd with football's most spectacular art. England, however, were determined not to pick up the same script in the second half.

During the half-time interval, Terry Venables and his coach, Don Howe, thanked Stuart Pearce for his efforts and replaced him with Jamie Redknapp in the hope of adding more attacking options to their left-hand side.

The change worked from the off. England were menacing and Redknapp, along with his Liverpool teammate, Steve McManaman, who had switched over to the right, began to probe ceaselessly at the Scotland defence with their skilful repertoire of long and short passes, timed and executed to perfection. It was with just such a pass that McManaman released Gary Neville on an overlapping run on the right eight minutes after the restart. Over came a cross which cleared a thicket of Scotland defenders and there was Alan Shearer arriving at the far post.

The goal should have lifted England to bigger and better, but in fact it was Scotland who came into the ascendency. With Ally McCoist on for Jon Spencer, and McCall and McAllister getting through a tremendous amount of work in midfield with seemingly little discomfort, Scotland dominated proceedings. Gascoigne was finding it increasingly difficult to stamp any presence on the game, let alone authority. And he appeared to have not the slightest notion as to how he could rectify the problem.

At the old Wembley there were two cushioned benches about

five yards long covered in deep purple leatherette, one behind the other. At the midway point on each bench was a strip of white tape. A printed card informed managers and coaches at the start of each game which team occupied which side of the bench. Invariably they sought to occupy the centre simply because it afforded an equal view of both halves of the pitch. Such was the case on this day, with me seated at the midway point. I had Craig Brown to my left and the England coach, Don Howe, on my right. Terry Venables had chosen to sit with the England reserves a few rows back since it gave him a slightly elevated view of play, so, thirteen minutes from time, I was surprised on glancing up to see Terry standing in front of me.

'Don! Take Gazza off,' said a vexed Venables, 'he's doing bugger all. Get Stoney (Steve Stone) on.'

This was good news. Gazza had indeed done little but, as everyone knew, he was the one player in the England team that day, capable of producing something exceptional, a 'rabbit-out-of-a-hat' that could turn a game on its head. Seeing Gascoigne substituted would give the Scotland players a lift and have an adverse effect on England.

'Stoney's not warmed up,' Don exclaimed.

'Take Gazza off. Now!' said Terry tersely.

Don told Steve Stone to get stripped and advised him once he got on the pitch, to run short sharp bursts to ease himself into the pace and tempo of the game. Suddenly, there was uproar.

McAllister beat two England players in the space of a hearthrug to send Gordon Durie bearing down on Seaman's goal. Gordon was not the most fleet-footed of forwards but had enough pace to keep ahead of Tony Adams who, seeing the Chelsea man displaying a pristine set of heels, decided to clip one of them.

For a split second both benches froze. Simultaneously Craig Brown gripped my arm, and me his. Don Howe's head fell forward and his eyes seemed transfixed to the ground as the referee, Mr Pairetto of Italy, pointed to the spot. Terry was fuming.

''king hell! Get Gazza off now!' Terry seethed through gritted teeth.

If I could have chosen one player to take a penalty in such a pressurised situation it would have been Gary McAllister, who had a record as reliable as daybreak. As he advanced to the ball,

I was convinced he would score and Scotland would go on to win.

Amidst a strangely hushed Wembley, Seaman stood erect as a Grecian pillar in the centre of his goal as McAllister made contact with the ball. Seaman immediately took off to his right, flung out his left arm above him and somehow managed to deflect the ball over the bar with his elbow.

Partly in an attempt to catch England before they could re-organise, partly to distance themselves from on-field disappointment as quickly as possible, Scotland took a quick corner. Too quick. The ball was hastily lofted into the penalty area and there was Seaman to collect with consummate ease. No sooner did Seaman have the ball in his hands then he released it, to Redknapp on the left, who re-labelled and re-despatched it to his fellow conspirator Gascoigne who had made a run into the Scotland half.

What happened next will be forever etched in the minds of those who witnessed it. With his left foot Gascoigne flicked the ball over the advancing Colin Hendry and, once around the big man, joyfully met the ball with his right to fire a low volley past Andy Goram. Gazza continued to run past Goram's far post before flinging himself to the ground a couple of feet from the touchline, whereupon with both hands he mimicked downing copious amounts of booze.

The England bench took to its feet, the fans pogoed with joy. Gazza's teammates gathered around him to proffer their congratulations. I suddenly felt a lead weight fall into my heart. I looked at my watch. There was ten minutes to go but I knew there was no way back.

Don Howe, still on his feet, with Steve Stone limpet-like by his side, turned to Terry Venables.

'Do you still want me to take Gazza off? asked Don.

There came a point when I felt I had to return to work in England. I loved working with both Scotland and Rangers, but I was missing family and home life on a daily basis. I took with me many great memories, not least that of the England-Scotland Euro 96 match, which shall remain with me always.

In the late nineties and throughout the 'noughties' I continued my peripatetic coaching at clubs such as Everton, Aston Villa, Leicester City and Birmingham City before returning to Watford and, from there, to Coventry City and then, at the invitation of Jim Smith, to Oxford United on a full-time basis. In between which, I ran numerous goalkeeping coaching courses for UEFA. In the main these were attended by goalkeepers wanting to be coaches themselves, such as Carlo L'Ami (Ajax goalkeeping coach in 2013) and Toni Tapalovic (Bayern Munich). A number of courses were for managers and attended by the likes of José Mourinho (who had qualified as a coach under Andy Roxburgh), Harry Redknapp, Filipe Scolari and Jupp Heyneckes.

I feel immense satisfaction at having devised and run courses for UEFA that have enabled numerous goalkeepers to attain licences that have, in turn, allowed them to become goalkeeping coaches and 'spread the gospel', so to speak.

I readily recall the first UEFA goalkeeping course I held. Twenty-four goalkeepers attended, which involved in the main practical sessions but also a written exam. Only four passed, among those being Tony Parkes (ex-Spurs) and Neil Sullivan who had played for Spurs, Chelsea, Leeds United and Scotland and was, at the age of forty-two, still keeping goal in 2012–13 for Wimbledon in League Two.

In essence the courses I devised for UEFA concentrated on three aspects of goalkeeping: the quality of touch – and by that I mean holding and catching a ball; mobility – where I concentrate on power work to improve such things as springing in the air or to either side so the goalkeeper becomes as proficient at saving a shot in the top right-hand corner as he does the bottom left; and what I call the 'Quality of Shape' – which has much to do with angles and positioning, whereby a goalkeeper must have an 'open window' when he looks at a striker. As teammates and opponents collect in front of him, through this open window the goalkeeper must have a clear vision of the ball and correct placement. This involves constant re-adjustment of position and also placement of his body so that he does not have to bring his right arm across his body to save a shot to his left, and vice versa.

By becoming highly competent at all three of the above, should a shot come to his left, the goalkeeper will call upon power to spring into the air in line with the open window and such will be his quality of touch that he should be able to collect the ball in his left hand.

The fact he is saving a shot in mid-air with his left hand rather than crossing his body with his right will save him a fraction of a second, which is often the difference between a save and a goal.

Such a save, as executed by Peter Schmeichel for Manchester United against Spurs in 1994, was brilliantly captured by *Sunday Express* sports photographer David Spurdells. His photo shows Peter flying through the air to his left at nigh on shoulder height. Peter's quality of touch is patently evident as he takes the ball in the palm of his left hand. The photograph won the World Press Photo Award for Best Sports Photograph, and numerous other awards. Peter made the save in the last minute of extra time with the score at 1–1. So delighted was Peter that something we had spent so much time working at on the training round had paid off, when he reached home (it was a mid-week match) he called me at two in the morning to express his glee.

'Peter, do you know what time it is?' I said blearily.

'Honey, Alan wants to know what time it is,' I heard him say to his wife, 'the clock's on your side.'

When I first joined Manchester United I spoke to Alex Ferguson about the importance to a team of a good goalkeeper, mentioning Gordon Banks and how Stoke City manager Tony Waddington had persuaded his board to pay a world record fee for a goalkeeper by telling them how many 'goals' Banksy would save in a season. When Peter Schmeichel eventually left Old Trafford, Alex called me to recall that conversation and inform me of a startling statistic. In terms of Premier League games, Peter kept a clean sheet in 42 per cent of the matches he played for United. As a goalkeeping coach, it is the sort of statistic I love to hear.

Coaching goalkeepers has much to do with needs and demands. The 'needs' encompass what a goalkeeper has to do, whereas the 'demands' entail what he has to do in order to be highly efficient at the former. It is also about creating good habits, and the earlier you do this the better. Decision making is also crucial to good goalkeeping; organising your defence, for example, is one aspect of this decision making.

You teach, you coach, then they play. Bob Stokoe once said, 'It is easy to be a good manager. All you have to do is sign good players. You don't have to teach good players what to do, they know.

The most difficult part of being a manager, however, is signing the good players.' Teach – coach – play, that is the formula for producing good players, be they outfield players or goalkeepers. The best players have the best technique and, again, the same applies to goalkeepers.

For a number of years I have lobbied the FA about creating a nationwide technical programme for goalkeepers. Without a shadow of a doubt, it is necessary if we are to produce generation after generation of top-class goalkeepers.

In 1970, when asked about other goalkeepers capable of playing for England, Gordon Banks memorably replied, 'Well, there's Peter Bonetti (Chelsea), Peter Shilton (Leicester City), Alex Stepney (Manchester United), Ray Clemence (Liverpool), Jimmy Montgomery (Sunderland), Gordon West (Everton), Joe Corrigan (Manchester City), Phil Parkes (QPR) and John Osborne (WBA). In addition to which Alan Hodgkinson (Sheffield United) and Peter Grummitt (formerly with Nottingham Forest, then with Sheffield Wednesday) are winding down their careers but still eminently capable. Apart from those, I don't think Alf Ramsey has much too much to choose from in the way of English goalkeepers capable of playing at international level.'

Banksy was undoubtedly teasing the questioner, but his answer speaks volumes about the standard of English goalkeepers at that time. There is an argument for saying it was not simply the quality of English but also British goalkeepers that was exceptional at the time, because the Football League also boasted Pat Jennings (Tottenham Hotspur and Northern Ireland), Bob Wilson (Arsenal and Scotland), Ian McFaul (Newcastle United and Northern Ireland), David Harvey (Leeds United and Scotland) and Gary Sprake (Leeds and Wales). It is testimony to the lack of quality home-grown goalkeepers in this country that in 2013 the England manager had only four regulars to choose from in the Premier League: Joe Hart (Manchester City), Ben Foster (West Bromwich Albion), Kelvin Davis (Southampton) and John Ruddy (Norwich City), albeit there may be a case for saying the latter two were not 'regulars' in 2013.

I believe the depth of quality in English football is the best in the world. Once you journey outside the top two divisions of Germany,

Spain and Italy, or simply the top divisions of any other European country, the quality markedly thins. In England we have teams in the Blue Square Conference and a number in the North and South divisions of that competition who could compete well against a team from, say, the French second division.

Whilst England may be lacking a surfeit of international-class goalkeepers, the depth of what I categorise as being 'good' goalkeepers is laudable and much of this has to do with the coaching received in recent years. Such is the lack of top-quality English goalkeepers in the Premiership, and the generally good standard of keepers through the divisions and into the higher echelons of non-League football, I envisage a day in the not too distant future when the England manager will call up a goalkeeper from League Two or the Blue Square Conference.

To provide the country with top-quality keepers in numbers, I would like our FA to undertake a National Coaching Strategy for Goalkeepers. One that would coach, educate and train goalkeepers from eight years of age through to internationals. The coaching programme would be tiered, with goalkeepers aiming to achieve and progress through a ladder of Key Stages of achievement via assessment.

If the FA is really serious about improving the standard of goalkeeping at all levels we need a Technical Programme such as this. When all is said and done, that is one of the reasons for the National Coaching Centre at Burton, is it not?

| CHAPTER THIRTEEN |

'The golden age is before us
not behind us'

Shakespearean Sonnet

On 5 September 1885, Dundee Harps beat Aberdeen Rovers 35–0 in the first round of the Scottish FA Cup. That evening beer and champagne flowed as the Dundee players and officials celebrated the record winning score for a British first-class football match. Just after 8 pm as the chairman of the football committee rose to make a speech to commemorate his club having made football history, Dundee Harps received unbelievable news. That very day, also in the Scottish FA Cup, Arbroath had beaten Bon Accord 36–0.

I can only imagine how those Dundee Harps players and officials must have felt as their emotions ran the gamut from joy to utter despair via shock and disbelief. Football can be a capricious and cruel mistress, but how can you fail to love a sport which produces such a longitudinal swing of the emotional pendulum?

It is because football has continued to affect emotions and produce such amazing stories, together with a few memorable experiences of my own, that I have remained in love with football. I have never been one of those people who say 'football was much better in my day'. It wasn't. It was, however, so very much different. Football today is indeed a beautiful game, one that has a place in the best of all possible worlds and, that was the case when I started back in 1953.

In 2012, I celebrated sixty years as a player and coach whilst working as goalkeeping coach for Oxford United.

At Oxford I had the pleasure of working with Ryan Clarke and Wayne Brown and the satisfaction of seeing Ryan develop into one of the best goalkeepers in the lower divisions, whilst helping Wayne achieve his ambition of becoming a goalkeeping coach himself. As 2012–13 marked my sixty years in football as player and coach, I thought this the right time to retire and tell my story in book form. I was obviously ready, because although I love the game and do miss the day-to-day involvement, I didn't feel as if an umbilical cord had been severed. Following the announcement of my retirement, Oxford United very kindly asked if I would return to the club to work a couple of days a week. Tempting as it was to work alongside Chris Wilder again, I respectfully thanked the club but declined the offer.

In 2012–13, I did some work for Bristol City at the request of their goalkeeping coach, Nigel Spinks, which involved me looking at and offering my assessment of goalkeepers with a view to their possible signing for Bristol City. I continue to offer my opinion on goalkeepers' talent and potential for clubs, which I enjoy as it enables me to get out and about and meet football people, who are, to my mind, the best of people.

Casting an eye over goalkeepers at League One or Two or top non-League matches in 2013 offered me yet another insight as to how the game had changed in recent years. Should you have attended a mid-week game in the equivalent of League Two in, say, the early nineties, you would have seen at least a dozen scouts and managers of other clubs present. I recall once attending a match at Northampton Town; the game took place on a Tuesday night and was one of only four taking place that evening. There must have been over twenty scouts and managers present, each one hoping to spot a gem. Should you go along to a mid-week match involving League Two clubs these days, you'll be lucky to find more than two scouts present.

Of course managers and scouts still do get out and about to matches, Crewe Alexandra being probably the most telling example. Crewe's assistant manager, Neil Baker, can be seen most nights at matches from Rochdale and Rotherham to Halifax and Hednesford Town. Rather than getting about and watching matches, however, quite a number of managers, especially in the higher divisions, now rely on agents with DVDs or downloads of players. It's not the same. You can't assess a player's worth and potential simply by watching video clips.

Nowadays we have instances of Chief Executives or owners of clubs recruiting players. I suppose they feel that having a large personal investment or key position in a club somehow qualifies them for such a role. Apart from this usurping the authority of the manager, 'cuckoo' players signed by owners or CEOs rarely, if ever, gel with the others in the dressing room. One is left to feel sorry for the player concerned, as it is, after all, none of his doing.

Premiership clubs no longer have a Chief Scout; the job title is now that of Head of Player Recruitment. One Premiership club in 2013 even deigned to give what was formerly their Chief Scout the title of 'Executive Assessor of Potential Human Resources (Playing)' – as pompous and fatuous a job title as you're every likely to hear.

Another aspect of the modern game I find disconcerting is the hypocrisy of some clubs in the way they view and deal with their own supporters. Many club PR departments are at pains to 'sell' to supporters the notion the club is 'their club' and fans should 'feel the passion'. Hand-in-hand with this illusion is a desire on the part of clubs to appear 'transparent'. Few, if any clubs, however, are truly transparent regarding financial dealings or anything else. Take transfers, for example. In the past all clubs readily publicised what they paid or received for players in the way of transfers. National and individual club records were kept, set and broken by way of fees received or paid. Given it was relative, how ambitious a club or board of directors was could be gauged by how much they paid for players. Nowadays, the vast majority of transfers are of the 'fee undisclosed' variety. So much so, it is rare to see an actual transfer fee recorded for the benefit of supporters and media. This has much to do with agents, their fees and other variables; however, the point remains that whilst supporters are entreated to believe the club is their club and they should 'invest' in it, the fee paid for the latest signing is none of their business.

The media coverage of football is terrific today, be it television, radio, internet or smart phones. When I think back to when I made the England team, the Football League would not even allow half-time scores to be broadcast on television or radio for fear such a service would affect attendances, which says much about the game's cheerless and funereal administrators' understanding of the power of television and radio. True, television in the UK was in its infancy in 1957; radio, however, certainly wasn't. Even in the 1980s we still heard protestations from FA and Football League officials that too much football on television would be detrimental to attendances, when most of us realised the reverse was true.

The multi-camera coverage of matches is fabulous and ensures the viewer misses nothing. This can, however, have a detrimental effect. What was once considered part and parcel of a game, such as players engaging in verbals with one another (in 99.9 per cent of cases this always ended in the respective players enjoying a beer together after the game) is now seized upon by those with no experience of playing the game at any decent level and condemned as bringing the game into disrepute. Likewise flailing arms, holding opponents and myriad other aspects of the game are frowned upon by those who officiate or commentate on football. All that these people are doing is offering evidence of not appreciating what to professional footballers happens to be reality. I heard one commentator say, 'Football, surely, must be played by the rules.' Professional football has never been played strictly to the rules; rather, to a consensus of the rules. In professional or semi-professional football, every time there is a corner there should be a penalty, if, that is, the game was played strictly to the rules. Referees also appreciate this. They don't give a penalty when they see pushing and shoving when there is a corner, simply because if they did, we would have no game and a match of a dozen penalties and more.

As fabulous as the media coverage of football is, it sadly suffers from Premiership myopia. One only has to look at the BBC Football website. The gossip column, which contains stories and rumours of transfers and news from clubs, in the main features only six clubs – both Manchester clubs, Liverpool, Chelsea, Arsenal and Spurs. Any other club appears as an afterthought. Day after day we read of players that these six clubs may or may not be interested in signing, or else stories of their own players seeking possible moves. It may interest TV executives and sports editors of newspapers to know that more people watch Football League matches every weekend than Premiership games.

Football has returned to being a family game, albeit one for those with decent disposable income. Rather like attending the theatre, cinema or a 'live' gig, it has, in recent times, become an 'occasion' rather than a couple of hours spent in leisure entertainment.

If there is one thing that gladdens my heart about the contemporary game, it is the attitude of the vast majority of supporters. For most, the sheer joy of watching football has not been tarnished by excessive hyperbole and the carpet baggers who have latched onto the game we love.

Those familiar with the history of the game know what Len Shackleton said, or, more to the point, did not say about football club directors. Directors in the fifties, sixties and seventies were football's central contradiction: amateurs who governed professionals. By and large, directors were either sensibly passive or incongruously obtrusive. To their credit, club directors of the past were not there to make money out of the football club. On the contrary, they were there to put money in and, in many cases, keep the club from going to the wall. Bob Lord, the former chairman of Burnley and also the Football League, was not everyone's cup of tea, but there is no disputing what he did for his local club. Asked by David Coleman what he would have been had he not been chairman of Burnley, Lord replied, 'A millionaire.'

Many directors of the past used the club as a private social club, a place to enjoy a bite to eat, a few drinks, or to do a little business networking. The boardroom was an enviable and desirable place to a man committed to his town and, in most cases, the game of football. The vast majority of directors were local businessmen. Today the directors of our top-flight clubs are, in the main, owners of multi-national companies, many based overseas. In essence there is nothing wrong in that, but they are not, by natural inclination, football people. The new breed of club owner appoints a CEO of similar business but not football background. The club is then little more than a money-making venture. There must be profit in everything and it is the 'everything' that irks the genuine supporter. Not so long ago, a local youngster was given the opportunity of being mascot for a match because it was his or her birthday, or simply because the opportunity to lead out their heroes guaranteed the club a supporter for life. Nowadays, parents have to pay for such a privilege, often handsomely so – at one Premiership club in 2013, an eye-watering £750. Some people might even call that exploitation.

In the 1990s, when big business and those adept at turning modest investment into massive profit woke up to the notion football clubs were a means of profit rather than philanthropic subvention, greed entered the game on a scale hitherto unknown. Moneyed people bought up football clubs comparatively cheaply with the aim of biding their time until the opportunity arose to sell the club for a massive profit to someone even richer than they. And so it goes on. Purchasing the local football club is now beyond every local business person unless the club is in the lower divisions and one step from going to the wall.

In recent times we have seen several instances of supporter groups coming to the rescue of a club which has been run into the ground. When a club has gone into administration and subsequently been saved from going out of existence by a group of loyal supporters, I find it unbelievable that the FA and Football League punish the new regime by deducting a considerable number of points, thus plunging the club into much further trouble. Luton Town were deducted thirty points and, as such, lost their Football League status; Chester and Halifax Town were relegated three divisions from the Blue Square Conference. When a supporters' group saves a club, the last thing they and the players need is a kick in the teeth from football's governing bodies whilst those who plunged the club into financial chaos walk away scot-free, but that's what happens. Football's governing bodies should be ashamed for the maleficence shown towards the likes of Luton Town, Wrexham, Chester and Halifax Town.

The technique (or skill, if you prefer) of today's players is, generally speaking, superior to players of the past. One only has to look at film of matches from the fifties or sixties for evidence of this. What helps today's player is the bowling-green pitches. Pitches today are a far cry from those of yesteryear which, in mid-winter, resembled either an ice-rink or molasses. The superb playing surfaces enable the ball to travel quicker.

Today's footballs are also lighter, a little under twelve ounces compared to the regulation sixteen ounces of the past. When I kept goal, the regulation Mitre football travelled true when hit, unless someone adept at swerving the ball bent a shot on purpose. When facing a long-distance shot, goalkeepers would take up a position and not have to re-adjust. Today, such is the deviation through the air of the lightweight ball, goalkeepers have taken to blocking or punching rather than catching. The unpredictable nature of the contemporary football has also resulted in goalkeepers blocking shots with their legs rather than smothering the ball, as used to be the case. The disadvantage to this, of course, is the goalkeeper immediately concedes possession. The trouble with a keeper going to ground and blocking a shot with his legs is he can't direct the ball with any accuracy, which is why we often see keepers saving a shot with his legs only to push the ball into the path of an on-rushing opponent, which results in a goal. This happens so regularly, I doubt if there is one edition of *Match of the Day* in which a goalkeeper does not concede in such a way.

The quality of the goalkeepers the England manager has at his disposal leaves much to be desired. This may appear to be a dichotomy, given there are so many goalkeeping coaches ('Hodgey's disciples' as Graham Taylor calls them) in the game. The depth in quality of goalkeepers in Britain is very good. Our top goalkeepers, that is those in the England squad, should be exceptionally good rather than very good, but in recent years this has not been the case. We are never going to produce goalkeepers of exceptional ability for the England team when the manager of the national team only has three top-flight keepers to select from.

It is not simply the lack of a retinue of international-quality goalkeepers that concerns me; when it comes to outfield players the England manager is also at a disadvantage. In one Premiership weekend in January 2013, only 29 per cent of the players who made it into the starting line-ups were English. On any given weekend, less than a third of the players on show in the Premiership are English. Compare this to La Liga in Spain, where in 2013 some 69 per cent of players were Spanish, or the Bundesliga (Germany), where the proportion of indigenous players was 64 per cent. The managers of Spain and Germany have twice as many players in the top flight from which to choose their squads as does the England manager.

Time was, we lovers of football still expected England to do well in major international tournaments, but the comparative dearth of really top-quality English players has served to engender in England supporters a lowering of expectation. Take the European Championships of 2012, or the 2010 World Cup: England flew out to both with, arguably for the first time in our football history, few if any supporters expecting anything much. In that we were not disappointed. It is the price we pay for having a bevy of glorious talent from overseas in the Premiership. Premiership clubs use international football as their 'supermarket', they go shopping for whoever takes their fancy. The Premiership, as high as the standard is, is not of the standard of La Liga; the Premiership, as well supported as it is, does not attract attendances to match those of the Bundesliga; the Premiership is the most expensive league in Europe regarding admission prices; the Premiership is, however, the richest league thanks to broadcasting deals, and so the overseas players keep coming. Even youngsters: one only has to look at the youth teams of Arsenal and Chelsea to see they are largely comprised of overseas players. I worry not so much about where tomorrow's top British players will come from, because we will always continue to produce them – but in what numbers?

The terrific football on show in the Premiership is only a part of it; every weekend there is good-quality, entertaining football in all three divisions of the Football League and in non-League. I have seen my share of dull matches, but I have also been highly entertained at Carlisle United, Torquay, Telford, Leek Town and more. Facilities in the lower divisions, non-League and throughout the Scottish League are far and away better than in the past. All of which engenders in me a firm belief that as good as football is now, it will become even better. A golden age is before us not behind us, though golden days we have indeed enjoyed and it is best we never forget them, because memory is the receptacle of all knowledge and by virtue of that, all future achievement.

I have thoroughly enjoyed every second of my sixty years in football. I feel truly blessed to have enjoyed a career of such longevity, from the days of Trevor Ford and Jackie Milburn through to the age of Robin Van Persie and Theo Walcott. In addition to which I have been fortunate to have Brenda, with whom I have enjoyed the happiest of marriages. We have a wonderful, loving family; how could I possibly ask for more? Happiness, for many, remains as elusive as a dream; for me it has been reality. The troubles I have encountered in my life: merely tools by which I was fashioned for the better. In my seventies I may be, but I like to think I still wear the rose of youth upon me. I don't think about age being a handicap to anything, it has certainly not been for me. I have always felt young, and still do. What is more I have, thank God, kept fit and healthy, even when working at Oxford United or some other club; fit enough to run two allotment gardens in addition to our gardens at home.

Age is a state of mind, they say. I would go one further and say to you, how old do you think you would be if you didn't know how old you are? Whatever, as Shakespeare said, no matter what age, we all have some salt of our youth in us, and perhaps that may be one of the contributing factors to me having worked for 60 years 'between the sticks'.

When I announced my retirement in 2012–13, two aspects of my life changed. In 2012 I spent my first Christmas Day in sixty years not at work. I loved it. Second, throughout my career, while I did my share around the house I never washed up as much as a single cup and saucer. As I told Brenda, placing my hands in washing-up water softens the skin and this is no good for a goalkeeper. So for all I painted and decorated, laid carpets, kept a steady flow of fresh fruit and vegetables coming to our table from the two allotments, in sixty years I never once put my hands into a washing-up bowl. On the day I retired, Brenda and I enjoyed a superb meal together that she had cooked (she's a brilliant cook and baker). We toasted my retirement with a glass of wine and I expressed my thanks to her for all the love and support she has given me. That done I said, 'Well, now I have retired, what shall I do with myself?'

'You can start by doing the washing up,' replied Brenda, quick as a flash.

I felt like Pontius Pilate, washing my hands of the daily grime and grind of work in football. No more would I don my tracksuit and fire shots at a goalkeeper on a misty Monday morning, or teach a young keeper how to collect a cross under pressure. No more to board a team bus bound for Plymouth Argyle or Hull City. No more one-hundred-mile drives on a Wednesday night to check out a goal-keeper at Preston or Tranmere. No more trips to Switzerland or France to hold UEFA coaching sessions for managers or aspiring goalkeeping coaches. No more to work a goalkeeper so hard the ground under his feet turned into the texture of Christmas pudding. No more to outline my ideas for a National Technical programme for goalkeepers to a seminar of goalkeeping coaches. No more trips to the USA to give practical lectures for NSL goalkeeping coaches. No more. Then, the phone rang ...

| ACKNOWLEDGEMENTS |

I would like to thank the following who, by way of expertise, access or friendship, significantly helped in the creation of this book: Julian Alexander and all at Lucas, Alexander Whitley; Sean Bean; Andy Boot; Craig Brown; Sir Alex Ferguson; Jimmy Greaves; Kevin McCabe (and for also saving Sheffield United!); Arthur Montford; Gordon Milne; Oxford United FC, in particular chairman Ian Lenagan and Owen Clark; Andy Roxburgh; Rory Scarfe and all at HarperCollins; Dave and Christine Scott; Sheffield United FC, in particular John Garrett; Peter Schmeichel; Jim Smith; Tommy Smith; Gerry Summers; Eric Steele; Graham Taylor.

I would particularly like to express my thanks and gratitude to Les Scott. Les is known and respected throughout football as being one of the very best writers on the game. I was familiar with his work on the books of George Best, Jimmy Greaves, Sir Stanley Matthews and Ian Rush to name but four. Having decided to commit my story to book form, it was Les I approached to assist me in the task. Thanks, Les, for everything, it has been great to work with you and fun too.

For Lauren and Ruby.

Alan Hodgkinson
2013

| INDEX |

AH indicates Alan
Hodgkinson.

AC Milan 177
Adams, Micky 271
Adams, Tony 296, 298
Adamson, Jimmy 185,
    201
Addison, Colin 246,
    247, 248, 260
Advocaat, Dick 286,
    290
Aitken, Senior 97, 113,
    114
Alford Town 14
Allchurch, Ivor 147
Allchurch, Len 142,
    143, 147, 151, 161,
    168, 190, 191, 193,
    206, 210, 212, 231
Allcock, Terry 132, 135
Allen, Ronnie 105
Anderson, Stan 54, 121,
    122, 180, 181
Appleton, Colin 148
Argentina 147, 184,
    185
Armfield, Jimmy 54,
    167, 186, 200, 223,
    224
Army Representative
    football team 53–5
Arsenal 47–50, 51, 54,
    65, 93, 97, 133, 141,
    144, 146, 148, 165,
    187–8, 205, 206, 207,

211, 213, 219, 220,
    235, 246, 261, 302,
    308, 312
Ash, Mick 224
Ashurst, Len 269
Aston Villa 28, 49, 53,
    93, 95, 98, 113, 117,
    122, 123, 214, 218,
    219, 228, 241, 279,
    299
Atyeo, John 91, 92, 94

Badger, Len 210, 211,
    213–14, 218, 235,
    239, 241, 256
Bailey, Gary 273, 279,
    280
Baker, Neil 121, 220–1,
    306
Banks, Gordon iii, 3,
    4–6, 31, 60, 148, 149,
    162, 164, 176, 202,
    233, 237, 280, 281,
    301, 302
Barclays Premiership:
    foreign players in 311,
    312
    friendlies and 32
    profit motive in 198,
    309–10
    quality of English
    players in 283, 303,
    311, 312
    reserve teams and 30
    scouting and 307
    squad system 138–40,
    238

television coverage
    307–8
working–class support
    supplanted in 120
Barlow, Frank 238
Barlow, Ray 105
Barrass, Malcolm 98
Bartram, Sam 14
Baxter, Jim 229, 230–1
Bell, Charlie 224
benevolent matches
    158–9
Best, George 1–6, 218,
    220, 258
Beverly Sisters 74–5, 88
Birchenall, Alan
    217–18, 219, 220,
    231, 232, 235, 238,
    240, 241, 243, 246–7,
    248, 250
Birmingham City 54,
    64, 66, 125, 196, 197,
    198, 206, 218, 219,
    235, 262, 299
Blackburn Rovers 55,
    64, 101, 102, 107,
    147, 148, 196, 199,
    205, 214, 215, 219
Blackpool 3, 42, 54,
    67, 78, 96, 146, 161,
    165–8, 176, 197, 199,
    205, 214, 222–3,
    224–5, 232, 240, 241,
    248, 260
Blanchflower, Danny 2,
    104, 261
Blyth, Jim 272

Boli, Basile 288–9
Bolton Wanderers 28,
    57, 60, 95, 109, 112,
    190, 197, 198, 199,
    205, 207–10, 214,
    227, 239, 262, 265
Bonetti, Peter 3, 176,
    237, 302
Booth, Colin 57
Bosnich, Mark 280
Boyd, Tommy 285, 296
Bradford City 21, 28,
    190
Bradley, Warren 57
Brazil 180, 184, 186–7,
    284, 285
Bremner, Billy 228, 233,
    247, 262
Bristol City 91, 119, 306
Bristol Rovers 134, 143
Broadbent, Peter 91,
    110, 111
Brook, Harry 129
Brown, Alan 78
Brown, Craig i, 284,
    285, 293, 296, 298
Brown, Wayne 306
Bruce, Steve 270, 271
Burgin, Ted 14, 34, 37,
    50, 251
Burnley 49, 55, 109,
    112, 127–8, 148, 150,
    165, 168, 174, 201,
    205–6, 214, 215, 228,
    231, 238, 242, 309
Burns, Tommy 286
Bury 59, 133, 168, 219,
    228
Busby, Matt 79, 97, 105,
    143, 220, 261, 278
Butler, Frank 161
Byrne, Johnny 177
Byrne, Roger 67, 80, 82,
    92, 94, 105

Caldow, Eric 57, 86
Cantwell, Noel 94
Carberry, Lee 177
Cardiff City 45, 46, 50,

    106, 107, 122, 123,
    163, 165, 247, 255,
    262
Carey, Johnny 29
Carlin, Willie 247, 248
Carlisle United 213,
    219, 247, 262
Carter, Raich 41, 230
Cass, Bob 239
Catterick, Harry 235
Celtic 14, 41, 58, 85,
    231, 234, 241, 278,
    286, 289, 290, 294,
    295
Central League 27–8,
    31, 38, 167, 210, 264,
    275
Chalmers, Len 148
Chapman, Herbert 47–8
Charles Buchan
    Football Annual/
    Football Monthly
    89, 162
Charlton Athletic 14,
    101, 133, 136, 137,
    227, 240, 256, 257
Charlton, Bobby 54, 55,
    73, 175, 182, 185, 258
Charlton, Jack 41, 234
Charnley, Ray 167, 223,
    224
Chelsea 3, 20, 49, 55,
    78, 111–12, 137, 162,
    163, 165, 176, 197,
    205, 211, 214, 229,
    240–1, 246, 258, 298,
    300, 302, 308, 312
Clarke, Allan 262
Clarke, Archie 113, 114
Clarke, Ryan 306
Clayton, Gordon 60
Clayton, Ronnie 55, 64,
    67, 82, 83, 84, 86, 147
Clemence, Ray 273,
    282, 302
Cliff, Phil 260
Clough, Brian 57,
    110–11, 128, 143,
    231–2, 247

Clyde 32, 33–4, 264
Co–op 17, 19, 20, 22,
    29, 96
Cobbold, John 178,
    214–15
Colchester United 261,
    270
Coldwell, Cec 40, 114,
    122, 127, 132, 149,
    151, 171, 189, 191,
    207, 209, 210, 212,
    213, 218, 222, 225,
    239, 242, 251, 253,
    262, 265
Coleman, Eddie 54
Coleman, David 309
Collins, Bobby 83, 85,
    87, 146, 165
Collins, John 285
Colquhoun, Eddie 255
Compton, Leslie 65
Cooke, Charlie 258
Coppell, Steve 274,
    277–8
Corrigan, Joe 272, 302
Coventry City 219, 243,
    249, 255, 259, 272,
    274, 275, 300
Cowan, Jimmy 14
Cowell, Bobby 42
Crawford, Billy 58
Crawford, Graeme 260
Crerand, Pat 3, 4–5,
    294
Crewe Alexandra 15,
    121, 128, 212, 220–1,
    306
Cross, Jack 43
Crystal Palace 177, 274,
    277, 283
Curran, Hugh 268
Currie, Tony 212,
    247–8, 260, 262
Curtis, Norman 251

Daily Express 55, 150,
    164–5, 260, 301
Daily Mirror 2, 46, 80,
    178, 213–14, 240

Davies, Wyn 207, 239, 240, 245
Davis, Kelvin 302
Dean, Dixie 49
Denmark 55, 56–7, 64, 91–2, 93
Derby County 41, 54, 59, 120, 134, 141, 143, 247
Digby, Frazer 272, 274
Dinnington Colliery Welfare team 17, 19, 27–8
Ditchburn, Ted 64, 66, 104
Dobing, Peter 102
Dobson, Colin 193
Docherty, John 210, 218, 231
Docherty, Tommy 83, 85, 87, 88, 158, 163, 197–8
Doncaster Rovers 21, 41, 57, 228, 265
Douglas, Brian 112
Dunmore, Dave 54
Durie, Davie 223, 224
Durie, Gordon 296, 298
Dyson, Jack 58
Dyson, Terry 104

Eastham, George 180
Eccleston, Tom 170, 171
Eckersley, Bill 78
Edwards, Duncan 54, 64, 66, 67, 86, 88, 92, 93–4, 105
Ellis, Keith 126, 252
Elsworthy, John 177
England (national team) 6, 14, 23–4, 33, 59–60, 264
  AH's coaching for 272–3
  AH's debut for 60–1, 67–89
  AH's full caps 60, 80–9, 91–2, 93, 94, 109–11, 139, 176
  European Championship and see European Championship
  managers see under individual manager name
  quality of players in modern team, AH on 311–12
  selection process 55, 56, 59, 64–7, 79–80, 92, 184–5, 186, 202
  under–18 272, 273
  under–21 273
  under–23 55–8, 60, 65, 79, 109, 110
  vs Hungary, 1953 64, 66, 76–7, 79, 80, 95, 100, 142
  World Cup and see World Cup
European Championship:
  1992 284–5, 287
  1996 284, 285, 293–9
  2012 312
European Cup:
  1955 78
  1956 79
  1967 14, 41, 241
Evans, Maurice 277
Everton iii, 28, 36, 49, 97, 146, 148, 163–4, 165, 168–70, 176, 188, 195, 199, 207, 210, 211, 214, 228, 232, 233, 234, 235, 236, 239, 242, 249, 258, 274, 279, 299, 302

FA see Football Association
FA Cup:
  1907–08 20
  1920–21 20–1
  1950–51 42
  1951–52 42
  1954–55 42
  1956–57 95–6
  1957–58 103–5, 106, 107, 112
  1959–60 123, 124–7, 128, 131, 132
  1960–61 137, 140, 146–53
  1961–62 168, 176
  1962–63 196, 198
  1963–64 210, 211
  1964–65 219
  1965–66 235–6
  1966–67 240–1
  1967–68 248, 249
  1969–70 259
  1970–71 261, 262
  1989–90 283
Fantham, John 126, 127, 236
Farrimond, Syd 207
Fell, Jimmy 165
Fenoughty, Tommy 224
Fenton, Ron 269
Ferguson, Sir Alex ii, 121, 213, 277–80, 282, 283, 290, 301
Fernie, Willie 83, 85, 87
FIFA 57, 184
Finlayson, Malcolm 161
Finnegan, Denis 168, 171
Finney, Alan 57, 126, 252
Finney, Jim 149
Finney, Tom 2, 67, 70, 72, 77, 91, 93, 94, 112
Finnigan, Denis 218, 220
Flowers, Ron 57, 161, 184, 185, 200
Fogarty, Ambrose 121
Football Association 73, 78, 79, 110–11, 181, 185–6, 200, 201, 227

Coaching Badge 79, 265

coaching schools, Lilleshall 79, 236, 268

Disciplinary Committee 233

England team and *see* England (national team)

nationwide goalkeeping technical programme, need for 302, 303

Selection Committee 55, 56, 59, 64–5, 66, 67, 79–80, 92, 185, 186

Football League 14, 15, 37, 41, 49, 54, 57, 73, 78, 79, 101, 102, 122, 128, 129, 130, 133, 156, 157, 158, 133, 161, 162–3, 176, 227, 229, 237, 258, 260, 264, 302, 307, 308, 309, 310, 312

Forbes, Alex 50

Ford, David 263

Ford, Trevor 45, 46, 49, 59, 312

Foster, Ben 302

Freeman, Reg 29, 31, 32, 34, 36, 40, 41, 45, 50, 51, 58, 97, 99

Fry, Keith 176–7

Fulham 60, 91, 107, 109, 110, 112, 156, 161, 165, 171, 172, 174, 188, 214, 215, 238, 239, 240, 248

Furphy, Ken 268

Gabriel, Jimmy iii, 146, 199

Gascoigne, Paul 289, 296, 297, 298, 299

Gillingham 212, 213, 269–70, 271

Godwin, Tommy 93, 94

Goram, Andy iii, 274, 275–7, 282, 285, 286, 288, 291, 296, 297, 299, 301

Grainger, Colin 67, 80, 86, 87, 91, 98

Gratrix, Roy 167

Graver, Andy 146

Gray, Eddie 262

Graydon, Ray 277

Greaves, Jimmy ii, 63, 112, 161, 162, 163, 177, 180, 182, 183, 184, 185, 186, 187, 200, 206, 216, 232, 233, 238, 258

Green, Geoffrey 77, 206

Greenwood, Ron 73, 165

Grimsby Town 104, 113, 114

Grummitt, Peter 176, 237, 302

Hackett, Desmond 260

Haddock, Harry 32

Hagan, Jimmy 34, 37, 43, 251

Halifax Town 197, 247, 301, 306, 310

Hall, Jeff 64, 66, 67, 83, 85

Hamilton, Willie 132

Hamlet (Shakespeare) 227, 267

Hannah, George 42, 43, 44, 147

Hardaker, Alan 73, 133, 157

Hardisty, Don 164–5

Harmston, Mick 256

Harper, David 261

Harris, Gordon 238

Harris, John 114–15, 122, 125, 126, 130, 131, 134–5, 136, 137,

138, 140, 142, 143, 152, 153, 159–61, 163, 164, 166, 171–3, 174, 177–8, 191, 193, 197, 210, 211, 213, 218, 221–2, 224, 228, 233, 238, 240, 243–4, 246, 248, 250, 252, 254, 257, 260, 262, 263, 264, 265, 268

Harrower, Alf 134

Hart, Joe 302

Hartle, Barry 138, 164, 190, 191, 193, 199, 207, 210, 218, 223

Hartlepool United 231–2

Harvey, Colin 258

Harvey, David 302

Hateley, Tony 177, 241

Haverty, Joe 93

Haynes, Johnny 91, 92, 94, 112, 161, 296

Heaton, Mick 224

Hemsley, Ted 255

Henry V (Shakespeare) 35

Herd, George 230

Hertha Berlin 54

Hewie, John 83, 85, 137, 227

Hickson, Dave 134

Hill, Freddie 207–8

Hill, Jimmy 156, 157

Hill, Mick 244, 245

Hillyard, Ron 270

Hitchens, Gerry 161–2, 184, 186–7

Hockey, Trevor 262

Hodgkinson, Alan: ball, on changes to modern 140, 310–11

birth 7–8

boots, on changes to 78, 214

burst ulcer 287–8

bypass, quadruple 287

childhood 7–18

coaching career i, ii, iii, 139, 265, 268–313 *see also under individual club name*

cricket, love of 35, 38

decline in entertainment factor of football after 1966, on 257–60

depth of quality in English game, on 302–3

England appearances *see* England (national team)

family *see under individual family member name*

Football League appearances *see* Sheffield United

gloves ii, 214, 239

height 55

injuries 59, 169–74, 207–10

kit changes, on 78, 95–6, 213–14, 229

Lord Mayor and Lady Mayoress of Sheffield, meets 68–72

maximum wage/ slavery contract, on 49, 79, 128–9, 155–6, 161–2, 163, 168, 177, 186

memorabilia, collects 14–15

National Service 51–5, 58, 98, 99, 108–9

near-death experience 287–8

PFA representative 129, 155–6

pitches, on quality of modern 140, 310

pre-match kick in, selects person from crowd to join in 232–3

pre-season training 114–18, 130–1, 157–9, 261, 264

press and 44, 64, 79, 88, 101, 202–3, 233, 240

profit motive in modern game, on 309–10

quality of English players in modern game, on 283, 303, 311, 312

retirement 306, 313

schooldays 15, 19

scouting in modern game, on 306–7

squad rotation, on modern 138–40, 238

superstitions/ goalkeeping paraphernalia 239

supporters, on treatment of modern 307, 309, 310

tactics, on changing 77–8, 96, 99–101, 236, 257

television coverage of modern game, on 307–8

testimonial 251–4

training 3, 4, 5–6, 114–18, 130–1, 139

training programmes, devises own 117–18

wages 19, 20, 22, 29, 49, 128, 155–7, 161–2, 163, 188

Hodgkinson, Andrew (son) 271

Hodgkinson, Brenda (wife) 16, 17, 19, 32,

38, 43, 53, 60, 105–6, 108, 126, 145, 165, 195, 225, 261, 269, 271, 312–13

Hodgkinson, Ivy (mother) 8–9, 10, 11, 19, 20, 23, 29, 37, 60, 72, 126

Hodgkinson, Karen (daughter) 145, 165, 195, 269

Hodgkinson, Len (father) 7–9, 10, 12, 15, 19, 23, 29, 32–3, 37–8, 43, 72, 108

Hodgkinson, Paula (daughter) 215, 269

Hodgson, Billy 98–9, 100, 132, 137, 144, 145, 161, 191, 207, 210, 251

Holden, Doug 57

Holland 54, 144, 157, 221, 228, 285

Holliday, Eddie 191

Holloway, Ian 121

Holton, Cliff 125

Hood, Harry 32

Hope, John 261, 263

Hopkinson, Eddie 60, 95, 109, 112, 207

Horne, Des 167

Howe, Don 57, 105, 180, 181, 297, 298

Hoyland, Tommy 37, 100, 116, 251

Huddersfield Town 15, 53, 59, 133, 260

Hull City 21, 42, 28, 42, 120, 121, 122, 212, 265, 313

Hungary 64, 76–8, 79, 80, 95, 100, 142, 184

Hunter, Norman 262

Hurley, Charlie 93, 121

Hurst, Geoff 73, 163

Iley, Jim 98

Inter Milan 162, 241

Ipswich Town 54, 107, 122, 123, 133, 136, 140–1, 144, 153, 159, 164, 165, 168, 174, 177, 178, 188, 194, 195, 201, 205, 214–15, 245

Ireland, Republic of 64, 75, 91, 92, 94, 95, 109, 121, 270

Jackson, Ernest 101, 114, 115, 116, 120–1, 122, 135, 151, 170, 171, 208

Jennings, Pat 3, 282, 302

Johnson, Peter 251

Johnston, Harry 78

Johnstone, Jimmy 231

Jones, Mick 210, 211, 212, 213, 217–18, 219, 220, 232, 233, 235, 239, 241, 243, 244–5, 247, 248, 250, 262

Julius Caesar (Shakespeare) 63, 205

Kay, Tony 126, 190, 192, 199

Keeble, Vic 42, 55

Kelsey, Jack 47

Kettleborough, Keith 132, 138, 164, 190, 191, 192, 210, 217, 218, 224, 231

Kevan, Derek 66–7, 86–7, 91, 105, 112

Keyworth, Ken 148

King Lear (Shakespeare) 265

King, Ian 148, 150–1

King, Ray 58–9

Knight, Alan 273

Knox, Archie 286

Knox, Bobby 227–8, 289

L'Ami, Carlo 300

Lacey, David 295

Langley, Jimmy 110, 111

Large, Frank 247

Latham, Harry 208

Laudrup, Brian 288

Law, Denis 161, 177, 294

Lawler, Chris 135

Lawther, Ian 122

Lawton, Tommy 49–50

Layne, David 'Bronco' 190–1, 192–3

Lazarus, Mark 261

Leach, Archibald 33

Leadbetter, Jimmy 177

League Cup:
1960–61 133–4
1964–65 218
1970–71 262

Lee, Francis 207

Leeds United 36, 41, 153, 201, 219, 228, 231, 233–4, 235, 244–5, 246–7, 248, 249, 254, 258, 261, 262, 300, 302

Leek, Ken 148, 151–2

Leggat, Graham 174

Leicester City 3, 31, 59, 95, 96, 148–53, 162, 197, 198, 206–7, 210, 214, 234, 246, 247, 248, 262, 264, 280, 299, 302

Leighton, Jim 280, 283, 285

Lewis, Kevin 122

Leyton Orient 101, 127, 133, 136, 261–2

Liddell, Billy 107–8

Lill, Micky 165

Lincoln City 101, 146, 210, 211

Lishman, Doug 50

Liverpool 15, 31, 97, 107–9, 120, 121, 122, 123–4, 133, 134, 136,

141, 144, 176, 198, 211, 215, 219, 220, 228, 231, 247, 249, 261

Lloyd, Cliff 156

Lord, Bob 309

Lord, Frank 247

Lorimer, Peter 262

Luton Town 146, 310

Lynn, Stan 117

Macedo, Tony 60

Mackay, Dave 54, 57, 206, 258, 294

Mackenzie, Ian 260

Mallender, Ken 218, 220

Manchester City 14, 28, 36, 45, 78, 127, 139, 165, 194, 195, 198, 207, 244, 272

Manchester United i, 1–6, 15, 79, 91, 95, 97, 105–6, 112, 144, 146, 148, 158–9, 165, 174–6, 177, 198, 201, 211, 215, 218–19, 220, 231, 233, 234, 240, 241, 249, 261, 267, 277–83, 286, 302

Mason, Cliff 137, 138, 146

Match of the Day, BBC 241–2

Matthews, Stanley 2, 65, 67, 70, 72, 78, 85, 86, 92–3, 95, 96, 161, 167

Matthewson, Reg 210, 211, 218, 237, 248

McColl, Ian 228

McCue, John 117

McDonald, Colin 55, 109, 112

McDonald, Malcolm 255

McFaul, Ian 302

McGrath, Paul 279

McGuinness, Wilf 57, 261
McIlmoyle, Hughie 247
McIlvanney, Hugh 241
McLeod, Ally 147
McLintock, Frank 148, 151
McMichael, Alf 42
McNab, Jimmy 121, 230
McNeill, Billy 231, 272, 294
Meagan, Mick 171
Medwin, Terry 104
Meek, George 36
Megson, Don 126, 127, 191, 193
Mercer, Joe 51, 53, 58, 63–4, 84, 95, 96–8, 99, 100, 101, 105, 106–7, 108, 113, 122, 142, 250
Merchant of Venice, The (Shakespeare) 243
Merrick, Gil 66
Middlesbrough 31, 128, 133, 136, 143, 144, 184, 187, 228
Midland League 20, 21, 55, 61
Milburn, Jackie 42–3, 44, 46, 50, 59, 147, 312
Mills, Mick 245
Mitchell, Bobby 43
Monkhouse, Alan 35
Monks, David 224
Montgomery, Jimmy 3, 237, 239, 302
Moore, Bobby 60, 73, 163, 183, 184, 185, 236, 258
Moore, Brian 269
Moran, Doug 177
Morris, Fred 22, 23, 24, 25
Morris, John 116, 151
Mortenson, Stan 78

Mourinho, José 7, 282, 300
Mudie, Jackie 78, 87, 88, 89
Mulhall, George 228
Mulholland, Ken 228
Mullery, Alan 216
Munich Air Disaster 105, 174
Munks, David 230
Murcott, Steve 272
Murray, Jimmy 55

National Service 51–5, 58, 98, 99, 108–9
Newcastle United 14, 34, 35, 37, 38, 39, 40–4, 147–8, 184, 231, 239–40, 244, 245, 255, 261, 263, 264, 265
Newport County 158–9, 228
Nibloe, Johnny 138
Nightingale, Albert 36
Norman, Maurice 104, 110, 180, 184
Norman, Richie 148
Northern Ireland 2, 65, 95, 109, 302
Northern League 42
Norwich City 127, 131–2, 133, 135–6, 143, 168
Nottingham Forest 59, 95, 125, 150, 165–6, 188, 198, 214, 219, 231, 243
Notts County 49, 101, 176, 212, 240, 247, 268–9
Nuse, Mel 228

O'Hare, John 230
O'Neill, Martin 121
Oldham Athletic 197, 274–6, 283, 286
Orr, Harry 164
Osborne, John 302

Oxford United 212, 257, 260, 263, 268, 277, 282–3, 300, 305–6, 313

Pace, Derek 98, 106, 121, 125, 127, 137, 143, 147, 149, 150, 152, 161, 165, 168, 191, 192, 193–4, 206, 210, 212, 251, 259
Paisley, Bob 135
Parkes, Phil 302
Parkes, Tony 300
Parkinson, Michael 202–3
Peacock, Alan 184, 186–7
Peacock, Keith 227
Pearson, Stan 29
Pegg, David 57, 92, 93
Pele 187
Penny, Alex 289
People, The 165
Perry, Arthur 28
Perry, Bill 78
Peterborough United 168
Peters, Martin 73
Peterson, Keith 167–8
PFA (Professional Footballers' Association) 129, 155–6, 161, 207
Phillips, Ted 177
Players' Union 156
Plymouth Argyle 56, 120, 132, 133, 218, 313
Pointer, Ray 168, 228
Poole, John 58–9
Port Vale 58–9, 60, 198
Portsmouth 124–5, 141, 262, 273
Potts, Harry 127
Powell, David 255
Preston North End 28, 34, 67, 77, 167, 176, 314

Price, Ken 270
Punton, Bill 132, 135, 241
Puskas, Ferenc 76, 77, 78

Quixhall, Albert 91

Ramsey, Alf 77, 78, 140–1, 177–8, 201, 202, 236, 257, 302
Rangers, Glasgow 286–7, 288–91, 294–5
Real Madrid 142–3
Redknapp, Harry 7, 300
Reece, Gil 228, 235, 256, 257, 260
Reilly, Hughie 85, 87
retain and transfer system 156, 162
'retained/not-retained letters' 128–9
Revie, Don 55, 78, 201, 233, 234
Richardson, Brian 99, 100, 116, 122, 150, 153, 189, 190, 192, 207, 217, 218, 251
Ridge, Roy 214, 218
Riley, Jimmy 151
Rimmer, Warwick 207
Ring, Tommy 34, 83, 84
Ringstead, Alf 93, 94, 129
Robb, George 78
Robeldo, George 184
Roberts, Dave 268
Robson, Bobby 105, 110, 112, 180, 182, 184, 186, 201, 273
Robson, Bryan 279
Rochdale 15, 251, 306
Romeo and Juliet (Shakespeare) 188
Rose, Henry 55
Rose, Mick 227
Rotherham United 21, 106, 107, 141, 190, 238, 265, 306

Rous, Sir Stanley 110, 111, 186
Rowley, Arthur 251, 254, 255–6, 257, 260
Roxburgh, Andy ii, 273, 274, 275, 276, 277, 282, 283, 284, 285, 300
Royal Signals Corps 51–2
Royle, Joe 274, 275–6
Ruddy, John 302
Rush, Ian iii
Russell, Billy 125, 127, 134, 143, 146

Salmons, Geoff 259
Sanders, Jim 106
Sargent, Sir Malcolm 230
Saul, Frank 216
Saward, Pat 93, 94
Schmeichel, Peter i, ii, 280–2, 283, 285, 301
Schwartzer, Mark 239
Scotland ii, 6, 14, 57–8, 60, 67, 72, 80–9, 91, 95, 99, 109, 147, 228, 255, 273–4, 276–7, 278, 283, 283–6, 293–9, 300
Scott, Alex 199
Scoular, Jimmy 42, 147
Sealey, Les 272, 280
Seaman, David 282, 296, 298, 299
Second World War 1939–45 11–12, 15, 33, 34
Setters, Maurice 54, 105
Sexton, Dave 272
Seymour, Stan 42
Shackleton, Len 309
Shankly, Bill 120, 124, 134, 135, 141, 231
Shaw, Bernard 211
Shaw, Graham 29, 54, 57, 99, 122, 137, 152, 153, 168, 190,

193, 200, 207, 217, 218, 237
Shaw, Joe 39, 41, 45–6, 59, 60, 100, 113, 114, 122, 130–1, 134–5, 145, 146, 147, 151, 152, 168, 169, 191, 192, 193, 199, 202–3, 207–8, 212, 217, 218, 220, 222, 223, 224, 225, 233, 234–5, 237, 245–6, 251, 253
Shearer, Alan 43
Sheffield Boys 17
Sheffield Star 18, 38, 44, 125, 194, 218, 242, 244
Sheffield United i, ii, 1–6, 14, 63, 89, 93, 94, 96
1952–53 season 21–2
1953–54 season 27–31
1954–55 season 35–50
1955–56 season 53
1956–57 season 58–60, 95–6, 98
1957–58 season 101–112
1959–60 season 113–28
1960–61 season 128–53
1961–62 season 155–78
1962–63 season 188–99
1963–64 season 205–15
1964–65 season 216–21
1965–66 season 225, 227–35
1966–67 season 237–42
1967–68 season 243–51
1968–69 season 254–7
1969–70 season 257–60

1970–71 season 260–1
AH leaves 263–5
AH plays for reserves
  27–31, 34, 35–6
AH signs as a
  professional for 29
AH signs as an
  amateur for 22–5
AH's amateur career
  at 25–9
AH's debut for first
  team 32–3
AH's Football League
  appearances for
  see (below) under
  individual season
AH's testimonial
  251–4
close-season tour to
  Canada and New
  Zealand, 1964 221–5,
  239
close-season tour to
  South America, 1967
  242
Football League
  debut, 1954 36–44,
  264
transfer policy 198–9,
  211–12, 228, 231,
  237–8, 248, 250
wage system after
  lifting of maximum
  wage 162
youth development
  policy 211–12, 231,
  237–8
Sheffield Wednesday
  26, 28, 31, 56, 57,
  91, 126–7, 133, 144,
  146, 157, 162, 163,
  182, 184, 188–94,
  198, 199, 211, 214,
  217–18, 219, 231,
  235–6, 241, 243, 249,
  251–2, 253, 262, 283,
  286
Sheils, Denis 122
Shepherdson, Harold

74–5, 185
Sheppard, Barry 210,
  240
Sherwood, Steve 272
Shilton, Peter 3, 273,
  302
Shipperley, Dave 270
Short, John 254–5, 256,
  262–3
Shrewsbury Town 254,
  255, 270
Sillett, Peter 55
Simpson, Ronnie 14,
  41–2, 43, 132, 135,
  137, 165, 206, 207,
  213
Sirrel, John 268–9
Smith, Bobby 91, 104,
  184
Smith, Denis 60
Smith, George 130–1
Smith, Jim i, 300
Smith, Joe 96
Smith, Tommy iii, 135
Smith, Trevor 54
Smith, Walter 286, 287,
  288, 289
Souness, Graeme 286,
  290
Southampton 56, 125,
  133, 136, 141, 196,
  198, 248, 302
Spinks, Nigel 306
Sprake, Gary 302
Springett, Ron 126,
  162, 163, 176, 182,
  183, 184, 185, 186,
  189, 190, 191, 192,
  193, 194, 202, 236,
  237, 241
Spurdells, David 301
St. John, Ian 128
Staniforth, David 260
Steele, Eric i, 272
Stepney, Alex 3, 237,
  302
Stevens, Denis 168, 199
Stockport County 212,
  231

Stoke City 3, 5, 28, 60,
  117, 133, 167, 197,
  214, 215, 217, 235,
  239, 243, 249, 280,
  301
Stokes, Ken 234
Stokoe, Bob 42, 147,
  301–2
Suart, Ron 167
substitutions first
  allowed in England
  227–8
Suckling, Perry 272, 274
Suddick, Alan 240
Sullivan, Derek 46
Sullivan, Neil 300
Summers, Gerry 99,
  100, 122, 127, 145–6,
  150, 164, 168–9, 171,
  189, 190, 191, 192,
  193, 207, 212–13,
  251, 268, 269–70, 271
Sunday Mirror 44, 249
Sunday People 187
Sunderland 3, 121, 122,
  136, 143, 144, 146,
  180, 196, 228–31, 259
Swan, Peter 126, 127,
  184, 190, 191
Swansea City 31, 123,
  137, 142, 211, 212,
  270
Swift, Frank 14
Switzerland 77, 314

Taming of the Shrew,
  The (Shakespeare)
  293
Tapalovic, Toni 300
Tapscott, Derek 50
Taylor, Ernie 78
Taylor, Gordon 207,
  272, 274
Taylor, Graham ii, 270,
  311
Taylor, Tommy 64, 66,
  91, 92, 94, 105
television, football and
  109–10, 162–3, 256

Tempest, The (Shakespeare) 113
Temple, Derek 169
Thompson, Des 134, 172, 174, 210
Thompson, Peter 176
Thompson, Tommy 67, 91
Thurcroft Main (cricket team) 35, 38
Times, The 77
Todd, Colin 59–60
Toner, Willie 29
Tottenham Hotspur 3, 20, 21, 64, 98, 104–5, 128, 144, 148, 150, 162, 165, 177, 197, 199, 206, 211, 216, 217, 228, 232, 234, 235, 238, 248, 262, 301
Trautmann, Bert 14, 15
Troilus and Cressida (Shakespeare) 155
Tudor, John 255, 259, 260, 262–3
Turner, Chris 279, 280
Turner, Edgar 165

UEFA: Goalkeeping Licenses/Award iii, 7, 283, 300–1, 314
Uphill, Dennis 125
Upton, Frank 197–8

Venables, Terry 293, 297, 298, 299
Vernon, Roy 164, 165, 169, 170, 171, 199

'W' formation 77, 78, 99, 123
Waddington, Tony 26, 280, 301
Wagstaff, Barry 224, 238
Wagstaff, Tony 207, 211, 218, 232, 235

Waiters, Tony 3, 167, 176, 237
Waldock, Ronnie 98
Walker, Billy 125
Walsall 36, 212
Walsh, Gary 279, 280
Walsh, Hughie 151
Walsh, Jimmy 150
Watford ii, 125, 164, 235, 247–8, 259, 270, 272, 274, 299
Wembley 295–6
Wenger, Arsène 213, 235, 282
West Bromwich Albion 28, 36, 37, 45, 54, 57, 67, 105, 106, 107, 110, 127, 180, 184, 214, 255, 302
West Ham United 54, 73, 107, 133, 163, 165, 177, 189, 198, 214, 215, 228, 231, 234, 235, 248, 249
West, Gordon 176, 199, 237, 239, 302
Whelan, Liam 'Billy' 93, 94
White, David 290
White, Dick 147
Whiteside, Norman 279
Wicks, Peter 241
Widdowson, Bob 172, 210, 224, 240
Wilder, Chris 306
Wilkinson, Derek 126, 127, 190, 193
Williams, Alex 272
Williams, Bert 66
Willie, Alf 59, 114
Wills, Len 149
Wilshaw, Denis 55
Wilson, Bob 206, 302
Wilson, Peter 80, 178
Wilson, Ray 180, 200
Wilson, Vince 2
Wimbledon 235, 256, 300
Winterbottom, Walter

55, 56, 64, 65–6, 67, 72, 73, 75, 78, 79–80, 85–6, 87, 88, 91, 95, 109, 111, 182, 184, 185, 200–1, 202
A Winter's Tale (Shakespeare) 179
Withers, Colin 206
Wolverhampton Wanderers 128, 147, 159, 161, 167, 188, 195, 198, 211, 219, 248
Woodward, Alan 212, 218, 219, 232, 235, 241, 257, 260
Woosnam, Phil 54
Worksop Town 6, 19, 20–5, 27, 55, 60–1, 82, 238
World Cup:
1950 78
1958 89, 95, 109, 112
1962 57, 176, 178, 179–87, 201
1966 200, 202, 225, 236–7, 257, 258
1976 147
1990 284
1998 285–6
2010 67, 312
Wragg, Dick 143, 199
Wrexham 197, 227, 255, 310
Wright, Billy 67, 73, 74, 75, 76–7, 82, 83, 84, 85, 86, 87, 91, 93
Wright, Reg 27, 31
Wylie, Ron 272

Yates, H. Blacow 33, 142, 144, 145
Yorkshire Post 142, 202–3
Young, Alex 57, 199
Young, George 82, 85, 86, 95
Younger, Tommy 82, 85, 86, 87, 88